# Principles of Econometrics

# Principles of Econometrics
## An Introduction (Using R)

NEERAJ R. HATEKAR

 **SAGE**   www.sagepublications.com
Los Angeles • London • New Delhi • Singapore • Washington DC

*First published in 2010 by*

**SAGE Publications India Pvt Ltd**
B1/I-1 Mohan Cooperative Industrial Area
Mathura Road, New Delhi 110 044, India
*www.sagepub.in*

**SAGE Publications Inc**
2455 Teller Road
Thousand Oaks, California 91320, USA

**SAGE Publications Ltd**
1 Oliver's Yard, 55 City Road
London EC1Y 1SP, United Kingdom

**SAGE Publications Asia-Pacific Pte Ltd**
33 Pekin Street
#02-01 Far East Square
Singapore 048763

Published by Vivek Mehra for SAGE Publications India Pvt Ltd, typeset in 11/13pt Minion Pro by Diligent Typesetter, Delhi and printed at Chaman Enterprises, New Delhi.

**Library of Congress Cataloging-in-Publication Data Available**

**ISBN:** 978-81-321-0469-8 (PB)

**The SAGE Team:** Reema Singhal, Pranab Jyoti Sarma, P.J. Mathew and Umesh Kashyap

*To my Parents, to Dr P.M. Bandivadekar and to Ishan*

'Camerado, this is no book,
who touches this, touches a man,
(Is it night? Are we here alone?)
It is I you hold, and who holds you,
I spring from the pages into your arms....'

— Walt Whitman

# Contents

# Contents

# List of Tables

# List of Figures

# Preface

As the name indicates, this text book on the first principles of econometrics is aimed at a student beginning to learn the subject. Let us imagine one such student. She probably has very little or no background in statistics or mathematics. She is keen to learn the subject but is a little bit unsure about what it will hold and whether she will be able to cope with the supposedly 'difficult' subject. I will consider this textbook successful if it can bring for her, some assurance in the initial phase and a genuine passion for the subject as the course unfolds. This textbook emphasizes real-world applications; econometrics is, after all, a way of making sense of the real world. This should enable the student to understand how the subject can help her comprehend the complex reality around her and endow her with a fascination for its methods. This is the main objective of the book.

Today, the teaching and learning of econometrics is inseparable from software. Programme code in R programming language is provided with every chapter. R is a widely popular programming language that is free to use. Students are strongly encouraged to experiment with these programs. If they keep experimenting with the programs, they will surely develop a good understanding of this very flexible and versatile programming language. It will also give the students a substantial professional edge.

The famous Caribbean cricket writer C.L.R. James once famously asked, 'What do they know of cricket who only cricket know?' The same question applies to understanding science. Science is not merely a dispassionate search for truth. It is also a social activity that scientists engage in. The objectives of science, its methods of judging scientific success and failure and its progress are inseparable from the wider social context within which scientists live and work. In this book, an attempt has been made to provide at least a fleeting introduction to the major dramatis personae. I hope this will provide some context to what otherwise may appear more asocial than it actually is.

Econometrics is a fascinating subject indeed. I have always been deeply fascinated by its method of getting so much information about the world that we inhabit, from apparently dry, dull and boring numbers arrayed in rows and columns with military tedium. My beginning in the subject was rather like the student we have just imagined and my journey has lived up to the promise of the hope that I hold out to her.

# Acknowledgements

Many individuals have contributed on the way, though none can be blamed for where I have failed to reach. My first debt is to my Alma Mater, The Department of Economics, University of Mumbai. The jovial, egalitarian and informal atmosphere has ingrained deeply human values among all those who went through its portals. It has created a space for each of us and allowed all to flourish. Teachers like Suhas Joglekar, Medha Deshpande, Abhay Pethe, Ajit Karnik, Ritu Dewan, Romar Correa, late Prof. M.J.M. Rao and colleagues like Avadhoot Nadkarni and Chandrahas Deshpande have shaped me as a student and teacher of econometrics as well as of economics. As a person and a researcher too, I owe much to these rare, warm and gifted individuals. I was particularly lucky to have had Prof. Dilip Nachane as my PhD guide. I cannot think of a way of repaying my debt to him. Friends like K. Sridhar, Geeta Chaddha, Rajesh Save, Mukund Vyas and T.P. Deo in my early student career fanned my passion for econometrics (as well as for several other things equally delightful though somewhat less exalted!). Friends like Biswamohan Pradhan and Rajan Padwal, whom I acquired in my later career keep egging me on, mostly by telling me everyday over innumerable cups of tea that I am the darkest possible blot on the fair face of scholarship.

I would not dare to call my wife Rajni a 'pillar', even in a metaphorical sort of way. She absolutely hates all construction activity. She has generally been a loving, caring wife, as long as she is not exasperated beyond a reasonable limit by my love for large German Shepherds who shed hair copiously on the drawing room sofa or by the occasional harmless tiny snake in my back pack. Our tom cat Mau has brought a fresh twist to life by giving us firsthand experience of living with a feline mafia don. He continues to be true to his birth and upbringing on the campus of a University by reck-lessly risking life and limb to satisfy what to lesser humans would be mere idle curiosity.

My greatest debt, however, is to several batches of students, who I have had the privilege to teach in various institutions and at the University of Mumbai as well as those students of the D.G. Ruparel College who sat through a course based on this book during their vacations in an unusually uncomfortable Mumbai summer. If I can call myself a tolerably good teacher, the credit should be entirely due to these long suffering personalities. I would like to record my thanks to each one of them. Some of my students, colleagues and friends have been good enough to give their time to reading various drafts of this book. I have benefited by comments made by Sandhya Krishnan, Krithika Subramanian, Vaidehi Tandel, Nupur Joshi, Ashutosh Sharma, Abodh Kumar, Sumedh Dalwai, Nisha Yadav, Pallavi Rege, Yogendra Sisodia, Wandana Sonalkar, Sneha Thayyil and finally Renita D'Souza as well as Savita Kulkarni, my bubbly pupils and prized project fellows, without whom this book would never have seen the light of the day. I am grateful to all of them, without ascribing to them any responsibility for the errors that might remain.

# Chapter 1

# Random Variables

## INTRODUCTION

A major objective in econometrics is to be able to make useful statements about parameters that we cannot observe directly. We aim to achieve this by examining data that we can actually observe. For instance, suppose we want to measure the average household income in Mumbai. To find the actual average household income in Mumbai, we will have to go to each household, find its income, add the incomes of all such households and then divide by the number of households. The difficulty of this task will become evident when we account for the fact that there are nearly three million households in Mumbai. We cannot realistically hope to ask each household what their income is. We will have to choose a sample of Mumbai households and infer the average household income for Mumbai on the basis of this sample of households. The number that we will arrive at is not the actual average household income in Mumbai, but an 'estimate' of that income. If we choose a different subset of households as our sample, we will get a different estimate. We can get different estimates of the average income if we choose different samples. We are constrained to make some reasonable statements about the actual average household income in Mumbai, on the basis of such imperfect information. A major part of this book will be concerned with how to make reasonably good guesses about such unobservable parameters from observable but imperfect bits of information. The concept of random variables is an integral part of the toolkit that we will build in order to achieve this. In this chapter, we will learn about:

1. The idea of a random variable.
2. The probability mass/distribution function of a random variable.
3. The mean and variance of a random variable as well as its skewness and kurtosis.
4. An introduction to some important random variables: Binomial, Poisson and the Normal distribution.

In addition to these statistical ideas, we will also learn about some basic commands in R, which you should try out on your own.

## 1.1 THE CONCEPT OF A RANDOM VARIABLE

Random variables are central to econometrics. In order to get some idea of what a random variable is, let us take an example. Suppose you and me are playing a game which involves tossing a coin. The coin can land heads up or tails up. A balanced coin is equally likely to land heads up or tails up. Suppose we describe the possible outcomes of our 'experiment' as follows:

$$S = \{\text{Head, Tail}\}$$

The set $S$ is called the 'sample space'. With each of the outcomes, 'head' and 'tail', we can assign a probability. Suppose we assign the probability 1 / 2 to the outcome that the coin lands up heads and 1 / 2 to the outcome that it lands up tails. Then, we can write this as shown in Table 1.1.

**Table 1.1**
**The probability distribution over the outcomes of a toss of an unbiased/balanced coin**

| Outcome | Probability of the given outcome |
|---------|----------------------------------|
| Head | 1 / 2 |
| Tail | 1 / 2 |

A useful way to understand the meaning of the sentence 'probability of a head = 1 / 2' is as follows: Suppose I toss a balanced coin ten times and count the fraction of heads and there were seven heads in this toss, so the fraction of heads = 7 / 10 = 0.7. As against this, let me throw the coin 100 times and then count the fraction of heads. Now, I might expect it to be closer to 0.5, say 0.6. As I keep on tossing the coin more and more times, I should expect the fraction of heads to get closer and closer to 0.5. It is this limiting value of the fraction of heads that we call the 'probability of a head'.

In effect, we have defined the 'probability distribution' of the outcomes of the experiment. Let us reconsider what we have done.

We have specified all the possible outcomes of our 'experiment', and then associated a unique real number between 0 and 1 to each of the outcomes, with the requirement that all such numbers add up to 1. Any such collection of numbers can be regarded as a prob-ability distribution.

For example, suppose our coin is not a balanced coin but the chance that it lands up 'heads' was thrice that of it landing 'tails', then we will have to re-specify our probability distribution as shown in Table 1.2.

**Table 1.2**
**The probability distribution over the outcomes of a toss of a biased/imbalanced coin**

| Outcome | Probability of the given outcome |
|---------|----------------------------------|
| Head    | 3 / 4                            |
| Tail    | 1 / 4                            |

Note that the occurrence of a head rules out the occurrence of a tail on the same toss. Such outcomes are called 'mutually exclusive'. The point is that we can assign any of the infinitely many possible numbers to each of our mutually exclusive outcomes, as long as each of the numbers lies between 0 and 1 (both inclusive), each outcome has a unique number associated with it and all such numbers sum to 1.

Now, suppose I decide to give you one rupee every time the coin comes up 'heads' and nothing if it lands as 'tails'. Then, you will either get one rupee or zero rupees whenever you toss the coin. That is, you are now re-representing the outcomes of your experiment in terms of real numbers, instead of 'heads' or 'tails'. Now, we can rewrite Table 1.1 in an expanded form, as shown in Table 1.3.

**Table 1.3**
**The probabilities and the payoffs associated with the outcomes of a toss of an unbiased/balanced coin**

| Outcome | The amount you earn | Probability of earning that amount |
|---------|---------------------|-----------------------------------|
| Head | 1 | 1 / 2 |
| Tail | 0 | 1 / 2 |

Notice that now, the phenomena of interest is not the outcome, heads or tails, but really the real numbers 1 or 0 associated with these outcomes. The probability that the outcome 1 occurs in Table 1.3, for example, is the same as the probability that the outcome 'head' occurs in Table 1.1. The outcome 'head' is being associated with a unique real number, just like in the assignment of probability. These real numbers are called 'random variables'. If I were to become more generous and decide to give you two rupees every time a head turns up and one rupee every time the coin shows up tails, the values of the random variable associated with the outcome 'head' would now change to 2 and the value associated with 'tail' would change to 1. We would then associate a probability 0.5 to your earnings taking the value 2 and a probability 0.5 to earnings taking the value 1.

We can think of more complex experiments. Suppose I now toss two coins at the same time. So, the set of possible outcomes of my experiment would be as follows:

$$S' = \{TH, HT, HH, TT\}$$

Here the outcome TT for example denotes the event that the first coin as well as the second coin both show 'tails' after landing. Since we have assigned the probability 1 /2 to the event 'heads' and

also to the event 'tails', it seems natural to assign the probability 1/2
× 1/2 = 1/4 to the event TH, or to any of the other three possible
events. Now suppose, I give you one rupee every time a coin shows
up heads and take away one rupee from you whenever a coin lands
tails, the situation can be shown in Table 1.4.

**Table 1.4**
**The real number values and the payoffs associated with the
outcomes of a toss of an unbiased/balanced coin**

| Outcome | Associated random variable | Associated probability |
|---|---|---|
| TH | 0 (−1 because of tail on the first toss and +1 because of head on the second toss) | 1 / 4 |
| HT | 0 | 1 / 4 |
| HH | 2 | 1 / 4 |
| TT | −2 | 1 / 4 |

I hope you have got some idea of what we mean by a random
variable. Let us think of what we have done.

We set up an experiment and enumerated the set of all the possible outcomes. We will denote this set by the term 'sample space'.
At the outset, let us assume that all of these events are mutually
exclusive. We associated a unique probability with each element of
the sample space (that is, with each possible outcome of the experiment). Any set of such real numbers, each of which is individually
non-negative and not greater than one, and which collectively add
up to one, would qualify as a probability distribution.

When we associate a probability with each possible value of
the outcome of our experiment, we are really defining a function,
$P(\omega_i)$ to R, where R is the real number line and $\omega_i$ is an element of
the sample space, $\Omega$ (we write this as $\omega_i \in \Omega$).

We require that $P(\omega_i)$ have the following two properties:

P1) $$0 \le P(\omega_i) \le 1 \text{ for all } \omega_i \in \Omega$$

P2) $$\sum_{i=1}^{n} P(\omega_i) = 1$$

where $n$ is the number of distinct elements of the sample space.

Once the function $P(\omega_i)$ has been specified, we can use that to calculate probabilities of events that are not explicitly specified in $S'$. For example, we might be interested in the event that there is a head on any of the two throws. Let us call this event $A$. Then, the events that will qualify are {TH, HH, and HT}. Three out of the four outcomes correspond to event $A$, and therefore, $P(A) = 3 / 4$. Similarly, we can be interested only in the event that the outcome on the second toss is a 'tail'. Let us call this event $B$. Then, the events that correspond to $B$ are {HT, TT}. Two of the four events in $S'$ correspond to $B$, and therefore, we might naturally assign a probability $1 / 2$ to this event. We can think of events as subsets of $S'$. Suppose $A$ and $B$ are two such subsets of $S'$. Then, we can think of the event that the event $A$ or the event $B$ occur as the event $A \cup B$. For example, let $A$ be the event {HH} and let $B$ be the event {HT}. Then, the event that there is a head on the first toss corresponds to the event that either HH or HT occurs, that is, {HH, HT} or $A \cup B$. The function $P(.)$ should allow us to compute probabilities of such events from our elementary outcomes in $S'$. In order to enable it to do this, we need to explicitly specify how the probability of $A \cup B$ relates to the probabilities associated with $A$ and $B$. This motivates the next restriction, P3:

P3)  $\qquad\qquad\qquad P(A \cup B) = P(A) + P(B)$

whenever $A$ and $B$ are disjoint events, that is, $A \cap B = \phi$.

For example, the events {HH} and {HT} are mutually exclusive events, in that you cannot have HH (head on the first toss and a head on the second toss) and HT (head on the first toss and tail on the second toss) occurring at the same time. Therefore,

$$P(\{HH\} \cup \{HT\}) = P(\{HH\}) + P(\{HT\})$$
$$= (1 / 4) + (1 / 4)$$
$$= (1 / 2)$$

In addition to specifying the probability distribution, we represented each outcome by a unique real number. For example, in Table 1.4, the outcome TH is represented by the number 0, whereas the outcome HH is represented by the number 2. Though more than one outcome can be described by the same real number (for example, both HT and TH are represented by number 0), there is a unique real number describing a given specific outcome.

### Definition 1.1: Random variable

A rule which associates a unique real number with each outcome of the experiment, in such a way that the probability associated with every such real number equals the probability associated with the outcome which the real number represents, is denoted by the term random variable.

In other words, 'a random variable is a function from the sample space to the real number line'. The probabilities associated with various values of the random variable can easily be computed from the probabilities that are associated with the corresponding elements of the sample space. For example, in Table 1.4, the random variable takes value 2 when the outcome of the experiment is HH. The probability of this outcome is 1 / 4. The random variable takes the value 0 if the outcome is either {HT, TH}, and therefore the probability associated with 0 must be 1 / 2. The probability associated with –2 will similarly be 1 / 4. We can write all this more succinctly as show in Table 1.5. $(HT, TH) = (+1, -1)$

**Table 1.5**
**The probability distribution over the values taken by the random variable**

| Value of the random variable | Associated probability |
| --- | --- |
| –2 | 1 / 4 |
| 0 | 1 / 2 |
| 2 | 1 / 4 |

For another example, suppose our experiment consists of rolling a die. You get one rupee every time the number on the upper most face of the die is even and you get two rupees if the same number is odd. Then, your earnings are a random variable taking values 1 and 2. Let us find the probabilities associated with your earnings. First, let us enumerate the sample space ($\Omega$) associated with the experiment:

$$\Omega = (\{1\}, \{2\}, \{3\}, \{4\}, \{5\} \text{ and } \{6\}).$$

In the next step, we need to associate the points in $\Omega$ with your earnings (in other words, define a function from $\Omega$ to the set of real numbers). You earn one rupee if the following events happen $=\{2\}, \{4\}, \{6\}$, and hence:

$$X(2) = X(4) = X(6) = 1$$

that is, you associate the number one with every element of the subset $\Omega_1$ of $\Omega$ where:

$$\Omega_1 = \{2, 4, 6\}$$

Similarly, you earn two rupees if the following events happen = $\{1\}, \{3\}, \{5\}$. Hence:

$$X(1) = X(3) = X(5) = 2$$

Hence, you would associate a number two with each of the elements of the subset $\Omega_2$ of $\Omega$ where:

$$\Omega_2 = \{1, 3, 5\}.$$

Having associated appropriate real numbers with various elements of $\Omega$, we need to find the probabilities to be associated with $X = 1$ and $X = 2$.

Finding probabilities associated with $X = 1$: We associate a value 1 with $X$ if any of the following three outcomes occur: $\{2\}, \{4\}$ and $\{6\}$. In the original experiment, it might be reasonable to associate a probability $1 / 6$ with each of the six outcomes $\{1\}, \{2\}, \{3\}, \{4\}, \{5\}$ and $\{6\}$. Hence, the probability that $X$ takes the value 1 is the event that either of the following number shows up on the uppermost face: $\{2\}, \{4\}$ and $\{6\}$. Since these events are mutually exclusive (that is, no two numbers can show up at the same time), we know that:

$$P(X = 1) = P(\{2\}) + P(\{4\}) + P(\{6\}) = 1 / 6 + 1 / 6 + 1 / 6 = 1 / 2$$

Hence, we say:

$$P(X = 1) = 1/2$$

Similarly, it can be seen that:

$$P(X = 2) = 1/2$$

We can define the probability function associated with the random variable $X$ as a function $P(.)$ having the following properties:

1. $P(X_i) \geq 0$

2. $\sum_{i=1}^{n} P(X_i) = 1$

3. The function $P(.)$ is such that $P(X_i)$ equals the probability associated with the event that the real number $X_i$ represents.

## Example 1.1

Suppose you have to determine the average monthly income of a family from Mumbai. Obviously, you cannot find out the incomes of all the families in Mumbai. You will perhaps choose a limited number of families, say 100, to interview. Let us assume that on finishing your survey, you calculated the mean value of family incomes in your sample and that it turned out to be 7,500. If you had taken a different set of 100 households to interview, you would most certainly have got a different number. Thus, the sample mean is a random variable. It can take different values as different elements of the population are selected for the sample.

## Example 1.2

Suppose we play the following game: A fair coin is tossed. If the coin lands heads, we toss it once again. If it lands tails, we toss it again twice. You will get ten rupees if it does not land heads at all and you must pay one rupee every time a head comes up. Consider your net earnings; $X$. $X$ is clearly a random variable, since it takes different values with different probabilities. Let us specify the probability distribution of $X$. Let us start by specifying the sample space, $S$:

$$S = (\{HH\}, \{HT\}, \{THH\}, \{THT\}, \{TTH\}, \{TTT\})$$

Principles of Econometrics

where {THT} for example stands for the event that there is a tail on the first toss, a head on the second and a tail again on the third. We must associate a probability with each of these outcomes. Since the coin is a balanced coin and the outcomes on subsequent tosses are independent, it seems reasonable to assign probability $(1/2) \times (1/2) = 1/4$ to outcomes like {HH} and {HT} and probability $(1/2) \times (1/2) \times (1/2) = 1/8$ to outcomes like {HTT}. More specifically, we have:

$$P(\{HH\}) = P(\{HT\}) = 1/4$$

and:

$$P(\{THH\}) = P(\{THT\}) = P(\{TTH\}) = P(\{TTT\}) = 1/8$$

The random variable of interest is your net earnings. From each element of the sample space, we can find the unique value of $X$ that corresponds to it. For example, {HH} and {THH} both correspond to a net earning of –2. The outcomes {HT}, {THT} and {TTH} correspond to the net earning value of –1, and the outcome {TTT} corresponds to net earnings of 10.

Therefore:

$$P(X = -2) = P(\{HH\} \cup \{THH\})$$

or, using P(3), we have:

$$P(X = -2) = P\{HH\} + P\{THH\} = 1/4 + 1/8 = 3/8$$

Similarly:

$$P(X = -1) = P\{HT\} + P\{THT\} + P\{TTH\}$$
$$= 1/4 + 1/8 + 1/8 = 1/2$$
$$P(X = 10) = P\{TTT\} = 1/8$$

The probability distribution for $X$ can be put into Table 1.6: As you can see, properties 1 and 2 are satisfied for $P(X)$.

### Exercise 1.1
Suppose the experiment consists of rolling a die. You get five rupees if the number on the uppermost face of the die is even and two rupees if it is odd. Suppose all six outcomes are equally likely.

Random Variables

**Table 1.6**
**The probability distribution over the values taken**
**by the random variable $X$**

| $X$ | $P(X)$ |
|---|---|
| -2 $P(HH) + P(THH)$ | 3 / 8 |
| -1 | 1 / 2 |
| 10 | 1 / 8 |

Describe the sample space, the associated probability distribution, and finally the amount you would get with each toss as a random variable associated with the experiment. Make sure that 1 and 2 are satisfied.

### Exercise 1.2

Suppose 100 families are living in a housing complex. Out of these 100 families, 25 families have a monthly income of Rs 15,000 and 25 have a monthly income of Rs 18,000. The remaining 50 have a monthly income of Rs 16,000. Suppose you randomly knock on any one family's door and find out their income. You can regard the answer that you will get as a random variable. Tabulate the values that the random variable will take and the associated probability function. Justify your answer.

### Exercise 1.3

Suppose a tribal village has 100 female children out of which 25 are underweight. Suppose you randomly pick a child, and classify her as 0 if she is underweight and as 1 otherwise. What is the sample space for this experiment? How will you associate the values of the random variable with the outcomes of the experiment? Show diagrammatically. Tabulate the probability distribution of the random variable associated with your experiment.

### Exercise 1.4

Suppose a box contains 10 balls, numbered successively from 1 to 10. The experiment consists of drawing a ball at random and recording the number on it. Call this random variable $X$ and associate a probability distribution with various values of $X$. Justify your answer.

### Exercise 1.5[1]

Suppose two desperadoes, say $A$ and $B$, are playing a game of Russian roulette. They have with them a revolver with a six-cylinder magazine, with a bullet in just one of them while the other five cylinders are empty. They take turns in putting the gun to their foreheads and pulling the trigger. After each attempt, the magazine is spun to a random position. The game ends when the trigger is pulled six times without the fatal shot being fired. Desperado $A$ begins the game. What is the distribution of the number of times Desperado $A$ pulls the trigger?

## 1.2 TYPES OF RANDOM VARIABLES

Random variables are broadly of two types, discrete and continuous.[2] Let us define the two types a bit more formally.

*Discrete Random Variables*: A discrete random variable is a variable that takes a finite number or a countably[3] infinite number of values.[4]

You will have noticed that all the examples that we have constructed so far are examples of discrete random variables. The function $P(X_i)$ is called a probability mass function (pmf) in the case of discrete random variables. The pmf for a discrete random variable will obviously have to satisfy P1 and P2. We will now see more such examples.

### Example 1.3

Suppose you are rolling a die once and let $X$ be the number that comes up on the uppermost face of the die. Then, $X$ is a random variable (you are familiar with it from Exercise 1.1) which takes the following set of values $\{1, 2, 3, 4, 5, 6\}$. This set consists of a finite number of elements and hence the number on the uppermost face of a die is a discrete random variable.

### Example 1.4 (The Bernoulli random variable)

Suppose we are dealing with someone who is engaged in shooting practice at a target. If he hits the target, we call it a 'success' and if he misses, we call it a 'failure'. We will assume that whether the shooter hits or misses the target on any particular attempt has nothing to do with his success or failure on any other attempts. So we are ruling out the possibility that the shooter improves with practice. Suppose the probability of a success is $p$ and therefore the probability of failure is $1 - p$, where $p$ is a constant between 0 and 1. Suppose we decide to represent 'success' and 'failure' numerically, by defining a new variable $X$, which equals 1 every time a 'success' occurs and which equals 0 whenever there is a 'failure'. Such an experiment is called a Bernoulli[5] trial, and $X$ will be called a Bernoulli random variable. We will follow the convention of representing a specific value of the random variable $X$ by the lower case letter $x$. The pmf of the Bernoulli random variable can be expressed as follows:

$$P(x) = P^x \times (1 - p)^{1-x}, x = 0, 1$$

If $x = 0$, $P(x) = 1 - p$, while if $x = 1$, $P(x) = p$.

**Example 1.5**

Suppose, for a Bernoulli random variable, $p = 0.4$. Then:

$$P(0) = 0.6, P(1) = 0.4$$

Let us construct the pmf of this random variable. Suppose the shooter shoots four times. The event that the shooter hits on the first trial, misses on the next two and hits on the last can be represented as the following sequence of 0s and 1s:

$$S = (1, 0, 0, 1)$$

The probability with which the shooter hits is $p$, while the probability with which she misses is $1 - p$. The events 'hit' or 'miss' on each trial are independent events, in the sense that whether the shooter hits or misses on any trial is independent of the chance of hitting or missing on any previous or subsequent trials. If $A$ and $B$ are independent events, the probability of observing $A$ and $B$ equals the probability of $A$ multiplied by the probability of $B$. Therefore, the probability of observing 1, 0, 0, 1 together is:

$$p \times (1 - p) \times (1 - p) \times p = p^2 \times (1 - p)$$

In general, the probability of observing any particular sequence of $x$ 1s and $n - x$ 0s in $n$ trials is $p^x \times (1 - p)^{n-x}$.

## Example 1.6

Suppose the probability that you find a seat in the suburban train on any given day is 0.2 and that the event that you get a seat on any particular day is independent of whether you get a seat on any other day. What is the probability that you will find a seat on Monday, Wednesday, Thursday and not find a seat on rest of the days including Sunday?

Let $X$ be the random variable that takes value 1 if you get a seat and 0 if you do not. Then, the event that you get a seat on Monday, Wednesday and Thursday but not on other days corresponds to the following sequence being observed:

$$S = (1, 0, 1, 1, 0, 0, 0)$$

Then, because the elements of the sequence are independent, we have

$$P(S) = p^3 \times (1 - p)^4$$
$$= 0.2^3 \times 0.8^4$$
$$= 0.003277$$

## Example 1.7

Suppose 32 per cent of the households in a certain district are classified as 'poor'. If you randomly pick ten households (with replacement), what is the probability that the first two households in the sample are poor, while the remaining eight are not?

Let us mark a household as 1 if that household is poor, and 0 if it is not poor. Then, we want to compute the probability of observing the sequence $S = (1, 1, 0, 0, 0, 0, 0, 0, 0, 0)$.

The probability of observing 1 is $p = 0.32$, while the probability of observing a zero is $1 - p = 0.68$. The occurrences of ones and zeros are independent events, and, therefore, we have a Bernoulli random variable. The probability of observing this specific sequence of ones and zeros is then:

$$p^2 (1 - p)^8 = 0.1481$$

## Example 1.8 (The Binomial Random Variable)

Suppose now, the shooter has fired his gun say four times and you are interested in the event that there are a certain number

14

of 'successes' out of these four attempts. The number of 'successes' can be thought as a random variable taking values between 0 and 4. Let $X$ be the number of successes. Suppose we are interested in finding $P(X = 2)$. How do we describe the sample space corresponding to this event? The outcome on the first shot could be success ($S$) or failure ($F$), so the first outcome could happen in two ways. Similarly, the second, third and fourth outcomes could each occur in two ways. Hence, the total number of possible outcomes would be $2 \times 2 \times 2 \times 2 = 2^4 = 16$ ways. Indeed, we can even describe the entire sample space:

$$\Omega = \{(S, S, S, S), (F, F, F, F), (F, S, S, S), (S, F, S, S), (S, S, F, S),$$
$$(S, S, S, F), (S, S, F, F), (S, F, F, S), (F, S, S, F), (F, F, S, S), (F, S, F, S),$$
$$(S, F, S, F), (S, F, F, F), (F, S, F, F), (F, F, S, F), (F, F, F, S)\}$$

which has 16 elements as expected. We are interested in $P(X = 2)$. The event $X = 2$ corresponds to the following subset of $\Omega$ which we will call:

$$\Omega' = \{(S, S, F, F), (S, F, F, S), (F, S, S, F), (F, F, S, S), (F, S, F, S),$$
$$(S, F, S, F)\}$$

There are six elements in $\Omega'$ and all elements are equally likely. Hence:

$P(X = 2)$ = number of elements in $\Omega'$ / number of elements in $\Omega$,

which is $6 / 16$. Instead of arriving at this number in this fashion, we can develop a simple rule to compute $P(X = 2)$. Let the probability of a success, $p$ be $1 / 2$ and consequently, that of failure, $q$, would be $1 - 1 / 2 = 1 / 2$. Two successes in four attempts implies two failures on the remaining attempts. Since the successes and failures on each individual attempt are independent, we have:

$$P(F, F, S, S) = p^2 \times q^2 = (1 / 2)^2 \times (1 / 2)^2 = (1 / 2)^4$$

But there are six such possible outcomes with two successes and two failures and therefore the probability that any one of them occurs is:

$$6 \times p^2 \times q^2 = 6 / 16$$

In general, let:

$$C_r^n = n!/(n-r)! \times r!$$

where $n! = (n \times (n-1) \times (n-2) \dots 3 \times 2 \times 1).[6]$

Then, if we set $n = 4$, $r = 2$, we have:

$$C_2^4 = 4!/(2! \times 2!) = (4 \times 3 \times 2 \times 1)/(2 \times 1 \times 2 \times 1) = 6$$

Therefore, the probability that there are two successes in four trials can be expressed as $C_2^4 \times p^2 \times q^2$. In general, we can express:

$$P(X = \textcircled{k}) = C_k^n \times p^k \times q^{n-k}$$

If $X$ has the above pmf, it is called a 'Binomial random variable',[7] with parameters $n$ and $p$. Alternatively, we can say that $X$ has a binomial distribution. This is a very commonly used model, and you must make sure that you understand it well.

### Example 1.9

Suppose you take an objective examination, where you are given 20 questions that you are supposed to mark 'true' or 'false'. Since you have not studied for the examination, you are randomly marking the answers 'true' or 'false'. Also, whether you mark a specific answer 'true' or 'false' does not depend upon how you have marked the previous answers or on how you will mark the future answers. In that case, the probability of 'success', defined as the event that an answer gets marked correctly, is 0.5. In effect, the number of successes is a Binomial random variable, with $p = 0.5$ and $n = 20$. You can use this model to answer some questions. For example, the probability that you will get exactly five answers correct is:

$$P(X = 5) = \binom{20}{5} \times 0.5^5 \times 0.5^{15}$$
$$= (20!/5! \times 15!) \times 0.5^5 \times 0.5^{15}$$
$$= 0.014786$$

The probability that you will get at least five answers right can also be obtained:

$$P(X \geq 5) = 1 - P(X < 5)$$
$$= 1 - (P(X = 0) + P(X = 1) + P(X = 2) + P(X = 3) + P(X = 4))$$

$$= 1 - \{ \binom{20}{0} \times 0.5^0 \times 0.5^{20} + \binom{20}{1} \times 0.5 \times 0.5^{19}$$

$$+ \binom{20}{2} \times 0.5^2 \times 0.5^{18} + \binom{20}{3} \times 0.5^3 \times 0.5^{17} + \binom{20}{4} \times 0.5^4 \times 0.5^{16} \}$$

$$= 1 - (0.00000095 + 0.00001907 + 0.00018120 + 0.00108719 +$$
$$0.00462055)$$

$$= 1 - 0.005909$$

$$= 0.994091$$

We can calculate such probabilities with the help of R. If you want to calculate the probability of five successes out of 10 trials, where the probability of success is say 0.5, you must type the following command in R:

```
dbinom(5,10,0.5)
```

The general command to calculate the probability of $x$ successes in $n$ trials where the probability of success is $p$ is as follows:

```
dbinom(x,n,p)
```

The graph in Figure 1.1 gives the number of successes on the X-axis and associated probabilities on the Y-axis for this specific example. The height of the histogram above 4, for example, shows the probability of four heads in 10 tosses. The continuous line simply draws a smooth curve joining such points. Note that the highest probability of occurrence is at 5 and the smooth curve is also symmetric around 5. The histograms show the relative frequencies of various numbers of heads that turn up, whereas the line is a smooth 'approximation'. The following R program commands will allow you to experiment more.

```
Size=10000
n=10
probab=0.5
x<-rbinom(Size,n,probab)
hist(x,xlim=c(min(x),max(x)),probability=TRUE,nclass=
max(x)-min(x)+1,col="lightblue",main="Fig 1.1:Binomial
Distribution X where n=10,p=0.5")
lines(density(x,bw=1),col="red",lwd=3)
```

## Figure 1.1
## Binomial Distribution of $X$ with $n = 10$, $p = 0.5$

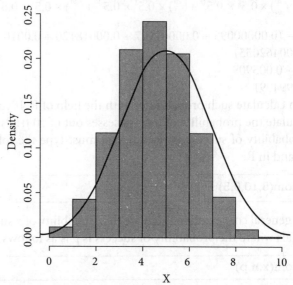

Here $n = 10$ means that 10 coins are to be thrown. *Probab* = 0.5 says that the assumed probability of a head is 0.5. $x$ is the number of heads that come up in a toss of $n$ coins. *Size* = 10000 means that the 10 coins are to be tossed 10000 times. The height of the histogram above each value of X shows the probability of those many successes in 10 tosses. The curve is a smooth approximation to the histograms. You can vary all these numbers and see how the graph changes.

### *Example 1.10*

Suppose $X$ is the number of successes in seven tosses of a balanced coin. What is the probability that there will be *(a)* exactly five heads; *(b)* there will be at least five heads; and *(c)* there will be at most three heads?

$$(a)\ P(X = 5) = \binom{7}{5}\, 0.5^5\, (1 - 0.5)^2$$
$$= 0.164063$$

You can find the answer in R by typing:

```
dbinom(5,7,0.5)
```

which is the probability of five heads in seven tosses when the probability of a head is 0.5.

*(b)* The event 'at least five heads' corresponds to the event that there are five, six or seven heads. The three events are mutually exclusive, and hence, in order to find the probability that one of them occurs, we must add the individual probabilities:

$$P(X \geq 5) = \binom{7}{5} 0.5^5 (1-0.5)^2 + \binom{7}{6} 0.5^6 (1-0.5)^1 + \binom{7}{7} 0.5^7 (1-0.5)^0$$

$$= 0.226532$$

The corresponding R syntax is:

```
dbinom(5,7,0.5)+dbinom(6,7,0.5)+dbinom(7,7,0.5)
```

*(c)* The event 'at most three heads' corresponds to the event that one of 0, 1, 2 or 3 heads occurs:

$$P(X \leq 3) = \binom{7}{0} 0.5^0 (1 - 0.5)^7 + \binom{7}{1} 0.5^1 (1 - 0.5)^6$$
$$+ \binom{7}{2} 0.5^2 (1 - 0.5)^5 + \binom{7}{3} 0.5^3 (1 - 0.5)^4 = 0.500002$$

## 1.2.1 The Cumulative Density Function of a Discrete Random Variable

Let $x$ be a specific value that the random variable $X$ takes. We can then ask the question: what is the probability that the random variable $X$ takes values at most equal to $x$? For example, in Example 1.6, you might want to know the probability that you get at most seven answers right. In general, we want the probability $P(X \leq x)$. This value obviously is a function of $x$. We will call it the Cumulative Density Function (cdf) of $X$. Figure 1.2 gives you the cdf for Example 1.6. To take an example, the probability $P(X \leq 4)$ can be read off from the graph, as the height of the bar over 4 on the X-axis. It turns out to be 0.377. Similarly, $P(X \leq 6)$ can be seen to be 0.8281. The smooth curve passing through the tops of all the vertical bars is a continuous approximation to this discrete random variable.

19

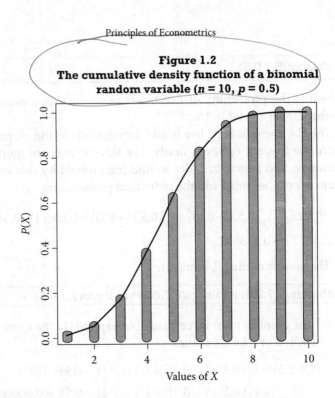

**Figure 1.2**
**The cumulative density function of a binomial random variable ($n = 10$, $p = 0.5$)**

To draw this graph on your own using R, you must type in the following program commands:

```
n=10
s1=c(rep(1,n))
i=0
repeat {
s1[i]=pbinom(i,n,0.5)
i=i+1
if(i>10)
break
}
plot(s1,type="h",col="yellow",lwd=20,main="Fig
1.11:Cumulative Density Function of a Binomial Random
Variable (n=10,p=0.5)",xlab="Values of X",ylab="p(X)")
lines(s1,col="red",lwd=5)
```

You can change any of the parameters as usual.

We call $K$ the 90 per cent percentile of the distribution if:

$$P(X \leq K) = 0.9$$

In general, we call $K$ the $100 \times x$th percentile if:

$$P(X \leq k) = x \text{ for } 0 < x < 1.$$

## 1.2.2 Calculating Percentiles of the Binomial Distribution Using R

Let $X$ be the number of heads in 10 tosses of a balanced coin. We might want to find the 90th percentile of $X$. The command to calculate this is:

```
qbinom(p,size,prob)
```

where $p$ is the required percentile/100, *size* is the number of trials and *prob* is the probability of success on any given trial. In our case, since we are looking for the 90th percentile, $p = 0.9$, *size* = 10 (since we have 10 tosses) and *prob* = 0.5, because of the assumption of a balanced coin.

Putting all this together, we type in the following command:

```
qbinom(0.9,10,0.5)
```

which generates the value 7. This means that the probability that there are at most seven heads in 10 tosses of a balanced coin is 0.9. This function, called the quantile function, is very important in hypothesis testing and hence we will encounter it often in Chapter 3.

### Exercise 1.6

Why does the cdf go from 0 to 1?

### Exercise 1.7

Suppose Mohan is throwing stones at a mango tree laden with fruit. If his stone hits a mango, it falls to the ground and Mohan gets to eat it. Mohan has 12 stones in his hand and that is the maximum number that he can throw. Mohan's aim is not very good, and hence, on any given attempt, the probability that his stone hits a mango is 0.3. Also, assume that whether Mohan succeeds in hitting a mango in any given attempt does not depend upon his succeeding or failing in any past or future attempt. Find the probability that Mohan gets (a) At most seven mangoes; (b) At least three mangoes.

## Exercise 1.8

Confirm that P1 as well as P2 are satisfied for the Example 1.5. (Hint: use the Binomial expansion).

## Example 1.11

It has been known since the 18th century that in reliable birth statistics based on a sufficiently large number, there is always a slight excess of male births over female births. For example, Laplace records that among the 215,599 births in 30 districts of France in the years 1800–1802, the proportions of boys and girls were 0.512 and 0.488 respectively. Let us regard 0.512 as the probability of observing a male birth and 0.488 as the probability of observing a female birth. Since the gender of a particular baby is independent of the gender of babies born previously or subsequently, we can regard a baby's gender as a binomial random variable with $p = 0.512$ and $(1 - p) = 0.488$. Can this be used to predict the number of boys and girls in a family? A certain A. Geissler undertook such an exercise in 1889, where he tried to predict the number of boys and girls in families having eight children in a large sample of 53,680 families. Geissler let $p$ (the probability of a male child being born) $= 0.5147$, while that of a female child being born, $(1 - p) = q = 1 - 0.5147 = 0.4853$. Here, $n$ is 8, while $r$ is the number of male children. The binomial probability that a family having eight children has $M$ number of male children ($M = 0, \ldots\ldots 8$) is given as follows:

$$P(M = 0) = C_0^8 (0.5147)^0 \times (0.4853)^8$$

$$= \frac{8!}{0!(8-0)!} \times (0.5147)^0 \times (0.4853)^8$$

$$= 0.003$$

$$P(M = 1) = C_1^8 (0.5147)^1 \times (0.4853)^7$$

$$= \frac{8!}{1!(8-1)!} (0.5147)^1 \times (0.4853)^7$$

$$= 0.0261$$

$$P(M = 2) = C_2^8 (0.5147)^2 \times (0.4853)^6$$

$$= \frac{8!}{2!(8-2)!} (0.5147)^2 \times (0.4853)^6$$

$$= 0.0969$$

$$P(M = 3) = C_3^8 (0.5147)^3 \times (0.4853)^5$$

$$= \frac{8!}{3!(8-3)!} (0.5147)^3 \times (0.4853)^5$$

$$= 0.205$$

$$P(M = 4) = C_4^8 (0.5147)^4 \times (0.4853)^4$$

$$= \frac{8!}{4!(8-4)!} (0.5147)^4 \times (0.4853)^4$$

$$= 0.272$$

$$P(M = 5) = C_5^8 (0.5147)^5 \times (0.4853)^3$$

$$= \frac{8!}{5!(8-5)!} (0.5147)^5 \times (0.4853)^3$$

$$= 0.231$$

$$P(M = 6) = C_6^8 (0.5147)^6 \times (0.4853)^2$$

$$= \frac{8!}{6!(8-2)!} (0.5147)^6 \times (0.4853)^2$$

$$= 0.122$$

$$P(M = 7) = C_7^8 (0.5147)^7 \times (0.4853)^1$$

$$= \frac{8!}{7!(8-1)!} (0.5147)^7 \times (0.4853)^1$$

$$= 0.0371$$

$$P(M = 8) = C_8^8 (0.5147)^8 \times (0.4853)^0$$

$$= \frac{8!}{8!(8-8)!} (0.5147)^8 \times (0.4853)$$

$$= 0.004$$

Suppose we want to find the number of families that might be expected to have three sons. Then, we must multiply the total number of families (53,680) with the probability that a given family has three sons, which is by multiplying these probabilities by the total number of families (53,680), we will get the number of families that are expected to have those many number of children, 0.205543. Table 1.7 gives the relevant findings for different numbers of boys.

**Table 1.7**
**The number of boys in families containing eight children**

| No. of Boys (M) | Observed No. of Families | Expected No. of Families | Binomial Probabilities P(M = m) |
|---|---|---|---|
| 0 | 215 | 165 | 0.003077 |
| 1 | 1,485 | 1,401 | 0.026105 |
| 2 | 5,331 | 5,202 | 0.096901 |
| 3 | 10,649 | 11,034 | 0.205543 |
| 4 | 14,959 | 14,628 | 0.272493 |
| 5 | 11,929 | 12,411 | 0.231201 |
| 6 | 6,678 | 6,581 | 0.122604 |
| 7 | 2,092 | 1,994 | 0.037152 |
| 8 | 342 | 264 | 0.004925 |

Source: Geissler (1889).[8]

As you can see, the agreement between the observed and the expected number of families is quite good, although there are rather too many families with all boys or all girls. There has been some controversy whether this slight departure from theory is a biological fact or whether there are some defects in the data. Though subsequent studies came to conflicting conclusions, the departure between the actual and expected numbers is rather small. Thus, the assumption that the gender of babies can be modelled using the binomial distribution seems a good approximation to reality.

## Example 1.12

Suppose it is known that in a particular district, 32 per cent of the households are below the poverty line. You are given 500 households chosen at random.

*(a)* What is the probability that exactly 200 of these households (40 per cent) are poor?

Let $X$ be equal to the number of poor households. Then:

$$P(X = 200) = \frac{500!}{200!(500-300)!}(0.32)^{200}(0.68)^{300}$$

We can answer this by using the R command:

```
dbinom(200,500,0.32)
```

which generates the answer 0.0000306488, which is a pretty small probability.

*(b)* Calculate the cdf of $X$ and graph it using R.

The following program will give us a CDF of $X$ for all values of $X$ from 0 to 500:

```
m=c(rep(0,501)) ## This command generates a column m
containing 501 0s
m[1]=dbinom(0,500,0.32)## Sets the first row of m to
dbinom(0,500,0.32)
i=1 ## starts a repeat loop
repeat {
m[i+1]=dbinom(i,500,0.32)+m[i]  ## i+1st row of m =
dbinom(I,500,0.32)+ith row of m
i=i+1 ## increases I by 1
if(i+1>501) ## condition for breaking the loop
break
}
plot(m,type="l",lwd=4,main="cdf   of   X",   xlab="X",
ylab="probability")
```

The output of the program is the following graph shown in Figure 1.3.

### Figure 1.3
### The cumulative density function of random variable $X$

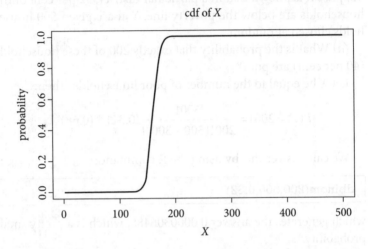

As has been pointed out above, the height of the cdf at $X = x$ gives $P(X \leq x)$. For example, the height of the curve above 200 is the probability of finding up to 200 houses below the poverty line in the random sample of 500.

## 1.2.3 The Poisson Distribution

*The Poisson distribution:* If, for the Binomial distribution, $p$ is small and $n$ is large such that $np = \lambda$ ( a fixed number), then as $n$ becomes large, the Binomial distribution tends to a distribution called the Poisson[9] distribution.[10]

This distribution has the following pmf:

$$P(X = k) = f(k;\lambda) = \frac{e^{-\lambda}\lambda^{k}}{k!}$$

where $e$ is the base of the natural logarithm, $k$ is the number of oc-currences of the random variable $X$, $\lambda$ is a positive natural number and $k!$ is the factorial of $k$.

The Poisson distribution is often used to model the probability of the number of events in a fixed period of time, if these events occur at a known average rate ($\lambda$) and independently of the time since the last occurrence.[11] Suppose a motorcyclist meets with one accident per year, on an average. Now, let us think of the motorcyclist setting out on his bike everyday. Suppose, on any given day, he is likely to meet with an accident with probability $p$, and is likely to have a safe ride with probability $1 - p$. Then, the event that he meets with an accident on any given day can be thought of as a binomial random variable with probability of a 'success' = $p$ and of a 'failure' = $1 - p$. The total number of days in a year = $n$ = 365, and hence we have $np = 365 \times p = 1$, since the average number of accidents during the year is 1. Now, instead of thinking of each day, we can think of each hour that the motorcyclist is actually riding his bike. In that case, there are many more Binomial trails, say $m > n$, such that $m \times p_1 = 1$, where $m$ is the total number of hours for which the motorcyclist rides his bike during the year and $-p_1$ is the probability that he meets with an accident during one of these hours. Clearly, since $m \times p_1$ and $m > n$, $p_1 < p$. As we think of smaller and smaller intervals in time, the number of such intervals will increase and since the expected number of accidents during the year is fixed at 1, the probability of having an accident during any of these small non-overlapping intervals must become smaller, in such a way that the product of the two remains the same. Clearly, as $n \to \infty$ we should have $p \to 0$ if $np$ is to remain constant. It can be shown that the expression for the Binomial distribution with parameters $n$ and $p$, such that $np = \lambda$ converges to the expression $\dfrac{e^{-\lambda}\lambda^{k}}{k!}$.

In order to get a feel for this intuitive idea, let us state the formal proof:

**Proof:** The Poisson as the limiting case of the Binomial as $p \to 0$, $n \to \infty$, $np$ a constant

Suppose we have a Binomial random variable with the pmf $\binom{n}{x} p^{x}(1-p)^{n-x}$. We rewrite the pmf as follows:

$$\frac{n(n-1)(n-2)......(n-x+1)}{x!} p^{x}(1-p)^{n-x} \qquad \text{Equation 1.1}$$

We have assumed that $np = \lambda$, a constant number. Therefore, we have $p = \dfrac{\lambda}{n}$. Using this, we can rewrite (1.1) as follows:

$$\frac{n(n-1)(n-2)......(n-x+1)}{x!}\left(\frac{\lambda}{n}\right)^{x}\left(n-\frac{\lambda}{n}\right)^{n-x} \qquad \text{Equation 1.2}$$

This can be further rewritten as:

$$\frac{1\left(1-\frac{1}{n}\right)\left(1-\frac{2}{n}\right)........\left(1-\frac{x-1}{n}\right)}{x!} \times (\lambda)^{x}\left[\left(1-\frac{\lambda}{n}\right)^{\frac{-n}{\lambda}}\right]^{-\lambda}\left(1-\frac{\lambda}{n}\right)^{-x}$$

Since:

$$\left(1-\frac{\lambda}{n}\right)^{n-x}=\left[\left(1-\frac{\lambda}{n}\right)^{\frac{-n}{\lambda}}\right]^{-\lambda}\left(1-\frac{\lambda}{n}\right)^{-x}$$

and the first part of the expression has been obtained by dividing $n(n-1)(n-2).....(n-x+1)$ by $n^x$.

Now, letting $n \to \infty$, while $x$ and $\lambda$ remains fixed:

$$\left(1-\frac{1}{n}\right)\left(1-\frac{2}{n}\right).....\left(1-\frac{x-1}{n}\right)\to 1, \left(1-\frac{\lambda}{n}\right)^{\frac{-n}{\lambda}}\to e$$

And hence the Binomial pmf converges to $\dfrac{\lambda^{x}e^{-\lambda}}{x!}$.

We use the Poisson model to model independent events occurring within such very small intervals, with very small probabilities. Therefore, it is sometimes said that the Poisson random variable models 'rare events'.

### Example 1.13

Suppose the number of 'wrong number calls' that you receive on your cell phone arrive randomly at an average rate of 4 calls per month. Then, we can model $X$, the number of 'wrong number calls' you receive as a Poisson random variable.

(a) What is the probability that you will receive exactly 10 such calls during the month?

$$P(X = 10) = e^{-4}\, 4^{10} / 10!$$
$$= 0.005292$$

The R syntax is:

```
f<-dpois(10,4)
```

where 10 is the number of calls and 4 is the value of $\lambda$.

*(b)*What is the probability that you will receive between 3 to 7 such calls in a month?

$$P(3 \le X \le 7) = (e^{-4}\, 4^3 / 3!) + (e^{-4}\, 4^4 / 4!)\, (e^{-4}\, 4^5 / 5!) + (e^{-4}\, 4^6 / 6!)$$
$$+ (e^{-4}\, 4^7 / 7!)$$
$$= 0.195367 + 0.195367 + 0.156293 + 0.104196$$
$$+ 0.059540$$
$$= 0.710763$$

The following graph (Figure 1.4) shows the pmf of a Poisson random variable with $\lambda = 4$. Notice that the graph peaks at 4.

**Figure 1.4**
**The probability mass function of random variable *X* that follows a Poisson distribution with lambda = 4**

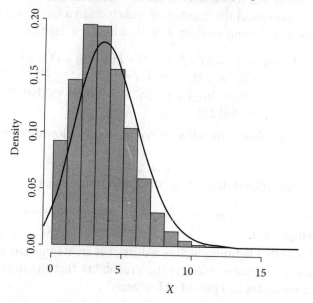

You can modify the program below to see how the shape of the distribution changes with $n$ (the number of observations) and $\lambda$. In this program, $\lambda$ has been set to 4 and $n = 1000000$. You can modify all these parameters and see how the distribution changes shape.

```
poidemo<-function(lambda,n)
{
x<-rpois(n,lambda)
hist(x,xlim=c(min(x),max(x)),probability=T,nclass=max(x)
-min(x)+1,col="lightblue",)
lines(density(x,bw=1),col="red",lwd=4)
}
poidemo(4,1000000)
```

## Example 1.14

The average number of snakebites in small village in India is four per year. Also, snakebites are completely accidental, so the time lapse between two cases of snakebites is independent of the time since last occurrence. What is the probability that in any given year, this village will see between three and six snakebites?

We can model the number of snakebites in a given year in this village as a Poisson random variable with $\lambda = 4$. Hence:

$$P(3 \leq X \leq 6) = P(X = 3) + P(X = 4) + P(X = 5) + P(X = 6)$$
$$= (e^{-4}\, 4^3 / 3!) + (e^{-4}\, 4^4 / 4!)\, (e^{-4}\, 4^5 / 5!) + (e^{-4}\, 4^6 / 6!)$$
$$= 0.195367 + 0.195367 + 0.156293 + 0.104196$$
$$= 0.651223$$

You can obtain this value by typing in the following commands in R:

```
x<-dpois(3,4)+dpois(4,4)+dpois(5,4)+dpois(6,4)
x
```

## Example 1.15

Suppose that lightning strikes a district at an average rate of three times in five years. What is the probability that the district will have no strikes in a period of five years?

Here, the conditions for the Poisson seem to be fulfilled, and hence we can treat the number of lightning strikes in a five-year period as a Poisson random variable with $\lambda = 3$. Therefore,

$$P(X = 0) = e^{-3}\, 3^0 / 0!$$
$$= 0.049787$$

What is the probability that there is at least one strike in five years?

$$P(X \geq 1) = 1 - P(X = 0)$$
$$= 1 - 0.049787$$
$$= 0.950213$$

## Example 1.16

Bortkiewicz (1898) used the Poisson distribution to model the number of deaths from horse kicks in the Prussian army in different years. From official records he extracted the numbers of deaths from horse kicks in 14 army corps over the 20 year period 1875–1894, (so that he had $14 \times 20 = 280$ observations, which we will call corps–years.).He argued that the chance that a particular soldier was killed by a horse kick was very small, but the number of soldiers was very large and hence the Poisson distribution would apply (since $p$ was very small and $n$ was very large).The total number of deaths in all the 14 corps over the 20 sample years was 196, so that the number of deaths per corps–year $= 196 / 280$ $= 0.70$. We can regard 0.70 as the rate at which deaths from horse kicks occurred for a given corps in a given year. Bortkiewicz uses 0.70 as an estimate for $\lambda$ and obtains the probabilities of observing the various number of deaths per corps per year. Multiplying the resultant probabilities for each number with 280 gives the numbers under the column 'Expected Frequency' in Table 1.8.[12] For example:

$$P(X = 0) = e^{-0.7}\, 0.7^0 / 0!$$
$$= 0.4965853$$

The expected number of corps years where no deaths occur $= 0.496585 \times 280 = 139.0438$. This can be rounded off to 139.

Bortkiewicz's complete set of findings is given in Table 1.8.

## Table 1.8
### The observed and expected frequency distributions over the number of deaths from horse kicks in the Prussian army

| Number of deaths | Observed Frequency | Expected Frequency |
|---|---|---|
| 0 | 144 | 139 |
| 1 | 91 | 97 |
| 2 | 32 | 34 |
| 3 | 11 | 8 |
| 4 | 2 | 1 |
| 5 and over | 0 | 0 |
| Total | 280 | $279^{13}$ |

We can see from this table that there is a close fit between the observed and the expected number of deaths.

### Exercise 1.9

Suppose in a large maternity hospital, there are on an average, two pairs of twins per week. Find the probability that 0, 1, 2 or 3 sets of twins are born in any given week.

The quantile function for the Poisson distribution can be calculated in R using the following command: qpois($p, \lambda$) where $p \times 10$ is the quantile that you are looking for while $\lambda$ is the relevant value of $\lambda$. For example, if $\lambda = 4$ then the 90th quantile can be calculated as:

```
qpois(0.9,4)
```

which generates the value 7.

## 1.2.4 Continuous Random Variables

Not all variables are discrete. Some variables may take infinitely many values which cannot be counted. Such variables are referred to as 'continuous random variables'. For example, weights and heights of individuals, time taken to complete a journey, the duration of a call on your cell phone, are all continuous random variables. In such a case, we say that the random variable $X$ takes all values between an interval, say $[a, b]$ where $a$ and $b$ are real numbers and $a < b$. You know that there are infinitely many points between $a$ and $b$. Since the possible values of $X$ cannot be counted, it does not really make sense to speak of the probability with which $X$ takes on any specific value. $P(X = x_i)$ becomes meaningless. But we can meaningfully speak of the probability with which $X$ takes values between any intervals. We deal with this by defining a function $f(x)$ for all values of $X$ between $a$ and $b$ such that $a \leq x_i \leq b$, such that:

C1: $f(x) \geq 0$ for all $a \leq x \leq b$

C2: $\int_{-\infty}^{\infty} f(x)dx = 1$

C3: For an interval such that $-\infty < a < b < \infty$, we have:

$$P(a \leq x \leq b) = \int_{a}^{b} f(x)dx$$

## Definition 1.2: Probability Density Function (pdf) of a Continuous Random Variable

For a continuous random variable $X$, if a continuous function $f$ satisfies the properties C1, C2 and C3 above, we call $f(x)$ the probability density function (pdf) of $X$.

If $f(x)$ is the pdf of a continuous random variable, then:

$$P(X \leq x) = f(x) = \int_{-\infty}^{x} f(x)dx$$

is its cumulative density function. It measures the probability that the random variable takes values less than or equal to $x$. It then follows that:

$$f(x) = \partial F(x) / \partial X.$$

I am sure that you are slightly bothered at this stage. If you were to actually measure weights of a set of people, say your classmates, the data would not take all values between the weights of the thinnest and fattest classmates. What do we then mean by a continuous random variable? What we have done is created an idealized description of the random variable $X$. We want to capture the fact that in principle, $X$ could take any value in an interval. We describe this situation by inventing the idea of a continuous pdf. This idea has considerable intuitive appeal and simplifies calculation. In mathematics, we often 'create' such objects for analytic convenience.

## Example 1.17

Suppose $X$ is a continuous random variable. Let the pdf of $X$ be given by:

$$f(x) = 2x \text{ for } 0 < x < 1$$

and:

$$f(x) = 0$$

in all other cases.

Clearly:

$$f(x) \geq 0, \int_{-\infty}^{\infty} 2x dx = 1,$$

so C1 and C2 are both satisfied. Suppose we want to compute the probability that $P(X \leq 0.5)$, using C3, we have:

$$P(X \leq 0.5) = \int_{0}^{0.5} 2x dx = 1/4$$

The cdf for this random variable is given by:

$$= f(x) = 0 \text{ if } x \leq 0$$
$$= \int_{0}^{x} 2s ds = x^2 \text{ if } 0 < x \leq 1$$
$$= 1 \text{ if } x > 1$$

## Example 1.18

Suppose the pdf of a continuous random variable is given as follows:

$$f(x) = 0 \text{ if } x < 0$$
$$= 2x/(1+x^2)^2) \text{ if } x \geq 0$$

Let us calculate:

$$P[3 \leq X \leq 5] = \int_3^5 (2x/(1+x^2)^2)dx$$

Let $u = -1/u\big|_{u=10}^{u=26}$. Then:

$$P[3 \leq X \leq 5] = \int_{10}^{26} (1/u^2)du$$

$$= -1/u\big|_{u=10}^{u=26} = (1/10) - (1/26) = 4/65$$

Several continuous random variables are crucial to econometrics.

## 1.2.5 The Exponential Distribution

A continuous distribution that is now being increasingly used in applied work is the exponential distribution. The exponential distribution can be used to model waiting time or survival time till an event takes place. Such variables can be modelled using the exponential distribution. Suppose an event occurs $\lambda$ times per second on an average. Then, the average number of times the event occurs in $t$ seconds must be $t\lambda$. Now, if the events are occurring at random, the number of times the event will occur in an interval of $t$ will be a Poisson random variable with mean $t\lambda$; in particular the probability that there is no occurrence of the event in $t$ seconds will be $e^{-\lambda t} (\lambda t)^0 / 0! = e^{-\lambda t}$. Therefore, if $T$ is the time taken for the first occurrence of the event, then:

$$P(T > t) = e^{-\lambda t}$$
$$P(T \leq t) = f(x) = 1 - e^{-\lambda t}$$

However, the latter is nothing but the cumulative density function of the distribution of waiting times. It is the CDF of the exponential distribution. It then implies that $f(x) = \lambda e^{-\lambda t}$. We say that $t$ follows an exponential distribution with parameter $\lambda$. In practice, we have observations on successive outcomes of the event at various times, like $t_1, t_2, \ldots, t_T$. Then, the differences between the times of successive occurrences, $t_2 - t_1, t_3 - t_2 \ldots t_T - t_{T-1}$ will follow the exponential distribution with parameter $\lambda$. For example, suppose the time for which you have to wait at your college canteen for a sandwich is exponentially distributed with $\lambda = 2$. Then, the probability that you will be served in 10 minutes at the most is:

$$P[t \leq 10] = 1 - e^{-2 \times 10}$$
$$= 0.999999997$$

Thus, you can be pretty sure that you will get your sandwich within 10 minutes.

### Exercise 1.10

Suppose the time (in minutes) you wait at the bus stop for your bus to arrive is exponentially distributed with $\lambda = 0.5$. Find the probability that you will have to wait at the bus stop for anything between 3 to 5 minutes.

### 1.2.6 The Normal Distribution

The normally distributed random variable is perhaps the commonest continuous random variable that you will encounter. Indeed, it is central to econometrics.

In general, we say that a random variable $X$, assuming all real values $-\infty < x < \infty$ has a normal (or Gaussian)[14] distribution if its pdf is of the form:

$$f(x) = (1/\sqrt{2\pi}\sigma)\exp(-(x-\mu)^2/2\sigma^2) \quad -\infty < x < \infty \quad \text{Equation 1.3}$$

where the parameter $\mu$ and $\sigma$ are both finite. $\mu$ is the mean of the distribution, whereas $\sigma$ is the standard deviation of the distribution. These two parameters fully describe the normal distribution.

The $\dfrac{1}{\sqrt{2\pi}\sigma}$ part ensures that $\int_{-\infty}^{\infty} f(x)dx$ equals 1. We will often write $f(x)$ in shorthand as $N(\mu, \sigma^2)$. The normal distribution is an excellent approximation to a large class of distributions that have great practical importance. There are some important features of the normal distribution. They are:

1. The distribution is symmetrical about the mean, which equals the median and the mode.

2. Sixty-eight per cent (approximately two-thirds) of the distribution lies within 1 standard deviation of the mean.
3. Approximately 95 per cent of the distribution lies within 2 standard deviations of the mean.
4. Approximately 99.5 per cent of the distribution lies within 3 standard deviations of the mean.

To understand the roles that $\mu$ and $\sigma^2$ play, we will see how the graphs change when we change these two parameters. The graph shown in Figure 1.5 is drawn with $\mu = 2$ and $\sigma = 2$.

**Figure 1.5**
**The normal distribution with mean 2 and std deviation 2**

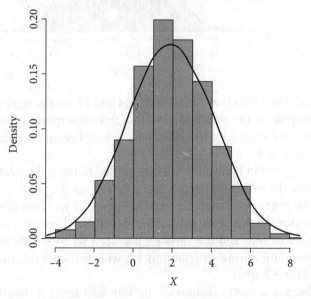

The graph peaks at 2 (which is the value of $\mu$ and most of the values on the x axis lie between –4 and 8, that is, at a distance of 3 × $\sigma$. Suppose we vary $\sigma$, keeping $\mu$ as it is.

Let us change $\sigma$ to 4 to get Figure 1.6.

The graph in Figure 1.6 is still peaking at 2, because we have kept $\mu$ unchanged. But because the standard deviation has now increased to 4, the spread of the values has now increased. The

**Figure 1.6**
**The normal distribution with mean 2 and std deviation 4**

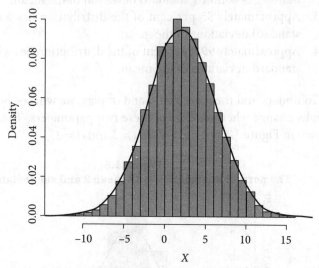

majority of values now lie between −14 and 14, that is, at a distance of three times the standard deviation from the mean. In the next graph (in Figure 1.7), we will change $\mu$ to 5, keeping the standard deviation at 4.

The graph in Figure 1.7 has now shifted to the right, peaking at 5. Thus, the two parameters $\mu$ and $\sigma$ determine the point on the $y$-axis for every point on the $x$-axis. In Figure 1.8 we show the graph of the normal distribution for $N(0, 1)$, that is, where the mean has been set to zero and the variance has been set to 1. This is called the 'standard normal distribution'. We will encounter this more explicitly in Chapter 3.

There is a useful feature of the standard normal distribution that we ought to take note of. Suppose, for the standard normal distribution we want to find the probability that $X$ takes values less than or equal to, say 1.96. Then, we find:

$$P(X \leq 1.96) = \int_{-\infty}^{1.96} f(x)dx = \int_{-\infty}^{1.96} (1/\sqrt{2\pi})\exp(-x^2)dx$$

$$= 0.975^{15}$$

**Figure 1.7**
**The normal distribution with mean 5 and std deviation 4**

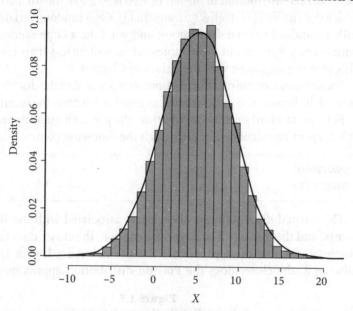

**Figure 1.8**
**The standard normal distribution with mean 0 and std deviation 1**

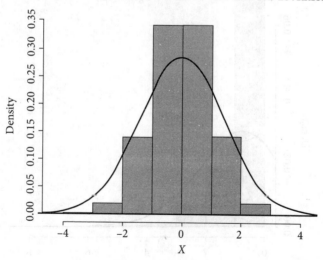

Thus, what we are really saying is that the area under the standard normal distribution to the left of 1.96 is 97.55 of the total area under the curve. This in effect means that if $X$ is a random variable with a standard normal distribution and you take a large random sample from $X$, 97.5% of the samples values will be less than 1.96. This idea is going to be very important in Chapter 3.

For the standard normal distribution, 99.5 per cent of the distribution will lie between $-3$ and 3 (that is, as usual, $3 \times \sigma$ from the mean).

For the standard normal distribution, the $p \times 10$th quantile and $P(X \leq x)$ can be calculated in R through the following commands:

```
pnorm(p)
qnorm(x)
```

The normal distribution is also closely associated with the Binomial and the Poisson. The larger you make $n$, the closer does the binomial distribution approximate the normal. Also, higher the value of $\lambda$, the closer does the Poisson distribution approximate

**Figure 1.9**
**Poisson distribution with lambda = 1**

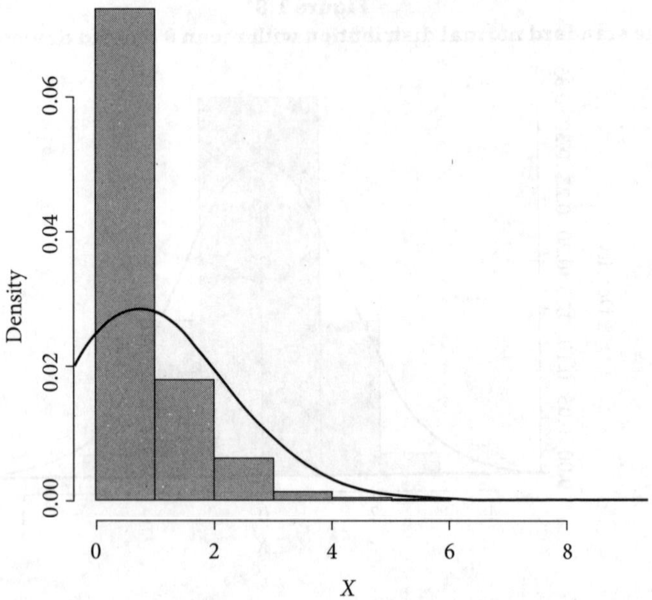

the normal. We show this graphically in Figures 1.9 to 1.12 for $\lambda = 1$, $\lambda = 2, \lambda = 4$ and $\lambda = 40$.

As can be seen from these graphs, as $\lambda$ goes on increasing, the curve becomes closer to the normal distribution. The Binomial distribution will tend to normal distribution as $n$ increases. This 'approaching the normal distribution' is a property shared by

**Figure 1.10**
**Poisson distribution with lambda = 2**

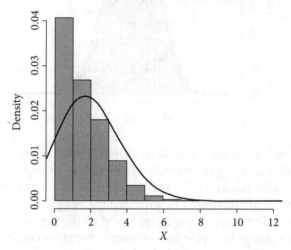

**Figure 1.11**
**Poisson distribution with lambda = 4**

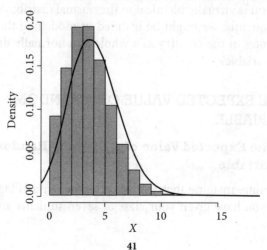

**Figure 1.12**
**Poisson distribution with lambda = 40**

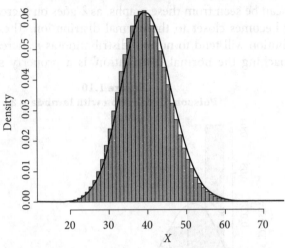

several important statistical distributions. Hence, many times, we are justified in using the normal distribution as an approximation even if we do not know the real distribution of the random variable that we are interested in, provided the sample size is moderately large. To take an example, we modelled the number of snakebites in a village in a year as a Poisson random variable with $\lambda = 4$. However, for India as a whole, there are an average number of 20,000 snakebites in a year. For a value of $\lambda$ that large, the Poisson distribution is virtually identical to the normal distribution.

Consequently, we might be justified in modelling the number of snakebites in the country as a whole as a normally distributed random variable.

## 1.3 THE EXPECTED VALUE OF A RANDOM VARIABLE

### 1.3.1 The Expected Value of a Discrete Random Variable

For a minute, imagine that you are a teacher in a village school. Suppose you have given your class of seven students an exam in poetry. The following are the marks scored by your students (the test is for 10 marks): (5, 7, 5, 8, 7, 8, 5). What are the average marks for the class? Obviously:

$$\text{Average marks} = (5 + 7 + 5 + 8 + 7 + 8 + 5) / 7$$

which equals:

$$((3 / 7) \times 5 + (2 / 7) \times 7 + (2 / 7) \times 8)), \qquad \text{Equation 1.4}$$

since there are 3 fives, 2 sevens and 2 eights respectively.

Now suppose we rephrase the problem. Let us take you away from your idyllic village. Instead of seeing the very same numbers as marks scored by students, we see them as numbers written on seven balls inside a box. Suppose the experiment consists of drawing a ball at random and noting the number on it, before putting the ball back in. Then, $X$, the number on the selected ball, can be thought as a random variable that takes values five, seven and eight. What is the probability that $X$ takes the value 5? Suppose we make a random draw from our urn and note the number on the draw. After that, we put the ball back in the urn, mix all balls thoroughly and take out a fresh ball. We again mark the number, and repeat the whole process again after replacing the ball. If we do this a very large number of times, what will be the limiting value of the fraction of times the number 5 is drawn? Clearly 3 / 7. Hence, we can think of 3 / 7 as the probability of drawing 5 from our set of numbers. The following table (Table 1.9) describes the random variable more fully:

**Table 1.9**
**The probability distribution of the random variable $X$**

| $Xi$ | $P(Xi)$ |
| --- | --- |
| 5 | 3 / 7 |
| 7 | 2 / 7 |
| 8 | 2 / 7 |

Notice that the $P(5)$ is precisely the fraction with which five has been multiplied in Equation 1.1. Similarly, $P(7)$ and $P(8)$ are also the fractions with which seven and eight have been multiplied in computing the average marks in Equation 1.1. So, if I multiply each value that a random variable takes with the probabilities with which it takes that value and then add up all such products, I should get something like the average in Equation 1.1. This sum of products of each value of the random variable with the associated probabilities is called the Expected Value of the Random variable and written as $E(X)$:

$$E(X) = \sum_{i=1}^{n} P(x_i) \times x_i \qquad \text{Equation 1.5}[16]$$

**Example 1.19**

Suppose we are rolling a die and let the random variable $X$ be the number on the uppermost face of the die: Then, the following table

**Table 1.10**
**The probability distribution over the outcomes of a throw of an unbiased die (X)**

| X | P(x) |
|---|---|
| 1 | 1/6 |
| 2 | 1/6 |
| 3 | 1/6 |
| 4 | 1/6 |
| 5 | 1/6 |
| 6 | 1/6 |

(Table 1.10) describes the values of the random variable and the associated probabilities.

$E(X) = 1 \times 1/6 + 2 \times 1/6 + 3 \times 1/6 + 4 \times 1/6 + 5 \times 1/6 + 6 \times 1/6 = 3.5$

Hence, the expected value of the number on the uppermost face of the die is 3.5. Let me sound a note of caution. The number 3.5 says that if you went on rolling a die, noting the number on the upper most face of the die and again rolling it, the average value of the numbers that you would get will be 3.5, provided you repeated the experiment sufficiently many times. The term 'expected value' could be a misnomer. You can never expect 3.5 to show up on any given trial. You must always remember this interpretation of the 'expected value'.[17]

### Example 1.20

Suppose you are tossing three balanced coins. Let $X$ be the number of heads that show up on any given toss. If you kept on doing this for a sufficiently long period, what would be the average of the number of heads on all tosses?

We are clearly calculating the expected value of the number of heads. Since three coins are being tossed, the set of possible values that $X$ can take will be (0, 1, 2, 3). To find the expected value, we must find the probability with which $X$ takes each value, multiply each value by this probability and add the resulting products. To obtain the probabilities, we must recognize that this is a case of a discrete random variable, the Binomial random variable in this case. Also, since the coins are balanced, it seems reasonable to assign probability 0.5 to the event that a head shows up as well as the event that a tail shows up. Also, since the two events are independent:

$$P(X = 0) = (3!/0!3!) \times (0.5)^0 \times (0.5)^3$$
$$= 0.125$$
$$P(X = 1) = (3!/1!2!) \times (0.5)^1 \times (0.5)^2$$
$$= 0.375$$
$$P(X = 2) = (3!/2!1!) \times (0.5)^2 \times (0.5)^1$$
$$= 0.375$$
$$P(X = 3) = (3!/3!0!) \times (0.5)^0 3(0.5)^0$$
$$= 0.125$$

Note that both P1 and P2 are satisfied in this case: Hence:

$$E(X) = 0 \times 0.125 + 1 \times 0.375 + 2 \times 0.375 + 3 \times 0.125$$
$$= 1.5$$

## Example 1.21

The Expected Value of a Binomial Random Variable.

Let $X$ be a binomial random variable with parameters $n$ and $p$. Let us try to find $E(X)$.

Since:

$$P(X = k) = \binom{n}{k} p^k (1-p)^{n-k}$$

we have:

$$E(X) = \sum_{k=0}^{n} (n! / (k-1)!(n-k)!) p^k (1-p)^{n-k}$$

Let $s = k-1$, so $k = s + 1$. Carrying out this substitution, we see that:

$$E(X) = \sum_{s=0}^{n-1} n \binom{n-1}{s} p^{s+1} (1-p)^{n-s-1}$$

$$= np \sum_{s=0}^{n-1} \binom{n-1}{s} p^s (1-p)^{n-1-s}$$

Notice that the term inside the summation sign is nothing but the sum of the Binomial probabilities with $n$ replaced by $(n - 1)$, and hence:

$$\sum_{s=0}^{n-1} \binom{n-1}{s} p^s (1-p)^{n-1-s} = (p + (1-p))^{n-1}$$

$$= 1$$

As a result, we have:

$$E(X) = np$$

## Example 1.22

Suppose we toss 10 balanced coins. Let $X$ be the number of heads that come up. Obviously, $X$ is a binomial random variable, with $n = 10$ and $p = 0.5$. Hence, the expected number of heads $= np = 0.5 \times 10 = 5$.

## Exercise 1.11

Suppose $X$ follows the Poisson distribution with $\lambda = 4$ and that $X$ can take values 0, 1, 2, 3 and 4. Find the expected value of $X$. What is remarkable about the result? Notice that the expected value of a Poisson random variable is exactly equal to $4(\lambda)$. This should not surprise you at all since we have defined the average rate of occurrence of $X$ in the first place.

Just like you can find the expected value of $X$, you can also find the expected value of $X^2$.

For example, in Example 1.20, the expected value of $X^2$ will simply be the sum of the products of the square of each value of $X$ multiplied by the probability that $X$ takes that value:

$$E(X^2) = 0^2 \times 0.125 + 1^2 \times 0.375 + 2^2 \times 0.375 + 3^2 \times 0.125$$
$$= 3$$

## Exercise 1.12

Suppose you are given the following values of $X$ and its pmf as given in Table 1.11:

**Table 1.11**
**The probability distribution of the random variable $X$**

| X | P(x) |
|---|------|
| 1 | 1 / 5 |
| 2 | 1 / 5 |
| 3 | 1 / 5 |
| 4 | 1 / 5 |
| 5 | 1 / 5 |

Calculate $E(X)$ and $E(X^2)$.

## 1.3.2 The Expected Value of a Continuous Random Variable

Think of a continuous random variable with pdf $f(x)$, defined over the range $-\infty < x < \infty$. Then, the expected value of the random variable is given by:

$$E(X) = \int_{-\infty}^{\infty} x f(x) dx^{18}$$

### Example 1.23

Suppose the pdf of $x$ is given by the following:

$$f(x) = 1 / (b - a) \text{ if } a \le x \le b$$
$$= 0$$

in all other cases.
Then:

$$E(X) = \int_{a}^{b} (x/(b-a)) dx$$

$$= (1/(b-a)) x^2/2 \Big|_{a}^{b}$$

$$= (a + b)/2$$

The distribution in this example is referred to as the uniform probability distribution. The expected value of a uniformly distributed random variable over the interval $[a, b]$ equals the midpoint of the interval.

### Example 1.24

The expected value of an exponential random variable:

If $X$ is an exponential random variable with parameter $\lambda$, then:

$$f(x) = \lambda e^{-\lambda x}$$

if $0 \le x \le \infty$
$= 0$
in all other cases.

$$E(X) = \int_{0}^{\infty} x \lambda e^{-\lambda x} dx$$

Integrating by parts, and letting $\lambda e^{-\lambda x} dx = dv$ and $x = u$, we obtain $v = -e^{-\lambda x}$, $du = dx$. Thus:

$$E(X) = \left[ -x e^{-\lambda x} \right]_{0}^{\infty} + \int_{0}^{\infty} e^{-\lambda x} dx = 1/\lambda$$

thus, higher the value of lower is $E(X)$.

## 1.3.3 Expected Value of a Sum of Two Random Variables

Suppose we roll two dice and let the random variable $X$ be the sum of the numbers on the uppermost faces of the two dice. We will represent the elements of the sample space by ordered pairs, where the first element will represent the number on the first die while the second will represent the number on the second die. The sample space:

$$\Omega = \{(1, 1), (1, 2), (1, 3), (1, 4), (1, 5), (1, 6)$$
$$(2, 1), (2, 2), (2, 3), (2, 4), (2, 5), (2, 6)$$
$$(3, 1), (3, 2), (3, 3), (3, 4), (3, 5), (3, 6)$$
$$(4, 1), (4, 2), (4, 3), (4, 4), (4, 5), (4, 6)$$
$$(5, 1), (5, 2), (5, 3), (5, 4), (5, 5), (5, 6)$$
$$(6, 1), (6, 2), (6, 3), (6, 4), (6, 5), (6, 6)\}$$

The random variable $X$ will take the following values:

$$X = \{2, 3, 4, 5, 6, 7, 3, 4, 5, 6, 7, 8, 4, 5, 6, 7, 8, 9, 5, 6, 7, 8, 9, 10,$$
$$6, 7, 8, 9, 10, 11, 7, 8, 9, 10, 11, 12\}$$

Thus, the lowest value that $X$ takes is two while the highest value is 12. It takes the value two once out of a possible 36. Hence, we will associate a probability 1 / 36 with the two. $X$ takes the value three twice and hence we will associate a probability of 2 / 36 with three. In a similar manner, we can write down Table 1.12 as:

$$E(x) = (1 / 36) \times 2 + (2 / 36) \times 3 + (3 / 36) \times 4 + (4 / 36) \times 5$$
$$+ (5 / 36) \times 6 + (6 / 36) \times 7 + (5 / 36) \times 8 + (4 / 36) \times 9$$
$$+ (3 / 36) \times 10 + (2 / 36) \times 11 + (1 / 36) \times 12$$
$$= 7.$$

Let us understand this number carefully. We rolled two dice, summed the numbers that appeared on the uppermost faces, and found the average of this sum. Initially, in Example 1.20, we had rolled just one die and found that the expected value of the number

**Table 1.12**
**The probability distribution over the sums of the numbers**
**on the uppermost faces of two dice resulting from a throw**
**of two unbiased dice**

| X | P(x) |
|---|---|
| 2 | 1 / 36 |
| 3 | 2 / 36 |
| 4 | 3 / 36 |
| 5 | 4 / 36 |
| 6 | 5 / 36 |
| 7 | 6 / 36 |
| 8 | 5 / 36 |
| 9 | 4 / 36 |
| 10 | 3 / 36 |
| 11 | 2 / 36 |
| 12 | 1 / 36 |

on the uppermost face of the dice was equal to 3.5. Now, we are rolling two such dice, and finding the expected value of the sum on their uppermost faces. This turns out to be exactly equal (3.5 + 3.5) to the sum on the uppermost faces of the two dice when rolled individually. This is to be expected, because it is not hard to see that the average of a sum is nothing but the sum of the individual averages. From this, we have the following rule:

$$E(X + Y) = E(X) + E(Y)$$

In general:

$$E(X_1 + X_2 + \ldots + X_n) = E(X_1) + E(X_2) + \ldots + E(X_n) \quad \text{Equation 1.6}$$

Also:

$$E(\alpha X) = \alpha E(X) \text{ where } \alpha \text{ is a constant} \qquad \text{Equation 1.7}$$

And:

$$E(X + c) = E(X) + c \qquad \text{Equation 1.8}$$

where $c$ is a constant

Equations 1.6, 1.7 and 1.8 together imply that $E(X)$ is linear. Equation 1.3 means that if you take the average of a sum, then that would be equal to the sum of the individual averages. Equation 1.4 implies that if you multiply all values of a random variable by a constant value, the average will also be multiplied by the same constant value. Equation 1.5 says that if you add a constant value to each of the values of a random variable and then take an average, the result will be identical to taking the average of the random variable first and then adding the constant. Collectively, Equations 1.6, 1.7 and 1.8 together imply the following:

$$E(\alpha X + \beta Y + c) = \alpha E(X) + \beta E(Y) + c \qquad \text{Equation 1.9}$$

### Exercise 1.13

If all the values of a random variable $X$ are equal to a constant $\alpha$, then $E(X) = \alpha$. Prove this statement.

We have seen in Example 1.1 that the sample mean is also a random variable. Suppose we have a sample of size $n$: $(X_1, X_2, \ldots X_n)$. Suppose further that each of the elements of this sample comes from a population with a mean $\mu$. To understand this statement better, think of an urn which contains 10 balls numbered from 1 to 10. The average of all the numbers on the balls in the urn is $(1 + 2 + 3 + 4 + 5 + 6 + 7 + 8 + 9 + 10) / 10 = 5.5$. We will denote this number, 5.5 by $\mu$. Suppose we decide to draw a ball at random, note the number written on it, and put the ball back in, before repeating the experiment. Then, we can draw as many balls as we want from this urn. Suppose we decide to draw 100 balls in this fashion and compute the sample mean. Then, we draw another set of 100 balls in the same manner and compute the sample mean. As we have seen above, the sample mean, *Xbar* is a random variable. What will be the expected value of *Xbar*?

$$E(Xbar) = E\left(\sum_{i=1}^{100} X_i / 100\right)$$

which, because of Equation 1.9 is

$$(1/100) \times E(X_1) + (1/100) \times E(X_2) + \ldots + (1/100) \times E(X_{100})$$

$$\text{Equation 1.10}$$

Now, let us consider what we understand by $E(X_1)$. We have taken out successive samples of 100 balls each. $X_1$ is a random variable denoting the number that comes up on the uppermost face of the first ball across all the samples we have taken. $E(X_1)$ is the average value of the numbers showing up on the first ball drawn across successive samples. What will this number be? Since any ball can be drawn the 'first' ball for a particular sample, the average of the numbers on the first ball will just be equal to the average of all the numbers in the urn, which is $\mu$. Hence, $E(X_1) = \mu$. But the same logic will hold for $E(X_2)$, and indeed for all $X_i$, for $i = 1, \ldots\ldots 100$. Hence, Equation 1.10 will become:

$$E(Xbar) = (1/100) \times \mu + (1/100) \times \mu + \ldots\ldots\ldots + (1/100) \times \mu$$
$$= 100 \times \mu \,/\, 100$$
$$= \mu$$

In general, if $X_1, X_2 \ldots\ldots X_n$ is a sample from a population with mean $\mu$, and $Xbar = \sum_{i=1}^{n} X_i \,/\, n$, then:

$$E(Xbar) = \frac{1}{n} \times E(X_1) + \frac{1}{n} \times E(X_2) + \ldots\ldots \frac{1}{n} \times E(X_n)$$
$$= \frac{1}{n} \times \mu + \ldots\ldots\ldots \frac{1}{n} \times \mu$$
$$n \times \frac{\mu}{n}$$
$$= \mu \qquad\qquad \text{Equation 1.11}$$

Equation 1.11 is saying something fundamental. It tells us that if we take many samples of size $n$ (in this example $n$ equals 100, but in general it can take any value) from a population where each unit drawn has a mean equal to $\mu$, the average value of the sample means will be equal to $\mu$. Therefore, it makes sense to use the sample mean as an 'estimator' of $\mu$.[19] An estimator which has the property that its expected value equals the population parameter, which it is meant to estimate, is called an 'unbiased estimator' of that parameter. The sample mean is an unbiased estimator of the population mean. We are going to study this property in greater detail in Chapter 4. Nevertheless, we will discuss it briefly here. How does this help in a practical context, where you are likely to have just one sample and hence only one value of the sample mean? Suppose you want to estimate the mean monthly income of a family in Mumbai. You collect data on monthly income from 1,000 randomly selected households and this number turns out to be 6,000. This is surely not equal to the mean income of a household in Mumbai. But the unbiased assertion is that though the sample mean that you have obtained is not equal to the population mean, the formula for computing the mean has the property that the average value of all the estimates that it yields will be equal to the mean family income in Mumbai, which you are seeking.

To see this more clearly, think of the following situation. Suppose we have 500 balls in an urn, such that the average value of the numbers on these balls equals zero. We draw 1,000 samples of size 500 with replacement (that is, putting the balls back in after noting the number). We will get 1,000 sample means. The graph below in Figure 1.13 plots the probability distribution of these 1,000 *Xbar* values.[20]

**Figure 1.13**
**Sampling distribution of the mean (sample size = 500)**

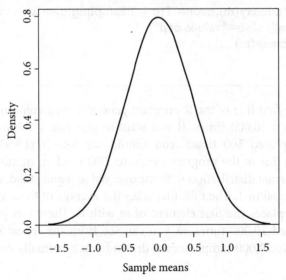

Sample means

This is called the 'sampling distribution' of the mean. We see that the probability distribution peaks over 0, the value of $\mu$. The average value of the entire 1,000 sample means in this case equals 0.0001045899, which is pretty close to zero, the population mean. You can carry out your own experiments using the R program given below. This program assumes that the population is normally distributed with mean 0 and standard deviation 1. It then draws 1,000 samples, each of size 500 from the population and computes the sample mean for each of them. Finally, it generates the probability distribution of the sample means. You can vary the numbers and see how the graphs change. The program is reproduced here:

```
m<-c(rep(1,10000))
i=1
repeat {
x<-rnorm(500,mean=0,sd=1)
xbar=mean(x)
m[i]=xbar
i=i+1
if(i>10000)
break
}
plot(density(m),main="Fig 1.2:Sampling distribution of the
mean", xlab="values of μ")
xx=mean(m)
xx
```

The first line of the R program generates $m$, a column of ones, repeated 10,000 times. If you want to generate a column of say 5s, repeated 500 times, you should say X<-c(rep(5,500)). The fourth line of the program generates 500 random numbers from the normal distribution with mean equal to 0 and standard deviation equal to 1. The fifth line takes the average of these numbers, and replaces the first element of $m$ with it. Then, this process is repeated 10,000 times, as you can see from the repeat loop. So, we have 10,000 sample means drawn from a normally distributed population with mean 0 and variance 1. Then, the density command generates the probability distribution of the sample means, which is then plotted. You should type in this program in R and experiment with it.

### 1.3.4 Substitution Rule for Random Variables

Suppose $X$ is a discrete random variable with a specified pmf. In some problems, we might want to calculate the expected value not of $X$ itself, but of some function of $X$, say $g(X)$. This is where the substitution rule helps. If $g(X)$ is a given real valued function, then $g(X)$ is itself a random variable and the expected value of $g(X)$ can be calculated directly from the probability distribution of $X$.

***Theorem 1.1***

For any function $g$ of the random variable $X$:

$$E(g(X)) = \sum_{i=1}^{n} g(x_i)P(X = x_i)$$

provided

$$\sum_{i=1}^{n} g(x_i)P(X = x_i) < \infty$$

This rule is called 'the substitution rule'. The proof of this rule is straightforward. If $X$ takes values $x_1, \ldots\ldots x_n$ with probabilities, $p_1, \ldots\ldots, p_n$, and suppose $g(x_i) \neq g(x_j)$, $i \neq j$, then $g(x_i)$ takes values with the probabilities identical to the probabilities associated with $x_i$. Therefore, we have the theorem. To see an application, suppose we are rolling a die and the random variable of interest is $g(X) = X^2 + 2$, where $X$ is the number on the uppermost face of the die. What is $E(g(X))$?

Let us specify the probability distribution of $X$ as well as $g(X)$ (see Table 1.13).

The key to understanding the substitution rule is that the probabilities associated with values of $X$ (given in column 2) and those associated with values of $g(X)$ (given in column 4) are identical. As a result:

**Table 1.13**
**The probability distribution of the random variable $X$ and over the values of $g(X)$**

| X | P(X) | g(X) | P(g(X)) |
|---|------|------|---------|
| 1 | 1 / 6 | 3 | 1 / 6 |
| 2 | 1 / 6 | 6 | 1 / 6 |
| 3 | 1 / 6 | 11 | 1 / 6 |
| 4 | 1 / 6 | 18 | 1 / 6 |
| 5 | 1 / 6 | 27 | 1 / 6 |
| 6 | 1 / 6 | 38 | 1 / 6 |

$$E(g(X)) = \sum_{i=1}^{n} g(x_i)P(X = x_i)$$

An important point to remember here is that, in general:

$$E(g(X)) \neq g(E(X)).$$

In the case of our example:

$$E(g(X)) = 17.166667$$

whereas:

$$g(E(X)) = g(3.5) = 3.5^2 + 2 = 14.25$$

## 1.4 VARIANCE OF A RANDOM VARIABLE

Suppose the straight line below represents a highway:

_____0__1__2__3__...

The point marked 0 is the starting point of the highway. There are milestones numbered 1, 2, and so on; one for every mile that you travel away from zero. Assume that your friend's house is situated exactly where the milestone numbered 1 stands, while your home is right on the milestone numbered 2. What is the distance of your home from your friend's house? An intuitively appealing answer would be 1 mile, which is obtained by subtracting the number on the milestone near your friend's house from the milestone near your house. However, this would not be entirely correct. By this logic, the distance of your friend's home from your home will be the result of subtracting the number on your milestone from the number on your friend's mile stone, which equals $1 - 2 = -1$. Not only can distances never be negative, the distance from your friend's house to your house must be the same as the distance from your house to your friend's house. There are two ways to achieving this. If you want to find the distance between points $A$ and $B$, subtract the number on the milestone at point $A$ from the number on the milestone at point $B$ and simply ignore the sign. Indeed, this is what we implicitly always do. The other method would be to subtract the number on the milestone at $A$ from the number on the milestone at $B$ and then square the resultant. This will also ensure that the distance from $A$ to $B$ is the same as the distance from $B$ to $A$ and that it is never negative. Statisticians normally prefer the second method of measuring distances. In other words, if $X_A$ and $X_B$ are milestones on point $A$ and $B$ respectively, the distance between $A$ and $B$ is given by $(X_A - X_B)^2$.

This should now help us to understand the idea of variance more clearly. Suppose we have three numbers 1, 2 and 3. Then, $(1-2)^2$ is the distance of one from two, $(3-2)^2$ is the distance of three from two, etc.

Therefore, $\{(1-2)^2 + (2-2)^2 + (3-2)^2\} / 3$ is the average distance (total distance divided by the number of individual distances) of an observation from 2. This is precisely the idea of variance. Note that in the above example, 2 is really the average of 1, 2 and 3. We will call this $\mu$ and assume that it is known before hand. (Think of the following situation: there are three balls in an urn, numbered 1, 2 and 3 and you know this fact.) Let one be $X_1$, let two be $X_2$ and let three be $X_3$, in general, you can think of $n$ such $X'_i s$. The average distance of a number in this set of numbers from the mean can be computed as follows:

$$\sum_{i=1}^{n} \frac{(X_i - \mu)^2}{n}$$

This number is referred to as the 'variance'. This is simply the sum of distances divided by the number of such distances. This number tells us the average distance of an observation from the mean. That is, suppose we have an urn in which we have balls numbered 1, 2 .... and so on. Assume that the mean of all such numbers in the urn is $\mu$. Suppose we withdraw a ball at random, noting the number on it, and putting the ball back into the urn. Then, we know that the average of all the numbers drawn will be a close approximation of $\mu$, provided we draw many such numbers. However, we will also want to know what would be the average 'distance' of any of the randomly drawn numbers from $\mu$. That answer is provided by the variance if we agree to measure distance as a squared difference. The square root of the variance:

$$\sigma = \frac{\sqrt{\sum_{i=1}^{n}(x_i - \mu)^2}}{n}$$

is known as the 'standard deviation'.

In general, we may not know $\mu$. In that case, we will replace it by its estimate from the sample:

$$Xbar = \sum_{i=1}^{n} x_i / n$$

and replace the unknown $\mu$ by $Xbar$. However, now there is an important consideration that we must pay attention to. We are aware from elementary statistics that the sum of the deviations around the sample mean, that is:

$$\sum_{i=1}^{n}(x_i - xbar) = 0$$

Think of numbers 1, 2 and 3. Now suppose we did not know beforehand that the mean of these numbers was equal to 2. (As might happen when you do not know the numbers on the balls in the urn beforehand, but notice them only after drawing them, and the three balls that you have randomly drawn have numbers

58

1, 2 and 3 on them respectively.) In this case, you will estimate the sample mean as $(1 + 2 + 3) / 3 = 2$. But now, we have $(1 - 2) + (2 - 2) + (3 - 2) = 0$. Suppose now, you know that the first ball drawn is 1, the second ball drawn in 2 and that the sample mean is 2. In that case, because the sum of the deviations around the mean has to be equal to zero, the third ball will necessarily have to be three. That means that there are only two deviations from the mean that can be independently determined; the third deviation is determined by the rule that the sum of the deviations around the mean has to be zero. Hence, to obtain the average distance from the mean, you really have only $n - 1$ independent distances. And therefore, if you have estimated the sample mean, the sum of the squared deviations from the mean must be divided by $n - 1$, not by $n$. We will define the number of elements of the data that can vary independently, when we are estimating a parameter as 'degrees of freedom'. In this case, there are $n - 1$ and not $n$ degrees of freedom because we have estimated one parameter, the sample mean. In general, if we are estimating $k$ parameters from $n$ observations, then the degrees of freedom are $n - k$. You can think of the idea of 'degrees of freedom' as involving the number of independent bits of information that you have in order to estimate a parameter. For example, suppose you are sitting in a group of five friends and wish to know the time. Let us assume that none of your friends have the exact time, but the time on their watches can differ from the real time by arbitrary unrelated amounts. A way to estimate the correct time could be to take an arithmetic average of the time on the watches of all your friends. However, suppose Ramesh has just set his watch exactly 5 minutes faster than that of Savita, another group member. In that case, we do not really have five independent times, but only four since the time on Ramesh's watch does not give you any additional information about the real time. We then say that we have only four and not five degrees of freedom. By this logic, 'the sample variance' is given by:

$$\hat{\sigma}^2 = \frac{\sum_{i=1}^{n}(x_i - xbar)^2}{n-1}$$

The square root of the sample variance:

$$\hat{\sigma} = \sqrt{\frac{\sum_{i=1}^{n}(x_i - xbar)^2}{n-1}}$$

is known as the 'sample standard deviation.'[21]

The critical idea is that the variance too, is an average. It is the mean of the squared deviations from the mean. Remembering this will make several things easy. For example, the sample mean is an unbiased estimator of the population mean. The sample variance is also a mean, and hence it must also be an unbiased estimator of the corresponding population feature, the population variance. We will show this more formally in a short while.

Since the variance is also an average, it must have a representation as an expected value of a random variable. Remember that $X$ is a random variable. Then, the square of the deviation of $X$ from its mean must also be a random variable. The variance is the mean, or the expected value of this random variable. Hence, we can write:

$$
\begin{aligned}
\sigma_x^2 &= E(X - E(X))^2 \\
&= E(X^2 - 2 \times XE(X) + E(X)^2) \\
&= E(X^2) - 2 \times E(X)^2 + E(X)^2 \quad \text{(from Equation 1.6)} \\
&= E(X^2) - E(X)^2 \quad \text{(Equation 1.12)}
\end{aligned}
$$

Thus, the variance of a random variable can be expressed as the average value of the squared random variable minus the square of the average value. Calculating the variance of a random variable is straightforward.

### Example 1.25

Suppose the experiment consists of rolling a die and letting $X$ be the number on the uppermost face of the die. We will calculate the variance of $X$ (see Table 1.14).

$$
\begin{aligned}
E(X^2) &= 1/6 \times 1 + 4 \times 1/6 + 1/6 \times 9 + 1/6 \times 16 + 1/6 \times 25 + 1/6 \times 36 \\
&= 15.166667 \\
\sigma_x^2 &= E(X^2) - E(X))^2 \\
&= 15.166667 - (3.5)^2 \\
&= 2.916667
\end{aligned}
$$

**Table 1.14**
**The calculation of the variance of X**

| X | X² | P(X) |
|---|---|---|
| 1 | 1 | 1 / 6 |
| 2 | 4 | 1 / 6 |
| 3 | 9 | 1 / 6 |
| 4 | 16 | 1 / 6 |
| 5 | 25 | 1 / 6 |
| 6 | 36 | 1 / 6 |

## Exercise 1.14

Find the variance of the random variable in Exercise 1.12.

## Exercise 1.15

Suppose you are given the values of the random variable $X$ and $P(X)$ (see Table 1.15). Find its variance.

**Table 1.15**
**The probability distribution of the random variable X**

| X | P(X) |
|---|---|
| 2 | 1 /36 |
| 3 | 2 /36 |
| 4 | 3 /36 |
| 5 | 4 /36 |
| 6 | 5 /36 |
| 7 | 6 /36 |
| 8 | 5 /36 |
| 9 | 4 /36 |
| 10 | 3 /36 |
| 11 | 2 /36 |
| 12 | 1 /36 |

## Exercise 1.16

An experiment consists of tossing four balanced coins. Let $X$ be the number of heads that come up. The number of heads out of four tosses follows the Binomial distribution, with $p = 0.5$. Find the expected value and variance of $X$.

### Exercise 1.17

Suppose the number of telephone calls that arrive in an hour $X = (0, 1, 2, 3, 4, 5)$ follows the Poisson distribution with $\lambda = 3$. Find the expected value and variance of $X$.

Let us go back to Example 1.25. Suppose, instead of thinking about $X$, we consider $10X$, so that every value of the random variable is multiplied by 10. We know from Equation 1.4 that the expected value will also go up by 10. What happens to the variance of $10X$?

Let us calculate that (see Table 1.16).

**Table 1.16**
**The calculation of the variance of $X$**

| $X$ | $X^2$ | $P(X)$ |
|---|---|---|
| 10 | 100 | 1/6 |
| 20 | 400 | 1/6 |
| 30 | 900 | 1/6 |
| 40 | 1,600 | 1/6 |
| 50 | 2,500 | 1/6 |
| 60 | 3,600 | 1/6 |

The value of $X$ has got scaled up by 10, so the value of $E(X^2)$ gets scaled up by 100. $E(X^2)$ also gets scaled up by 100, following Equation 1.4. Also $E(X)$ gets scaled up by 10, so that $E(X^2)$ gets scaled by 100. Hence, we have:

$$\text{Variance}(10X) = 100 \times E(X^2) - 100 \times E(X)^2$$
$$= 100 \times \text{Variance}(X)$$

In general,

$$\text{Variance}(\alpha X) = \alpha^2 \text{Variance}(X) \qquad \text{Equation 1.13}$$

We can also think of the variance of the sum of independent random variables.

## 1.4.1 Variance of a Sum of Random Variables

Let $X_1, \dots \dots X_n$ be $n$ independent random variables.[22] Then, the variance of the sum equals the sum of the individual variances. That is

$$\sigma^2_{x_1+x_2+\dots x_n} = \sigma^2_{x_1} + \sigma^2_{x_2} + \dots \dots \dots + \sigma^2_{x_n} \quad \text{Equation 1.14}$$

## 1.4.2 The Variance of the Sample Mean

We know that the sample mean has an expected value equal to the population mean. So, if we have just one sample, we know that the sample mean is generally different from the population mean, the value that we are trying to estimate. If we knew the average distance that any given sample mean will lie from the population mean, it would be helpful. But this is the variance of the sample mean. Let us now consider this quantity. Suppose we have a sample of size $n$, $(x_1, x_2, \dots \dots x_n)$, where all the $X_i$ are independent and come from a population with mean $\mu$ and variance $\sigma^2$:

$$\text{Variance}(xbar) = \text{Variance}\left(\frac{\sum_{i=1}^{n} x_i}{n}\right)$$

$$= \text{Variance}\left(\frac{x_1}{n} + \frac{x_2}{n} + \dots \dots + \frac{x_n}{n}\right)$$

$$= \frac{1}{n^2} \times \sigma^2 + \frac{1}{n^2} \times \sigma^2 + \dots \dots \dots + \frac{1}{n^2} \times \sigma^2 \quad \text{where the sum involves } n \text{ terms}$$

$$= \frac{\sigma^2}{n}$$

What this means is that if we have a random sample of size $n$ from a population which has mean $\mu$ and variance $\sigma^2$, the sample mean *Xbar* will have a sampling distribution with mean equal to $\mu$ and variance equal to $\dfrac{\sigma^2}{\text{sample size}}$. That is, suppose we collect a random sample of size 100 from a population with mean equal to 200 and variance equal to 100, the sample mean will have a sampling distribution with mean equal to 200 (the same as the population) but a variance equal to 1 (population variance divided by the sample size). This then implies another desirable property of the sample mean: as the sample size increases, the variance of the sample mean declines. That is, the average value of the sample mean gets closer and closer to the population mean as the sample size increases. Figures 1.14 and 1.15 demonstrate this. The first graph plots the sampling distribution of the sample mean for a sample size of 10, where the sample is chosen from a population that follows the standard normal distribution. Clearly, the value of the population mean is zero. The mean of every sample will be an unbiased estimator of the population mean, but individual sample means will not always be equal to zero.

Here, we see that the sample mean is an unbiased estimator of the population mean, but individual values can be as far apart as –3 and +3.

In Figure 1.15, we increase the sample size from 10 to 100.

We see that again, the sample mean continues to be unbiased. But the individual values are now spread much closer to the val-

**Figure 1.14**
**Sampling distribution of the mean (sample size = 10)**

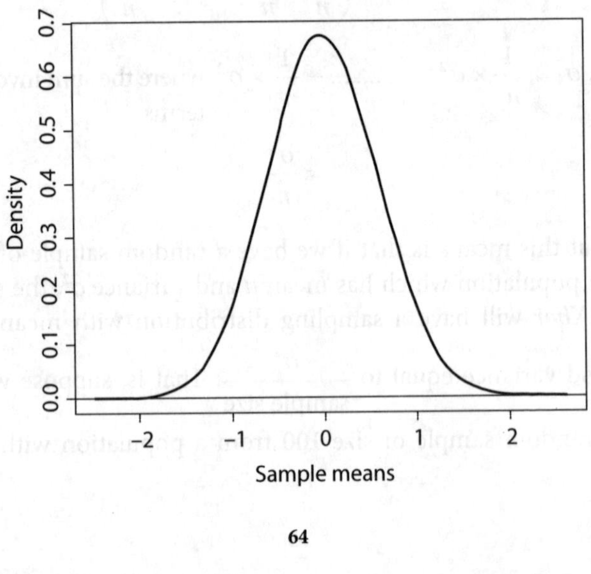

**Figure 1.15**
**Sampling distribution of the mean (sample size = 100)**

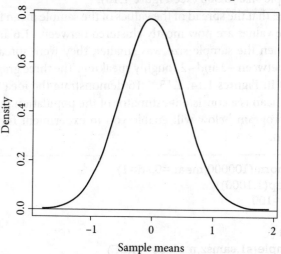

Sample means

ue of the population mean. The variance of the sample mean has

**Figure 1.16**
**Sampling distribution of the mean (sample size = 500)**

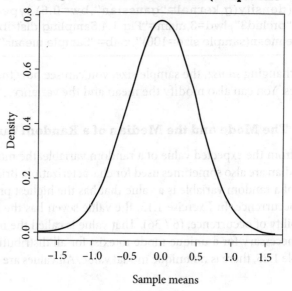

Sample means

fallen as the sample size has increased. Now suppose we increase the sample size to 500 (see Figure 1.16).

We see that the spread of the values of the sample mean falls further. The values are now mostly clustered between −1.6 and +1.6, while when the sample size was smaller, they were spread more widely, between +2 and −2 roughly speaking. The three graphs represented in Figures 1.14, 1.15, 1.16 demonstrate the idea that the sample mean is a consistent estimator of the population mean.

The program below will enable you to experiment further on your own.

```
s1<-rnorm(100000,mean=0,sd=1)
g=c(rep(1,1000))
samsz=100
i=1
repeat {
d=sample(s1,samsz,replace=TRUE)
g[i]= mean(d)
i=i+1
if(i>1000)
break
}
plot(density(g,kernel="gaussian",bw=0.5),type="l",
col="orchid3", lwd=3,main="Fig 1.4:Sampling distribution
of the mean(sample size=100)",xlab="Sample means")
```

By changing *samsz*, the sample size, you can see how the graph changes. You can also modify the mean and the variance.

### 1.4.3 The Mode and the Median of a Random Variable

Apart from the expected value of a random variable, the mode and the median are also sometimes used for characterization. Briefly, the mode of a random variable is a value that has the highest probability of occurrence. In Exercise 1.15, the value seven has the highest probability of occurrence, (6 / 36). That value is called the mode. It is not necessary for a unique mode to exist for all distributions. In Example 1.25, there is no unique modal value. All values are equally likely. The median is a value that divides the distribution into two symmetric parts. You can see that in the case of Exercise 1.15, seven is also the median value. Unlike the mode, the median always exists. In Example, 1.25, there is no modal value, but 3.5 is the value which divides the distribution into two equal halves.

The relationship between the mean, median and mode (whenever all three exist) can be used to characterise the skewness of the distribution as we will see below.

### 1.4.4 Kurtosis and Skewness

Variations in the logarithm of stock market indices, exchange rates and many other financial assets are often of interest to econometricians. They can be placed in relation to the normal distribution, even when they themselves are not necessarily nor-

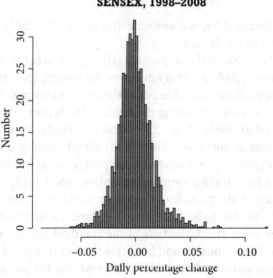

**Figure 1.17**
**Distribution of daily percentage changes in the SENSEX, 1998–2008**

mally distributed. Figure 1.17 shows the distribution of percentage daily returns on the Bombay Stock Exchange Sensex.

**Figure 1.18**
**Probability distribution of the daily percentage returns on the BSE SENSEX, 1998–2008**

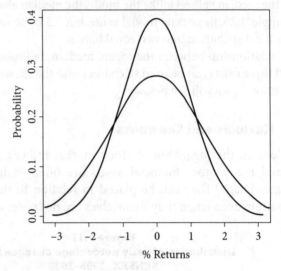

In Figure 1.18, we examine the pdf of the daily percentage changes in the Sensex.

The curve with the shorter tail is the graph of the probability distribution of daily per cent returns on the Sensex. The curve with the more spread-out tail is the pdf of the standard normal distribution. There are some interesting differences. The Sensex returns curve is confined to values –3 to +3, whereas the standard normal graph is more spread out. This results in the distribution of daily per cent changes in the Sensex have a higher peak(close to 0.4) as against the peak of the standard normal distribution, which is slightly less than 0.3. As a result, the tails of the Sensex distribution decline quickly, and can be seen to be 'fatter' than the standard normal distribution. On the other hand, the tails of the standard normal distribution taper off much further and hence are thinner compared to the standard normal distribution. Distributions like the per cent returns distribution, which are 'peaked' relative to the normal, are called 'leptokurtic'. The degree of 'peakedness' of a distribution is referred to as its 'kurtosis'. The kurtosis of the normal distribution is zero. Distributions which have the same peakedness as the normal distribution are called 'mesokurtic'. A distribution with a kurtosis less than that of the normal distribution is called 'platykurtic'. Many asset market percentage returns would have leptokurtic distributions. Formally, the degree of kurtosis is measured as:

$$\text{Kurtosis} = \frac{\sum_{i=1}^{n}(x_i - xbar)^4}{(n-1) \times \sigma^4} - 3 \qquad \text{Equation 1.15}$$

where $\sigma$ is the standard deviation, $n$ is the number of data points. The kurtosis of the normal distribution is 3, so Equation 1.12 measures excess kurtosis.

### Skewness

Skewness is a measure of the lack of symmetry in a distribution. A distribution is said to be symmetric if it looks the same from the left as well as the right. The distribution of daily returns of the Sensex is symmetric. This means that negative and positive returns have the same probability. But if you look at Figure 1.19, the distribution has a long tail to the right, and therefore is asymmetric. This is an example of a 'positively skewed distribution'. A distribu-

**Figure 1.19**
**Positively skewed distribution**

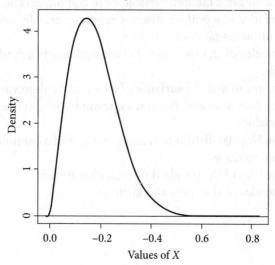

tion having a similar long tail, but to the left, will be called 'a negatively skewed distribution'.

Pearson's coefficient of skewness can be calculated as '(mean-mode)/standard deviation'.[23] The normal distribution is symmetric, which means the mean and the mode are the same. Thus, the Pearson coefficient of skewness for the normal distribution is zero. The normal distribution has zero excess kurtosis and zero skewness. It is fully described by its mean and standard deviation. Skewness is extremely important in finance and investing. Many data sets including stock prices and asset returns, may exhibit either negative or positive skewness, rather than follow the normal distribution. By knowing which way the data are skewed, one can better estimate whether a given (or future) data point will be more or less than the mean. Most advanced economic analysis models study data for skewness and incorporate this into their calculations. Skewness risk is the risk that a model assumes for a normal distribution when, in fact, the data are skewed to the left or to the right.

## CONCLUSION

In this chapter, we have encountered the following ideas:

1. The idea of a random variable, both continuous and discrete.
2. The idea of a pmf for discrete random variables and pdf for continuous random variables.
3. The idea of an expected value and variance of a random variable.
4. The mean and the variance of a sum of random variables.
5. The Binomial and Poisson as examples of discrete random variables.
6. The Normal distribution as an example of a continuous random variable.
7. The idea of the standard normal distribution.
8. The idea of skewness and kurtosis

Make sure that you have grasped each of these ideas. It will help if you experiment with the R code given here. In the next chapter, we will understand the joint distribution of a pair of random variables.

## NOTES

1. H. Tijms, *Understanding Probability: Chance Rules in Everyday Life* (Cambridge: Cambridge University Press, 2004), 31.
2. Though some can be 'mixed', a combination of discrete and continuous types. For details, see Paul L. Meyer, *Introductory Probability and Statistical Applications*, 2nd edition (New Delhi: Oxford and IBH, 1970), 73–74.
3. When we are counting the elements of a set, we are putting them into a one-to-one correspondence with the set of positive integers, so that we have a 'first' element, a 'second' element and so on.
4. By countably infinite objects, we mean that objects can be counted, but the counting process does not ever come to an end.
5. Jacques or Jacob Bernoulli (born 27 December 1654; died 16 August 1705), was the eldest child in a Swiss protestant family of three generations of mathematicians. The Bernoullis were passionate about science and mathematics. Jacob's brother, Johannes, famously threw his son out of the house for having won a prize from the French Academy of Sciences for which he himself had competed! Jacques published many articles on infinite series and did pioneering work in the theory of probability. His great treatise on probability, *Ars Conjenctandi*, was published eight years after his death, in 1713. In addition to probability, Jacob developed differential and integral calculus from where Newton and Leibnitz had left it. His contribution to calculus of variations is of the highest importance. For an interesting piece on the Bernoulli family, see E.T. Bell, *The Men of Mathematics* (New York: Simon and Schuster, 1986).
6. To understand this formula better, see Vijay Rohatgai, *Statistical Inference* (New York: Dover, 2003), 33–41; or Chung Kai Lai and Farid Ait Sahlia, *Elementary Probability Theory with Stochastic Processes and an Introduction to Mathematical Finance*, Chapter 3 (Springer, 2003).
7. This is called a Binomial random variable because it takes only two values. The general case is known as the multinomial random variable.
8. This is reproduced from M.G. Bulmer, *Principles of Statistics* (New York: Dover, 1979), 89.
9. Simeon Denis Poisson (born 21 June 1781; died 25 April 1840) was a French mathematician. This was the hot period for mathematics in France. Poisson worked alongside other greats like Laplace, Legendre and Lagrange, whose names are inseparable from modern mathematics. He is reported to have said that life was good only for two things: discovering mathematics and teaching

mathematics. An interesting anecdote has it that since Poisson preferred to be preoccupied with one idea at a time, he wrote down whatever research ideas occurred to him when he has already working on other things and kept the notes in his wallet. After he finished working on the first idea, he would fish out another idea from his wallet and start work on it. He eventually published 300 to 400 works on mathematics, including applications to electricity, magnetism and astronomy. Poisson's most important work is a series of papers on definite integrals and his advances in Fourier series. The Poisson distribution first appeared in 1837, in his book *Recherchés sur la probabilité des jugements*.

10. Even though we have explained Poisson distribution here in relation to the Binomial, the Poisson distribution is very important in its own right.

11. Ladislaus Bortkiewicz, a Russian economist and statistician of Polish descent, in a book published in 1898, showed that the number of soldiers in the Prussian army, who died of horse kicks every year, followed the Poisson distribution. The other examples he used were suicides by children in different years, the number of suicides of women in different regions and years and the number of accidental deaths in different years in eleven trade associations.

12. Confirm these numbers for yourself.

13. This is not exactly 280 because of rounding off error.

14. Johann Carl Friedrich Gauss (born 30 April 1777; died 23 February 1855), a German mathematician and scientist, known as the 'Prince among mathematicians' has had a deep influence on many branches of mathematics and is associated with the normal family of distributions as he analysed astronomical data using them in 1809. The first use of the Normal distribution itself is to be attributed to Abraham De Moivre (born 26 May 1667; died 27 November 1754) in an article in 1733. The term 'normal distribution' was first used around 1875 by Charles Sanders Peirce, Francis Galton and Wilhelm Lexis. The distribution is sometimes called 'the bell shaped curve'. The great 20th century statistician R.A. Fisher (1890–1962), changed the form of the normal distribution principally by presenting the case with the non-zero mean as the typical case.

15. You can find this number by typing the following command in R: d<-pnorm (1.96,mean=0,sd=1), which will give the $P(X \leq 1.96)$.

16. A technical condition that needs to be satisfied for this is: $\sum_i |x_i| p(x_i) < \infty$. Also, surprising as it may seem, not all random variables have expected values.

17. This is just one of the several instances where statistics has borrowed a term from the English vocabulary, but subtly altered its meaning.

18. This convergent expression need not always exist, unless $\int_{-\infty}^{\infty} |x| f(x) dx$ is finite.

19. An estimator is a function of the sample observations. The formula used to obtain the mean is the estimator, whereas the specific value that it yields is the estimate.

20. The graph looks a bit jagged. What do you think could be the reason?

21. If we divide the sum of squared deviations from the sample mean by $n$ instead of $n - 1$, we will be creating a downward bias to the extent of $(n - 1) / n$. This would matter if $n$ were a small number. But as $n$ becomes larger and larger, this bias would become smaller. Hence, for large sample sizes, it does not matter so much whether we divide the sum of squared deviations around the mean by $n$ rather than $n - 1$.

22. Informally, two random variables are said to be independent if the values that one takes have no bearing on the values taken by the other, and hence the probability of their joint occurrence is simply the product of their individual probabilities of occurrence. You will obtain a more formal treatment in Chapter 2.

23. Karl Pearson (born 27 March 1857; died 27 April 1936) was a pioneer in the application of statistics to problems of heredity and evolution. His book, the *Grammar of Science* (1892) is remarkable in that it anticipated some ideas of relativity theory. Pearson also coined the term 'standard deviation' in 1893. He developed the chi–square test of statistical significance in 1900. Pearson, or KP, as he was referred to, was also a noted historian and Germanist. In his first book, *The New Werther*, Pearson gives a clear indication of why he studied so many diverse subjects: 'I rush from science to philosophy and from philosophy to our old friends the poets; and then, over-wearied by too much idealism, I fancy I become practical in returning to science. Have you ever attempted to conceive all there is in the world worth knowing—that not one subject in the universe is unworthy of study? The giants of literature, the mysteries of many-dimensional space, the attempts of Boltzmann and Crookes to penetrate Nature's very laboratory, the Kantian theory of the universe, and the latest discoveries in embryology, with their wonderful tales of the development of life—what an immensity beyond our grasp!'. Pearson, unfortunately, was an aggressive Eugenicist, who declared an open war on the so called 'inferior races'. Paradoxically, he was a committed socialist, who refused a knighthood in 1935! Darwin's ideas have had a very productive impact on statistics, but the political ideas of Pearson were the unfortunate fallout of mistaken applications of Darwinism to the social world.

# Chapter 2

# Jointly Distributed Random Variables

## INTRODUCTION

In this chapter, we will study random variables that are jointly distributed. For example, we might be interested in studying the relationship between family incomes and savings by households. We might want to ask questions like 'What is the average savings for households that have an income of Rs 10,000 per month?' 'What is the overall relationship between average savings and household income?' 'What is the variance of savings for households earning Rs 7,500 per month? Is it greater than that for households earning Rs 150,000 per month?' Answering such questions will presume an understanding of the joint probability distribution of income and savings. In general, instead of thinking of savings or income as individual random variables taking various values, we can think of a new random variable, that takes two specific values, one each for income and savings. Previously, we thought of our random variable as a function from the sample space to the real number line. The random variables in the previous chapter took values like 1, 2, 3, and so on, on the real number line. Now, our new random variables will take values in the $XY$ plane, one value for $X$ and another for $Y$. For example, it might take values like (1, 2), (3, 2), (0, 1), and so on, where, for each ordered pair, the first number represents values taken by the first random variable, while the second number represents values taken by the second random variable. The whole pair represents the 'value' taken by our bi-variate random variable. In this chapter, we are going to understand such random variables. As you will no doubt appreciate, the analysis will be more complex and richer than the one in the previous chapter. This chapter will help us understand the following concepts:

1. Joint and marginal distribution of two random variables.
2. Conditional probability and conditional probability distributions.
3. Conditional means and conditional variances.
4. The idea of the regression function.
5. The ideas of covariance and correlation as measures of co-movement of random variables.

In addition to these ideas, we will become familiar with some programs in R, which you are strongly encouraged to experiment with.

## 2.1 JOINTLY DISTRIBUTED RANDOM VARIABLES

### Example 2.1

Suppose we are tossing four coins. Let $X$ be the number of heads appearing on the first three tosses, while $Y$ is the number of heads appearing on all four tosses. Then, $X$ and $Y$ are jointly distributed random variables.

Let us examine Example 2.1 in greater depth. Let us first enumerate $\Omega$, the sample space:

$\Omega$ = ({HHHH}, {HHHT}, {HHTH}, {HTHH}, {THHH}, {TTTT},
{TTTH}, {TTHT}, {THTT}, {HTTT}, {HHTT}, {TTHH},
{HTHT}, {THTH}, {HTTH}, {THHT})

The first outcome, {HHHH} corresponds to three heads on the first three tosses and four heads on all four tosses. Hence, in this case, we set $X = 3$, $Y = 4$, writing this as $(3, 4)$. For {HHTH}, we set $X = 2$ and $Y = 3$, or $(2, 3)$, whereas for {HHHT}, we set $X = 3$ and $Y = 3$, which becomes $(3, 3)$. Now, we are associating each outcome in the sample space with a point in the $XY$ plane, rather than on the real number line. We are now dealing with a two-dimensional random variable, rather than with a random variable with just one dimension, like in the previous chapter. Apart from this modification, the definition of a random variable as a function from the sample space to the real number line remains unchanged.

Let us enumerate all the values of the random variable in Example 2.1:

$Z = \{(3, 4), (3, 3), (2, 3), (2, 3), (2, 3), (0, 0), (0, 1), (1, 1), (1, 1), (1, 1), (2, 2), (1, 2), (2, 2), (1, 2), (1, 2), (2, 2)\}$

Just like the random variables in Chapter 1, we can associate probabilities with each of the Zs. This can be done in the following table (Table 2.1):

**Table 2.1**
**The joint distribution of the random variables $X$ and $Y$**

|  | $Y = 0$ | $Y = 1$ | $Y = 2$ | $Y = 3$ | $Y = 4$ | $f(X)$ |
|---|---|---|---|---|---|---|
| $X = 0$ | 1/16 | 1/16 | 0 | 0 | 0 | 2/16 |
| $X = 1$ | 0 | 3/16 | 3/16 | 0 | 0 | 6/16 |
| $X = 2$ | 0 | 0 | 3/16 | 3/16 | 0 | 6/16 |
| $X = 3$ | 0 | 0 | 0 | 1/16 | 1/16 | 2/16 |
| $f(Y)$ | 1/16 | 4/16 | 6/16 | 4/16 | 1/16 | – |

This table is to be interpreted as follows; on the $Y$-axis, we have enumerated all the values that $Y$ can take. On the $X$-axis, all the possible values of $X$ have been listed. The entry 1 / 16 in the cell $X = 0$, $Y = 0$ is the probability associated with the value $(0, 0)$ of $Z$. The random variable $Z$ takes value $(0, 0)$, in one case out of the sixteen possible and equally likely cases, and hence it seems reasonable to associate the probability 1 / 16 with that outcome. Similarly, the probability associated with the random variable $(2, 2) = 3/16$, because it occurs three times out of a possible 16.

How do our requirements P1 and P2 of Chapter 1 change now? Recall that in Chapter 1:

P1: $P(X = x_i) \geq 0$ for any value of $X = x_i$.

This requirement will become now:

P1': $P(X = x_i, Y = y_j) \geq 0$ where $P(X = x_i, Y = y_j)$ is the entry in the box where $X$ takes the specific value $x_i$ and $Y$ takes the specific value $y_j$. Remember that now our random variable is $Z$, an ordered pair, and what we are now saying is simply that the probability associated with each $Z$ must be non-negative. It is just that $Z$ is now an ordered pair, instead of being a simple number like in Chapter 1.

Similarly, in Chapter 1:

P2: $\sum_{i=1}^{n} P(X = x_i) = 1$ The relevant generalization for the jointly distributed random variable.

This will now become:

P2': $\sum_{j=1}^{m} \sum_{i=1}^{n} P(X = x_i, Y = y_j) = 1$

That is, now the function $P(X, Y)$ must sum to 1 when the summation is over values of $X$ as well as $Y$. The function $P(X, Y)$ is called the probability function of $(X, Y)$.

## 2.1.1 Cumulative Distribution Function of a Two Dimensional Random Variable

Let $Z = (X, Y)$ be a two-dimensional random variable. The cumulative distribution function (cdf) of $Z$ is defined as:

Cumulative Density Function of a Two-Dimensional Random variable: $F(x, y) = P(X \leq x, Y \leq y)$, that is, the probability of the event that $X$ takes a value less than a specific value, $x$ and $Y$ takes a value less than a specific value $y$.

In the case of Table 2.1, $F(1, 1)$ is the probability that there are at most one heads on the first three tosses and at most one heads on all four tosses. Thus:

$$P(X \leq 1, Y \leq 1) = 1/16 + 1/16 + 0 + 3/16$$
$$= 5/16$$

### Exercise 2.1

Find $F(3, 2)$.

In addition to the cdf, we can think of the probability distributions of $X$ and $Y$ alone. The function $f(Y)$ suggests that $Y$ takes various values, irrespective of the values of $X$. For example:

$$f(Y = 0) = 1 / 16$$

gives the probability that $Y$ takes the value 0, irrespective of the various values of $X$. $P(X = 1) = 6 / 16$, which is the probability that $X$ takes the value 1, irrespective of values of $Y$. This probability is obtained simply by summing over the probabilities of various values of $Y$ for which $X = 1$. In other words:

$$P(X = 1) = P(X = 1, Y = 0) + P(X = 1, Y = 1) + P(X = 1, Y = 2) +$$
$$P(X = 1, Y = 3) + P(X = 1, Y = 4) = 6 / 16$$

More generally:

$$\text{M1: } P(X = x_i) = \sum_{j=i}^{m} P(X = x_i, Y = y_j)$$

Note that:

$$\text{M2: } \sum_{i=1}^{n} P(X = x_i) = \sum_{i=1}^{n} \sum_{j=i}^{m} P(X = x_i, Y = y_j) = 1 \text{ from P2}'$$

Hence, $P(X = x_i)$ are also probabilities. In fact, $P(X = x_i)$ gives you the probability that $X$ takes the value $x_i$, irrespective of the values taken by $Y$. This is called the 'marginal distribution of $X$'. The marginal distribution of $X$ for Table 2.1 is shown in the extreme right hand column of the table. Similarly, the marginal distribution of $Y$ is shown in the bottom row of the table.

### Exercise 2.2

Find $P(X = 2)$.

### Example 2.2

Suppose we are rolling two dies. Let $X$ be the number on the uppermost face of the first dice, and $Y$ the number on the uppermost face of the second dice. Then, we can think of:

$$Z = (X_i, Y_i)$$

as a two dimensional random variable with $X$ and $Y$ taking various values between one and six. The sample space $\Omega$ is:

$$\Omega = \{(1, 1), (1, 2), (1, 3), (1, 4), (1, 5), (1, 6), (2, 1),(2, 2), (2, 3),$$
$$(2, 4), (2, 5), (2, 6), (3, 1), (3, 2), (3, 3), (3, 4), (3, 5), (3, 6),$$
$$(4, 1), (4, 2), (4, 3), (4, 4), (4, 5), (4, 6), (5, 1), (5, 2), (5, 3),$$
$$(5, 4), (5, 5), (5, 6), (6, 1), (6, 2), (6, 3), (6, 4), (6, 5), (6, 6)\}$$

The joint distribution of $X$ and $Y$ can be represented in Table 2.2:

**Table 2.2**
**The joint distribution of the random variables $X$ and $Y$**

|         | $Y = 1$ | $Y = 2$ | $Y = 3$ | $Y = 4$ | $Y = 5$ | $Y = 6$ |
|---------|---------|---------|---------|---------|---------|---------|
| $X = 1$ | 1 / 36  | 1 / 36  | 1 / 36  | 1 / 36  | 1 / 36  | 1 / 36  |
| $X = 2$ | 1 / 36  | 1 / 36  | 1 / 36  | 1 / 36  | 1 / 36  | 1 / 36  |
| $X = 3$ | 1 / 36  | 1 / 36  | 1 / 36  | 1 / 36  | 1 / 36  | 1 / 36  |
| $X = 4$ | 1 / 36  | 1 / 36  | 1 / 36  | 1 / 36  | 1 / 36  | 1 / 36  |
| $X = 5$ | 1 / 36  | 1 / 36  | 1 / 36  | 1 / 36  | 1 / 36  | 1 / 36  |
| $X = 6$ | 1 / 36  | 1 / 36  | 1 / 36  | 1 / 36  | 1 / 36  | 1 / 36  |

As can be seen from the table, each value of $Z$ is equally likely. That is to be expected, because when we carried out a similar experiment in Chapter 1, with just one dice being rolled, each value of $Z$ also turned out to be equally likely. Suppose we want to compute the marginal distribution of $X$. Then:

$$P(X = 1) = P(X = 1, Y = 1) + P(X = 1, Y = 2) + P(X = 1, Y = 3)$$
$$+ P(X = 1, Y = 4) + P(X = 1, Y = 5) + P(X = 1, Y = 6)$$
$$= 1 / 36 + 1 / 36 + 1 / 36 + 1 / 36 + 1 / 36 + 1 / 36$$
$$= 6 / 36$$
$$= 1 / 6$$

But this was just the probability that the number on the uppermost face of the dice equals 1, when we were just rolling one dice.

**Exercise 2.3**

Obtain the marginal distributions of $X$ and $Y$.

## Example 2.3

Suppose, for a pair of discrete random variables $X$ and $Y$, the joint distribution of $X$ and $Y$ can be expressed in Table 2.3.

**Table 2.3**
**The joint and marginal distributions of the random variables $X$ and $Y$**

|         | $Y = 0$ | $Y = 1$ | $Y = 2$ | $Y = 3$ | $Y = 4$ | $Y = 5$ | $f(X)$ |
|---------|---------|---------|---------|---------|---------|---------|--------|
| $X = 0$ | 0       | 0       | 0       | 0       | 0       | 0       | 0      |
| $X = 1$ | 0       | 0       | 0       | 0       | 0       | 0       | 0      |
| $X = 2$ | 0       | 0       | 1 / 6   | 0       | 0       | 0       | 1 / 6  |
| $X = 3$ | 0       | 0       | 0       | 0       | 2 / 6   | 0       | 2 / 6  |
| $X = 4$ | 0       | 0       | 0       | 1 / 6   | 2 / 6   | 0       | 3 / 6  |
| $X = 5$ | 0       | 0       | 0       | 0       | 0       | 0       | 0      |
| $f(Y)$  | 0       | 0       | 1 / 6   | 1 / 6   | 4 / 6   | 0       | –      |

Since we know the marginal distributions of $X$ and $Y$, we can easily calculate $E(X)$ and $E(Y)$:

$$E(X) = P(X = 0) \times 0 + P(X = 1) \times 1 + P(X = 2) \times 2 + P(X = 3) \times 3$$
$$+ P(X = 4) \times 4 + P(X = 5) \times 5$$
$$= 0 + 0 + 2 \times (1 / 6) + 3 \times (2 / 6) + 4 \times (3 / 6) + 0$$
$$= 3.333333$$

Similarly, we can find variance of $X$:

$$\sigma_x^2 = E(X^2) - E(X)^2$$
$$= 4 \times (1 / 6) + 9 \times (2 / 6) + 16 \times (3 / 6) - (3.333333)^2$$
$$= 0.555558$$

We will call this value the unconditional variance of $X$, since it does not depend upon $Y$ taking a particular value.

## Exercise 2.4

Find $E(Y)$ and the unconditional variance of $Y$.

## Finding E(XY)

Given a pair of random variables $X$ and $Y$, we can find $E(XY)$ as follows:

$$E(XY) = \sum_i \sum_j x_i y_j P(X = x_i, Y = y_j)$$

where the summation extends over all $(x_i, y_j)$ pairs. Let us refer to Table 2.3. The formula for $E(XY)$, for this specific example, becomes:

$$E(XY) = \sum_{i=1}^{5} \sum_{j=1}^{5} x_i y_j P(X = x_i, Y = y_j)$$

To calculate the product, we first fix the value of $X$, multiply this value of $X$ with all the values of $X$ and the corresponding entries in the joint distribution. Then, we do the same thing for the next value of $X$. We repeat this for all values of $X$ and then sum all the products. Let us carry this out here. Let $X = 0$. Then, we have:

$$\sum_{j=1}^{5} 0 \times y_j P(X = 0, Y = y_j) = 0$$

Now, let $X = 1$. Again, we have:

$$\sum_{j=1}^{5} 1 \times y_j P(X = 1, Y = y_j) = 0$$

Next, let $X = 2$. We have:

$$\sum_{j=1}^{5} 2 \times y_j P(X = 2, Y = y_j) = 4/6 = 0.66$$

For $X = 3$:

$$\sum_{j=1}^{5} 3 \times y_j P(X = 3, Y = y_j) = 24/6 = 4$$

For $X = 4$:

$$\sum_{j=1}^{5} 4 \times y_j P(X = 4, Y = y_j) = (12/6) + (32/6) = 44/6 = 7.33$$

Finally, for $X = 5$, we have:

$$\sum_{j=1}^{5} 5 \times y_j P(X=5, Y = y_j) = 0$$

In the last stage, we add all these sums to get:

$$0.666667 + 4 + 7.333333 = 12 \text{ (to round off)}$$

### Exercise 2.5

Compute $E(XY)$ for the joint distribution in Table 2.2.

## 2.2 CONDITIONAL PROBABILITY, CONDITIONAL EXPECTATION AND CONDITIONAL VARIANCE

Let us go back to Example 2.1. The joint and marginal distributions of $X$ and $Y$ is reproduced in Table 2.4.

**Table 2.4**
**The joint and marginal distributions of random variables $X$ and $Y$**

|  | $Y = 0$ | $Y = 1$ | $Y = 2$ | $Y = 3$ | $Y = 4$ | $f(X)$ |
|---|---|---|---|---|---|---|
| $X = 0$ | 1 / 16 | 1 / 16 | 0 | 0 | 0 | 2 / 16 |
| $X = 1$ | 0 | 3 / 16 | 3 / 16 | 0 | 0 | 6 / 16 |
| $X = 2$ | 0 | 0 | 3 / 16 | 3 / 16 | 0 | 6 / 16 |
| $X = 3$ | 0 | 0 | 0 | 1 / 16 | 1 / 16 | 2 / 16 |
| $f(Y)$ | 1 / 16 | 4 / 16 | 6 / 16 | 4 / 16 | 1 / 16 | – |

Suppose now we are interested in finding the probability that there are two heads on the first three tosses, given that there are three heads on all four tosses. That is, we are trying to find the probability that $X = 2$ given $Y = 3$, written as $P(X = 2 / Y = 3)$. The requirement $Y = 3$ now restricts the sample space to the following:

$$\Omega' = \{(HHHT), (HHTH), (THHH), (HTHH)\}$$

Hence, there are now four possible outcomes. Out of which, we are interested in the outcome $X = 2$. That is the second, third and the fourth outcomes among the four listed earlier. Hence:

$$P(X = 2 / Y = 3) = 3 / 4$$

A more direct way to obtain this is to use the definition of conditional probability:

$$P(X = 2 / Y = 3) = P(X = 2, Y = 3) / P(Y = 3)$$

where the numerator is the probability of the joint occurrence $X = 2$ and $Y = 3$ and the denominator is the marginal probability of $Y = 3$:

$$P(X = 2, Y = 3) / P(Y = 3) = (3 / 16) / (4 / 16) = 3 / 4$$

Similarly:

$$P(X = 1 / Y = 1) = P(X = 1, Y = 1) / P(Y = 1)$$
$$= (3 / 16) / (4 / 16) = 3 / 4$$

In general, we have:

$$P(X = x_i / Y = y_j) = P(X = x_i, Y = y_j) / P(Y = y_j)$$

### Exercise 2.6

From Table 2.1, find $P(X = 3 / Y = 4)$ and $P(X = 0 / Y = 0)$. From Table 2.2, find $E(X = 3 / Y = 3)$ and $E(X = 4 / Y = 6)$. Interpret these numbers.

## 2.2.1 Conditional Expectation

Now, suppose, I want to ask the following question: what is the average number of heads on the first three tosses given that there are three heads on all the four tosses? That is, we are looking for $E(X/Y = 3)$, or the conditional expectation of $X$, given that $Y$ takes the value 3.

This expectation is found as follows:

$$E(X / Y = 3) = \sum_{i=1}^{n} x_i \times P(X = x_i / Y = 3)$$

That is, each value of $X$ is now multiplied by the conditional probability that $X$ takes that value and then the products are summed. So far, we have been only considering unconditional expectations of $X$. For example, if you were to obtain $E(X)$ from the marginal distribution of $X$, you would get the unconditional mean of $X$, since the probabilities involved are unconditional probabilities.

Let us find $E(X / Y = 0)$:

$$
\begin{aligned}
E(X / Y = 0) &= 0 \times P(X = 0 / Y = 0) + 1 \times P(X = 1 / Y = 0) \\
&+ 2 \times P(X = 2 / Y = 0) + 3 \times P(X = 3 / Y = 0) \\
&= 0 \times 1 + 1 \times 0 + 2 \times 0 + 3 \times 0 \\
&= 0
\end{aligned}
$$

That is, the average number of heads on three tosses when there are no heads on all the four tosses is naturally zero:

$$
\begin{aligned}
E(X / Y = 1) &= 0 \times P(X = 0 / Y = 1) + 1 \times P(X = 1 / Y = 1) \\
&+ 2 \times P(X = 2 / Y = 1) + 3 \times P(X = 3 / Y = 1) \\
&= 0 \times 1/4 + 1 \times 3/4 + 2 \times 0 + 3 \times 0 \\
&= 3/4
\end{aligned}
$$

$$
\begin{aligned}
E(X / Y = 2) &= 0 \times P(X = 0 / Y = 2) + 1 \times P(X = 1 / Y = 2) \\
&+ 2 \times P(X = 2 / Y = 2) + 3 \times P(X = 3 / Y = 2) \\
&= 0 \times 0 + 1 \times 3/6 + 2 \times 3/6 + 3 \times 0 \\
&= 1.5
\end{aligned}
$$

$$
\begin{aligned}
E(X / Y = 3) &= 0 \times P(X = 0 / Y = 3) + 1 \times P(X = 1 / Y = 3) \\
&+ 2 \times P(X = 2 / Y = 3) + 3 \times P(X = 3 / Y = 3) \\
&= 0 \times 0 + 1 \times 0 + 2 \times 3/4 + 3 \times 1/4 \\
&= 2.25
\end{aligned}
$$

$$
\begin{aligned}
E(X / Y = 4) &= 0 \times P(X = 0 / Y = 4) + 1 \times P(X = 1 / Y = 4) \\
&+ 2 \times P(X = 2 / Y = 4) + 3 \times P(X = 3 / Y = 4) \\
&= 0 \times 0 + 1 \times 0 + 2 \times 0 + 3 \times 1 \\
&= 3
\end{aligned}
$$

It is clear that $E(X / Y)$ depends upon specific values of $Y$. Suppose we were to plot $E(X / Y = i)$ as a function of $i$. In this case, we will get a straight line, representing the conditional expectation of $X$ given $Y$ as a function of $Y$. This is plotted in Figure 2.1.

**Figure 2.1**
**$E(X/Y)$ as a function of $Y$**

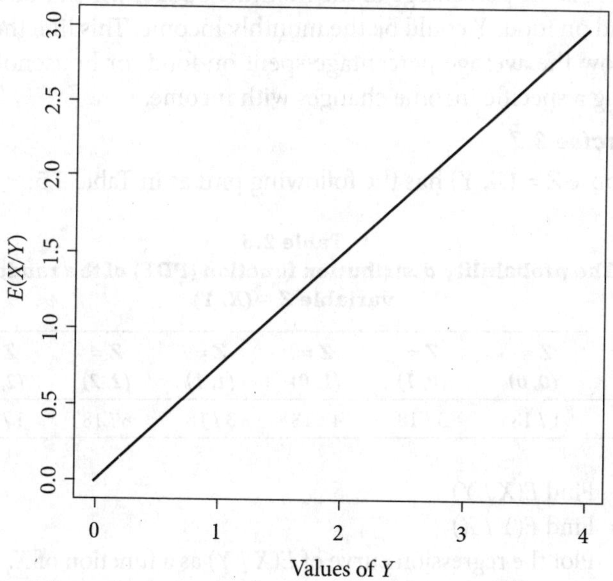

Since the graph is a straight line, we can express $E(X / Y)$ as a linear function of $Y$:

$$E(X/Y) = \alpha + \beta Y$$

$\beta$ is the 'slope' of the line, that is, it tells us how much $E(X / Y)$ changes whenever $Y$ changes by one unit. $\alpha$ is the intercept. $\alpha$ and $\beta$ are called 'regression parameters'. In our example, we can see whenever $Y$ increases by 1 unit, $E(X / Y)$ increases by exactly 0.75 units. Also, the line begins from zero, and hence $\alpha$ must be equal to zero. We will call this line the regression line.[1]

Therefore:

$$E(X / Y) = 0 + 0.75Y$$

This 'regression line' must not be confused with the 'regression method' of finding the slope and the intercept, that is, estimating regression parameters, of such a line from observed data. The regression method will be studied extensively in later chapters. The regression line tells us how the conditional mean of $X$ varies with $Y$. This might be very useful in certain contexts. For example, suppose $X$ is the percentage of the monthly budget which households spend on food. $Y$ could be the monthly income. This line then tells us how the average percentage spent on food for households enjoying a specific income changes with income.

### *Exercise 2.7*

Suppose $Z = (X, Y)$ has the following pmf as in Table 2.5:

**Table 2.5**
**The probability distribution function (PDF) of the random variable $Z = (X, Y)$**

|       | $Z =$ (0, 0) | $Z =$ (0, 1) | $Z =$ (1, 0) | $Z =$ (1, 1) | $Z =$ (2, 2) | $Z =$ (2, 1) |
|-------|------|------|------|------|------|------|
| $P(Z)$ | 1 / 18 | 3 / 18 | 4 / 18 | 3 / 18 | 6 / 18 | 1 / 18 |

a) Find $E(X / Y)$
b) Find $E(Y / X)$
c) Plot the regression curve of $E(X / Y)$ as a function of $X$.

## 2.2.2 Conditional Expectations and Independent Random Variables

### *Theorem 2.1: If X and Y are independent random variables, $E(X / Y) = E(X)$*

Proof: We will try to prove this by arguing as follows:
Consider $E(X / Y = 1)$:

$$\sigma^2_{X/Y} = \sigma^2_X$$

But if $X$ and $Y$ are independent, we know that

$$P(X = x_i / Y = 1) = P(X_i)$$

Hence,

$$E(X / Y = 1) = x_1 \times P(x_1) + x_2 \times P(x_2) + \ldots + x_n \times P(x_n)$$

$$= \sum_{i=1}^{n} x_i \times P(X = x_i)$$

$$= E(X)$$

## Exercise 2.8

In the case of Example 2.2, find $E(X / Y)$ for $Y = 1, 2, 3, 4, 5, 6$. Plot the regression line of $X$ on $Y$. How does it relate to theorem 2.1?

## 2.2.3 Conditional Variance

Just like the conditional expectation, we think of the conditional variance of a random variable.

$$\sigma^2_{x/y} = E(X^2 / Y) - E(X / Y)^2 \qquad \text{Equation 2.1}$$

That is, the conditional variance of $X$ given $Y$ is the expected value of the square of $X$ given $Y$ minus square of the expected value of $X$ given $Y$.

## Example 2.4

Returning to Table 2.1, suppose I want to calculate the variance of $X$ given $Y = 3$. Then,

$$\sigma^2_{x/y=3} = E(X^2 / Y = 3) - E(X / Y = 3)^2$$

$$E(X^2 / Y = 3) = 0^2 \times P(X = 0 / Y = 3) + 1^2 \times P(X = 1 / Y = 3)$$
$$+ 2^2 \times P(X = 2 / Y = 3) + 3^2 \times P(X = 3 / Y = 3)$$
$$= 0 \times 0 + 1 \times 0 + 4 \times 3 / 4 + 9 \times 1 / 4$$
$$= 5.25$$

$$\sigma^2_{x/y=3} = 5.25 - (2.25)^2$$

$$= 0.1875$$

Suppose you want to calculate $\sigma^2_{X/Y=3}$. Then,

$$E(X^2 / Y = 0) = 0^2 \times P(X = 0 / Y = 0) + 1^3 \times P(X = 1 / Y = 0)$$
$$+ 2^2 \times P(X = 2 / Y = 0) + 3^2 \times P(X = 3 / Y = 0)$$
$$= 0 + 0 + 0 + 0$$
$$= 0$$

We have seen earlier that:

$$E(X / Y = 0) = 0$$

Therefore:

$$E(X / Y = 0)^2 = 0$$

Therefore:

$$\sigma^2_{x/y=0} = 0$$

How will you interpret the finding that $\sigma^2_{x/y=0} = 0$? This implies that the variance of the number of heads on the first three tosses of the coin, given that there are no heads on any of the four tosses equals zero. That is intuitively right, because the only event which corresponds to this is {TTTT}. When you have just one event in the sample space, its variance is bound to be zero.

### Exercise 2.9

Show that $\sigma^2_{x/y=1} = 0.1875$ and $\sigma^2_{x/y=2} = 0.25$.

Just like $E(X / Y)$ was a function of $Y$ and could be plotted against $Y$, $\sigma^2_{x/y}$ is also a function of $Y$ and will in general change with $Y$.

### Exercise 2.10

Suppose a box contains 10 blue balls and 10 red balls. Four balls are drawn at random from the box. Let $X$ be the number of blue balls drawn and let $Y$ be the number of red balls drawn. The sample space is as follows:

$$\Omega = \{(bbbb), (bbbr), (bbrb), (brbb), (rbbb), (rrrr), (rrrb), (rrbr),$$
$$(rbrr), (brrr), (bbrr), (rrbb), (brrb), (rbbr), (brbr), (rbrb)\}$$

where the outcome (bbbb) corresponds to four blue balls being drawn, the outcome (rbrb) corresponds to the first ball drawn being red, the second ball drawn being blue and so on.

The two dimensional random variable $Z = (X, Y)$ corresponding to this sample space takes the following values:

$(4, 0), (3, 1), (3, 1), (3, 1), (3, 1), (0, 4), (1, 3), (1, 3), (1, 3), (1, 3),$
$(2, 2), (2, 2), (2, 2), (2, 2), (2, 2), (2, 2)$

The joint distribution of $X$ and $Y$ can be expressed in Table 2.6:

**Table 2.6**
**The joint distribution of the random variables $X$ and $Y$**

|  | $Y = 0$ | $Y = 1$ | $Y = 2$ | $Y = 3$ | $Y = 4$ |
|---|---|---|---|---|---|
| $X = 0$ | 0 | 0 | 0 | 0 | 1 / 16 |
| $X = 1$ | 0 | 0 | 0 | 4 / 16 | 0 |
| $X = 2$ | 0 | 0 | 6 / 16 | 0 | 0 |
| $X = 3$ | 0 | 4 / 16 | 0 | 0 | 0 |
| $X = 4$ | 1 / 16 | 0 | 0 | 0 | 0 |

1. Find the marginal distribution of $X$ and $Y$.
2. Find $E(X / Y = 2)$.
3. Draw the regression line of $X$ on $Y$.
4. Find $\sigma^2_{x/y=3}$.

The idea of the conditional variance, just like the conditional mean idea, is highly useful. For example, let $X$ be the percentage of their budgets that households spend on education of their children and let $Y$ be the household's annual income. Then, the conditional variance of $X$ for various values of $Y$ tells us how the spread of household expenditure shares on education changes with household incomes. Do poorer households have less variable budget shares as against rich households? This question can be answered, just by plotting the conditional variance of $X$ for specific values of $Y$ against those values, just like our regression line. For example, suppose we classify households into four income brackets: I for the poorest one-fourth of the households, II for the second poorest 25 per cent, III for the next 25 per cent and IV for the richest 25 per cent. That means, if a household belongs to the second poorest slot, we label it II and so on. Now, suppose we have got the following data where the first element refers to the household's expenditure share in (in percentage) on education (which we will call $X$), and the second refers to which of the four divisions it belongs to (which we will call $Y$):

(30, I), (25, II), (30, II), (20, II), (5, IV), (6, IV), (15, III), (15, IV), (20, III), (10, III), (20, IV), (5, I), (10, I), (7, II)

Suppose the data are randomly chosen, so we can think of each of the pairs as equally likely. Then, we can express the joint distribution of income classes and budget shares as shown in Table 2.7:

**Table 2.7**
**The joint distribution of the variables income class and budget share (percentage) spent on education**

| | Income group = I | Income group = II | Income group = III | Income group = IV | $f(X)$ |
|---|---|---|---|---|---|
| $X = 5$ | 1 / 14 | 0 | 0 | 1 / 14 | 2 / 14 |
| $X = 6$ | 0 | 0 | 0 | 1 / 14 | 1 / 14 |
| $X = 7$ | 0 | 1 / 14 | 0 | 0 | 1 / 14 |
| $X = 10$ | 1 / 14 | 0 | 1 / 14 | 0 | 2 / 14 |
| $X = 15$ | 0 | 0 | 1 / 14 | 1 / 14 | 2 / 14 |
| $X = 20$ | 0 | 1 / 14 | 1 / 14 | 1 / 14 | 3 / 14 |
| $X = 25$ | 0 | 1 / 14 | 0 | 0 | 1 / 14 |
| $X = 30$ | 1 / 14 | 1 / 14 | 0 | 0 | 1 / 14 |
| $f(Y)$ | 3 / 14 | 4 / 14 | 3 / 14 | 4 / 14 | – |

Now let us proceed to find:

1. How $E(X/Y)$ changes with $Y$, that is, how does the average budget share on education change with income.
2. How the variance of the budget share changes with income.

Unconditional expectation of $X$ and the unconditional variance of $X$ can also be obtained from the marginal distribution. $E(X) = 15.571429$. That means that on an average, a sample household spends 15.57 per cent of its budget on education. The variance of budget shares is 72.530599.

Now, we proceed to calculate $E(X / Y)$ for each value of $Y$:

$$E(X / Y = 1) = 5 \times P(X = 5 / Y = 1) + 6 \times P(X = 6 / Y = 1)$$
$$+ 7 \times P(X = 7 / Y = 1) + 10 \times P(X = 10 / Y = 1)$$

$$+ 15 \times P(X = 15 \,/\, Y = 1) + 20 \times P(X = 20 \,/\, Y = 1)$$
$$+ 25 \times P(X = 25 \,/\, Y = 1) + 30 \times P(X = 30 \,/\, Y = 1)$$
$$= 5 \times 1\,/\,3 + 0 + 0 + 10 \times 1\,/\,3 + 0 + 0 + 0 + 30 \times 1\,/\,3$$
$$= 15$$

This means that the average expenditure share for a household with income in the lowest 25 per cent of the income distribution is 15 per cent:

$$\sigma^2_{X/Y=1} = E(X^2 \,/\, Y = 1) - E(X \,/\, Y = 1)^2$$
$$= 25 \times 1\,/\,3 + 100 \times 1\,/\,3 + 900 \times 1\,/\,3 - (15)^2$$
$$= 116.666667$$

Similarly, you can compute the other values. It turns out that

$$E(X \,/\, Y = 2) = 20.5$$
$$E(X \,/\, Y = 3) = 15 \text{ and}$$
$$E(X \,/\, Y = 4) = 11.5$$

We can plot $E(X \,/\, Y)$ against $Y$ as shown in Figure 2.2:

**Figure 2.2**
**Sample regression curve: Regression of budget share on income class**

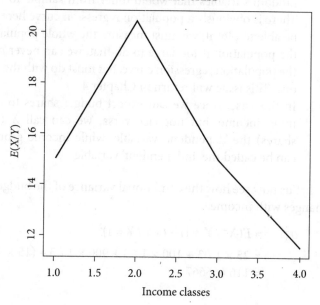

Income classes

Note three important aspects here:

1. The relationship between budget shares and income classes seems to be described by a curve rather than a line like in Figure 2.1. In this case, as income increases, the budget share on education first increases and then falls. That is perhaps because households that are very poor cannot afford to allocate a large fraction of their budget to education, whereas rich households do not need to, since their budgets are large in absolute quantity.

2. More importantly, this is a regression curve calculated from an observed sample. The regression curve (really the line) that we calculated and subsequently plotted in Figure 2.1 was a population regression curve, since it calculated from all the possible values that $X$ and $Y$ could conceptually take. This is not the case in Figure 2.2. Here, we have obtained just a subset of the population values, since there are several thousand households that we could have sampled from. If we obtain a different sample, we would get a different curve. Hence, you must regard the parameters of this curve like its slope as random variables that would differ from sample to sample. There is obviously a population regression curve here, but to be able to plot it, we must measure the whole population. If the population is too large to do that, we can never observe the population regression curve, but must do with the sample one. This issue will return in Chapter 4.

3. In this case, since we can expect budget shares to depend upon income, but not vice versa, we can call $X$ (budget shares) the 'dependent' variable, while income groups ($Y$) can be called the 'independent' variable.

Let us now see how the conditional variance of the budget share changes with income:

$$\sigma^2_{X/Y=1} = E(X^2 / Y = 1) - E(X / Y = 1)^2$$
$$= 25 \times 1 / 3 + 100 \times 1 / 3 + 900 \times 1 / 3 - (15 \times 15)$$
$$= 116.666667$$

$$\sigma^2_{X/Y=2} = E(X^2 / Y = 2) - E(X / Y = 2)^2$$
$$= 493.5 - 420.25$$
$$= 73.25$$
$$\sigma^2_{X/Y=3} = E(X^2 / Y = 3) - E(X / Y = 3)^2$$
$$= 241.666667 - 225$$
$$= 16.666667$$
$$\sigma^2_{X/Y=4} = E(X^2 / Y = 4) - E(X / Y = 4)^2$$
$$= 171.5 - 132.25$$
$$= 39.25$$

Thus, we see that the variability of the budget share declines with income except for the richest income group. This can also be plotted just like Figure 2.2.[2]

### Theorem 2.2

If $X$ and $Y$ are independent random variables, $\sigma^2_{X/Y} = \sigma^2_X$.
The proof is similar to Theorem 2.1 (see Figure 2.3).

**Figure 2.3**
**Conditional variance of budget shares against income**

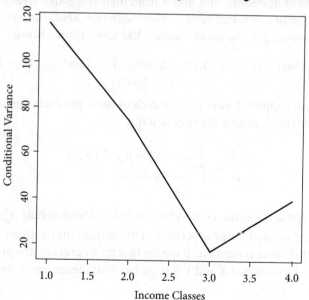

The idea of changing conditional variance is very important in the financial world. Conditional variance of a share price is referred to as its volatility. For example, instead of taking data on budget shares, you could take data on the daily percentage change in the closing price of the BSE Sensex. Instead of taking income classes, you could take days of the week, and assign them numbers 1, 2, 3, 4, 5, one for each working day (assuming Saturday is non-working). Then, you could take random samples of data and see how the conditional variance of the daily percentage returns on the BSE Sensex. In courses on time series econometrics, such problems are routinely dealt with.

## 2.3 COVARIANCE AND CORRELATION

Suppose we have a two-dimensional random variable $Z = (X, Y)$ where $X$ takes values $x_1, x_2, .......... x_n$ and $Y$ takes values $y_1, y_2, .......... y_n$. Let $Xbar$ be the mean of $X$ and $Ybar$ be the mean of $Y$, both assumed to be known beforehand. Suppose I now subtract $Xbar$ from each value of $X$ and $Ybar$ from each value of $Y$. Then, I would get a series of deviations of $X$ and $Y$ from their respective means. Suppose, further, I multiplied $(x_i - Xbar)$ with $(y_i - Xbar)$ for each value of $i$, I would get a series of $n$ values, like those shown below:

$$(x_1 - Xbar) \times (y_1 - Xbar), (x_2 - Xbar) \times (y_2 - Xbar), ....... (x_n - Xbar) \times (y_n - Xbar)$$

Now, suppose I were to sum each of these products and divide the sum by $n$, calling the resultant $\sigma_{xy}$.

$$\sigma_{xy} = \frac{\sum_{i=1}^{n}(x_i - Xbar)(y_i - Ybar)}{n}$$

Suppose $\sigma_{xy}^2$ turned out to be $-20$. What does it mean? $\sigma_{xy}^2$ is the average value of the product of deviations from the mean for $X$ and $Y$. If this value is negative, it means that on an average, the product of the deviations of $X$ and $Y$ is negative. That means, on an average, if $(x_i - Xbar)$ is positive, $(y_i - Ybar)$ must be negative, or the other way round. Effectively, it means that on an average, if a value of $X$ is above its mean, the corresponding value of $Y$ must be below the mean of $Y$ and vice versa. This in turn means that on an average, $X$ and $Y$ move in opposite directions relative to their own means. On the other hand, if $\sigma_{xy}$ is positive, it implies that $X$ and $Y$ move in the same direction relative to their means. If $\sigma_{xy}$ equals zero, it means that $X$ and $Y$ move independently vis-à-vis each other. $\sigma_{xy}$ is called the 'covariance of $X$ and $Y$'. It is a measure of how much the two variables change together.

Note that $\sigma_{xy}$ is also an average, the average of the product of deviations from the mean. Therefore, like all averages, it can be written as an expected value. Indeed:

$$\sigma_{xy} = E[(X - E(X))(Y - E(Y))]$$
$$= E[XY - XE(Y) - YE(X) + E(X) \times E(Y)]$$

by using simple multiplication.
Since:

$$E(X + Y) = E(X) + E(Y)$$

and:

$$E(E(X)) = E(X)^3$$

this becomes:

$$= E(XY) - E(X)\,E(X) - E(Y)\,E(X) + E(X) \times E(Y)$$
$$= E(XY) - E(X) \times E(Y)$$

## Exercise 2.11

If $X=Y$, what would be $\sigma_{xy}$?

## Theorem 2.3

If $X$ and $Y$ are independent then $E(XY) = E(X) \times E(Y)$.
    Proof: Since $X$ and $Y$ are independent, $\sigma_{xy} = 0$. Therefore:
$0 = E(XY) - E(X) \times E(Y)$ which then yields the theorem.

## Theorem 2.4

For two random variable $X_1$ and

$$X_2, \sigma^2_{x_1+x_2} = \sigma^2_{x_1} + \sigma^2_{x_2} + 2 \times \sigma_{x_1 \times x_2}, \sigma^2_{x+y}$$

$$= E((X + Y - E(X + Y))^2$$
$$= E((X - E(X)) + (Y - E(Y)))^2$$
$$= E(X - E(X))^2 + E(Y - E(Y))^2 + 2 \times E((X - E(X))(Y - E(Y)))$$
$$= \sigma_x^2 + \sigma_y^2 + 2 \times \sigma_{xy}$$

### Theorem 2.5

If $X_1$ and $X_2$ are independent random variables, then:

$$\sigma_{x_1+x_2}^2 = \sigma_{x_1}^2 + \sigma_{x_2}^2$$

### Exercise 2.12

Prove theorem 2.5.

This holds for any number $n$ of independent random variables, so that:

$$\sigma_{x_1+x_2+\dots\,x_n}^2 = \sigma_{x_1}^2 + \sigma_{x_2}^2 + \dots\dots\dots + \sigma_{x_n}^2$$

But this is Equation 1.11 from Chapter 1. In that chapter, we had simply assumed the result, now we have proved it.

## 2.3.1 The Sample Covariance

Suppose you have a sample of size 7, on $X$ and $Y$: (1, 3), (3, 4), (4, 6), (3, 5), (3, 2), (4, 6), (3, 6).

Just like the sample regression line, you can compute 'the sample covariance' as follows:

$$\hat{\sigma}_{xy} = \frac{\sum_{i=1}^{n}(x_i - Xbar)(y_i - Ybar)}{n-1}$$

The $n-1$ in the denominator is the degrees of freedom correction that we have mentioned in Chapter 1.

### Example 2.5

In the sample given above, $Xbar = 3, Ybar = 4.571429$. Hence, we get the following values of $(X_i - Xbar)$ and $(Y_i - Ybar)$ for $i = 1$, 2, ... 7:

**Table 2.8**
**The values of (*X–Xbar*) and (*Y–Ybar*) and those of their product**
**(*X–Xbar*) and (*Y–Ybar*)**

| (*X_i - Xbar*) | (*Y_i - Ybar*) | (*X_i - Xbar*) × (*Y_i - Xbar*) |
|---|---|---|
| −2 | −1.571429 | 3.142858 |
| 0 | −0.571429 | 0 |
| 1 | 1.428571 | 1.428571 |
| 0 | 0.428571 | 0 |
| 0 | −2.571429 | 0 |
| 1 | 1.428571 | 1.428571 |
| 0 | 1.428571 | 0 |

Having obtained $(X_i - Xbar) \times (Y_i - Ybar)$ for each value, we must now find

$$\sigma_{xy} = \frac{\sum_{i=1}^{n}(X_i - Xbar)(Y_i - Ybar)}{n-1}$$

$$= 6/6$$
$$= 1$$

This can be done in R. The program below explains how to estimate covariance in R:

```
x<-c(1,3,4,3,3,4,3)
y<-c(3,4,6,5,2,6,6)
cova<-function(x,y)
{
x1=(x-mean(x))
y1=(y-mean(y))
dd=x1*y1
dd
cov1 = sum(dd)/(length(y)-1)
}
m=cova(x,y)
m
```

The first and the second lines read the data into two columns, $x$ and $y$. The third line defines a function, *cova*, which will calculate covariance. Covariance between any two series, $x$ and $y$ can be obtained using this function. The curly brackets enclose the calculations. $x1 = (x - \text{mean}(x))$ creates a set of values of $x$ minus the mean of $x$. Similarly, $y1 = (y - \text{mean}(y))$ creates a set of values of $y$ minus the mean of $y$. The next line, $dd = x1 \times y1$ creates a series of the products of the deviations from their means. $Cov1 = \text{sum}(dd)/\text{length}(y - 1)$ sums the products of covariances and divides it by the number of items in $y - 1$, which is $n - 1$. The curly brackets then close the calculations. The output of this program is the single number covariance between $x$ and $y$. If you want to read the data from a file (say named data.txt (saved as 'tab delimited' and stored on drive C:) file, where the data are stored under the column headings $x$ and $y$, the program will read like this:[4]

```
data <-read.table("c:\\data.txt",header=TRUE,sep="")
attach(data)
m=cova(x,y)
m
```

### Example 2.6
Suppose we have a two-dimensional random variable:

$$Z = (3, 5), (3, 6), (6, 9), (4, 6), (5, 7), (6, 8), (5, 4), (4, 6), (2, 5),$$
$$(1, 1), (0, 5), (4, 5)$$

where the first value in each pair refers to the value of $X$, while the second value refers to $Y$. Find $\sigma_{XY}$.

### Exercise 2.13
Table 2.9 gives the marks scored by 10 students in Maths ($X$) and English ($Y$). Find $\sigma_{XY}$.

## 2.3.2 The Coefficient of Correlation

Covariance is a measure of the co-movement of two variables. However, it has one major drawback. Covariance changes if the

**Table 2.9**

**The marks scored by ten students in Maths (X) and English (Y)**

| Roll No. | X | Y |
|---|---|---|
| 1 | 34 | 45 |
| 2 | 50 | 56 |
| 3 | 46 | 52 |
| 4 | 23 | 56 |
| 5 | 76 | 75 |
| 6 | 82 | 72 |
| 7 | 69 | 65 |
| 8 | 58 | 54 |
| 9 | 52 | 43 |
| 10 | 48 | 23 |

scale of measurement of the two variables is altered. That is suppose both $X$ and $Y$ are multiplied by a scalar $\alpha$.

**Theorem 2.6**

$$\sigma_{\alpha X \alpha Y} = \alpha^2 \sigma_{XY}$$

**Proof:**

$$\sigma_{\alpha X \alpha Y} = E[(\alpha X - E(\alpha X))(\alpha Y - E(\alpha Y))]$$
$$= E[(\alpha X - \alpha E(X))(\alpha Y - \alpha E(Y))]$$
$$= E[\alpha(X - E(X))\alpha(Y - E(Y))]$$
$$= \alpha^2 E[(X - E(X))(Y - E(Y))$$
$$= \alpha^2 \sigma_{XY}$$

What Theorem 2.3 indicates is that if both $X$ and $Y$ are multiplied by a scalar $\alpha$, the covariance between $X$ and $Y$ will be multiplied by $\alpha^2$. The measure of co-movement between $X$ and $Y$ should ideally not depend upon the units of measurement of $X$ and $Y$. However, covariance does depend upon the units of measurement. Hence, we need to adjust for this deficiency. The coefficient of correlation is one such measure which does not depend upon the unit of measurement. We define the 'coefficient of correlation' between $X$ and $Y$ as follows:

$$r = \frac{\sigma_{XY}}{(\sigma_X \sigma_Y)}$$

That is, the correlation between $X$ and $Y$ is the covariance between $X$ and $Y$ divided by the product of the standard deviations of $X$ and $Y$. To see why it is invariant to scaling by $\alpha$, recall from Chapter 1 (Equation 1.10) that:

$$\text{Variance}(\alpha X) = \alpha^2 \, \text{Variance}(X)$$
$$\sigma_{\alpha X} = \sqrt{\text{Variance}(\alpha X)}$$
$$\sigma_{\alpha X} = \sqrt{\alpha^2 \text{Variance}(X)}$$
$$= \alpha \sqrt{\text{Variance}(X)}$$
$$= \alpha \sigma_X$$

Now, suppose both $X$ and $Y$ get scaled by a constant $\alpha$. Then, the correlation between $\alpha X$ and $\alpha Y$:

$$= \frac{\sigma_{\alpha X \alpha Y}}{(\sigma_{\alpha X}) \times (\sigma_{\alpha Y})}$$
$$= \frac{\alpha^2 \sigma_{XY}}{\alpha^2 \times (\sigma_X) \times (\sigma_Y)}$$
$$= \frac{\sigma_{XY}}{(\sigma_X) \times (\sigma_Y)}$$
$$= r$$

Of course, dividing covariance between $X$ and $Y$ by the product of the standard deviations is not the only way to get rid of the scale factor. It is easy to see that $\frac{\sigma_{XY}}{(Xbar) \times (Ybar)}$ would also achieve the same result. What is special about the coefficient of correlation?

The coefficient of correlation has a further desirable property that $-1 \leq r \leq 1$, which measures like $\dfrac{\sigma_{XY}}{(Xbar) \times (Ybar)}$ would not have.

Suppose $X$ and $Y$ are the same variables. Then:

$$\frac{\sigma_X}{(\sigma_X)(\sigma_Y)} = \frac{\sigma_X^2}{(\sigma_X)(\sigma_X)} = 1$$

On the other hand, if $Y = -X$, then we would have $\dfrac{\sigma_{XY}}{(\sigma_X)(\sigma_Y)}$ $= \dfrac{-1 \times \sigma_X^2}{(\sigma_X)(\sigma_X)} = -1$. Thus, the strongest possible positive correlation is $+1$, while the strongest possible negative correlation is $-1$.

### Example 2.7

Find the correlation between $X$ and $Y$ in Table 2.9. In that example:

$$r = \frac{\sigma_{XY}}{\sigma_X \times \sigma_Y}$$

$\sigma_{XY} = 146.52$, $\sigma_X = 18.225745$ and $\sigma_Y$ 15.132379. Hence:

$$r = \frac{\sigma_{XY}}{\sigma_X \times \sigma_Y}$$

$$= 0.531257$$

Alternatively, the R code to calculate correlation for Example 2.8 is as follows:

```
x<-c(34,50,46,23,76,82,69,58,52,48)
y<-c(45,56,52,56,75,72,65,54,43,23)
x1=(x-mean(x))
y1=(y-mean(y))
dd=sum(x1*y1)/length(y-1)
correl= dd/(sd(x)*sd(y))
correl
```

The first and the second lines read in the data. The next two lines, $x1$ and $y1$, calculate the series for the deviation from the mean. The next line calculates the covariance (*dd*). The line following computes the correlation, and the final line prints it. You are encouraged to try this out on different data sets. You can also read the data from a file using the read.table command as given in the R code for calculating covariance.

### Theorem 2.7

If two variables are independent, the correlation between them is zero.

### Example 2.8

Prove Theorem 2.4.

### Exercise 2.14

But the converse of Theorem 2.4 is *not* true. We may find $X$ and $Y$ to be uncorrelated, but $X$ and $Y$ might not be independent. Consider the following table showing the joint distribution of $X$ and $Y$ (see Table 2.10):

**Table 2.10**
**The joint and marginal distributions of the random variables $X$ and $Y$**

|          | $X = -1$ | $X = 0$ | $X = 1$ | $f(Y)$ |
|----------|----------|---------|---------|--------|
| $Y = -1$ | 1 / 8    | 1 / 8   | 1 / 8   | 3 / 8  |
| $Y = 0$  | 1 / 8    | 0       | 1 / 8   | 2 / 8  |
| $Y = 1$  | 1 / 8    | 1 / 8   | 1 / 8   | 3 / 8  |
| $f(X)$   | 3 / 8    | 2 / 8   | 3 / 8   | –      |

First, let us calculate $E(XY)$:

$$= 1/8 \times 1 + 1/8 \times 0 + 1/8 \times -1 + 1/8 \times 0 + 0 \times 0 + 1/8 \times 0$$
$$+ 1/8 \times -1 + 1/8 \times 0 + 1/8 \times 1$$
$$= 1/8 - 1/8 - 1/8 + 1/8 = 0$$

$$E(X) = 3/8 \times -1 + 2/8 \times 0 + 3/8 \times 1 = 0$$
$$E(Y) = 3/8 \times -1 + 2/8 \times 0 + 3/8 \times 1 = 0$$

Hence:

$$\sigma_{XY} = E(XY) - E(X) \times E(Y) = 0$$

By Theorem 2.1, if the $X$ and $Y$ are independent:

$$E(Y / X) = E(Y)$$

Let us check that out:

$$E(Y / X = -1) = -1 \times 1 / 3 + 0 \times 1 / 3 + 1 \times 1 / 3 = 0$$
$$E(Y / X = 0) = -1 \times 1 / 2 + 0 \times 0 + 1 \times 1 / 2 = 0$$
$$E(Y / X = 1) = -1 \times 1 / 3 + 0 \times 1 / 3 + 1 \times 1 / 3 = 0$$
$$E(X / Y = -1) = 0, E(X / Y = 0) = 0, E(X / Y = 1) = 0$$

Now let us see whether the condition implied by Theorem 2.2 is satisfied:

$$\sigma^2_{X/Y=0} = 1 / 2 \times 1 + 1 / 2 \times 1 = 1$$
$$\sigma^2_{X/Y=-1} = 1 / 3 \times 1 + 1 / 3 \times 1 = 2 / 3$$

Hence, we find that the conditional variance of $X$ given $Y = 0$ is different from the conditional variance of $X$ given $Y = -1$. As an implication, $X$ and $Y$ are not independent. But they are uncorrelated.

The coefficient of correlation, though a popular and useful measure, must be interpreted with care. It is not uncommon for numerically large and statistically significant correlation coefficients to denote nonsense relationships. A classic example can be found in a paper by G. Udny Yule (Yule, 1926).[5] Yule used annual data from 1866 to 1911 for the death rate in England and Wales and for all marriages solemnised in the Church of England during each of these years. Yule found a correlation of +0.95 between the two series! Clearly, this is a nonsensical correlation. Whenever we observe some correlation between two variables, we should be able to think of a sensible relationship between the two series. To take another example, Plosser and Schwert (1987),[6] using annual data from 1897 to 1958, found a correlation of +0.91 between the log of the national income in the United States and the log of accumulated sunspots. Hendry (1980) has found a positive (albeit a somewhat non-linear) relationship between the accumulation of annual rainfall and the inflation rate for the United Kingdom.[7]

A strong reason for such nonsensical correlations in economic variables is their being subject to trends in time. Series that are not related in any way can still share the same trend-like movement and exhibit a correlation. For example, both, the price level as well as per capita incomes, show upward movements in time. As a result, they might show significant positive correlation, which vanishes when the effect of the trend is removed from both the series. One of the ways of guarding against such spurious correlations is to analyse the correlation not between the series themselves, but in the 'first differences' of these series. Suppose $X_t$ and $Y_t$ are the values of two series $X$ and $Y$ for time period $t$. Then, the first differences of $X$ and $Y$ are defined as $\Delta X_t = X_t - X_{t-1}$ and $\Delta Y_t = Y_t - Y_{t-1}$. Many series show high correlation between $X$ and $Y$ but negligible correlation between $\Delta X_t$ and $\Delta Y_t$. This result would generally indicate a spurious correlation. On the other hand, if there is a genuine causal mechanism linking the two series, we would observe some correlation also between first differences.

## CONCLUSION

In this chapter, we have studied the idea of a jointly distributed (bivariate) random variable. The following are the key concepts in this chapter:

1. The idea of a joint and marginal distribution
2. The idea of conditional mean and conditional variance and their contrast with the ideas of unconditional mean and variance
3. The ideas of independence, covariance and correlation between two random variables.

You should make sure that you understand these ideas clearly.

## NOTES

1. The earliest example of the regression line can perhaps be found in Francis Galton's work (born 16 February 1822; died 17 January 1911). Galton was trying to see whether children of relatively taller parents are shorter than them

and vice-versa, which is the tendency for the regression to the mean. However, in this context, he drew the first regression line, that is conceptually similar to the line we have drawn earlier. Galton's line was a plot of seed weights and was presented at a Royal Institution lecture in 1877. Galton had seven sets of sweet pea seeds labelled K to Q and in each packet the seeds were of the same weight. He distributed these packets to a group of friends throughout Great Britain who planted them. At the end of the growing season the plants were uprooted and returned to Galton. He found that the weights of the offspring seeds were normally distributed, like their parents, and that if he plotted the mean diameter of the offspring seeds against the mean diameter of their parents he could draw an upward sloping straight line through the points—the first regression line. This confirmed Galton's point about 'inheritability' of characters; mean 'offspring' weight increased with mean 'parent' weight. This is another instance of the impact of Charles Darwin's ideas on statistics, apart from the fact that Galton was Darwin's cousin. Galton funded the Biometric laboratory where Karl Pearson did nearly all his work.

2. But this curve will not be called a 'regression' curve in Galton's sense, because it does not plot the conditional mean of $X$, but plots the conditional mean of $(X - E(X))^2$ against $Y$.

3. By a law called the Law of Iterated Expectations.

4. Data can be saved as .txt by using the command 'save as' in Excel.

5. G.U. Yule, 'Why Do We Sometimes Get Nonsense Correlations between Time Series?' *Journal of the Royal Statistical Society*, Series A, General, 89 (1926): 1–69.

6. Charles Plosser and William Schwert, 'Money, Income and Sunspots: Measuring Economic Relationships and the Effect of Differencing', *Journal of Monetary Economics*, 4 (1987): 637–60.

7. David F. Hendry, 'Econometrics—Alchemy or Science', *Economica*, 47 (1987): 387–406.

# Chapter 3

# Elements of Hypothesis Testing

## INTRODUCTION

Think of the following hypothesis: 'The average income of a household in Mumbai is greater than that of a household in Delhi'. This is an assertion which, in principle, you can verify with the help of actual data. However, it is almost impossible to collect data on all households in Mumbai and Delhi. At the same time, finding a few households in Delhi that have a higher income than a few households in Mumbai does not refute our hypothesis. What we need is a methodology which will enable us to say something about the comparative income of an average household in Mumbai vis-à-vis an average household in Delhi, on the basis of a sample that is smaller than (and usually only a small fraction of it) the whole population of households in Mumbai and Delhi. The theory of statistical inference provides one such methodology. In this chapter, we will examine its elements.[1] In particular, we will learn about the following:

1. The standard normal distribution, testing hypothesis about the mean when the population variance is known and creating confidence intervals.
2. The Central Limit Theorem.
3. The Chi-Square distribution and comparing sample variance with that of the population.

4. The F distribution that allows us to compare two sample variances.
5. The Student's t distribution to be used when the sample size is small and when the population variance is not known, but replaced by its sample estimate.
6. The idea of the 'Power of a Test' and how to compute the power function of a given test with the help of R.
7. We will also learn how to write programs in R to do these routine tests.

## 3.1 THE Z DISTRIBUTION AND HYPOTHESIS TESTING

Suppose a random variable $X$ follows the normal distribution with mean $\mu$ and variance $\sigma_x^2$. We write this as $X{\sim}N(\mu, \sigma_x^2)$. Now, suppose we have a sample of size $n$ whose values are the realizations of $X$, $(X_1, X_2, \ldots\ldots X_n)$. Suppose we subtract $\mu$ from each value of $X_i$ and divide the resultant by $\sigma_x$. That is, we think of a new random variable, $Z$, each of whose value is a particular value of $X$ from which the mean of $X$ has been subtracted and the resultant has been divided by the standard deviation of $X$.

$$Z_i = \frac{(X_i - \mu)}{\sigma_x}$$
Equation 3.1

Let us find:

$$E(Z) = E\left(\frac{(X-\mu)}{\sigma_x}\right) = \frac{1}{\sigma_x}E(X-\mu) = \frac{1}{\sigma_x}E(X) - \frac{1}{\sigma_x}\mu$$

$$= \frac{1}{\sigma_x}\mu - \frac{1}{\sigma_x}\mu = 0$$

Hence, the mean of $Z$ is zero. Let us now find the variance of $Z$:

$$\mathrm{Var}(Z) = \mathrm{Variance}\left(\frac{(X-\mu)}{\sigma_x}\right)$$

$$= \frac{1}{\sigma_x^2}(\text{Variance}(X-\mu))$$

Let us consider Variance$(X - \mu)$. The variance of $X$ is $\sigma_x^2$. $(X_i - \mu)$ is simply each value of $X$ minus its mean. This will shift the location of the distribution but not its spread. Hence, the variance of the distribution will remain the same, that is, $\sigma_x^2$. Therefore, the:

$$\text{variance of } Z = \frac{1}{\sigma_x^2}\text{Variance}(X_i - \mu).$$

$$= \frac{1}{\sigma_x^2}\sigma_x^2 = 1$$

Therefore, $Z \sim N(0,1)$, or in other words, $Z$ is normally distributed with mean 0 and variance 1. You will recognize this as the standard normal distribution from Chapter 1. For convenience, we have plotted it in Figure 3.1:

**Figure 3.1**
**The standard normal distribution**

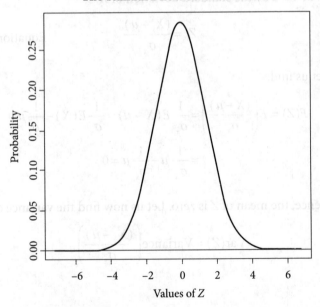

The probability that $Z$ lies between any two points on this curve can be calculated by calculating the area under the curve between any two points. The following program will allow you to do this:

```
up=1.96
lp=-1.96
x=pnorm(up)-pnorm(lp)
x
```

In this program, we are calculating the area under the curve that lies between an upper point (*up*) and a lower point (*lp*). For example, the area under the curve between –1.96 and 1.96 is equal to 0.95. You can find the area between any other two values by changing the values for *up* and *lp*. For example, the area under the curve between –1.65 and 1.65 is equal to 0.901057.

Figure 3.2 illustrates this.

In Figure 3.2, the area under the standard normal curve that is bounded by the two lines (line *ab* and line *cd*) on both sides

**Figure 3.2**
**Area under the standard normal curve (–1.65 < Z < 1.65)**

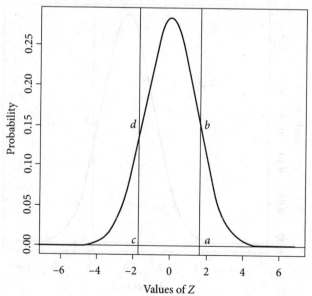

consists of 90 per cent of the area under the curve. Five per cent of the area under the curve is to the left of *cd* and the remaining 5 per cent is to the right of *ab*.

Suppose you want to find a value z of $Z$ such that

$$P(z \leq Z) = 0.95$$

You can type in the following commands:

```
x=qnorm(0.95)
x
```

The program will type $x = 1.644854$. The value of $x = 1.644854$ will indicate that the area of the curve to the left of 1.644854 equals 0.95. This means that 95 per cent of the values of $Z$ are less than 1.644854. Similarly, you can confirm that the area to the left of 1.96 is 0.975. This means that 97.5 per cent of the values of $Z$ are less than 1.96.

Figure 3.3 illustrates this graphically.

**Figure 3.3**
**Area under the standard normal curve ($Z < 1.96$)**

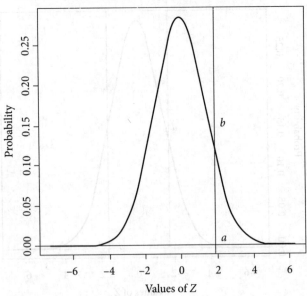

In Figure 3.3, 97.5 per cent of the area under the curve is to the left of line *ab*. The area to the right of *ab* contains 2.5 per cent of the distribution.

**Exercise 3.1**

Find the value *x* such that 99 per cent of the values of *Z* are less than *x*.

It is important to note that if:

$$X \sim N(\mu, \sigma_x^2)$$

then:

$$Z = \frac{(X_i - \mu)}{\sigma_x} \sim N(0, 1)$$

Let:

$$Xbar = \sum_{i=1}^{n} X_i / n$$

We know from Chapter 1 that: *(a)* $E(Xbar) = \mu$; and *(b)* Variance$(Xbar) = \dfrac{\sigma_x^2}{n}$.

We also know that *Xbar* is normally distributed because each of the $X_i$ are normally distributed. Hence:

$$Z = (Xbar - \mu) / \sigma_{Xbar} = (Xbar - \mu) / \sigma_x / \sqrt{n}$$
$$= \sqrt{n} \times (Xbar - \mu) / \sigma_x \sim N(0, 1)$$

This fact can be used for testing certain hypotheses under specific assumptions.

**Example 3.1**

Suppose you are given a sample of weights (in kg) of eight individuals, selected randomly. Suppose the weights are (60, 70, 58, 78, 73, 63, 59 and 74). Suppose you are told that the weights come from a normally distributed population with variance equal to 16. Could the mean weight of the population $\mu$ be equal to 65?

We can answer this question with the help of the information that we already have. The sample mean,

$$Xbar = (60 + 70 + 58 + 78 + 73 + 63 + 59 + 74) / 8 = 66.875$$

Suppose we start by assuming that this sample does come from a population with a mean = 65. It is entirely possible for us to observe a sample whose mean weight is different from the population mean weight because of sampling fluctuations. We have seen in Chapter 1 that $Xbar$ is a random variable, and has a distribution with mean equal to $\mu$. Here, we will start by assuming that $Xbar$ indeed comes from a population with a mean weight of 65. This hypothesis, which we assume as true in order to construct a test of the hypothesis, is called the 'null hypothesis', and is denoted by $H_o$. The idea is to start by presuming an assertion, which is in principle capable of being refuted, and then see whether we find enough evidence to make the assumed assertion unlikely to be true. The important point to remember is that our test procedure is designed to test the falsity of the null hypothesis. It is not designed to test for its truth. Hence, we will be able to reject the null hypothesis if the evidence is overwhelmingly against it, but will never be able to accept the null. We might fail to reject the null for different null hypotheses that are not mutually compatible. Therefore, failure to reject the null cannot be construed as 'acceptance' of the null, since the various nulls that we have posited could be mutually contradictory. So, suppose, in our example, we start with the null hypothesis that $\mu = 65$. Thus,

$$H_o : \mu = 65$$
$$H_A : \mu \neq 65$$

The alternative hypothesis, $H_A$ is something that we contrast with the null hypothesis.[2]

Assuming the null is true, we must have $Xbar \sim N\left(65, \dfrac{16}{8}\right)$.

Therefore, $\dfrac{\sqrt{n} \times (Xbar - \mu)}{\sigma_x}$ must be $Z \sim N(0, 1)$. In such a case

the values of $\dfrac{\sqrt{n} \times (Xbar - \mu)}{\sigma_x}$ are expected to lie between $-1.96$ and

+1.96, 95 per cent of the time. What this means is that if you took 100 samples of size $n$ from this population, and calculated *Xbar* from each of them, in 95 of these cases, $\dfrac{\sqrt{n} \times (Xbar - \mu)}{\sigma_x}$ would be expected to lie between −1.96 and +1.96. We have all the values, $n$, *Xbar* and the assumed $\mu$ and $\sigma_x$. The calculated value of $Z$, we will refer to as the test statistic, $Z_{calc}$. The value for our parameters turns out to be 1.3258. This is consistent with our expectation that given our assumed null hypothesis, 95 per cent of the values of $Z$ are expected to lie between −1.96 and +1.96. Hence, we cannot say that we have accumulated enough evidence to reject the null hypothesis. Please note that we could not have started with the null hypothesis that $\mu \neq 65$ and the alternate hypothesis that $\mu = 65$. In that case, we would not have been able to maintain that $\dfrac{\sqrt{n} \times (Xbar - \mu)}{\sigma_x}$ would lie between −1.96 and +1.96, 95 per cent of the time. In other words, we would not have been able to devise a testing procedure in the manner that we have done here. It does not mean that such a hypothesis cannot be entertained or tested in real life. All that it means is that if we start by assuming the null that $\mu \neq 65$, we would not be able to develop a test on the lines indicated in this chapter. Please remember that the null hypothesis must be a statement that is, at least in principle, capable of being refuted. Therefore, we cannot start with the null hypothesis that $\mu$ is equal to the sample mean. In that case, $\dfrac{\sqrt{n} \times (Xbar - \mu)}{\sigma_x}$ would always be zero, and our expectation that it lies between −1.96 and +1.96 would always be fulfilled. Therefore, such an assertion would be one that cannot be refuted in principle.[3]

Suppose, instead of drawing the sample (60, 70, 58, 78, 73, 63, 59, 74), we would have drawn the sample (70, 73, 65, 69, 80, 83, 58, 72). The sample mean, *Xbar* for this sample equals 71.25. The value of $Z$ would now become:

$$\frac{\sqrt{8} \times (71.25 - 65)}{4} = 4.41$$

This value of $Z$ would have less than 5 per cent probability of occurrence, given our null hypothesis. The set of values $Z \leq -1.96$ and $Z \geq 1.96$ are referred to as the 'critical region of size 5 per cent'. This means that under the assumption that the null hypothesis is true the probability that $Z$ takes any values in this critical region is only 5 per cent at the most. This critical region is illustrated in Figure 3.4.

**Figure 3.4**
**5% critical region for $Z$**

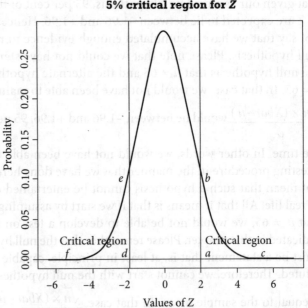

The area of the curve between points $def$ (to the left of the line $de$) and the area of the curve between points $abc$ (to the right of the line $ab$) together constitute the 5 per cent critical region. Each of the two sub regions $abc$ and $def$ enclose 2.5 per cent of the area under the curve.

Similarly, values of $Z$ such that $Z \geq 2.575829$ and $Z \leq -2.575829$ constitute a 'critical region of size 1 per cent', since, if the null hypothesis is true, only 1 per cent of the values of $Z$ are expected to fall in this region. Now, we have found a value of $Z$ that lies in the 1 per cent critical region. That is, if the null hypothesis is true, then, less than 1 per cent of the sample means will result in a $Z$ statistic, that is as large as 4.41. We might therefore regard ourselves as justified in saying that this constitutes sufficient evidence against the null hypothesis. That is, we have found a value of $Z$ that is 'surprising' if the null hypothesis were true. Therefore, we may go ahead and reject the null hypothesis. However, remember that even when the null hypothesis is true, there is a 1 per cent chance of observing values lying in the critical region of size 1 per cent. That is, if we reject the null hypothesis, there is a 1 per cent chance that the null hypothesis may be rejected wrongly. Rejecting the null hypothesis when it is in fact true is called a type I error in statistics. The size of the critical region is the maximum probability of the type I error. It is also sometimes referred as the '$p$ value'.[4] To be very precise, in this example, the size of the critical region for $Z \geq 4.41$ is only 0.00004. Sometimes, the analyst might set a maximum acceptable limit to the probability of a type I error, which is called the 'level of significance'. The conventional levels of significance are 5 per cent and 1 per cent. The null hypothesis is rejected if the size of the critical region is smaller than this pre-assigned significance level. In this example, we will reject the null hypothesis since the size of the critical region is smaller than 5 per cent, and we will say that the null hypothesis has been rejected at a 5 per cent level of significance. (In this example, it is rejected at even a 1 per cent level of significance.)

The following program will enable you to find the size of the critical region for any value of $z$:

```
crit=1-pnorm(x)
crit
```

If you want the size of the critical region such that $Z \geq x$ or $Z \leq x$, this can be obtained as:

```
crit2=2*(1-pnorm(x))
crit2
```

**Example 3.2**

Suppose we have the following sample from a normally distributed population with variance = 4:

Sample = (24, 32, 18, 20, 19, 15, 22, 24, 25, 20, 27, 19, 17, 28). Say whether this sample could have come from a population with a mean of 24.

**Step 1:** Calculate the sample mean:

$$Xbar = (24 + 32 + 18 + 20 + 19 + 15 + 22 + 24 + 25 + 20 + 27 +$$
$$19 + 17 + 28) / 14$$

$$= 22.1429$$

**Step 2:** Form the Z statistic:

$$\sqrt{n} \times (Xbar - \mu) / \sigma_x$$
$$= \sqrt{14} \times (22.1429 - 24) / 2$$
$$= -3.4743$$

This statistic falls within the 1 per cent critical region, since $-3.4743 < -2.575829$. As a result, we can reject the null hypothesis at 1 per cent. The size of the critical region such that $x \leq -3.4743$ or $x \geq 3.4743$ is given by:

```
Crit2=2*(1-pnorm(3.4743))
Crit2
```

Crit2 turns out to be 0.00051218. If we choose to reject the null hypothesis, we can say that we reject the null hypothesis that $\mu = 24$ at a 0.00051218 level of significance. In other words, the maximum probability of a type I error in this case is as small as 0.00051218.

**Exercise 3.2**

Suppose the following sample comes from a normally distributed population with mean $\mu$ and variance = 9.

Sample = (20, 30, 25, 32, 18, 28, 32, 36, 38, 35, 32, 30, 29, 21, 28, 18)

Say whether this sample could have come from a population with $\mu = 27$. Use a critical region of size 1 per cent.

## Exercise 3.3

Suppose the following sample comes from a normal population with mean $\mu$ and variance 4. Say whether the sample could have come from a population with $\mu = 18$.

Sample = (20, 24, 18, 24, 22, 20, 16, 15, 19, 17, 18, 20, 22, 21)

We have defined the maximum probability of type I error as the level of significance. Like the type I error which occurs when we wrongly reject the null, we can think of a 'type II error' as occurring when we fail to reject the null, in spite of its not being true. We can define the 'power of a test' as (1 – probability of type II error), that is, the probability with which a test might be expected to correctly reject the null.[5] The higher the power of a test, the better it is.[6]

Suppose, $X \sim N(\mu, 1)$ with $\mu \neq 0$. Suppose we test the following null and alternate hypothesis:

$$H_o : \mu = 0$$
$$H_A : \mu \neq 0$$

Suppose we have a sample of $n$ values of $X$ and construct:

$$Xbar = \frac{\sum_{i=1}^{n} X_i}{n}$$

We then construct the $Z$ statistics to test the null given above as:

$$Z = \frac{Xbar}{\frac{1}{\sqrt{n}}}$$

Suppose we find the value of $Z$ such that $-1.96 \leq Z \leq 1.96$. We will then fail to reject the null, even if the null is not true. This is an example of a type II error. Intuitively, the probability of a type II error will depend on the value of $\mu$. If the value of $\mu$ is very close to 0, say 0.001, then the test might find it difficult to distinguish 0.001 from 0, specially if the data has a fair amount of variance. As the value of $\mu$ goes further and further away from zero, the ability of the test to distinguish the true value of $\mu$ from zero is expected to increase. Hence, the power of a test can be written as a function of $\mu$, $\Pi(\mu)$. This is called 'the power function'. The program given below will help you to understand these ideas better. The program functions in two stages:

1. In the first stage, it fixes the value of $\mu$ as $-3$. It then generates 50 random numbers each of which is normally distributed with the mean equal to the fixed value of $\mu$ and variance equal to 1. It then takes a test of hypothesis for the null of $\mu = 0$ against the alternative of $\mu \neq 0$. This procedure is repeated 300 times, and the fraction of times the null hypothesis fails to get rejected is noted. That is the probability of a type II error for $\mu = -3$.

2. In the second stage, we increase the value of $\mu$ by a small amount, say to $-2.98$, and repeat step 1. This will give us the probability of a type II error for $\mu = -2.98$. The value of $\mu$ changes in this fashion till it reaches $+3$. Finally, the power function is calculated as $\Pi(\theta) = 1$ – probability of a type II error for each value of $\theta$.

```
n=50
 rem=c(rep(1,300))     ## This creates a column of 300 ones
                       to store the values of rem in the repeat
                       loop
 mo=c(rep(1,300))      ##This creates a column of 300 ones
                       to store the values of mo in the repeat
                       loop
 mu=-3                 ##This sets the initial value of mu
 i=1
 repeat {
 pimu=1-(pnorm(3-sqrt(n)*mu)-pnorm(-3-sqrt(n)*mu))
                       ##This generated the Z test and
 rem[i]=pimu           ## measures the probability that null
                       fails to get rejected
 mo[i]=mu
 mu=mu+0.02
 i=i+1
```

```
if(i>300)
break
}
rem
mo
plot(mo,rem,type= "l",col="darkgreen", lwd=3, maim="Power
                    Function", xlab="mu", ylab="power")
```

The program generates graph like Figure 3.5.

**Figure 3.5**
**Power function**

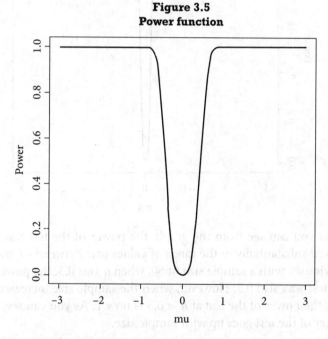

As you can see from the graph, the power of the test statistic is pretty low for values of $\mu$ close to but not equal to zero. For example, when $\mu = 0.5$, the power of the test is only 0.5, that is, in 50 per cent of the cases, it will wrongly fail to reject the null. The sample size ($n$) is equal to 50, which very often is more than the number of observations that we work with in real life. It is only when the value of $\mu$ starts to cross $-1$ or $+1$ does the test become completely reliable. Let us see how the power of the test changes with the sample size. Instead of 50, let us make the sample size 500 and then examine this graph (see Figure 3.6).

**Figure 3.6**
**Power function (sample size = 500)**

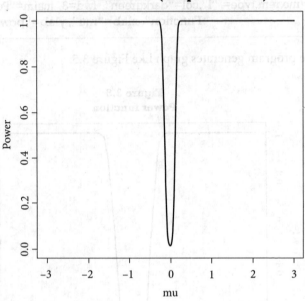

As you can see from the graph, the power of the test has improved substantially in the range of values of $\mu$ between −1 and 1. Previously, with a sample size of 50, when $\mu$ was 0.5, the power of the test was also 0.5. However, when the sample size increased to 500, the power of the test at $\mu = 0.5$ is now 1. As you can see, the power of the test goes up with sample size.

## 3.2 ONE TAILED VERSUS TWO TAILED TESTS

### Example 3.3

Suppose we have a sample of students' marks from a test (out of 10 marks): (4, 7, 8, 9, 5, 6, 8, 5, 7, 8) coming from a normal population with mean $\mu$ and variance 4. Suppose now we want to test whether the sample mean equals population mean = 5 against whether the sample mean is greater than 5 (and not just 'not equal to'). We set up the following null and alternate hypotheses:

$$H_0 : Xbar = 5$$
$$H_A : Xbar > 5$$

This is an example of the so called 'one-tailed test'. In which case, one proceeds as follows:

**Step 1:** Form the $Z$ statistic as usual:

$$\sqrt{10} \times (6.7 - 5) / 2$$
$$= 2.6879$$

Now, in this case, the critical region $Z \leq -2.6789$ is irrelevant, since even if $Z$ was to lie in that region, that would not constitute support against the null hypothesis and favouring the alternative. Consequently, this test uses only the critical region to the right of the test statistic, $Z \geq 2.6789$, and hence the size of the critical region is obtained as:

$$1 - \text{Probability}(Z \leq 2.6789)$$

This can be calculated in R as follows:

```
Crit= (1-pnorm(2.6789))
Crit
```

This turns out to 0.0000044, which is the level of significance. Thus, the level of significance of a one-tailed test is only the size of the one-sided critical region, as against the two-tailed test where $H_A: Xbar \neq \mu$ involves two critical regions.

For example, the 5 per cent critical region for the one-sided test in this example is given in the graph given in Figure 3.7.

The one-sided critical region of size 5 per cent is given by the area of the curve that is enclosed by points *abc*, to the right of the line *ab*. If we are using a 5 per cent one-sided critical region, we will say that we have a test of size 0.05. Compare this with Figure 3.4, which gives the 5 per cent critical region for a two-tailed test.

**Figure 3.7**
**5% critical region for Z (one-tailed test)**

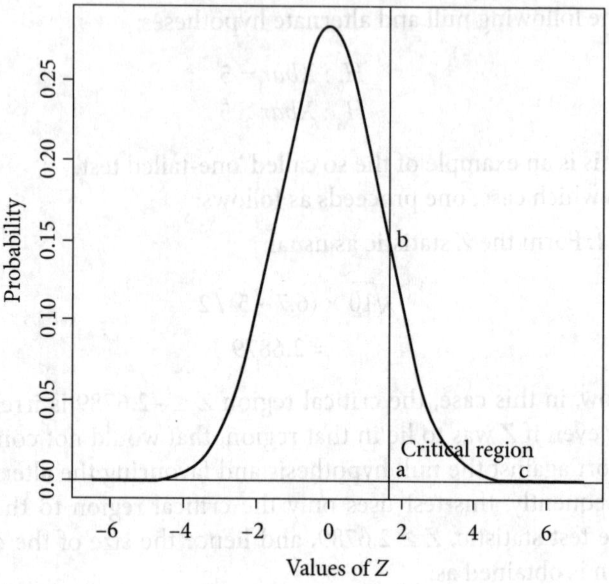

## Exercise 3.4

Suppose you are given the following sample from a normally distributed population with mean $\mu$ and variance 4:

Sample = (23, 34, 28, 28, 27, 29, 30, 32, 34, 33, 25, 30, 32, 33, 35, 37, 32)

Test the null hypothesis that the sample has come from a population with mean equal to 26, against the alternative that the population mean is greater than 26. Use a one-sided test with a 5 per cent level of significance.

## Exercise 3.5

You are given the following sample from a normally distributed population with mean $\mu$ and variance 25:

Sample = (200, 175, 150, 350, 230, 245, 250, 300, 335, 290, 200, 250, 240, 235)

Test the null that the sample has come from a population with mean 250 against the alternative that the population mean is less than 250. Use a one-sided test of size 0.01.

## 3.3 CONFIDENCE INTERVALS FOR THE MEAN

So far, we have dealt with examples where we have a sample of size $n$ from a normally distributed population, with an unknown population mean $\mu$ and a known population variance, $\sigma_x^2$. We have then demonstrated that $Z = \dfrac{\sqrt{n}(Xbar - \mu)}{\sigma_x}$ is such that

$$P(-1.96 \le Z \le 1.96) = P(-1.96 \le \sqrt{n} \times (Xbar - \mu)/\sigma_x \le 1.96) = 0.95$$

Hence, it follows that:

$$P(Xbar - 1.96 \times \sigma_x / \sqrt{n} \le \mu \le Xbar + 1.96 \times \sigma_x / \sqrt{n}) = 0.95$$

Equation 3.2

which follows from a simple rearrangement of terms.

What Equation 3.2 says is that if the null hypothesis is true, then $\mu$ will lie between the two points $\left(Xbar - 1.96 \times \dfrac{\sigma_x}{\sqrt{n}}, Xbar + 1.96 \times \dfrac{\sigma_x}{\sqrt{n}}\right)$ with 95 per cent probability. In other words, if you take say 1,000 samples of size $n$ from a normally distributed population with mean $= \mu$ and variance $= \sigma_x^2$, and construct around each of the sample means the interval:

$$\left(Xbar - 1.96 \times \frac{\sigma_x}{\sqrt{n}}, Xbar + 1.96 \times \frac{\sigma_x}{\sqrt{n}}\right)$$

Then, 950 of these intervals from a total of 1,000 can be expected to contain $\mu$. Such intervals are called 'confidence intervals'.[7] The confidence interval approach recognizes that our estimate of the parameter of interest is not accurate, but we can still say something about the interval in which the true value of the parameter may be expected to lie. Here, we have created a 95 per cent confidence interval, but you can create confidence intervals with other levels of confidence. For example:

$$\left(Xbar - 1.64 \times \frac{\sigma_x}{\sqrt{n}}, Xbar + 1.64 \times \frac{\sigma_x}{\sqrt{n}}\right)$$

would give a 90 per cent confidence interval. In general, the confidence associated with an interval is one minus the size of the critical region associated with the chosen value of $Z$.

### Example 3.4

Suppose we have the following sample coming from a normally distributed population with mean $\mu$ and variance $\sigma_x^2 = 4$:

Sample = (23, 32, 28, 25, 30, 33, 32, 24, 22, 34, 36, 24)

Construct a) a 95 per cent Confidence interval for $\mu$;
b) a 90 per cent Confidence interval for $\mu$

a) Let us calculate the 95 per cent confidence intervals for $\mu$. We know that $P(-1.96 \leq Z \leq 1.96) = 0.95$. Therefore, we have:

$$\left(P -1.96 \leq \frac{\sqrt{n} \times (Xbar - \mu)}{\sigma_x} \leq 1.96\right) = 0.95$$

$$Xbar = (23 + 32 + 28 + 25 + 30 + 33 + 32 + 24 + 22 + 34$$
$$+ 36 + 24) / 12$$
$$= 28.58$$

Therefore, the 95 per cent confidence interval is:

$$\left(28.58 - 1.96 \times \frac{2}{\sqrt{12}}, 28.58 + 1.96 \times \frac{2}{\sqrt{12}}\right)$$

$$= (27.45, 29.71)$$

b) To calculate the 90 per cent confidence interval, we have

$$P(-1.64 \leq Z \leq 1.64) = 0.90$$

Or:

$$P(-1.64 \leq \sqrt{n} \times (Xbar - \mu) / \sigma_x \leq 1.64) = 0.90$$

Therefore:

$$P(Xbar - 1.64 \times \sigma_x / \sqrt{n} \leq \mu \leq Xbar + 1.64 \times \sigma_x / \sqrt{n}) = 0.90$$

Substituting the value, we get the following confidence interval:

$$(28.58 - 1.64 \times 2 / \sqrt{12}, 28.58 + 1.64 \times 2 / \sqrt{12})$$
$$= (27.63, 29.53)$$

Thus, the 90 per cent confidence interval is narrower than the 95 per cent interval, as would be expected. Also, higher the value of $n$, the narrower the confidence intervals, while greater the value of $\sigma_x^2$, the wider the confidence interval.

### Exercise 3.6

You are given the job of estimating the average yield on an acre of land for all the districts in Maharashtra. You are told that yields are normally distributed around a mean $\mu$, with variance of 36. You have collected data on per acre output from 100 randomly chosen farms in Maharashtra. The sample mean works out to be 300 kg. Find the 95 per cent confidence interval for the true average yield per acre for Maharashtra, $\mu$.

### Exercise 3.7

Suppose the average weight of a sample of 220 school children has mean equal to 32 kg. You are told that the weights of school children are distributed normally with an unknown mean $\mu$ and variance of 9. Calculate the 90 per cent confidence interval for the unknown $\mu$.

## 3.4 THE CENTRAL LIMIT THEOREM

The methodology developed above would seem to have limited applicability in the real world because its validity seems to depend upon two crucial assumptions:

1. That the population variance $\sigma_x^2$ is known.
2. The population will be normally distributed.

This difficulty is more apparent than real. At the moment, we will assume that requirement (1) continues to hold, but will convince

Principles of Econometrics

ourselves that requirement (2) can generally be relaxed, provided the sample size is sufficiently large. This is made possible by the celebrated Central Limit Theorem.

### Theorem 3.1: Central Limit Theorem[8]

Let $X_1, X_2, \ldots\ldots X_n$ be a sequence of independent random variables, such that:

$$E(X_i) = \mu$$

and:

$$\text{Variance}(X_i) = \sigma_x^2$$

(where both the mean and variance are finite), for all $i$. Let:

$$X = X_1 + X_2 + \ldots X_n$$

Then, under certain general conditions (which we will not explicitly state here):

$$Z_n = \frac{(X - n\mu)}{\sqrt{n}\sigma_x} \qquad \text{Equation 3.3}$$

has an approximate $N(0, 1)$ distribution, with the approximation getting closer as $n$ increases.

In other words, we can reformulate the Central Limit Theorem as follows:

If $X_1, X_2, \ldots\ldots X_n$ are independent random variables each having the same distribution with expected value $\mu$ and standard deviation $\sigma$, then the sum $X_1 + X_2 + \ldots X_n$ is approximately normally distributed with expected value $n\mu$ and standard deviation $\sigma\sqrt{n}$ when $n$ is sufficiently large.[9]

This theorem states the remarkable result that the sum of $n$ independent random variables with finite means and variances will be approximately normal, independent of the distribution of the original random variables![10]

We can divide the numerator and denominator of the left-hand side (L.H.S.) of Equation 3.3 by $n$, and we will get:

$$Z_n = (Xbar - \mu)(\sigma_x / \sqrt{n}) \qquad \text{Equation 3.4}$$

126

But we know from Chapter 1 that if $X_1, X_2, \ldots\ldots X_n$ comes from a population with mean $\mu$ and variance $\sigma_x^2$, then $Xbar$ has mean $\mu$ and variance $\dfrac{\sigma_x^2}{n}$. This is irrespective of the distribution of $X_1, X_2, \ldots\ldots$ $X_n$. What the Central Limit Theorem tells us is that not only will $Xbar$ be distributed with mean $\mu$ and variance $\dfrac{\sigma_x^2}{n}$, but it will be approximately normally distributed, with the approximation getting better as the sample size increases. This is one of the most fundamental theorems in statistics. It then says that irrespective of the distribution of $X_i$'s, we can still regard $\dfrac{(Xbar - \mu)}{\dfrac{\sigma}{\sqrt{n}}}$ as having distribution $N(0, 1)$.[11]

To get an intuitive feel for this very important theorem, let us carry out an experiment in R. Suppose a random variable follows the Poisson distribution with $\lambda = 0.02$.

By construction, this is not a normally distributed variable. We will now take random samples of size 10 from this distribution, compute the sample mean, and examine its distribution. Remember, in this case:

$$E(X_i) = \lambda = 0.02 \text{ and } Variance(X_i) = \lambda = 0.02$$

Figure 3.8 graphs the distribution of:

$$Z_{10} = \sqrt{10} \times (Xbar - 0.02) / \sqrt{0.02}$$

Compare the graph presented in Figure 3.8 to the graph of a standard normal variable as shown in Figure 3.1. As you can see from the graph, the distribution is not $N(0, 1)$. The graph in Figure 3.9, shows the distribution of:

$$Z_{100} = \sqrt{100} \times (Xbar - 0.02) / \sqrt{0.02}$$

where $n$ has been increased from 10 to 100.

This is still not a graph of a standard normal variable. We now raise n = 1,000, and compute the distribution of:

**Figure 3.8**
**Distribution of Z, n = 10**

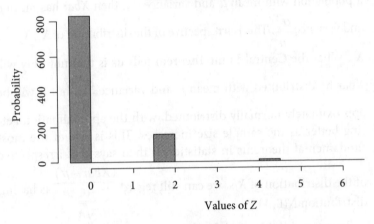

**Figure 3.9**
**Distribution of Z, n = 100**

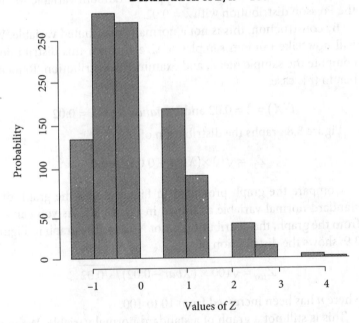

$$Z_{1000} = \sqrt{1000} \times (Xbar - 0.02) / \sqrt{0.02}$$

This is shown in Figure 3.10.

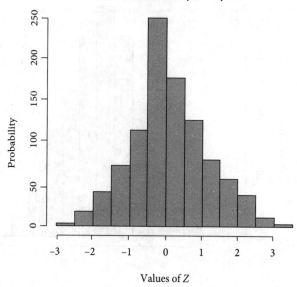

**Figure 3.10**
**Distribution of Z, n = 1,000**

Values of Z

The graph of:

$$Z_{1000} = \sqrt{1000} \times (Xbar - 0.02) / \sqrt{0.02}$$

looks a closer approximation to the graph of the standard normal distribution. Finally, let us increase $n$ to 500,000. The graph in Figure 3.11 looks like an even closer approximation to the normal distribution.

The program given after the figure will enable you to generate these graphs (Figures 3.8, 3.9, 3.10 and 3.11). The first line sets the value of $\lambda = 0.02$ for the Poisson distribution. The next line generates 100,000 Poisson random variables with $\lambda = 0.02$ and stores them in a variable *x*. *samsz* allows you to choose the sample size. *Repl* = 1,000 says to take 1,000 samples of size *samsz* are to be taken from *x*. The command *sample()* takes random samples of size *samsz* from *x* with replacement:

```
z10 = (sum(d) - samsz × lambda) / sqrt(samsz × lambda)
```

generates:

## Figure 3.11
### Distribution of *Z*, *n* = 500,000

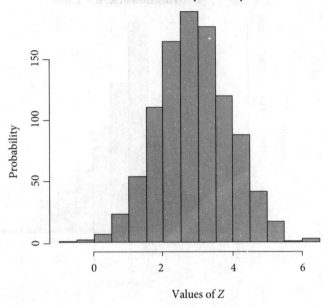

Values of *Z*

$$Z = \sqrt{samsz} \times (Xbar - lambda) / \sqrt{samsz}$$

for each sample. Thus, if *repl* is set to 1000, then 1000 values of *Z* will be generated. Finally, the histogram of these values will be plotted by the last command. You can experiment with this program by changing any of the parameters. You can change the distribution from Poisson to any other you wish. For example, *rt(n,df)* will generate *n* random variables with *df* degrees of freedom.

```
lambda=0.02
x=rpois(100000,lambda)
samsz=500000
repl=1000
rl=c(rep(1,repl))
i=1
repeat {
d=sample(x,samsz,replace=TRUE)
z10=(sum(d)-samsz*lambda)/sqrt(samsz*lambda)
```

```
rl[i]=z10
i=i+1
if(i>repl)
break
}
rl
hist(rl,col="seagreen",lwd=5, main="Distribution of Z,
n=500000", ylab="probability", xlab="values of Z")
```

As we can see from these graphs, even when the original data is not normally distributed, the sample means can be regarded as 'approximately normally distributed', provided 'the sample is sufficiently large'. The requirement that values of the random variable $X$ come from a normally distributed population can be relaxed. However, there is a cost to pay: we cannot apply the $Z$-test to samples that are rather small, because the approximation to standard normal distribution might not be very good in small samples. For small samples, we will have to ensure that the sample indeed comes from a normally distributed population. The other requirement, that the population variance, $\sigma_x^2$ be known will also be relaxed at the end of the chapter.

## Example 3.5

A coin is tossed 100 times. Calculate a 95 per cent confidence interval for the total number of heads on a toss of 100 coins.

Let $S_n$ be the total number of heads, $n = 100$, and $p$, the probability of a head = 0.5. Each of the outcomes of the toss $X_i$ is a binomial random variable, with $E(X_i) = p$ and variance $p \times (1 - p)$. Thus, according to the Central Limit Theorem:

$$Z_n = (S_n - n \times p) / \sqrt{n \times p(1-p)}$$

follows the standard normal distribution:

$$np = 100 \times 0.5 = 50$$

and:

$$\sqrt{n \times p \times (1-p)} = \sqrt{100 \times 0.5 \times 0.5} = 5.$$

Therefore,

$$P(-2 \leq (S_n - 50) / 5 \leq 2)$$
$$P(-1.96 \leq (S_n - 50) / 5 \leq 1.96) = 0.95$$

This gives the interval $(50 - 1.96 \times 5, 50 + 1.96 \times 5) = (40.2, 59.8)$.

### Example 3.6

For Example 3.5, calculate the probability that the number of heads is between 40 and 60.

$$P(40 \leq S_n \leq 60) = P((40 - 50) / 5 \leq (S_n \leq 50) / 5 \leq (60 - 50) / 5))$$
$$= P(-2 \leq (S_n - 50) / 5 \leq 2)$$
$$= 0.9544997$$

Since $(S_n - 50) / 5$ is standard normal variable (since 100 is a large number and the Central Limit Theorem can be invoked).

The required probability can be calculated using R as follows:

```
x=pnorm(2)-pnorm(-2)
x
```

The value of $x$ that will be printed out will be the area of the standard normal distribution between –2 and 2.

### Exercise 3.8

In a toss of 100 coins, calculate the probability that there are at least 45 heads.

### Exercise 3.9

Suppose you are given a sample of monthly incomes of a hundred households from Mumbai. Suppose $Xbar$ = Rs 7,500, and you know that the population variance is 225. Calculate a 95 per cent confidence interval for the mean monthly population income.

## 3.5 THE LAW OF LARGE NUMBERS[12]

Suppose we have a random variable with a finite expected value. For example, the expected value of the number on the uppermost

face of a balanced dice is 3.5. However, suppose you roll the dice
only five times and take an arithmetic average of the numbers on
the uppermost face. The average will in probability not be equal to
3.5. According to the Law of Large Numbers, as you keep on rolling the dice for more times, the arithmetic average of the numbers
on the uppermost face will get closer to 3.5. To take another example, suppose we toss a coin and associate the number one with
a head and number zero with a tail. The expected value of this random variable is 0.5. However, in a small number of tosses, the sum
of ones divided by the total number of tosses will be quite different
from 0.5. As you keep on tossing the coin more times, the fraction
of ones will be observed to get closer to 0.5. This is shown in the
graph given in Figure 3.12:

**Figure 3.12**
**The fraction of heads in *n* coin tosses as *n* increases**

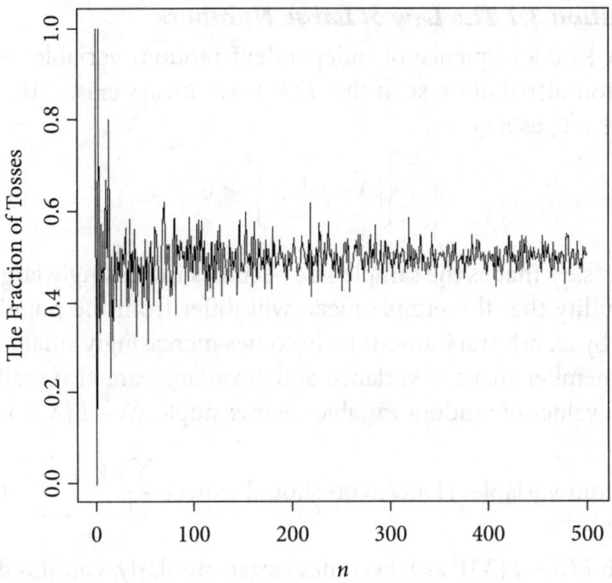

This graph represents the results of an actual experiment, where
we threw a balanced coin an increasing number of times, from
one to 500. Each time, we calculated the fraction of heads. We see
that when the number of tosses is small, the fraction fluctuates a lot.

However, as the number of tosses increases, it becomes more stable, with the values being more and more closely clustered around 0.5, which is the theoretical expected value.

To give a formal proof of the Law of Large Numbers is outside the scope of this text book. However, let us try to state the Law as rigorously as possible as follows:[13]

> If a certain chance experiment is repeated an unlimited number of times under exactly the same conditions, and if the repetitions are independent of each other, then the fraction of times a given event A occurs will converge with probability 1 to a number that is equal to the probability that A occurs in a single repetition of the experiment.

For those who would want a formal statement, it is given below:

### Definition 3.1 The Law of Large Numbers

Let $\{X_n\}$ be a sequence of independent random variables with a common distribution such that $E(X_n) = \mu$ always exists. Then, for every $\varepsilon > 0$, as $n \to \infty$:

$$P\left\{ |\bar{X} - \mu| > \varepsilon \right\} \to 0$$

This says that as the sample size becomes increasingly large, the probability that the sample mean will differ from the population mean by an arbitrary amount $\varepsilon$ becomes increasingly small.

Remember that the variance and covariance are also really expected values of random variables. For example, $(X - E(X))^2$ is also:

a random variable. Hence, you should expect $\dfrac{\sum_{i=1}^{n}(X_i - \bar{X})^2}{n}$ to approach $E(X - E(X))^2$ as $n$ becomes larger. Similarly, you should expect the sample covariance $\dfrac{\sum_{i=1}^{n}(X_i - \bar{X})(Y_i - \bar{Y})}{n}$ to get increasingly closer to $E(X - E(X))(Y - E(Y))$ as $n$ becomes larger.

## 3.6 THE CHI-SQUARE DISTRIBUTION

### Definition 3.2

Suppose $Z_1, Z_2, ....., Z_n$ are independent standard normal variables. Then:

$$X = \sum_{i=1}^{n} Z_i^2$$                    Equation 3.5

The distribution of $X$ is referred to as the Chi-square distribution with $n$ degrees of freedom and expressed as $\chi^2 (n)$.

Consider two standard normal variables, $Z_1$ and $Z_2$. You now know how the distribution of the individual $Z$'s looks. Let us graph the distribution of $X = Z_1^2 + Z_2^2$. From Equation 3.5, this will be $\chi^2 (2)$. The graph below (in Figure 3.13) shows the $\chi^2 (2)$ distribution. Note that the distribution peaks over 2.

**Figure 3.13**
**Chi-square distribution with 2 degrees of freedom**

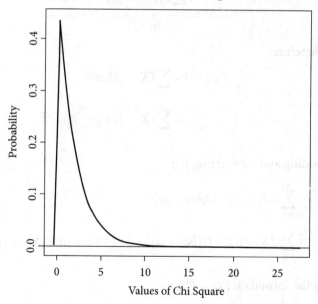

If, $Z = \chi^2 (n)$, $E(Z) = n$ and Variance$(Z) = 2n$.

The chi-square distribution is used widely in statistics. Theorem 3.2 is extremely important:

## Theorem 3.2

If $X_1, X_2, \ldots\ldots X_n$ is a random sample from a normally distributed population with variance $\sigma_x^2$, and if:

$$S^2 = \frac{\sum_{i=1}^{n}(X_i - Xbar)^2}{(n-1)}$$

then:

$$\frac{S^2(n-1)}{\sigma_x^2} = \frac{\sum_{i=1}^{n}(X_i - Xbar)^2}{\sigma_x^2}$$

is a $\chi^2 (n-1)$ variable.

Proof:

$$S^2 = \frac{\sum_{i=1}^{n}(X_i - Xbar)^2}{(n-1)}$$

Therefore:

$$S^2(n-1) = \sum_{i=1}^{n}(X_i - Xbar)^2$$

$$= \sum_{i=1}^{n}(X_i - \mu + \mu - Xbar)^2$$

(adding and subtracting $\mu$):

$$= \sum_{i=1}^{n}((X_i - \mu) - (Xbar - \mu))^2$$

$$= \sum_{i=1}^{n}((X_i - \mu)^2 + (Xbar - \mu)^2 - 2 \times (Xbar - \mu) \times (X_i - \mu))$$

using the formula for $(a - b)^2$:

$$= \sum_{i=1}^{n}(X_i - \mu)^2 + \sum_{i=1}^{n}(Xbar - \mu)^2 - 2 \times \sum_{i=1}^{n}(Xbar - \mu) \times (X_i - \mu)$$

$$= \sum_{i=1}^{n}(X_i - \mu)^2 + n \times (Xbar - \mu)^2 - 2 \times (Xbar - \mu) \sum_{i=1}^{n}(X_i - \mu)$$

$$= \sum_{i=1}^{n}(X_i - \mu)^2 + n \times (Xbar - \mu)^2 - 2 \times (Xbar - \mu) \times (\sum_{i=1}^{n} X_i - n \times \mu)$$

$$= \sum_{i=1}^{n}(X_i - \mu)^2 + n \times (Xbar - \mu)^2 - 2 \times (Xbar - \mu) \times n \times (Xbar - \mu)$$

$$= \sum_{i=1}^{n}(X_i - \mu)^2 + n \times (Xbar - \mu)^2 - 2n \times (Xbar - \mu)^2$$

$$= \sum_{i=1}^{n}(X_i - \mu)^2 - n \times (Xbar - \mu)^2$$

Dividing L.H.S. and right-hand side (R.H.S.) by $\sigma_x^2$:

$$\frac{S^2(n-1)}{\sigma_x^2} - \frac{(Xbar - \mu)^2}{\dfrac{\sigma_x^2}{n}}$$

$$= \left(\frac{(X_i - \mu)}{\sigma_x}\right)^2 - \left(\frac{(Xbar - \mu)}{\sqrt{n}}\right)^2$$

The first term on the R.H.S. is nothing but a sum of squares on $n$ standard normal variables, and hence is $\chi^2 (n)$. The second term on the R.H.S. is nothing but the square of the (sample mean – population mean) / (variance of the sample mean), which is a $\chi^2 (1)$. Hence, the degrees of freedom of the R.H.S are:

$$\chi^2 (n) - \chi^2 (1) = \chi^2 (n - 1)$$

Therefore, $\dfrac{S^2(n-1)}{\sigma_x^2}$ is a $\chi^2$ variable with $n - 1$ degrees of freedom.

This theorem is a very useful one. Suppose you have a sample $(X_1, X_2, \ldots\ldots X_n)$ from a population with variance = $\sigma_x^2$, and if

137

$$S^2 = \frac{\sum_{i=1}^{n}(X_i - Xbar)^2}{(n-1)}$$

is the sample variance (as seen in Chapter 1), then $\frac{S^2(n-1)}{\sigma_x^2}$ is a $\chi^2$ variable with $(n-1)$ degrees of freedom. This fact can be used to construct a test statistic that will allow us to examine hypotheses about the sample mean and the population mean.

### Example 3.7

Suppose you are given the following sample of randomly chosen values of $X$ from a normally distributed population:

Sample = (12, 10, 11, 9, 4, 15, 13, 7, 19, 15, 9, 10, 13, 14)

Could this sample have come from a population with variance 14?

As usual, we set up the null hypothesis that the population variance equals 14:

$$H_o : \sigma_x^2 = 14$$
$$H_A : \sigma_x^2 \neq 14$$

Assuming the null hypothesis is valid:

$$T = \frac{S^2(n-1)}{\sigma_x^2}$$

must be a $\chi^2$ variable with $n-1$ degrees of freedom. Since $S^2$ is the sample variance, $\frac{\sum_{i=1}^{n}(X_i - Xbar)^2}{(n-1)}$ :

$$S^2 = 14.26$$

The null hypothesis implies that the value:

$$T = \frac{S^2 \times (n-1)}{\sigma^2} = 14.26 \times 13/14 = 13.25$$

should be fairly plausible. Suppose we choose to work with a 10 per cent level of significance. We will reject the null hypothesis if the value of the test statistic lies in the critical region of size 5 per cent in the left tail of the distribution or in the critical region of size 5 per cent in the right tail of the distribution. The left hand side critical value $X_1$ such that:

$$P(T \le X) = 0.05$$

under the null hypothesis can be found using R as follows:

```
qchisq(0.05,13)
```

which generates the value 5.891864.

Similarly, the value of $X$ such that $P(T \ge X) = 0.05$ can be obtained as:

```
qchisq(0.95,13)
```

which generates the value 26.36203.

Since $T = 13.25$, we have $X_1 \le T \le X_2$ which means that we cannot reject the null at 10 per cent level of significance.

Graphically, the distribution of $\chi^2$ with 13 degrees of freedom is shown below (in Figure 3.14). The area to the left of the left hand

**Figure 3.14**
**5% critical region for Chi-square distribution with 13 degrees of freedom**

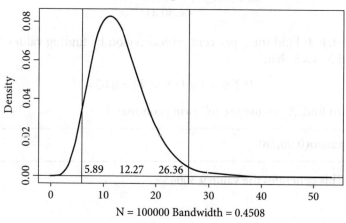

N = 100000 Bandwidth = 0.4508

side vertical straight line and the area to the right of the right hand side vertical straight line constitute the 10 per cent critical region. As you can see, the value of $T$ lies outside the critical region and therefore, the null hypothesis cannot be rejected in this case.

### Example 3.8

Suppose you collect the weights (in kg) of your classmates, which we will assume realistically, are normally distributed with a finite population mean and variance. Suppose you have observed the following sample:

Sample = (63, 56, 78, 54, 65, 68, 48, 57, 59, 70, 85, 65, 56, 72, 69, 54, 50, 55, 63)

Could the variance of the population from which the sample has been taken be equal to 55?

The null hypothesis for this example is:

$$H_o : \sigma_x^2 = 55$$
$$H_a : \sigma_x^2 \neq 55$$

**Step 1:** First find the sample variance. It turns out to be 92.929825.

**Step 2:** Form the quantity:

$$T = S^2(n-1)/\sigma_x^2$$
$$S^2(n-1)/\sigma_x^2 = 92.93 \times 18 / 55$$
$$= 30.41$$

**Step 3:** Find the 5 per cent critical region by finding values $X_1$ and $X_2$ such that:

$$P(T \leq X_1) = P(X_1 \geq T) = 0.05$$

To find, $X_1$ we use the following command:

```
qchisq(0.05,18)
```

This generates the value 9.300455.

To find $X_2$, the following command can be used:

```
qchisq(0.95,18)
```

which generates the following value: 28.8693.

Since $T = 30.41$, we can reject the null hypothesis at 10 per cent level of significance. Suppose we now decide to use the 5 per cent level of significance instead of 10 per cent. That is, we must look for $X_1$ and $X_2$ such that:

$$P(T \leq X_1) = P(T \geq X_2) = 0.025$$

assuming that the null hypothesis is true. $X_1$ can be calculated by typing the command:

```
qchisq(0.025,18)
```

which generates the value 8.230746.

$X_2$ can be calculated by typing the command:

```
qchisq(0.975,18)
```

which generates the value 31.52638. Since $T = 30.41$, we have $X_1 < T < X_2$ and we cannot reject the null at 5 per cent level of significance.

Intuitively, the numerator is the sample variance multiplied by the degrees of freedom, while the denominator is the hypothesized population variance. The test rejects the null hypothesis if the ratio $\frac{S^2(n-1)}{\sigma_x^2}$ is too large or too small, that is, the estimated sample variance is too large when compared to the hypothesized population variance when allowance is made for the degrees of freedom.

We can also calculate the $p$-value associated with any test statistic under the null hypothesis. Remember that the $p$-value calculates the maximum probability associated of rejecting the null wrongly. This $p$-value can be compared with a pre-assigned level of significance in order to determine whether the null hypothesis can be rejected. The program below illustrates how this can be done for an illustrative data set:

```
x<- c(63,56,78,54,65,68,48,57,59,70,85,65,56,72,69,54,50,
55,63)#(This ##command will read in your data into a vari-
able x.)
y= k ##(where k is the hypothesized value of the popula-
tion variance, in this ##example it is 55)
chi= (length(x)-1)*var(x)/k
chi
##(This will compute the chi squared calculated  value)
prob=(1-pchiq(chi,length(x)-1)+(pchisq(chi,length(x)-1)
prob
```

(*prob* will print out the size of the critical region [see Figure 3.15] below for better clarity, *prob* will equal the maximum probability of a type 1 error, or the probability of wrongly rejecting the null, assuming the null is true. If *prob* is less than a pre-assigned level of significance, then the null can be rejected. Otherwise, we will fail to reject the null).

You can try out the above program for any data set and any hypothesized value of population variance.

### Exercise 3.10

Using the R program mentioned above, say whether the following random sample from a normally distributed population could have come from a population with variance equal to 36 or whether it comes from a population with a greater variance:

$$X = (20, 22, 29, 38, 33, 35, 30, 13, 34, 36, 32, 38, 40, 15, 18)$$

Suppose we are testing the null given below against a one sided alternative as follows:

$$H_o : \sigma^2 = 36$$

$$H_A : \sigma^2 > 36$$

We can use the 5 per cent and 1 per cent level of significance. Let us start with the problem of calculating a value $X_1$ such that, if the null hypothesis is true:

$$P(T \geq X_1) = 0.05$$

where:

$$T = (S_x^2 / \sigma_x^2) \times 14$$

This can be obtained using R by typing in the following commands:

```
qchisq(0.95,14)
```

The value of $x$ that is printed out is 23.68479.

The critical region of size 5 per cent, for 14 degrees of freedom in this case corresponds to values greater than 23.6848. See Figure 3.15 below.

**Figure 3.15**
**5% critical region for Chi-square with 14 degrees of freedom**

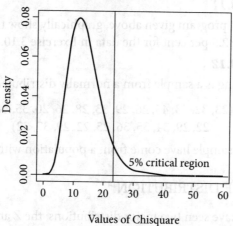

The area of the curve to the left of the vertical line, which is enveloped consists of 5 per cent of the distribution. If the test statistic $S_x^2(n-1)/\sigma_x^2$ falls in that region, we can reject the null hypothesis at 5 per cent level of significance, that is, at a 5 per cent risk of a type 1 error (rejecting the null wrongly). The following program will help you draw similar graphs:

```
df=14
x=rchisq(100000,df)
plot(density(x,bw=1),col= "violetred",lwd=4,main= "Fig
3.9:5% Critical region for Chi square variable
with 18 df",col.main= "salmon3",xlab= "values of Chi
square", ylab= "probability")
abline(v=qchisq(0.95,df) ,col= "seagreen",lwd=4)
```

For this example:

$$S_x^2 = 80.12380$$

so that:

$$(S_x^2 / \sigma^2) \times 14 = (80.12380 / 36) \times 14 = 31.159$$

Since 23.68 < 31.159 we reject the null hypothesis in favour of the alternative at 5 per cent level of significance.

Type this program in R and experiment with various options.

### Exercise 3.11

Using the R program given above, graphically show the critical region of size 2.5 per cent for the data in Exercise 3.10.

### Exercise 3.12

The following is a sample from a normally distributed population:

Sample = (23, 32, 33, 45, 26, 29, 33, 28, 26, 20, 35, 40, 38, 35, 26, 22, 29, 34, 35, 36, 25, 22, 29, 37, 32)

Could this sample have come from a population with variance 4?

## 3.7 THE F DISTRIBUTION[14]

So far, we have seen two major distributions, the Z and the $\chi^2$. Another important distribution is the F distribution.

### Definition 3.3

Let $Z_1 = \chi^2(n)$ and $Z_2 = \chi^2(m)$. Then, the ratio:

$$F = \frac{\left(\dfrac{Z_1}{n}\right)}{\left(\dfrac{Z_2}{m}\right)} = \left(\frac{Z_1}{Z_2}\right) \times \left(\frac{m}{n}\right)$$

follows the *F* distribution with *n* and *m* degrees of freedom. *n* is known as the numerator degrees of freedom and *m* is known as the denominator degrees of freedom.

Figure 3.16 graphs the *F* distribution with 3 (numerator) and 15 (denominator) degrees of freedom:

**Figure 3.16**
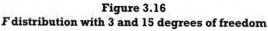
**F distribution with 3 and 15 degrees of freedom**

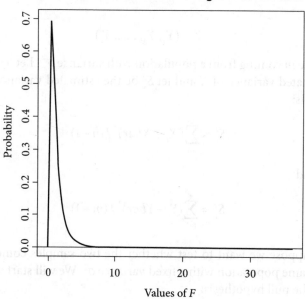

By experimenting with various values in the program below (particularly the degrees of freedom 3 and 15), you can see how the graph changes. You are encouraged to experiment with this program in R. In particular, you must see how the mean and skewness of the distribution change with *n* and *m*:[15]

```
x=rf(100000,3,15)
plot(density(x,bw=1),col= "darkblue",lwd=4, main= "F dis-
tribution with 3 and 15 dfs", xlab= "values of F", ylab= "prob-
ability", col.main= "orange")
```

The $\chi^2$ test can be used to compare sample variance with population variance, whereas the $F$ test can be used to compare between two sample variances. The test is constructed as follows:

Suppose we have two samples:

$$X = (X_1, X_2, \ldots\ldots X_n)$$

of size $n$ from a normally distributed population with variance $\sigma_x^2$ and:

$$Y = (Y_1, Y_2, \ldots\ldots Y_n)$$

of size $m$ coming from a population with variance $\sigma_y^2$. Let $S_x^2$ be the estimated variance of $X$ and let $S_y^2$ be the estimated variance of $Y$. That is:

$$S_x^2 = \sum_{i=1}^{n}(X_i - Xbar)^2 / (n-1)$$

and:

$$S_y^2 = \sum_{i=1}^{n}(Y_i - Ybar)^2 / (m-1)$$

Suppose we want to test whether the two samples come from the same population with a fixed variance $\sigma^2$. We will start assuming the null hypothesis:

$$H_o : \sigma_x^2 = \sigma_y^2$$
$$H_A : \sigma_x^2 \neq \sigma_y^2$$

Then, under the null hypothesis, according to Theorem 3.2, $S_x^2(n-1)/\sigma_x^2$ is a $\chi^2$ with $(n-1)$ degrees of freedom. Similarly, $S_y^2(m-1)/\sigma_y^2$ is a $\chi^2$ with $(m-1)$ degrees of freedom. Therefore:

$$F_{n-1, m-1} = S_x^2/\sigma_x^2 / S_y^2/\sigma_y^2$$
$$= S_x^2 / S_y^2$$

We reject the null hypothesis if the probability of finding the calculated value of $F$ assuming the null hypothesis is true and is small.

**Example 3.9**

Suppose:

$$X = (23, 32, 34, 43, 23, 33, 36, 39, 31, 29, 28, 27, 26)$$

and:

$$Y = (32, 33, 37, 38, 32, 30, 25, 26, 28, 30, 31, 33, 33, 36, 34)$$

For this example:

$$S_x^2 = 35.743590,$$
$$S_y^2 = 13.838095$$

Let $n$ be the number of observations on $X$. Then:

$$(n - 1) = 12$$

Let $m$ be the number of observations on $Y$, so:

$$m - 1 = 14.$$

Thus, the:

$$F \text{ ratio} = S_x^2 / S_y^2$$
$$= (35.743590) / (13.838095)$$
$$= 2.58$$

We will now proceed to find two values which can act as 5 per cent critical values, so that the null hypothesis can be rejected if the test statistic is either less than or greater than these values. Let $X_1$ be the value such that $P(Z \leq X_1) = 0.025$ and let $X_2$ be the value such that $(1 - P(Z \leq X_2)) = 0.025$. We want to calculate the probability $P(Z \leq X_1) + P(Z \geq X_2)$.

The two values can be calculated using the following R commands:

```
X1=qf(0.025,12,14)
```

which generates a value = 0.03119. Similarly, $x_2$ can be calculated using the following command:

```
X2=qf(0.975,12,14)
```

which generates the value 3.050155. If the test statistic is either less than or more than this value, we reject the null. However, since our test statistic equals 2.58, we do not reject the null at 5 per cent level of significance.

We can also approach the hypothesis testing idea by calculating the size of the critical region that is associated with the calculated value of $T$ and then taking a decision on whether to reject or fail to reject the null depending upon whether the critical region is less than or greater than the pre-specified level of significance.

The program given below allows you to calculate the size of the critical region for the following test against a one-sided alternative:

$$H_o : \sigma_x^2 = \sigma_y^2$$
$$H_A : \sigma_x^2 > \sigma_y^2$$

It also illustrates it with hypothetical data.

```
## programme for F test to compare two sample variances
(one tailed test)
x<-c(23,32,34,43,23,33,36,39,31,29,28,27,26)
y<-c(32,33,37,38,32,30,25,26,28,30,31,33,33,36,34)
x1=length(x)-1
y1=length(y)-1
s1=var(x)
s2=var(y)
f=(s1/s2)
critreg=(1-pf(f,x1,y1))
critreg
```

The program will print out the calculated $F$ and the probability of a type 1 error for that value of $F$. You can then decide whether to reject or fail to reject the null given the value of $e$.

## Example 3.10

Let:

$$X = (23, 34, 33, 30, 25, 27, 29, 20, 25, 24, 20, 45, 43, 42)$$
$$Y = (34, 32, 30, 36, 38, 29, 34, 34, 31, 26, 25, 29, 28, 36, 39, 34)$$

be two samples from a normally distributed population. Test whether the two samples could have come from the same population with identical variance = $\sigma^2$ against the alternative that the variance of the population from which the first sample has come is higher than the variance of the population that has generated the second sample.

Let us solve this problem using the program given above. Let $\sigma_x^2$ and $\sigma_y^2$ be the variances of the population from which the first and the second sample have been respectively generated. We form the null and alternative hypothesis:

$$H_o : \sigma_x^2 = \sigma_y^2$$
$$H_A : \sigma_x^2 > \sigma_y^2$$

We can use the previous program above to test the null and alternative pair.

The following is the output of the program:

```
f
1] 4.085566
> critreg
[1] 0.04672
```

The maximum probability of a type 1 error is 0.04672. Since this is less than 5 per cent, we can feel confident about rejecting the null hypothesis.

## Example 3.11

Suppose we have the following random samples from a normally distributed population:

$$X = (0.23, 0.34, 0.34, 0.45, 0.56, 0.23, 0.45, 0.43, 0.37, 0.76)$$
$$Y = (0.2, 0.56, 0.9, 0.01, 0.8, 0.7, 0.5, 0.3, 0.4)$$

Suppose now we want to test the null against the one sided alternative:

$$H_o : \sigma_x^2 = \sigma_y^2$$

$$H_A : \sigma_x^2 > \sigma_y^2$$

We will reject the null in favour of the alternative if $S_x^2 / S_y^2$ is surprisingly large if the null hypothesis is assumed valid. We will reject the null hypothesis if the size of the one-sided critical region is less than a pre-specified level of significance, say 5 per cent. The following program will generate the size of the critical region for this combination of the null and the alternative hypotheses:

```
## Programme for F test to compare two sample variances
(one tailed test)
x<-c(0.23,0.34,0.34,0.45,0.56,0.23,0.45,0.43,0.37,0.76)
y<-c(0.2,0.56,0.9,0.01,0.8,0.7,0.5,0.3,0.4)
x1=length(x)-1
y1=length(y)-1
s1=var(x)
s2=var(y)
f=(s1/s2)
critreg=(pf(f,×1,y1))
critreg
```

This generates a critical region of size 0.044, which is less than the pre-specified 5 per cent level of significance. As a result, we reject the null in favour of the alternative.

### Exercise 3.13

Suppose you are given the following two normally distributed samples:

$$X = (3, 4, 5, 6, 2, 3, 7, 8, 5, 6, 3, 4, 6, 8, 9, 0, 1, 2, 3, 4, 5, 6)$$
$$Y = (4, 5, 6, 7, 3, 4, 6, 7, 8, 9, 3, 4, 5, 6, 7, 8, 9, 0, 2, 4, 5, 6,$$
$$7, 4, 3, 4, 5, 6, 7, 8, 9, 2, 3, 4, 5, 6, 7, 8, 9)$$

Examine whether the two samples could have come from a populations with identical variance.

We have so far examined the standard normal, the $\chi^2$, and the $F$ distributions. Another important distribution is the student's $t$ distribution, to which we now turn.

## 3.8 THE STUDENT'S $t$ DISTRIBUTION[16]

We will start by defining the $t$ distribution.

### Definition 3.4

Let $Z \sim N(0, 1)$, and let $K$ be a $\chi^2$ $(n)$. Then, we say that $Z / \sqrt{K / n}$ follows the Student's $t$ distribution with $n$ degrees of freedom.

The Student's $t$ distribution can be thought of as the ratio of a standard normal variable to the square root of a chi-squared variable divided by its own degrees of freedom. This definition is very useful to us. When using the tests based on the $Z$ distribution at the beginning of the sample, we were forced to make the rather restrictive assumption that the population variance $\sigma_x^2$ be known. What if we do not know $\sigma_x^2$, but estimate it from the sample, by using the formula:

$$S^2 = \frac{\sum_{i=1}^{n}(X - Xbar)^2}{(m - 1)}$$

and then replace the unknown $\sigma_x^2$ with its known estimate $s^2$? Theorem 3.3 is extremely useful in that it tells us that the quantity $\frac{(Xbar - \mu)}{S}$ is a ratio of a standard normal to the square root of a chi-square variable divided by its degrees of freedom, and hence follows the Student's $t$ distribution with $n - 1$ degrees of freedom.

The Student's $t$ distribution has the following properties:

1. If $X$ has a Student's $t$ distribution with $n$ degrees of freedom, $E(X) = 0$.
2. If $X$ has a Student's $t$ distribution with $n > 2$ degrees of freedom, variance$(X) = (n / (n - 2))$.
3. For $n > 3$, skewness $= 0$.
4. Excess kurtosis $= 6 / (n - 4)$ for $n > 4$.

Figure 3.17 gives the graph of the $t$ distribution for 5 degrees of freedom (the thick line), comparing it to the standard normal distribution (the thin line).

**Figure 3.17**
**Student's $t$ distribution with 5 degrees of freedom**

Probability

0.25
0.20
0.15
0.10
0.05
0.00

-10   -5   0   5   10   15

Values of $t$

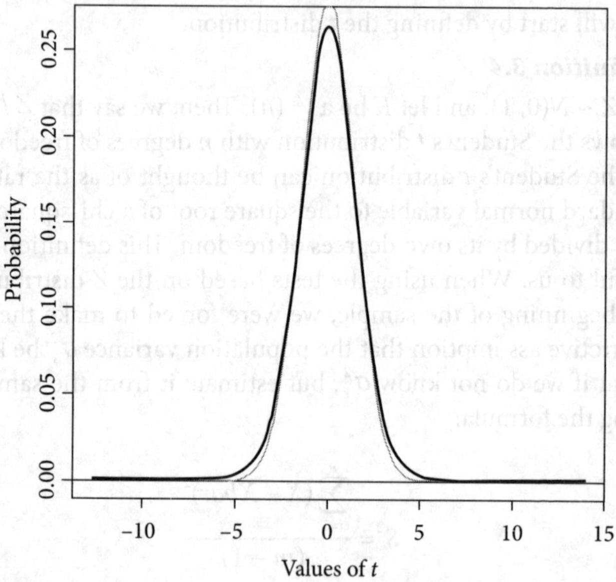

As can be seen from the graph, student's $t$ distribution is just like the normal distribution, but a bit wider and lower. In particular, its tails are fatter than the tails of the standard normal distribution. As the degrees of freedom go up, the $t$ distribution becomes an increasingly better approximation to the normal. In Figure 3.18, we plot the student's $t$ distribution with 30 df (the thick line) and compare it to the standard normal (the thin line).

As can be seen from Figure 3.18, the student's $t$ distribution with 30 degrees of freedom is a better approximation to the standard normal compared to the distribution with 5 degrees of freedom. As a result, for sample sizes great than 30, the difference in results when the $t$ distribution is used as against the use of the standard normal distribution will be negligible.

**Figure 3.18**
**Student's *t* distribution with 30 degrees of freedom**

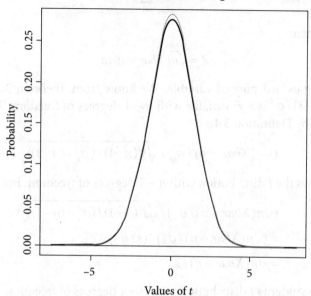

Values of *t*

The important theorem given below enables us to apply the *t* distribution to problems of hypothesis testing.

### Theorem 3.3

Let $X_1$, $X_2$, ...... $X_n$ be a random sample of size $n$ from a population that is normally distributed with mean $\mu$ and variance $\sigma^2$. Let:

$$s^2 = \sum_{i=1}^{n} (X_i - Xbar)^2 / (n-1)$$

where:

$$Xbar = \sum_{i=1}^{n} X_i / n$$

Then, $\sqrt{n}(Xbar - \mu)/s$ follows the student's *t* distribution with $n - 1$ degrees of freedom.

Proof:

Let $X_1$, ......... $X_n$ be a random sample that is distributed normally with mean $= \mu$ and variance $= \sigma_x^2$. Let:

$$Xbar = \sum_{i=1}^{n} X_i / n$$

Then:

$$Z = \sqrt{n}(Xbar - \mu)/\sigma_x$$

is a standard normal variable. We know from Theorem 3.2 that $s^2(n-1)/\sigma_x^2$ is a $\chi^2$ variable with $n - 1$ degrees of freedom. Therefore, by Definition 3.4:

$$(\sqrt{n}(Xbar - \mu)/\sigma_x)/\sqrt{s^2(n-1)/(\sigma_x^2 \times (n-1))}$$

follows the $t$ distribution with $n - 1$ degrees of freedom. But:

$$(\sqrt{n}(Xbar - \mu)/\sigma_x)/\sqrt{s^2(n-1)/(\sigma_x^2 \times (n-1))}$$
$$=(\sqrt{n}(Xbar - \mu)/\sigma_x)/(s/\sigma_x)$$
$$=\sqrt{n}(Xbar - \mu)/s$$

has a student's $t$ distribution with $n - 1$ degrees of freedom.

How do we use this theorem? The following example makes this clear.

### Example 3.12

Suppose we have a sample coming from a population with unknown men and variance:

Sample = (12, 13, 23, 24, 18, 17, 16, 23, 22, 20, 26, 21, 19, 18, 15, 23, 24, 20, 19, 17, 16, 15)

Could this sample have come from a population with mean = 17?
Let us state the null and alternative hypotheses:

$$H_o : \mu = 17$$
$$H_A : \mu \neq 17$$

We know, by using the central limit theorem that $\sqrt{n} \times (Xbar - \mu)/\sigma_x$ (where $\sigma_x$ is the unknown population standard deviation) is a standard normal variable. We also know that

$$s^2(n-1) / \sigma_x$$

where

$$s^2 = \sum_{i=1}^{n}(X_i - Xbar)^2 / n - 1$$

is a chi-square variable with $n - 1$ degrees of freedom. Thus, $\sqrt{n} \times (Xbar - \mu)/s$ must follow the Student's $t$ distribution with $n - 1$ degrees of freedom. We can use this fact to test our hypothesis as follows:

**Step 1:** Calculate:

$$s^2 = \sum_{i=1}^{n}(X_i - Xbar)^2 / n - 1$$

It turns out to be 14.59, and $s$ turns out to be 3.82. The sample mean:

$$Xbar = 19.13$$
$$n = 22$$

so:

$$n - 1 = 21$$

**Step 2:** Calculate the test $t$ statistic:

$$t_{calc} = \sqrt{21} \times (19.13 - 17) / 3.82 = 2.56$$

**Step 3:** Find the size of the critical region for $t_{calc}$. Since this is a

```
x=2*(1-pt(2.56,21))
x
```

two-tailed test, this can be done in R by typing the following:
The value of $x$ that is printed out is 0.01824218.
Thus:

$$P(x \le -2.56) + P(x \ge 2.56) = 0.01824218$$

In other words, assuming the null hypothesis is true, the probability that the calculated value of $t$ takes a value less than or equal to –2.56 or greater than or equal to 2.56, is 0.01824218. If we go by the conventional 5 per cent size of the critical region, we can feel safe in rejecting the null. In other words, assuming that the null is true, the maximum probability of rejecting the null wrongly would be 0.01824218.

The following $R$ program will help you solve similar problems:

```
## Programme for t test of mean
X<c(12,13,23,24,18,17,16,23,22,20,26,21,19,18,15,23,24,20,
19,17,16,15)
hyp=17
s1=sd(x)
n=length(x)-1
tcalc= sqrt(n)*(mean(x)–hyp)/s1
critregion= 2*(1-pt(tcalc,n))
tcalc
critregion
```

In this program, $hyp = 17$ refers to the hypothesized mean that has been set to 17 in this example. You can also obtain values $x$ such that $P(t \leq x) = 0.975$ so that areas to the left of $-x$ and right of $x$ together form a 5 per cent critical region. In this case, for 21 degrees of freedom, we can find this value by using the following R command:

```
x=qt(0.975,21)
x
```

The value of $x$ that gets printed is 2.07. This critical value defines the following critical regions shown in Figure 3.19.

In this graph, the vertical lines $df$ and $ac$ have been drawn at –2.07 and 2.07 respectively. The area to the left of $ac$, enclosed in the curve $def$, and the area to the right of the line $ac$, enclosed in the points $acb$, form two critical regions of size 2.5 per cent respectively. If the calculated $t$ falls within any of these regions, we can reject the null at the 5 per cent level of significance.

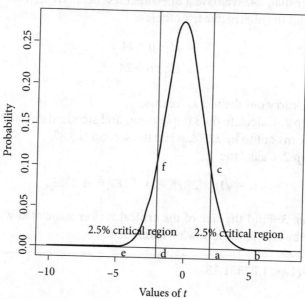

**Figure 3.19**
**5% critical region for a two-tailed test for the *t* distribution with 21 degrees of freedom**

## Exercise 3.14

Suppose we have the following sample:

$X = (4, 3, 5, 6, 7, 4, 5, 6, 3, 4, 6, 7, 8, 2, 3, 4, 6, 4, 9, 3, 4, 3, 5, 6, 3, 8, 6)$

Test if the sample could have come from a population with mean 5.

## Exercise 3.15

Suppose we have the following sample:

$X = (12, 34, 23, 43, 26, 43, 20, 34, 33, 36, 32, 21)$

Test whether this sample could have come from a population with a mean of 20.

## Example 3.13(One-tailed test)

Suppose we have the following sample:

$X = (23, 22, 21, 25, 27, 19, 18, 20, 22, 24, 26, 28, 23, 20,$
$19, 18, 20, 28, 30)$

Test the null that the sample has come from a population with a mean of 24, against the alternative that the population mean is greater than 24. We have a one-sided test here. We first set up the null and the alternative hypotheses:

$$H_o : \mu = 24$$
$$H_A : \mu > 24$$

We carry out the test as follows:

**Step 1:** Calculate the sample mean and standard deviation. The first turns out to be 22.78, while the second is 3.87.

**Step 2:** Calculate:

$$t = \sqrt{18} \times (22.78 - 24) / 3.87 = -1.23881$$

**Step 3:** Find the size of the critical region associated with this value by typing the following command:

```
x<-(1-pt(1.23881,18))
x
```

This turns out to be 0.1156. That is, the probability of wrongly rejecting the null, given the value of test statistic equals 1.23881, equals 0.1156. This is higher than the 5 per cent conventional value, and hence, we do not feel confident in rejecting the null.

Alternatively, we can find the value $x$ such that:

$$P(t \geq x) = 0.05$$

assuming the validity of the null hypothesis. That value can be found by typing in the following command:

```
qt(1.23881,18)
```

The number that gets printed out is 1.734064. The calculated value of $t$ is less than this value, so we do not reject the null.

## Exercise 3.16

Suppose you are given the following sample:

$$X = (3, 2, 4, 5, 6, 3, 4, 5, 6, 7, 8, 2, 3, 4, 5, 6, 7, 8, 5, 6, 8, 0, 1, 2, 0, 1, 5, 8)$$

Test the null hypothesis that the population mean is 3 against the alternative that the population mean is greater than 3.

## 3.9 CONFIDENCE INTERVALS USING THE $t$ DISTRIBUTION

### Example 3.14

Suppose we have the following sample:

$$X = (2, 4, 3, 5, 6, 7, 3, 6, 8, 9, 12, 11, 10, 4, 6, 7, 8, 9)$$

Suppose we want to form a 95 per cent confidence interval for the population mean $\mu$. The degrees of freedom in this case are 17. The value of $x$, such that Prob$(t \leq x) = 0.975$, is 2.86. This value can be found in R simply by typing:

```
qt( 0.975,17).
```

Hence:

$$P(-2.86 \leq t \leq 2.86) = 0.95$$

Therefore:

$$P(-2.86 \leq t \leq 2.86) = 0.95$$

$$P(-2.86 \leq \sqrt{17} \times (Xbar - \mu)/s_x \leq 2.86) = 0.95$$

$$P(Xbar - 2.86 \times s_x / \sqrt{17} \leq \mu \leq Xbar + 2.86 \times s_x / \sqrt{17}) = 0.95$$

```
X<-c(3,2,4,5,6,3,4,5,6,7,8,2,3,4,5,6,7,8,5,6,8,0,1,2,0,1,5,8)
N=length(X)-1
Co = 0.975
G=qt(Co,n)
sl=sd(X)
cfl= mean(X)-G*sl/sqrt(N)
cfu=mean(X)+G*sl/sqrt(N)
cfl
cf
```

*Xbar* in this case equals 6.666667, while the standard deviation of $X$ equals 2.869720. Substituting these values, we get the 95 per cent confidence interval (4.68,8.66).

You can calculate a confidence interval in R by running the above program.

You can of course change the level of confidence. Suppose you want 90 per cent confidence intervals, then you should change Co from 0.975 to 0.95.

### Exercise 3.17

Suppose you are given the following sample:

$$X = (9, 8, 7, 6, 9, 10, 11, 13, 15, 13, 12, 9, 7, 9, 6, 8, 5, 9, 6, 8, 7, 9, 4,$$
$$6, 7, 8, 9, 5, 7, 8, 9)$$

Calculate a 90 per cent confidence interval for the population mean $\mu$.

## CONCLUSION

In this chapter, we have got acquainted with the basics of statistical inference. We learnt about:

1. The standard normal distribution, testing hypotheses about the mean when the population variance is known and creating confidence intervals.
2. The Central Limit Theorem.
3. The Chi-squared distribution and comparing sample variance with that of the population.

4. The $F$ distribution that allows us to compare two sample variances.

5. The $t$ distribution to be used when the sample size is small and when the population variance is not known, but replaced by its sample estimate.

6. We learnt how to write programs in R to do these routine tests.

Make sure that you have internalized these concepts well.

## NOTES

1. Hypothesis testing is largely the product of Ronald Fisher (born 17 February 1890; died 29 July 1962), William Gosset (born 13 June 1876; died 16 October 1937), Jerzy Neyman (born 16 April 1894; died 5 August 1981), and Egon Pearson (Karl Pearson's son, born 11 August 1895; died 12 June 1980). Fisher was a statistician who emphasized rigorous experimental design and methods to extract a result from few samples assuming Gaussian distributions. Neyman (who teamed with the younger Pearson) emphasized mathematical rigour and methods to obtain more results from many samples and a wider range of distributions. Modern hypothesis testing is an (extended) hybrid of the Fisher versus Neyman/Pearson formulation, methods and terminology developed in the early 20th century.

2. This was Jerzy Neyman's (born 16 April 1894; died 5 August 1981) major discovery. Neyman is one of the greats of modern statistics. Karl Person had tried to see whether the data followed some distribution without positing an alternative. Neyman argued that significance testing made no sense unless there were at least two possible hypotheses. The choice of these alternatives dictates the manner in which the significance testing is carried out. The names 'alternative hypothesis' and the 'null hypothesis' were developed by Neyman and Egon Pearson in order to distinguish the alternative from the null hypothesis that is used to compute the $p$ = value.

3. Sir Karl Raimund Popper (born 28 July 1902; died 17 September 1994) held that a theory that is always verified is not a good scientific theory. On the contrary, a good scientific theory is one that is, in principle, capable of being refuted. There are some outcomes that a good scientific theory says will not occur. If these are actually observed to occur, the theory will be refuted. A 'pseudoscientific' theory, on the other hand, is one that will always be verified, if one is looking for verifications. Every empirical observation can be 'fitted' into the theory. Such theories, according to Popper, are not good scientific theories. Note that Popper was not a classical empiricist, but believed that scientific theories are abstract in character, just like modern microeconomic

theories. They can be tested only by implications. He held that no amount of verification validates a theory, but a single counterexample will do. This is perhaps the main difference between Popper's view of falsifiability and statistical inference. For statistical inference, the number of events that occur counter to the theory must be a statistically significant number. Though Popper's approach to good scientific theory is different from the statistical approach to hypothesis testing, the emphasis on potential falsifiability connects the two.

4. The exact interpretation of the p-value remains an uncomfortable issue. If the p-value is used to show that the hypothesis under which it was calculated is false, what does it really mean? It has nothing to do with reality. It is not the physical, real world probability of any kind of error that we may make. It is not the probability that the null hypothesis is in fact true. It is just a way of saying which tests will work better than others. In this formulation, the scientist pre-selects some $p$ value, say 0.05, and rejects the null hypothesis whenever he/she finds a $p$ value less than or equal to 0.05. In this way, the statistician will reject a true null hypothesis exactly 5 per cent of the time. In that sense, the p-value is a probability. Its intellectual pedigree can be traced to John Venn (born 4 August 1834; died 4 April 1923), who argued that long-run frequencies of events could be termed as probabilities (*Logic of Chance*, published in 1866). That is, if you toss a coin many times, the fraction of the times you get heads could be thought as the 'probability' of a head. This is called the frequentist definition of probability. John Maynard Keynes, in his *Treatise on Probability* (1921), strongly argued against this formulation, showing it had fundamental inconsistencies. However, statisticians have continued to use the frequentist approach. During World War II, Abraham Wold expanded on Neyman's adoption of Venn's definition to develop the field of statistical decision theory.

5. In the Neyman–Pearson formulation of hypothesis testing, the p–value is calculated to test the null hypothesis, but the power refers to how the p–value will behave if the alternative hypothesis were in fact true.

6. This also means that the set of alternative hypotheses cannot be too large. The power of a test must be judged in the context of a specific set of alternatives; no test can be powerful against all possible alternatives. In 1956, Leonard Savage and Raj Raghu Bahadur showed that the class of alternatives does not have to be very wide for hypothesis testing to fail. Neyman himself developed the idea of restricted hypothesis testing during the 1950s. This idea roughly says that tests against very narrowly defined hypotheses have better power compared to hypotheses that are more inclusive.

7. This was another of Neyman's fundamental contributions to statistics. Neyman presented the outlines of this approach in a paper presented before the Royal Statistical Society in 1934. It is worth reiterating that Neyman's approach to probability is a frequentist one. In keeping with this approach, the 95 per cent confidence interval implies that in the long run, 95 per cent

of the intervals will include the true parameter. It does not imply statements like 'I am 95 per cent sure that the parameter lies between these two specific limits'. Such statements require a different approach to probability, namely the subjective probability approach, which was developed by Leonard Savage and Bruno de Finetti, among others.

8. This is the Lindberg–Levy Central Limit Theorem. It requires all the $X_i$ to be independently distributed with the same mean and the same variance. The more general theorem, allows each $X_i$ to have a different mean and a different variance.

9. In the more general formulation of the Central Limit Theorem, it is essential that the random variables $X_k$ are independent, but it is not necessary for them to have the same distribution. When the random variables have different distributions with $X_k$ having the mean $\mu_k$ and standard deviation $\sigma_k$, the Central Limit theorem still holds if we replace $n\mu$ with $\sum_{k=1}^{n} \mu_k$ and $\sigma \sqrt{n}$ with $(\sum_{k=1}^{n} \sigma_k^2)^{1/2}$.

10. Sir Francis Galton, who we have already met in the previous chapter, had the following to say about this 'I know of scarcely anything so apt to impress the imagination as the wonderful form of cosmic order expressed by the "Law of Frequency of Error". The law would have been personified by the Greeks and deified, if they had known of it. It reigns with serenity and in complete self-effacement, amidst the wildest confusion. The huger the mob, and the greater the apparent anarchy, the more perfect is its sway. It is the supreme law of Unreason. Whenever a large sample of chaotic elements are taken in hand and marshalled in the order of their magnitude, an unsuspected and most beautiful form of regularity proves to have been latent all along.'

11. The earliest version of this theorem was formulated by the French-born mathematician Abraham de Moivre who, in an article published in 1733, used the normal distribution to approximate the distribution of the number of heads resulting from many tosses of a fair coin. This finding was nearly forgotten until the famous French mathematician Pierre-Simon Laplace rescued it from obscurity in his *Théorie Analytique des Probabilités*, (published 1812). Yet again the finding received little attention in Pascal's own life time. In 1901, the Russian mathematician Aleksandr Lyapunov defined it in general terms and showed precisely how it worked mathematically. Nowadays, the central limit theorem is considered to be the unofficial sovereign of the probability theory.

12. The Law of Large Numbers was first described by Jacob Bernoulli in his *Ars Conjenctandi*. He names it the 'golden theorem'. In 1835, S.D. Poisson further described it under the name 'La loi des grandes nombres' (the law of large numbers). This name gradually stuck. Chebyshey, Markov, Borel, Cantelli and Kolmogrov all contributed to the refinement of this law.

13. The mathematical basis for the (strong) Law of Large Numbers was given for the first time by the famous Russian mathematician, A.N. Kolmogrov in the

20th century. A so-called weak version of the law had already been formulated by Jacob Bernoulli in the *Ars Conjenctandi*.

14. This distribution is also known as the Fisher–Snedecor distribution.
15. The mean for the *F* distribution is $m / m - 2$ (for *m* greater than 2).
16. William Sealy Gosset (born 13 June 1876; died 16 October 1973), who was known by his pen-name Student, developed this distribution. Gosset was employed with the famous brewers, Guinness in order to help Guinness select the best varieties of barley for brewing. A previous researcher at Guinness had published a paper about their trade secrets. As a consequence, Guinness prohibited its employees from publishing any papers irrespective of the content. Gosset had done substantial work with small samples, unlike Karl Pearson's work on large samples. Pearson had depended on large samples in his quest for exact estimates of parameters of probability distributions. Pearson and Gosset had a good relationship and Gosset published most of his papers, including the 'The Probable Error of a Mean' in Pearson's *Biometrica*. The Student's *t* distribution is widely used today, but when Pearson sent Gosset's small sample work to R.A. Fisher, he wrote, 'I am sending you a copy of Student's Tables as you are the only man that's ever likely to use them!' Pearson strongly disliked Fisher. Fisher appreciated Gosset's work, and modified Gosset's statistic slightly.

# Chapter 4

# Point Estimation and the Method of Ordinary Least Squares

## INTRODUCTION

In this chapter, we will learn about estimation of parameters. This chapter will cover the following:

1. The idea of an estimator as a random variable.
2. Some desirable properties of estimators: Unbiasedness, Efficiency, Consistency.
3. The Ordinary Least Squares (OLS) estimator for a two variable regression model: Estimating the parameters using the method of least squares and properties of OLS estimator.
4. Properties of the OLS estimators, and that they are BLUE under certain assumptions.
5. Goodness of fit measures and model selection criteria for the two-variable linear regression model.
6. The use of the F statistic in the context of the two-variable linear regression model.
7. Using dummy variables to model qualitative explanatory variables.
8. Testing for structural break using the Chow test.

9. Log-Log and Semi Log Regression.
10. Regression with standardised coefficients.
11. Prediction using two-variable linear regression model.
12. Estimating two-variable linear regression in R.

## 4.1 ESTIMATING PARAMETERS

The objective is to estimate population parameters which are generally not observable with any degree of certainty. For example, we might be interested in finding $p$, the proportion of heads that will be observed if a balanced coin is tossed indefinitely many times. However, it is not possible to physically throw a balanced coin infinitely many times. We can throw it only finitely many times. We will observe a finite sequence of heads and tails. This is the sample we will have and based on this sample, we have to make an estimate of $p$. As one of many possible strategies to estimate $p$, we might decide to sum the total number of heads observed in our sample and divide this by the total number of tosses we have made in order to obtain an estimate of $p$. Remember that this is an estimate of $p$, not $p$ itself.

Just to fix ideas, think of the following situation: You are anchored in the deep sea on a ship and somewhere far away, somebody plays the same song everyday on a violin. Depending upon the wind direction and other parameters, you get to hear just some snatches, and those too rather imperfectly. Your problem is to make a reasonable guess about which song is being played by repeatedly listening to the bits that you can hear. In many ways, the problem of estimating unobservable parameters is similar. We can only 'estimate' the actual parameters.[1] Lest we forget this, we will represent the estimate of $p$ by $\hat{p}$. Suppose we have tossed the coin 100 times and 47 of these have turned out to be heads. Then, one of our possible estimates of $p$, $\hat{p}$, will be $47 / 100 = 0.47$, if we stick to our rule of obtaining the estimate of $p$ by dividing the total number of observed heads by the total number of tosses. If we toss the coin again, we will obtain another sample and another value of $\hat{p}$. Thus, $\hat{p}$, the estimated value of $p$, is a random variable, with a probability distribution. Different samples associated with the same experiment (of tossing a balanced coin 100 times) will result in different values of $\hat{p}$.

On the other hand, $p$, the parameter that we are trying to estimate, is a fixed number. Also, though dividing the total number of heads by the total number of tosses seems a natural way to estimate $p$, it is only one among all possible ways of using the sample information to obtain an estimate of $p$. Another way (though a somewhat more roundabout one) of estimating $p$ could be to argue that since the coin is balanced, the proportion of tails to the total number of tosses could be an estimator of the proportion of heads, since heads and tails are equally likely! This way of estimating $p$ is different from estimating $p$ by dividing the total number of heads by the total number of tosses. It is a different 'estimator'. In general, 'an estimator is a function from the sample to the set of real numbers, and value of the function is an estimate of the parameter'. When we decided to estimate $p$ by summing the number of heads in the sample and dividing by the number of tosses, we were combining the various data points in the sample into a one single number and interpreting the value of this number as the estimate of $p$, $\hat{p}$. Suppose we threw the coin 20 times and obtained the following sample:

$$S = (H, T, T, H, H, T, H, H, T, H, H, T, T, H, T, H, H, T, T, H)$$

We have 11 heads out of 20 tosses. Suppose we think of a series of variables $X_i$, such that $X_i = 1$ if the $i$th toss is a head, and 0 otherwise. Then, $S$ can be written as:

$$S' = (1, 0, 0, 1, 1, 0, 1, 1, 0, 1, 1, 0, 0, 1, 0, 1, 1, 0, 0, 1)$$

That is, we have defined a function from the sample space to the set of real numbers, which is how we understand random variables. Now, when we take an average of the numbers in $S'$, we define a new function from $S'$ to the set of real numbers. For example, we can take the arithmetic average of the numbers in $S'$. In that case, we will be associating one real number (the value of this average) with the elements of $S'$. This function is called an estimator. Our estimator of $p$:

$$\hat{p} = \sum_{i=1}^{n} X_i / 20 = 11 / 20 = 0.55$$

In this example, the formula $\sum_{i=1}^{n} X_i / 20$ is the estimator (which is more general in that you can apply it to any sample), while 0.55 is the estimate, which is a particular value for this specific sample. For a different sample, the application of the same formula might give a different value.

To take yet another example, let us assume that we want to estimate the number of mangoes that you can find on any randomly picked tree on a given day in our locality. So, you take a sample of 30 trees and count the number of mangoes on each tree. Let the data be as follows:

$S'' = $ (456, 500, 435, 550, 456, 600, 590, 456, 600, 623, 567, 589, 634, 601, 456, 200, 599, 245, 299, 356, 365, 380, 434, 456, 421, 333, 321, 302, 368, 390)

One way of finding the number of mangoes that you would find on any randomly picked tree is to take an average across all the numbers in $S''$, which turns out to be 452.73. You can argue that any randomly picked tree will have 453 mangoes (rounding off the number 452.73). But this is not the only estimate that you can form. Looking closely at the data, you will notice that the number 456 appears more frequently compared to any other number, four times out of 30. Thus, about 13 per cent of the trees in the sample have 456 mangoes. That could be used as another candidate to estimate the number of mangoes on a tree. The point that I am trying to emphasize here is that there are more than one way in which the same parameter can be estimated.

### Exercise 4.1

Suppose an urn contains an unknown number of balls, all numbered sequentially starting from one. How many different ways can you think of estimating the number of balls in the urn?

As we have seen, we can generally find more than one estimator to guess the value of an unknown parameter. How do we select among them? On what basis can we say that one estimator is better than another? Can we think of an 'ideal' estimator? For that, we need to know what makes an estimator an ideal estimator. That is done in Section 1. In Chapter 2, we have seen how $E(Y / X)$ can be modelled as a linear function of $X$, namely:

$$E(Y / X) = a + bX$$

In this chapter, we will examine a popular estimator of $a$ and $b$, which is called the ordinary least squares estimator. This is done in Section 2 of this chapter. In Section 3, we will demonstrate that, provided some assumptions that we have made the ordinary least squares estimators of $a$ and $b$ will have many of the properties that make an estimator desirable, as per the criteria given in Section 1. In Section 4, we deal with rather special ways of modelling $E(Y / X)$ as a function of $X$.

## 4.2  DESIRABLE PROPERTIES FOR ESTIMATORS TO HAVE

In this section, we will discuss some of the properties that can help us make a choice between alternative estimators. Classically, we judge estimators on the basis of their performance in small samples and their performance as the sample size becomes large. The former properties are called 'small sample' properties while the latter ones are called 'large sample' properties. Small sample properties are those that hold for any finite sample of size $n$, provided $n$ is larger than the number of parameters being estimated. Large sample properties are 'asymptotic', that is, they hold as the sample size tends to infinity. The small sample properties that will be studied in this chapter are

1. Unbiasedness
2. Efficiency
3. Linearity

The large sample property to be studied will be the property of consistency. Of course, this does not exhaust the list of estimator properties that have been studied in the literature. We choose to focus on these because they are directly relevant to our discussion.

## 4.2.1 Unbiasedness[2]

Think again of the problem of estimating the proportion of heads in infinitely many tosses of a balanced coin. In reality, we will only have the outcomes of a finite number of tosses. Suppose we decide to estimate $p$ by $n / N$ where $n$ is the total number of heads in $N$ tosses that constitute our sample. Let:

$$\hat{p} = n / N$$

If we were to toss the coin again $N$ times, the total number of heads in the sample of size $N$ will now differ and we will get a fresh value of $\hat{p}$. Thus, our estimator, that is, the rule of obtaining the estimate of $p$ by dividing the total number of heads by the sample size, will result in a different estimate every time. $\hat{p}$ is a random variable, taking different values with different probabilities. The question that naturally arises is: What is the relationship between $\hat{p}$, which is a random variable, and $p$ itself, which is the fixed population parameter that we are unable to observe directly but want to estimate? What connects the two? The concept of an unbiased estimator provides one such connection. We say $\hat{p}$ is an 'unbiased estimator' of $p$ if:

$$E(\hat{p}) = p.$$

That is, if the average value of all possible different values of $p^\wedge$ equals $p$, we will say that it is an unbiased estimator of $p$. This does not rule out specific individual values of $p^\wedge$ based on specific samples being very different from $p$. We have already come across this concept in Chapter 1, where we demonstrated that the sample mean, $\sum_{i=1}^{n} x_i / n$ is an unbiased estimator of the population mean. The sample mean is an estimator, because it is a rule for obtaining an estimate of the population mean. Different samples will give you different values of the estimator, even when the estimator is the same. We will now examine whether dividing the number of heads by the total number of tosses is an unbiased estimator of $p$. Let us decide to represent a head by the number 1 and a tail by the number 0. Then, we can think of $X$, the outcome of any given toss, as being a random variable that takes values 1 or 0, with:

$$\text{Probability } (X = 1) = p$$

and

$$\text{Probability}(X = 0) = 1 - p$$

We have

$$E(X) = p \times 1 + (1 - p) \times 0 = p$$

Now, suppose we have got $n$ 1's and $N - n$ 0's in $N$ tosses. Then,

$$\hat{p} = \sum_{i=1}^{N} X_i / N$$

Let us check whether $\hat{p}$ is an unbiased estimator of $p$.

$$E(\hat{p}) = E(\sum_{i=1}^{N} X_i / N)$$
$$= (1 / N)E(X_1) + \ldots\ldots (1 / N)E(X_n)$$
$$= (1 / N)p + \ldots\ldots (1 / N)p$$
$$= Np / N = p$$

Hence, $p^\wedge$ is indeed an unbiased estimator of $p$. It says that on an average, $p^\wedge$ will yield the correct value of $p$, though in individual instances, there is no such guarantee. That is, in any particular sample, $p^\wedge$ will not necessarily be equal to $p$, but if you average the values of $p^\wedge$ over many samples, then the resultant average value will be equal to $p$.[3] More formally, we will define an unbiased estimator as follows:

**Definition 4.1**

Let $\hat{\theta}$ be an estimator of $\theta$. We say that $\hat{\theta}$ is an unbiased estimator of $\theta$ if $E(\hat{\theta}) = \theta$.

## Example 4.1

Suppose we are given that the number of accidents happening at railway crossings in Mumbai on any given day follows a Poisson distribution with parameter $\lambda$. If we can estimate this parameter, we will be able to say a lot about the probability with which different numbers of accidents might be expected to happen. Suppose we collect data on the number of accidents that have already occurred at railway crossings for $n$ randomly chosen days. Let the sample be $\{X_1, X_2, \ldots\ldots X_n\}$ where $X_i$ is the number of accidents on the $i$th day. As we know, we can think of different alternative ways of estimating $\lambda$. Suppose we estimate $\lambda$ by:

$$\hat{\lambda} = \sum_{i=1}^{n} X_i / n$$

that is, the sample average. Is this an unbiased estimator of $\lambda$? Each of the $X_i$ follows the Poisson distribution with:

$$E(X_i) = \lambda$$

by hypothesis. $\hat{\lambda}$ will be an unbiased estimator of $\lambda$ if we can show that

$$E(\hat{\lambda}) = E(\sum_{i=1}^{n} X_i / n) = \lambda$$

This is easy to show since:

$$E(\sum_{i=1}^{n} X_i / n) = (1/n) \times E(X_1) + (1/n) \times E(X_2) + \ldots\ldots + (1/n) \times E(X_n)$$
$$= (1/n) \times \lambda + (1/n) \times \lambda + \ldots\ldots\ldots + (1/n) \times \lambda$$
$$= n\lambda / n$$
$$= \lambda$$

Therefore, $\sum_{i=1}^{n} X_i / n$ is an unbiased estimator of $\lambda$.

## Example 4.2

Assume that we have balls labelled from 1 to $N$ ($N \geq 2$). Suppose we want to estimate the number $N$. Let us draw one ball at random with replacement and note the number on it. Let $X$ be this number. $X$ could be one estimate of $N$. Is $X$ an unbiased estimator of $N$? Let us examine this issue carefully. The number on any ball drawn at random is a random variable. Each ball is equally likely to be drawn, and hence, each number has an equal probability of being drawn. Hence:

$$P(X = x) = 1 / N$$

It follows that:

$$E(X) = \sum_{i=1}^{N} P(X_i = k) \times k = \sum_{k=1}^{N} k \times (1 / N)$$

$$= 1 / N + 2 / N + 3 / N + ... + (N - 1) / N + N / N$$
$$= 1 / N + 2 / N + 3 / N + ... + [1-(1 / N)] + 1$$
$$= 2 + 2 / N + 3 / N + ... + (N - 2) / N$$
$$= 2 + 2 / N + 3 / N + ... + [1 - (2 / N)]$$
$$= 3 + 3 / N + 4 / N + ... + (N - 3) / N$$
$$= 4 + 4 / N + ... + (N - 4) / N$$

Continuing in this fashion, we will come to the middle number of the list of numbers from 1 ... $N$:

$$= N / 2 + [N - (N / 2)] / N$$
$$= (N + 1) / 2$$

Hence, $E(X)$ is not an unbiased estimator of $N$, but it estimates the mid-point of all the possible numbers that the ball can take. This is not surprising. Since each number is equally likely to be drawn, it has a discrete uniform distribution between 1 to $N$. The mean of this distribution is $(N+1)/2$. We can see that $X$ is not an unbiased estimator of $N$, as $E(X) \neq N$. But all is not lost. If we use $2X-1$ as an estimator of $N$, instead of $X$ itself, we will get an unbiased estimator of $N$ because:

$$E(2X - 1) = 2E(X) - 1$$
$$= [2 \times (N + 1) / 2] - 1$$
$$= N$$

Hence, even if $X$ is not an unbiased estimator of $N$, $2X - 1$ is.

## Example 4.3

Suppose we have a random sample of size $N$, $X_1, X_2, \ldots\ldots X_N$, where each observation comes from a population with mean equal to $\mu$ and variance equal to $\sigma^2$. Imagine that we want to estimate $\mu$. We might want to estimate $\mu$ by averaging over all the $X_i's$. But in doing so, we forget to take the last sample observation even while we continue to divide the sum by $N$. That is, instead of having:

$$Xbar = \sum_{i=1}^{N} X_i / N$$

we have:

$$Xbar' = \sum_{i=1}^{N-1} X_i / N$$

What is the impact of this lapse on $Xbar'$? Let us find the expected value of $Xbar'$:

$$E(Xbar') = E(\sum_{i=1}^{N-1} X_i / N) = ((N-1) \times \mu) / N \neq \mu$$

Hence, $Xbar'$ is not an unbiased estimator of $\mu$. Yet, you may argue that this is a relevant point only if $N$ is small. As $N \to \infty$, $(N-1)/N \to 1$ which in turn implies that $Xbar'$ will be a close approximation to $\mu$ if $N$ is rather large. In that sense, the lack of unbiasedness might not be such a serious concern if the sample size tends to infinity. Yet, it might be a cause for concern if the sample is small.

## Example 4.4

Unbiased Estimator of the Population Variance:

Suppose $X_1, \ldots\ldots X_n$ is a random sample from a random variable $X$ with $E(X) = \mu$ and variance $\sigma^2$. Let:

$$S^2 = \sum_{i=1}^{n} (X_i - \overline{X})^2 / (n-1)$$

be the sample variance. Is this an unbiased estimator of the population variance? Let us find out $E(S^2)$. We start by writing:

$$\sum_{i=1}^{n}(X_i - \bar{X})^2 = \sum_{i=1}^{n}(X_i - \mu + \mu - \bar{X})^2$$

(adding and subtracting $\mu$ does not make a difference):

$$= \sum_{i=1}^{n}[(X_i - \mu)^2 + 2 \times (\mu - \bar{X}) \times (X_i - \mu) + (\mu - \bar{X})^2]$$

(using the expansion for $(a+b)^2$ with $a = (X - \mu)$ and $b = (\mu - \bar{X})$)

$$= \sum_{i=1}^{n}(X_i - \mu)^2 + 2 \times (\mu - \bar{X}) \times \sum_{i=1}^{n}(X_i - \mu) + n \times (\mu - \bar{X})^2$$

(since $(\mu - \bar{X})$ is a constant, it can be taken out of the bracket):

$$= \sum_{i=1}^{n}(X_i - \mu)^2 + 2 \times (\mu - \bar{X}) \times (\sum_{i=1}^{n}X_i - n\mu) + n \times (\mu - \bar{X})^2$$

$$= \sum_{i=1}^{n}(X_i - \mu)^2 - n \times (\bar{X} - \mu)^2$$

Therefore:

$$E((1/(n-1)) \times \sum_{i=1}^{n}(X_i - \bar{X})^2)$$

$$= (1/(n-1)) \times \left( E(\sum_{i=1}^{n}(X_i - \mu)^2) - n \times E(\bar{X} - \mu)^2 \right)$$

$$= (1/(n-1)) \times [n \times \sigma^2 - n \times \sigma^2/n]$$

$$= \sigma^2$$

On the other hand, if we estimate the population variance by:

$$S'^2 = \sum_{i=1}^{n}(X_i - \bar{X})^2 / n$$

you should be able to show, using the proof above that:

$$E(S'^2) = (n-1)/n \times \sigma^2 \neq \sigma^2$$

Consequently, the latter estimator would be a biased estimator of the population variance.

## 4.2.2 Efficiency

Suppose we succeed in finding an unbiased estimator $\hat{\lambda}$ for a parameter $\lambda$. This means that if we average over various values of $\hat{\lambda}$ emanating from various different samples, the average of these values will equal $\lambda$. However, we will not generally have the luxury of having many samples, We have to do with just one sample and hence just one value of $\hat{\lambda}$. In that case, we would be concerned with the following question: How far away would a randomly chosen value of $\hat{\lambda}$ lie from the true $\lambda$? We have seen in Chapter 1 that this is a question about the variance of $\hat{\lambda}$. Since $\hat{\lambda}$ is an unbiased estimator of $\lambda$, the variance of $\hat{\lambda}$ gives us the average distance at which values of $\hat{\lambda}$ will lie from $\lambda$. Clearly, the lower this value, the better it is. In general, suppose $\hat{\lambda}_1$, $\hat{\lambda}_2$, ........ $\hat{\lambda}_n$ are all possible and different unbiased estimators of $\lambda$, and suppose the variance of $\hat{\lambda}_1$ is lower than the variance of all the other estimators in this list. $\hat{\lambda}_1$ is then said to be an efficient estimator of $\lambda$. In other words, an efficient estimator is an unbiased estimator such that no other unbiased estimator has a variance lower than this estimator. More formally, we will define an efficient estimator as follows:

### Definition 4.2

Let $\hat{\theta}$ be an unbiased estimator of $\theta$. We say that $\hat{\theta}$ is an efficient estimator of $\theta$ if for all estimators $\theta*$ such that $E(\theta*) = \theta$, variance$(\hat{\theta})$ $\leq$ variance$(\theta*)$.

### Example 4.5

Suppose we have a random sample of size $n$, coming from a population with mean $\mu$, $(X_1, X_2, ...... X_n)$ from a population with variance equal to $\mu_x^2$ and suppose we form two estimators of $\mu$:

$$Xbar = \frac{\sum_{i=1}^{n} X_i}{n}$$

and another estimator:

$$Xbar' = \sum_{i=1}^{n} \alpha_i X_i$$

with:

$$\sum_{i=1}^{n} \alpha_i = 1$$

You can see that both the estimators are unbiased. We are already familiar with the first one. The variance of $Xbar$ is $\dfrac{\sigma_x^2}{n}$. As far as the second one is concerned, we have

$$E\left( \sum_{i=1}^{n} \alpha_i X_i \right) = E\left( \sum_{i=1}^{n} \alpha_i E(X_i) \right) = \sum_{i=1}^{n} \alpha_i \mu = \mu \sum_{i=1}^{n} \alpha_i = \mu$$

Let us compute the variance of $Xbar'$.

$$\text{Variance}\left( \sum_{i=1}^{n} \alpha_i X_i \right) = \alpha_1^2 \text{Variance}(X_1) + \dots + \alpha_n^2 \text{Variance}(X_n)$$

$$= \sigma_x^2 \left( \sum_{i=1}^{n} \alpha_i^2 \right)$$

Unless $\left( \sum_{i=1}^{n} \alpha_i^2 \right) < \dfrac{1}{n}$, the variance of $Xbar'$ will be greater than the variance of $Xbar$.

## 4.2.3 Consistency

Many estimators are biased in small samples, but the bias tends to become smaller as the sample size increases. Such estimators would not be very useful if the sample is rather small, but can still be used with reasonable confidence as the sample size increases. To return to the example that we have taken earlier, suppose we have $X_1, X_2, \dots\dots X_n$, a random sample of size $n$ from a population having mean $\mu$ and variance $\sigma^2$. Suppose we use $Xbar'$ as an estimator of $\mu$, where $Xbar' = \sum_{i=1}^{n-1} X_i / n$, that is, we sum the first $n - 1$ values of $X$ and divide by $n$, the total sample size. Let us say we forgot to add the last value, but continued to divide by $n$, the size of the full sample. What is the implication of our omission?

First, $Xbar'$ is no longer an unbiased estimator for $\mu$. This is easy to see:

$$E(Xbar') =$$

$$E(\sum_{i=1}^{n-1} X_i / n) = (1/n) \times E(X_1) + (1/n) \times E(X_2) + \ldots + (1/n) \times E(X_{n-1})$$

$$= (1/n) \times \mu + (1/n) \times \mu + \ldots + (1/n) \times \mu$$

$$= ((n-1)/n) \times \mu$$

$$\neq \mu$$

However, the size of the bias, $(n - 1) / n = 1 - (1 / n)$ decreases with sample size. In fact, you can see that as $n \to \infty$, $(n-1)/n \to 1$. In other words, if we let $E(Xbar') = ((n - 1) / n) \times \mu$, we have $E(Xbar') \to \mu$ as $n \to \infty$. This means that though $Xbar'$ might be far from $\mu$ in small samples, it will get closer and closer to $\mu$ as the sample size increases. We can drive the probability that $Xbar'$ differs from $\mu$ by any finite distance as close to zero as we want by choosing a sufficiently large value for $n$. This is called the property of consistency. This is a large sample property as against unbiasedness and efficiency which are supposed to hold in small samples and hence are more restrictive.

As another example of consistency consider the following estimator of variance:

$$S^2 = \frac{\sum_{i=1}^{n} (X_i - Xbar)^2}{n}$$

where $Xbar$ is the sample mean. Here, the squared deviations from the mean are divided by $n$ and not $n - 1$. We have shown above that the estimator is a biased estimator of the population variance $\sigma^2$ since:

$$E(S^2) = ((n-1) / n) \times \sigma^2$$

But, you can see that as $n$ becomes larger, $E(S^2)$ gets closer to $\sigma^2$. Hence, as the sample size becomes larger, $S^2$ becomes an increasingly acceptable estimator of $\sigma^2$.

More formally, we have the following definition of consistency:

**Definition 4.3**

Let $\hat{\theta}$ be an estimator (based on a sample $X_1, \ldots\ldots X_n$) of a parameter $\theta$. We say that $\hat{\theta}$ is an unbiased estimator of $\lim\limits_{n \to \infty} \text{Prb}\left( \left| \hat{\theta} - \theta \right| > \varepsilon \right)$ for all $\varepsilon > 0$.

Let us try to understand this definition. $\left| \hat{\theta} - \theta \right|$ measures the absolute difference between the value of $\hat{\theta}$ and $\theta$. The definition requires that the probability that this difference is greater than any given positive number tends to zero as the sample size increases. That is, as the sample size increases, the probability that $\hat{\theta}$ equals $\theta$ should get closer to 1.[5] How do you check whether this condition is indeed satisfied by any given estimator? It is here that the following theorem, (which we state without proof) is helpful:[6]

**Theorem 4.1**

If $\hat{\theta}$ is an estimator of $\theta$, based on a sample of size $n$, and if $\lim\limits_{n \to \infty} E(\hat{\theta}) = \theta$ and if $\lim\limits_{n \to \infty} \text{variance}(\hat{\theta}) = 0$, then $\hat{\theta}$ is a consistent estimator of $\theta$.

Thus, if you can show that the estimator tends towards the true population parameter and its variance tends to zero as the sample size increases, you have a way of checking whether a given estimator is consistent.

For example, suppose we have a sample $(X_1, X_2, \ldots\ldots X_n)$ from a Poisson population with mean and variance equal to $\lambda$. The problem is to estimate $\lambda$. Suppose we use the sample mean:

$$\text{Xbar} = \frac{\sum_{i=1}^{n} X_i}{n}$$

as an estimator for $\lambda$. Then, it is easy to check whether *Xbar* is an unbiased estimator of $\lambda$:

$$E(Xbar) = E(\sum_{i=1}^{n} X_i / n) = (1/n)E(X_1) + \ldots\ldots(1/n) \times E(X_n)$$

$$= (1/n) \times \lambda + (1/n) \times \lambda + \ldots(1/n) \times \lambda$$

$$= n\lambda / n$$

$$= \lambda$$

Is *Xbar* a consistent estimator of $\lambda$? It will be a consistent estimator if the conditions (*a*) and (*b*) of Theorem 4.1 are satisfied. Condition (*a*) is trivially satisfied since $E(Xbar)$ equals $\lambda$ even for small *n*, instead of just tending to it as *n* becomes bigger. The second condition, that the variance of *Xbar* should tend to zero as *n* becomes bigger needs to be checked out. We will do that below:

$$\text{Variance}(Xbar) = \text{Variance}\left(\frac{\sum_{i=1}^{n} X_i}{n}\right)$$

$$= \frac{1}{n^2} \times \text{Variance}(X_1) + \ldots\ldots + \frac{1}{n^2} \times \text{Variance}(X_n)$$

$$= \frac{1}{n^2} \times \lambda + \ldots\ldots\ldots\ldots + \frac{1}{n^2} \times \lambda$$

$$= \frac{\lambda n}{n^2}$$

It can be seen from the above that as *n* becomes bigger and bigger, Variance(*Xbar*) becomes smaller and smaller. Thus, condition (*b*) of Theorem 4.1 is satisfied and *Xbar* is a consistent estimator of $\lambda$.

## Assertion 4.1

For any random variable with a finite mean $\mu$ and finite variance $\sigma^2$, the sample mean based on $n$ randomly chosen observations, is an unbiased and consistent estimator of $\mu$.

## Exercise 4.2

Prove Assertion 4.1.

Finally, we consider best linear unbiased estimators or the so called BLUE estimators.

## Definition 4.4

Suppose $(X_1, X_2, \ldots\ldots X_n)$ is a random sample and $\theta$ an unknown parameter. We say that $\hat{\theta}$ is a best linear unbiased estimator (BLUE) of $\theta$ when:

1. $E(\hat{\theta}) = \theta$.
2. $\hat{\theta}$ is an efficient estimator, that is, no other unbiased estimator of $\theta$ has variance less than $\hat{\theta}$.
3. $\hat{\theta} = \sum_{i=1}^{n} a_i \times X_i$, that is $\hat{\theta}$ can be written as a sum where each value of $X$ is multiplied by a constant number and the resultant numbers are summed to yield $\hat{\theta}$. For example, the sample mean is a linear estimator of the population mean, since $Xbar = \dfrac{1}{n} \times X_1 + \ldots\ldots + \dfrac{1}{n} \times X_n$.

In fact, you already know that the sample mean also satisfies properties ($a$) and ($b$). Hence, the sample mean is a 'Best Linear Unbiased Estimator or BLUE' of the population mean. The important thing about linearity is that it sometimes helps us to find the probability distribution of $\hat{\theta}$. Remember that $\hat{\theta}$ is also a random variable because every time we take a different sample, we will get a different value of $\hat{\theta}$. Hence, we will need to know the probability distribution of $\hat{\theta}$ in order to make probabilistic statements about it or take tests of hypothesis. Suppose each of the $X_i$ are normally distributed; then $\hat{\theta}$ will also be normally distributed since a weighted sum of $n$ normally distributed variables is also normally distributed. Thus, the linearity property is a useful property in that it enables us to derive the probability distribution of our estimator. We will encounter best linear unbiased estimators quite often in what follows.

## 4.3 THE ORDINARY LEAST SQUARES (OLS) ESTIMATOR

The OLS estimator is one of the most popular estimators used in applied work. To understand this estimator, it will be helpful to start by thinking of the joint distribution of two random variables $(X, Y)$ that we encountered in Chapter 2. In that chapter, we saw how conditional expectation of $X$ given $Y$, $E(X/Y)$ can be plotted as a function of various values of $Y$. In this chapter, we will put more structure on this relationship. We will be concerned with modelling $E(Y/X)$ as a function of $X$. As an example, consider the case of rolling two dies. Let $Y$ be the random variable which describes the outcome on the uppermost face of the first die, while $X$ is the random variable that describes the outcome on the uppermost face of the second die. So, if we were to enumerate the sample space associated with this experiment, we would have:

$$\Omega = \{(1, 1), (1, 2), (1, 3), (1, 4), (1, 4), (1, 6), (2, 1), (2, 2), (2, 3),$$
$$(2, 4), (2, 5), (2, 6), (3, 1), (3, 2), (3, 3), (3, 4), (3, 5), (3, 6),$$
$$(4, 1), (4, 2), (4, 3), (4, 4), (4, 5), (4, 6), (5, 1), (5, 2), (5, 3),$$
$$(5, 4), (5, 5), (5, 6), (6, 1), (6, 2), (6, 3), (6, 4), (6, 5), (6, 6)\}$$

where $(1, 3)$ for example, corresponds to $Y$ taking the value 1 and $X$ taking the value 3. The joint distribution of $X$ and $Y$ can now be written as done in Table 4.1.

**Table 4.1**
**The joint and marginal distributions of the random variables $X$ and $Y$**

| $X \downarrow Y \rightarrow$ | 1 | 2 | 3 | 4 | 5 | 6 | $f(X)$ |
|---|---|---|---|---|---|---|---|
| 1 | 1 / 36 | 1 / 36 | 1 / 36 | 1 / 36 | 1 / 36 | 1 / 36 | 1 / 6 |
| 2 | 1 / 36 | 1 / 36 | 1 / 36 | 1 / 36 | 1 / 36 | 1 / 36 | 1 / 6 |
| 3 | 1 / 36 | 1 / 36 | 1 / 36 | 1 / 36 | 1 / 36 | 1 / 36 | 1 / 6 |
| 4 | 1 / 36 | 1 / 36 | 1 / 36 | 1 / 36 | 1 / 36 | 1 / 36 | 1 / 6 |
| 5 | 1 / 36 | 1 / 36 | 1 / 36 | 1 / 36 | 1 / 36 | 1 / 36 | 1 / 6 |
| 6 | 1 / 36 | 1 / 36 | 1 / 36 | 1 / 36 | 1 / 36 | 1 / 36 | 1 / 6 |
| $f(Y)$ | 1 / 6 | 1 / 6 | 1 / 6 | 1 / 6 | 1 / 6 | 1 / 6 | |

where the values of $Y$ are represented along the columns, the values of $X$ are represented along the rows, entries inside the table are probabilities of observing $(Y = y_i, X = x_i)$ and the last column and last row are the marginal distributions of $X$ and $Y$ respectively. Since $X$ and $Y$ are independent random variables,

$$E(Y / X = 1) = E(Y / X = 2) = E(Y / X = 3) = E(Y / X = 4) =$$
$$E(Y / X = 5) = E(Y / X = 6) = 3.5$$

(You are encouraged to do the computations yourself and check out the result). The graph in Figure 4.1 shows $E(Y/X)$ as a function of $X$.

**Figure 4.1**
**E(Y/X) as a function of X**

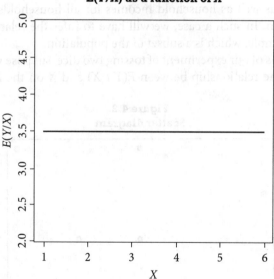

We have been able to draw the horizontal line that is parallel to the X-axis at $E(Y / X) = 3.5$, since we knew the specific experiment and could enumerate the set of all possible outcomes. Since we know all possible realizations of the pair of random variables, the relationship depicted in the graph is a population relationship. In the real world, we cannot generally enumerate all the possible values that a pair of jointly distributed random variables will attain.

For example, if we are looking at the relationship between family incomes ($X$) and composite nutritional status of the families ($Y$), then we might be interested in knowing $E(Y / X)$ as a function of $X$, that is, the relationship between average composite nutritional status of the family and family incomes. For example, does the average composite nutritional status of the household increase with family income? However, in this case, we will not be able to enumerate all the values taken by composite nutritional status of the household and household incomes for all the households in the population. The model that generates various values of $X$ and $Y$ will not always be as obvious as it was in the case of rolling of two dies. Also, if the population is even moderately large, it might well be impossible to actually measure composite household nutritional status as well as household incomes for all households in the population. In such a case, we will have to infer the relationship from a sample, which is a subset of the population.

In terms of our experiment of tossing two dice, suppose we have to infer the relationship between $E(Y / X)$ and $X$ on the basis of

**Figure 4.2**
**Scatter diagram**

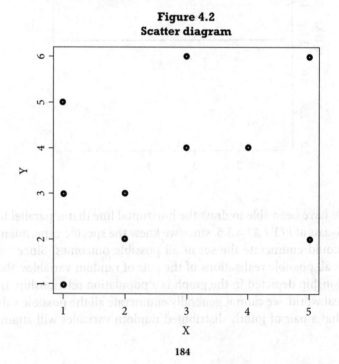

outcomes of 10 actual tosses rather than a full knowledge of the relevant experiment that generated the data. Suppose the observed outcome is like this {(1, 1), (2, 3), (3, 6), (5, 2), (4, 4), (1, 5), (3, 4), (1, 3), (2, 2), (5, 6)}. Now, we will have to infer $E(Y / X)$ from this data. Let us first write down the joint probability distribution of the observed sample. We will first just plot the data in the $X$–$Y$ plane. Such a diagram is known as a scatter diagram (see Figure 4.2).

From this scatter diagram in Figure 4.2, it can be seen that the values of $Y$ increase with the values of $X$, or in other words, $E(Y / X)$ increases with $X$. We will now make an important assumption.

## Assumption 4.1

We will assume that $E(Y / X)$ is a 'linear function' of $X$, that is, $E(Y / X_i) = a + bX_i$. $Y$ is referred to as the dependent variable, while $X$ will be referred to as the independent variable. We will assume that this relationship is 'linear in parameters', which not only allows relationships like:

$$E(Y / X_i) = a + bX_i$$

but also:

$$E(Y / X_i) = a + bX_i^2$$

or:

$$E(Y / X_i) = a + b \log(X_i)$$

but not relationships that involve powers or logs of the parameters $a$ and $b$. The parameters $a$ and $b$ must enter the regression equation in a linear form, irrespective of the form of the explanatory variable, which can be transformed as logs, squares, cubes, or any higher power, or square root, or reciprocal, as necessary. For a specific value of $E(Y / X_i)$, the individual values of $Y$ are clustered around $E(Y / X_i)$. For example, in our example, $E(Y/X = 1)$ is 3.5. However, $Y$ takes values 1, 2, 3, 4, 5 and 6, when $X = 1$. Let the gap between $Y_i$ and $E(Y/X = 1) = Y_i - E(Y / X = 1) = Y_i - 3.5 = e_1$. For our example, $e_1$ takes the following values:

$$e_{11} = 6 - 3.5 = 2.5$$

$$e_{21} = 5 - 3.5 = 1.5$$
$$e_{31} = 4 - 3.5 = 0.5$$
$$e_{41} = 3 - 3.5 = -0.5$$
$$e_{51} = 2 - 3.5 = -1.5$$

and:

$$e_{61} = 1 - 3.5 = -2.5$$

In general, we can think of the variable $e_j$ as the random variable $Y_i - E(Y \mid X = x_j)$.
We then have:

$$e_1 = Y_1 - E(Y \mid X = x_1), e_2 = Y_2 - E(Y \mid X = x_2), ..., e_1 = Y_i - E(Y \mid X = x_i).$$

More generally, we have the following 'population regression function':

$$Y_i = a + bX_i + e_i$$

Here, $e_i$ is a random variable with a well defined probability distribution for every $i$, $I = 1, 2, ..., n$. In order to put more structure in the population regression function, we need to specify the structure of the probability distribution of $e_i$. For the OLS method, this is achieved by making the following assumptions (known as the classical assumptions).

### 4.3.1 Classical assumptions about $e_i$

**E1**

$$E(e_i \mid X_i) = 0$$
$$i = 1, 2 \, .... \, n$$

The conditional expectation of $e_i$, conditional on $X_i$ is zero.

**E2**

Variance$(e_i) = \sigma^2$, $i = 1, 2....n$ is constant. Each of the $n$ distinct random variables $e_i$ are assumed to have the same variance $\sigma^2$.

This assumption has a specific name: 'the assumption of ho-moskedasticity'. This implies that the spread of the values of $e$ around our line does not increase or decrease as we change the values of $X$.

**E3**

We will also assume that all values of $e$ are uncorrelated with their previous or future values, which then implies that $\text{Cov}(e_i, e_j)=0$ whenever $e_i$ and $e_j$ are different random variables. In particular, suppose our data have been collected in time, so that the different pairs $(X, Y)$ are observed at different points in time. In that case, the random variables $e_i$ will be defined over time so that it will be more appropriate to write $e_t$, for $t = 1, 2, 3, \ldots T$ if we have in all $T$ observations on the pairs $(X, Y)$. In that case, the assumption of $\text{Cov}(e_i, e_j) = 0$ can be stated as $\text{Cov}(e_t, e_{t-j}) = 0$, for all $j \neq 0$.

This is called the 'assumption of no autocorrelation'.

**E4**

We will assume that each of the $e_i$ are normally distributed.

**E5**

We will assume that $e_i$ and $X_i$ are independent for every $i$, implying:

$$E(e_i X_i) = E(e_i)E(X_i) = 0$$

using the property that if $X$ and $Y$ are independent random variables, $E(XY)=E(X)E(Y)$ and assumption E1.

**E6**

We will assume that not all values of $X_i$ are the same.

In the specific example above, since we know the population model, we also know that $a = 3.5$ and $b = 0$. However, as a general rule, we do not know the population model in advance. We have to 'infer' the values of $a$ and $b$ from the scatter diagram of the sample available to us. Obviously, the values of $a$ and $b$ that we will find the most appropriate to define the relationship between $Y$ and $X$ in a given sample will depend upon that specific sample. Given our sample, in Figure 4.2, since values of $Y$ seem to increase with the values of $X$, we might claim that $b > 0$. If we make the tosses again, a fresh sample will be obtained, which will indicate a different scatter and hence a different set of values of $a$ and $b$. Thus, the estimates of $a$ and $b$ that we obtain from a specific sample, which we will indicate by '$a\wedge$ and $b\wedge$, are random variables'. The problem is to approximate the observed scatter with an appropriate straight line through a judicious choice of $a\wedge$ and $b\wedge$. This straight line that we fit to the sample is called the 'sample regression function', as against the actual line shown in Figure 4.1, which we have called the population regression function. The population regression function is unobservable to us, so we must infer its parameters, $a$ and $b$, from the sample, and approximate the population regression function by the sample regression function. This will require us to work with a sample. This motivates the next assumption:

## M1

We have a random sample of $n$ observations $(X_i, Y_i)$ for $i = 1 \ldots n$ from the model describing the population regression function.

Suppose we decide to approximate the scatter in Figure 4.2 by a straight line with intercept, $a$, equal to one and slope, $b$, equal to 0.8, as done in Figure 4.3.

Note that we are attempting to represent a scatter by a straight line. Clearly, it is impossible that every point in the scatter will lie precisely on our line. Points will in general lie above or below our line. For example, consider the pair $X = 3$, $Y = 4$ which is one of our observed outcomes. However, when we substitute the value of $X$ in our line, we get:

$$Y = 1 + 0.8 \times 3 = 3.4$$

which is lower than 4, the observed value of $Y$. This difference, between the value of $Y$ expected by our line (3.4) and the actual value of $Y$ (4), is represented in Figure 4.3 by the segment $hi$. The segment $gh$ represents the value of $Y$ that our line would lead us to expect given that $X = 3$, while the length of $hi$ represents the difference of the actual value, 4, from our line, which is 3.4. You will

**Figure 4.3**
**Approximating the scatter with a straight line**

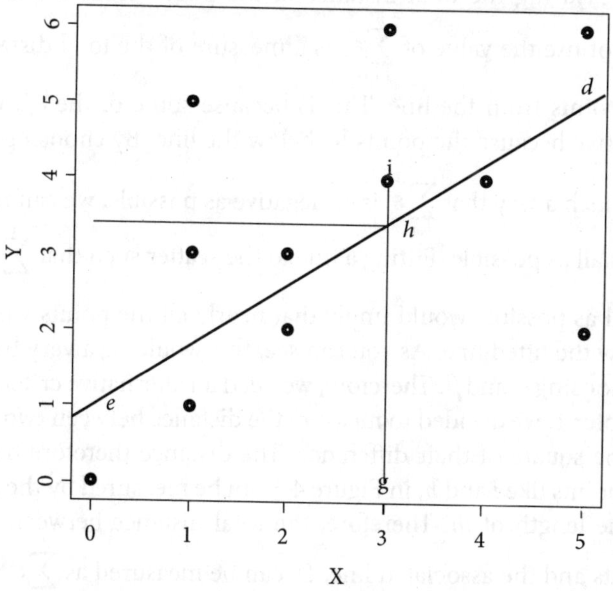

be able to do this with each observed $X - Y$ pair, given our line. In general, for $X = X_i$, we can then write:

$$Y_i = \alpha + \beta X_i + \varepsilon_i$$

where $\alpha + \beta X_i$ corresponds to the distance from the X-axis to the straight line (in the case of $X = 3$, and $Y = 4$, this distance is the length of the segment $gh$) and $\varepsilon_i$ corresponds to the length of the segment $hi$. For different $(X, Y)$ pairs, there will be different values of $\varepsilon_i$.

We are now sufficiently well-armed to develop a general method for approximating a scatter like Figure 4.2 by a straight line. For a moment, examine Figure 4.3 again. A reasonable criterion for approximating the scatter with a straight line would be that the straight line should pass through the scatter in such a manner that the points lie as close to the line as possible. That is, the line should be fitted in such a way that the total distance of all the points from the lines should be as small as possible. We need to find out a way of measuring the total distance of the points from the line. We cannot use the value of $\sum_{i=1}^{n} \varepsilon_i$ as a measure of the total distance of the points from the line. This is because some of the $\varepsilon_i$'s will be negative because the points lie below the line. By choosing $\alpha$ and $\beta$ in such a way that $\sum_{i=1}^{n} \varepsilon_i$ is as negative as possible, we can make it as small as possible. Fitting a line to the scatter such that $\sum_{i=1}^{n} \varepsilon_i$ is as small as possible would imply that nearly all the points would be below the fitted line. As you can see, this would be a very bad way of choosing $\alpha$ and $\beta$. Therefore, we need an alternative criterion. In Chapter 1, we decided to measure the distance between two points by the square of their difference. The distance therefore between the points like $i$ and $h$, in Figure 4.3 can be measured by the square of the length of $ih$. Therefore, the total distance between all the points and the associated line, $D$, can be measured as $\sum_{i=1}^{n} \varepsilon_i^2$. Thus, we must fit our line in such a way that $\sum_{i=1}^{n} \varepsilon_i^2$ is as small as possible. This criterion leads to our method of fitting the line (which is the same thing as finding $a$ and $b$, its intercept and slope) being called the method of 'Ordinary Least Squares (OLS)'.[7]

Since:

$$Y_i = \alpha + \beta X_i + \varepsilon_i$$

we have:

$$\varepsilon_i = Y_i - \alpha - \beta X_i$$

Hence:

$$D = \sum_{i=1}^{n} \varepsilon_i^2 = \sum_{i=1}^{n} (Y_i - \alpha - \beta X_i)^2$$

This way of writing expresses the total distance from the line as a function of $a$ and $b$. Minimising this involves taking the partial derivatives of $D$ with respect to $\alpha$ and $\beta$, setting them to zero and solving for values of $\alpha$ and $\beta$.

$$\partial D / \partial \alpha = \partial \sum_{i=1}^{n} e_i^2 / \partial \alpha = 0$$

$$= \partial \sum_{i=1}^{n} (Y_i - \alpha - \beta X_i)^2 / \partial \alpha = 0$$

$$= -2 \times \sum_{i=1}^{n} (Y_i - \alpha - \beta X_i) = 0$$

Using the chain rule of differentiation, –2 cannot be equal to zero, hence:

$$\sum_{i=1}^{n} (Y_i - \alpha - \beta X_i) = 0$$

Opening the brackets results in the following equation:

$$\sum_{i=1}^{n} (Y_i - \alpha - \beta X_i) = \sum_{i=1}^{n} Y_i - \sum_{i=1}^{n} \alpha - \beta \sum_{i=1}^{n} X_i = 0$$

$$= \sum_{i=1}^{n} Y_i - n\alpha - \beta \sum_{i=1}^{n} X_i$$

$$\therefore n\alpha = \sum_{i=1}^{n} Y_i - \beta \sum_{i=1}^{n} X_i$$

As result, you would get:

$$\alpha = \sum_{i=1}^{n} Y_i / n - \beta \sum_{i=1}^{n} X_i / n$$

or:

$$\alpha = \overline{Y} - \beta \overline{X} \qquad \text{Equation 4.1}$$

At this juncture we will bring in an important point. The formula for obtaining *a* tells us how to obtain an estimate of *a*, from a particular sample. The real *a* is perhaps not observable:

$$\alpha = \overline{Y} - \beta \overline{X}$$

is a general formula for computing an estimate of *a* from any given sample. To emphasize this, we will denote $\overline{Y} - \beta \overline{X}$ by $a^{\wedge}$, the estimator of *a*.

However, Equation 4.1 is not very helpful in finding the value of $a^\wedge$, because the expression for $a^\wedge$ involves the value of $\beta$, which we still do not know. Therefore, we must now obtain a similar expression for $\beta$. A similar expression for $\beta$ can be obtained by differentiating $D$ with respect to $\beta$:

$$\partial D / \partial \beta = \partial \sum_{i=1}^{n} (Y_i - \alpha - \beta X_i)^2 / \partial \beta = 0$$

$$= -2X_i \sum_{i=1}^{n} (Y_i - \alpha - \beta X_i) = 0$$

This implies that:

$$X_i \sum_{i=1}^{n} (Y_i - \alpha - \beta X_i) = 0$$

and, therefore:

$$\sum_{i=1}^{n} X_i Y_i = \alpha \sum_{i=1}^{n} X_i + \beta \sum_{i=1}^{n} X_i^2 \qquad \text{Equation 4.2}$$

Equations 4.1 and 4.2 give us two equations in two unknowns, $\alpha$ and $\beta$ that we are trying to estimate. These equations are referred to as 'normal equations'. Solving the two equations simultaneously, (by substituting the formula for $a^\wedge$ into Equation 4.2) we have:

$$\sum_{i=1}^{n} X_i Y_i = (\sum_{i=1}^{n} Y_i / n - \beta \sum_{i=1}^{n} X_i / n) \sum_{i=1}^{n} X_i + \beta \sum_{i=1}^{n} X_i^2$$

$$\sum_{i=1}^{n} X_i Y_i = \sum_{i=1}^{n} X_i \sum_{i=1}^{n} Y_i / n - \beta (\sum_{i=1}^{n} X_i)^2 / n + \beta \sum_{i=1}^{n} X_i^2$$

$$\sum_{i=1}^{n} X_i Y_i - \sum_{i=1}^{n} X_i \sum_{i=1}^{n} Y_i / n = \beta ((\sum_{i=1}^{n} X_i)^2 - (\sum_{i=1}^{n} X_i)^2 / n)$$

$$n \sum_{i=1}^{n} X_i Y_i - \sum_{i=1}^{n} X_i \sum_{i=1}^{n} Y_i = \beta (n \sum_{i=1}^{n} X_i^2 - (\sum_{i=1}^{n} X_i)^2)$$

$$b^\wedge = (n \sum_{i=1}^{n} X_i Y_i - \sum_{i=1}^{n} X_i \sum_{i=1}^{n} Y_i) / (n \sum_{i=1}^{n} X_i^2 - (\sum_{i=1}^{n} X_i)^2)$$

$$\text{Equation 4.3}$$

where the $\wedge$ symbol after $b$ also indicates that it is an estimator for the generally unobservable $b$. The expression for $b\wedge$ can be written more simply and in a more transparent manner. Let us denote:

$$x_i = (X_i - \bar{X})$$

that is, deviation of the $i$th observation of $X$ from its mean. Similarly, we can write:

$$y_i = (Y_i - \bar{Y})$$

Note that:

$$\sum_{i=1}^{n} x_i^2 = \sum_{i=1}^{n}(X_i - \bar{X})^2 = \sum_{i=1}^{n} X_i^2 - 2\sum_{i=1}^{n} X_i \bar{X} + \sum_{i=1}^{n} \bar{X}^2$$

$$= \sum_{i=1}^{n} X_i^2 - 2\bar{X}\sum_{i=1}^{n} X_i + \sum_{i=1}^{n} \bar{X}^2$$

$$\because \sum_{i=1}^{n} X_i = n\bar{X}, \sum_{i=1}^{n} \bar{X}^2 = n\bar{X}^2$$

$$\therefore \sum_{i=1}^{n} x_i^2 = \sum_{i=1}^{n} X_i^2 - 2n\bar{X}^2 + n\bar{X}^2$$

$$= \sum_{i=1}^{n} X_i^2 - n\bar{X}^2$$

If we divide the denominator of Equation 4.3 by $n$, we will get:

$$\sum_{i=1}^{n} X_i^2 - \sum_{i=1}^{n} X_i \sum_{i=1}^{n} X_i / n$$

$$= \sum_{i=1}^{n} X_i^2 - \bar{X}\sum_{i=1}^{n} X_i$$

$$= \sum_{i=1}^{n} X_i^2 - n\bar{X}^2$$

But as we have seen, this is nothing but $\sum_{i=1}^{n} x_i^2$.

Similarly, for the expression in the numerator of Equation 4.3:

$$n\sum_{i=1}^{n} X_i Y_i - \sum_{i=1}^{n} X_i \sum_{i=1}^{n} Y_i$$

Dividing by $n$, we have:

$$\sum_{i=1}^{n} X_i Y_i - \bar{X} \sum_{i=1}^{n} Y_i$$

$$= \sum_{i=1}^{n} X_i Y_i - \sum_{i=1}^{n} Y_i \bar{X}$$

$$= \sum_{i=1}^{n} Y_i (X_i - \bar{X})$$

$$= \sum_{i=1}^{n} x_i Y_i - \bar{Y} \sum_{i=1}^{n} x_i$$

The second term in the last equation can be subtracted because its value is zero, as it involves the sum of deviations of $x$ around its mean. The last equation can then be rewritten as $\sum_{i=1}^{n} x_i y_i$. Hence, if we divided the numerator and denominator of Equation 4.3 by $n$, we can rewrite:

$$b^\wedge = \sum_{i=1}^{n} x_i y_i \Big/ \sum_{i=1}^{n} x_i^2 \qquad \text{Equation 4.4}$$

To obtain $a^\wedge$, the expression for $b^\wedge$ can be substituted in Equation 4.1, so we have:

$$a^\wedge = \bar{Y} - \left(\sum_{i=1}^{n} x_i y_i \Big/ \sum_{i=1}^{n} x_i^2\right) \bar{X} \qquad \text{Equation 4.5}$$

Let us examine Equation 4.4 closely. It can be re-written as:

$$b^\wedge = \sum_{i=1}^{n} x_i y_i / n \Big/ \sum_{i=1}^{n} x_i^2 / n \qquad \text{Equation 4.6}$$

Here the numerator as well as the denominator have been divided by $n$, keeping the fraction unchanged. Supposing $n$ to be fairly large, the numerator of the fraction is the estimated sample covariance between $X$ and $Y$ while the denominator is the variance of $X$. $b^\wedge$ measures the change in $Y$ per unit of change in $X$ (the slope of the $Y$ function). Equation 4.5 says that the marginal impact of $X$ on $Y$ (that is, $b$), can be estimated by dividing the covariance between $X$ and $Y$ by the variance of $X$. If the covariance of $X$ and $Y$ is small relative to the variance of $X$ (even if $X$ moves a lot, $Y$ shows little movement), then the estimated value of $b^\wedge$ should be small. On the other hand, if $Y$ is rather sensitive to variations in $X$, then even small variation in $X$ should result in a large covariance of $Y$ with $X$, implying a relatively larger value of $b^\wedge$. Therefore, the sample covariance of $X$ and $Y$ per unit of sample variance of $X$ is a reasonable estimator of the change in $Y$ per unit of change in $X$.

### Example 4.6

The data in Table 4.2 presents the educational development index (EDI, a composite index of primary and upper primary school enrolment rates), and net per capita state domestic product (NSDP) for the year 2006–07 for 17 states.

**Table 4.2**
**The Educational Development Index and Per Capita NSDP of 17 States/Union Territories for the year 2006–07**

| State/UT | Educational Develop- ment Index | Per Capita NSDP (Rs at constant prices) | State/UT | Educational Develop- ment Index | Per Capita NSDP (Rs at constant prices) |
|---|---|---|---|---|---|
| Andhra Pradesh | 0.67 | 22,835 | Mizoram | 0.661 | 20,618 |
| Assam | 0.477 | 15,623 | Orissa | 0.487 | 15,096 |
| Bihar | 0.321 | 7,598 | Puducherry | 0.771 | 38,488 |
| Haryana | 0.612 | 35,779 | Punjab | 0.654 | 30,158 |
| Himachal Pradesh | 0.707 | 28,415 | Rajasthan | 0.582 | 15,420 |
| Jharkhand | 0.381 | 15,904 | Sikkim | 0.662 | 22,001 |
| Kerala | 0.772 | 27,824 | Tamil Nadu | 0.741 | 25,898 |
| Madhya Pradesh | 0.481 | 12,577 | Uttar Pradesh | 0.526 | 11,898 |
| Manipur | 0.598 | 19,625 | | | |

We want to model the relationship between EDI and NSDP. The population regression function is:

$$E(EDI/NSDP) = a + b \times NSDPi$$

This implies the following population regression function:

$$EDI_i = a + bNSDP_i + e_i$$

The idea is to estimate $a$ and $b$ from the sample above. First, let us plot the scatter of EDI versus NSDP for all the 17 states.

**Figure 4.4**
**Scatter diagram of EDI versus NSDP**

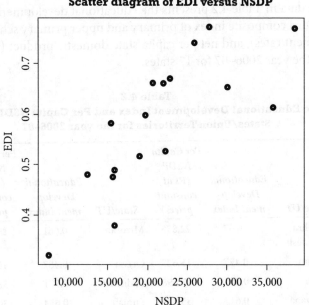

From Figure 4.4 it seems that as the per capita net state domestic product increases, one can see an improvement in the education development index of the state.

We can use the formulae in Equations 4.4 and 4.5 to obtain values of $a\wedge$ and $b\wedge$. Let $Y_i$ and $X_i$ represent the educational development index and the net state domestic per capita income respectively. The average value of $X$, denoted by $Xbar = 21515.12$ and the

## Table 4.3
## The calculation required for the estimation of $\hat{a}$ and $\hat{b}$

| State/UT | EDI (Y) | NSDP (X) | $(X_i - Xbar)$ | $(Y_i - Ybar)$ | $(X_i - Xbar) \times (Y_i - Ybar)$ | $(X_i - Xbar)^2$ |
|---|---|---|---|---|---|---|
| Andhra Pradesh | 0.67 | 22,835 | 1,319. 88 | 0.08 | 99.92 | 1,742,089.43 |
| Assam | 0.477 | 15,623 | −5,892.12 | −0.12 | 691.11 | 34,717,050.37 |
| Bihar | 0.321 | 7,598 | −13,917.12 | −0.27 | 3,803.47 | 193,686,163.60 |
| Haryana | 0.612 | 35,779 | 14,263.88 | 0.02 | 252.55 | 203,458,339.78 |
| Himachal Pradesh | 0.707 | 28,415 | 6,899.88 | 0.11 | 777.66 | 47,608,376.48 |
| Jharkhand | 0.381 | 15,904 | −5,611.12 | −0.21 | 1,196.82 | 31,484,641.25 |
| Kerala | 0.772 | 27,824 | 6,308.88 | 0.18 | 1,121.13 | 39,801,996.54 |
| Madhya Pradesh | 0.481 | 12,577 | −8,938.12 | −0.11 | 1,012.64 | 79,889,947.07 |
| Manipur | 0.598 | 19,625 | −1,890.12 | 0.00 | −7.00 | 3,572,544.72 |
| Mizoram | 0.661 | 20,618 | −897.12 | 0.07 | −59.84 | 804,820.07 |
| Orissa | 0.487 | 15,096 | −6,419.12 | −0.11 | 688.73 | 41,205,071.37 |
| Pondicherry (now Puducherry) | 0.771 | 38,488 | 16,972.88 | 0.18 | 2,999.21 | 288,078,735.37 |
| Punjab | 0.654 | 30,158 | 8,642.88 | 0.06 | 516.03 | 74,699,415.37 |
| Rajasthan | 0.582 | 15,420 | −6,095.12 | −0.01 | 74.93 | 37,150,459.13 |
| Sikkim | 0.662 | 22,001 | 485.88 | 0.07 | 32.9 | 236,081.66 |
| Tamil Nadu | 0.741 | 25,898 | 4,382.88 | 0.15 | 642.99 | 19,209,637.72 |
| Uttar Pradesh | 0.526 | 11,898 | −9,617.12 | −0.07 | 656.79 | 92,488,951.84 |
| Total | | | | 14,500.04 | | 1,189,834,341.76 |

average value of $Y$, denoted by $Ybar = 0.59$ (the figures are rounded off to the closest two decimal places). The relevant calculations are illustrated in Table 4.3

We can estimate

$$b\wedge = \sum_{i=1}^{n}(X_i - Xbar)(Y_i - Ybar) / \sum_{i=1}^{n}(X_i - Xbar)^2$$

$$= 14500.04 / 1189834341.76$$
$$= 0.0000128$$

Similarly,

$$a\wedge = Ybar - b\wedge\, Xbar$$
$$= 0.594 - (0.0000128) \times 215151.12$$
$$= 0.311$$

The R program below will enable us to calculate the value of $b\wedge$ and $a\wedge$ from Equations 4.4 and 4.5.

```
d<-read.table("c:\\book3.xls",header=TRUE,sep="")
attach(d)
DNSDP=(NSDP-mean(NSDP)) ## This line takes the devia-
tion of NSDP from its
## mean, calling the deviations DNSPD
DEDI=(EDI-mean(EDI)) ## This line takes the deviation of
EDI from its mean
## calling the deviations DEDI
bhat=sum(DNSDP*DEDI)/sum(DNSDP*DNSDP) ## This line
computes b^.
bhat ## This line prints b^
ahat=mean(EDI)-bhat*mean(NSDP) ## This line computes
a^
ahat ## This line prints a^.
```

The first line reads the data from the file 'book3.xls' and assigns it to a data frame called $d$ (the student will have to enter the data provided in the text into an excel file called book3.xls). A data frame is a list or array with a certain structure. Variables will have to be extracted from this array. The command *attach(d)* allows us to deal individually with the data series NSDP and EDI. The next line generates the values of NSDP minus the mean of NSDP and the values of EDI minus the mean of EDI. The value of *bhat* and *ahat* are then calculated. If you run the program, it will give you this output:

```
bhat
[1] 1.256873e-05
ahat
[1] 0.3115857
```

The same output can be achieved by typing:

```
d<-read.table("c:\\book3.xls",header=TRUE, sep="")
attach(d)
lm(EDI~NSDP)
```

The *lm(EDI~NSDP)* command estimates a 'linear model' and gives the following output:

```
Coefficients:
(Intercept) NSDP
3.116e-01 1.257e-05
```

The values generated by the two programs are very close to each other.

From these values, we have:

$$EDI = 0.3115857 + 0.00001256873 \times NSDP$$

This equation can be used to fit a line to the scatter. The graph in Figure 4.5 shows this line along with the scatter.

The dark line, starting at 0.3115857 on the Y-axis and moving upwards to the right with a slope of 0.00001256873 is our sample regression function. This means that if the NSDP goes up by Rs 1,000, the value of the EDI increases by 0.00001256873 units on an average. Again, remember that the values of $a^\wedge$ and $b^\wedge$ are sample specific. A different sample (say data for a different year) will in general lead to a different set of parameter estimates. The value 0.00001256873 is an estimate of $b$, not $b$ itself. How is it related to $b$? That is what we examine in the next section.

**Figure 4.5**
**EDI versus NSDP (scatter and linear approximation)**

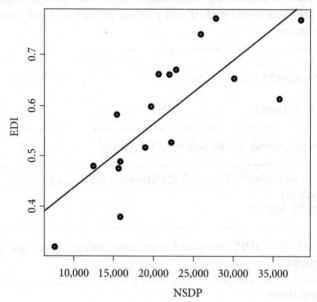

## 4.4 SECTION III THE GAUSS–MARKOV THEOREM

In the beginning of this chapter, we examined some desirable properties that an estimator should have. Do our OLS estimators have those properties? In particular, can they be said to be BLUE? In what follows, we will check whether the OLS estimator:

$$b^\wedge = \sum_{i=1}^{n} x_i y_i \Big/ \sum_{i=1}^{n} x_i^2$$

is BLUE.

It will help us to introduce some short hand notation at this stage:

We will henceforth denote:

$$x_i \Big/ \sum_{i=1}^{n} x_i^2 \text{ as } k_i$$

Note the following properties of $k_i$:

1. $$\sum_{i=1}^{n} k_i = \sum_{i=1}^{n} x_i / \sum_{i=1}^{n} x_i^2 = 0$$

    since $\sum_{i=1}^{n} x_i$ is zero, being the sum of deviations of $X$ around its mean.

2. $$\sum_{i=1}^{n} k_i^2 = 1 / \sum_{i=1}^{n} x_i^2$$

3. $$\sum_{i=1}^{n} k_i X_i = \sum_{i=1}^{n} k_i (X_i - \overline{X})$$

    (since, by property 1)

$$\sum_{i=1}^{n} k_i (X_i - \overline{X}) = \sum_{i=1}^{n} k_i X_i - \overline{X} \sum_{i=1}^{n} k_i = \sum_{i=1}^{n} k_i X_i$$

$$= \sum_{i=1}^{n} x_i^2 / x_i^2 = 1$$

## Theorem 4.2: Linearity of the OLS estimator

$$b^\wedge = \sum_{i=1}^{n} x_i y_i / \sum_{i=1}^{n} x_i^2$$

$$= \sum_{i=1}^{n} k_i (Y_i - \overline{Y})$$

$$= \sum_{i=1}^{n} k_i Y_i - \overline{Y} \sum_{i=1}^{n} k_i$$

$$= \sum_{i=1}^{n} k_i Y_i$$

$$= (x_1 / \sum_{i=1}^{n} x_i^2) Y_1 + (x_2 / \sum_{i=1}^{n} x_i^2) Y_2 + \ldots\ldots + (x_n / \sum_{i=1}^{n} x_i^2) Y_n$$

$$= \alpha_1 Y_1 + \ldots\ldots\ldots + \alpha_n Y_n$$

But this is part (c) of definition 4.4. $b^\wedge$ is a linear function of the values of $Y$.

### Theorem 4.3

If assumptions **E5** (that $e_i$ and $x_i$ are independent random variables for every $i$) and **E1**, that is, $E(e_i) = 0$ hold for every $i$, then $b^\wedge$ is an unbiased estimator of $b$, that is, $E(b^\wedge) = b$.

**Proof:**

$$b^\wedge = \sum_{i=1}^{n} x_i y_i \Big/ \sum_{i=1}^{n} x_i^2$$

$$= \sum_{i=1}^{n} x_i (Y_i - \bar{Y}) \Big/ \sum_{i=1}^{n} x_i^2$$

$$= \sum_{i=1}^{n} x_i Y_i \Big/ \sum_{i=1}^{n} x_i^2 - \sum_{i=1}^{n} x_i \bar{Y} \Big/ \sum_{i=1}^{n} x_i^2$$

$$= \sum_{i=1}^{n} k_i Y_i - \bar{Y} \sum_{i=n}^{n} k_i$$

$$= \sum_{i=1}^{n} k_i Y_i$$

(since we know from property a) above that

$$\sum_{i=1}^{n} k_i = 0$$

$$= \sum_{i=1}^{n} k_i (a + bX_i + e_i)$$

$$= a \sum_{i=1}^{n} k_i + b \sum_{i=1}^{n} k_i X_i + \sum_{i=1}^{n} k_i e_i$$

$$= 0 + b + \sum_{i=1}^{n} x_i e_i \Big/ \sum_{i=1}^{n} x_i^2 \qquad \text{Equation 4.7}$$

(using the properties $(a)$ and $(c)$ respectively, and the definition of $k_i$, respectively).

Therefore, we have:

$$E(b^\wedge) = b + E\left( \sum_{i=1}^{n} x_i e_i \Big/ \sum_{i=1}^{n} x_i^2 \right)$$

(remember that $b$, the unknown population parameter that we are trying to estimate, is a constant and therefore $E(b) = b$).

Since we have assumed that $X_i$ and $e_i$ are independent for each $i$ and therefore:

$$E(X_i e_i) = E(X_i)E(e_i)$$

using assumption E5. But:

$$E(\sum_{i=1}^{n} x_i / \sum_{i=1}^{n} x_i^2)E(e_i) = 0$$

since assumption E1 claims that $E(e_i) = 0$. As a result, we have:

$$E(b^\wedge) = b$$

or that:

$$b^\wedge = \sum_{i=1}^{n} x_i y_i / \sum_{i=1}^{n} x_i^2$$

is an unbiased estimator of $b$.

Therefore, if $x$ and $e$ are not independent, the OLS estimators will not be unbiased.

### Exercise 4.3

Show that the OLS estimator $\hat{\alpha} = \bar{Y} - \hat{\beta}\,\bar{X}$ is an unbiased estimator of $\alpha$.

Let us pause here to absorb the import of the theorem that we just proved. We are trying to estimate the impact on $Y$ on a one unit change in $X$, which we call $b$. Since the parameter $b$ is itself unobservable, we obtain an estimate of $b$ by applying the formula $b^\wedge$ (the OLS estimator) to the data on $X$ and $Y$ from a given sample. Obviously, the particular value that we obtain as an estimate of $b$, will not generally be equal to the real $b$. The actual estimated value is a random variable, and there will be different realizations of this random variable from different samples. Theorem 4.2 says that if assumptions E1 and E5 hold, then, the probability distribution of the estimated values of $b$ will be such that the expected value will be precisely $b$. We have used the example of the experiment of rolling two balanced dies and estimating $a$ and $b$ in the relationship $E(Y / X) = a + bX$. The value of the real $b = 0$, since the slope of the population regression function in Figure 4.1 is zero. Yet, when we obtained a sample and attempted to approximate the relationship between $Y$ and $X$ with a straight line, the graph appears to be upward sloping (Figure 4.3).

What the statement about the unbiasedness of $b^\wedge$ means is that if we generate many different samples and compute the slope using the formula for $b^\wedge$, for each of these samples, then the average value of all the $b^\wedge$'s that we will get will be close to zero, though in each individual case it might not be so. This, in the particular case of OLS estimators, of course requires assumptions E1 and E5 to hold. If these assumptions are satisfied, in each particular sample, the best linear approximation for $Y$ will be an upward sloping or a downward sloping line, but the 'average line' will have a slope of zero. In the real world, assumptions E1 and E5 may not always be satisfied except for the simplest models. If these assumptions are not satisfied, the OLS estimators will not be unbiased.

We will now do a simulation exercise in order to show that the OLS estimator $b^\wedge$ is unbiased when $x$ and $e$ are independent, and correspondingly, are biased when $X$ and $e$ are not independent.

Suppose we have the following 15 observations on $X$:

$$X = (12, 32, 12, 43, 24, 54, 34, 54, 50, 49, 42, 34, 36, 38, 34)$$

**Step 1:** We will use these 15 observations to generate 15 values of $Y$ as follows:

$Y_i = 2 + 3 \times X_i + e_i$

where $e_i$ is the $i$th value of a normally distributed random variable with mean zero and variance equal to 1, which is by construction independent of $X$. We can generate the required values of $e$ by the R command:

```
rnorm(15,0,1)
```

which generates 15 normally distributed random variables with mean zero and variance 1.

**Step 2:** In step 2, we calculate $a\wedge$ and $b\wedge$.

**Step 3:** We repeat step 1, 10,000 times.

**Step 4:** We plot the density of the 10,000 values of $b\wedge$ that we have and check if $E(b\wedge) = b = 3$ and $E(a\wedge) = a = 2$.

The R program below achieves this:

```
X=C(12,32,12,43,24,54,34,54,50,49,42,34,36,38,34)  ##This
reads the data
k=c(rep(0,10000)) ## generates a column vector of 10000
zeros
i=1
repeat {
e=rnorm(15,0,1) ## generates 15 random numbers with
mean zero and variance 1
Y=2+3*X+e ##generates Y
c1=coef(lm(Y~X)) ## regresses y on X and stores the coef-
ficients in a column c1
k[i]=c1[2] ## stores the second row of c1, the estimate of
b^ in k
i=i+1
if(i>10000)
break
}
plot(density(k,bw=1),lwd=4, main="Density of b^")  ##
plots the density of k
```

This generates the graph in Figure 4.6.

As you can see from the graph, the density of $b\wedge$ is symmetric around the true value of $b = 3$, and therefore, $E(b\wedge) = b$ as we have proved earlier.

In the next program, we will generate a correlation between $X$ and $e$ and then examine the impact on the density of $b\wedge$. In the new regression, we will keep $X$ the same, but generate:

$$Y_i = a + bX_i + v_i$$

where:

$$v_i = e_i + 2 \times X_i$$

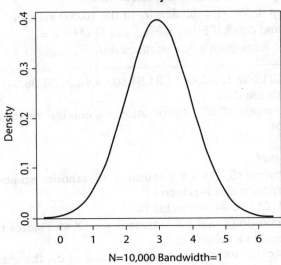

**Figure 4.6**
**Density of $b^\wedge$**

Note that

$$\text{Cov}(X_i, v_i) = E((X_i - E(X))(v_i - E(v_i)))$$
$$= E((X_i - E(X))(e_i + 2X_i - 2E(X)))$$
$$= E(e_i(X_i - E(X))) + 2 \times E(X_i - E(X))^2$$
$$= 2\sigma_x^2$$
$$\neq 0$$

We will now see the implication of this change on the distribution of $b^\wedge$. The following program makes this modification.

```
X=C(12,32,12,43,24,54,34,54,50,49,42,34,36,38,34)
k=c(rep(0,10000))
i=1
repeat {
e=rnorm(15,0,1)
Y=2+3*X+(e+2*X)##this line generates a correlation be-
tween X and the error term.
c1=coef(lm(Y~X))
```

```
k[i]=c1[2]
i=i+1
if(i>10000)
break
}
plot(density(k,bw=1),lwd=4, main="Density of b^")
k[i]=c1[2]
```

The program generates the graph as shown in Figure 4.7.

**Figure 4.7**
**Density of $b^\wedge$**

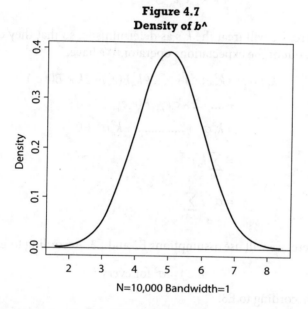

N=10,000 Bandwidth=1

As you can see, the distribution of $b^\wedge$ has shifted to being symmetrical around 5 rather than 3. Therefore, $E(b^\wedge)=5$. Thus, we can see that when the error term and the independent variable are correlated, the OLS estimators are not unbiased.

We have just proved that the OLS estimators are unbiased if certain assumptions hold. What about efficiency? Can we show that if there is any other unbiased estimator of $b$, its variance will not be any smaller that that of the OLS estimator? It turns out that we can, provided assumptions E2 and E3 hold. First, let us find the variance of the OLS estimator $b^\wedge$.

## 4.4.1 The Variance[8] of $b^{\wedge}$

Since we know that $b^{\wedge}$ is an unbiased estimator of $b$, the variance of $b^{\wedge}$ is given by:

$$E(b^{\wedge} - E(b^{\wedge}))^2 = E(b^{\wedge} - b)^2$$

$$= E(\sum_{i=1}^{n} x_i e_i / \sum_{i=1}^{n} x_i^2)^2 = E(\sum_{i=1}^{n} k_i e_i)^2$$

$$= E(k_1^2 e_1^2 + k_2^2 e_2^2 + \dots + k_n^2 e_n^2 + 2k_1 k_2 e_1 e_2 + \dots$$

$$+ k_n k_{n-1} e_n e_{n-1})$$

Here, we will treat the $k_i$'s as deterministic, so that they can be taken out of the expectations operator. We have:

$$k_1^2 E(e_1^2) + k_2^2 E(e_2^2) + \dots + k_n^2 E(e_n^2) + 2k_1 k_2 E(e_1 e_2)$$

$$+ \dots + 2 \times k_n k_{n-1} E(e_n e_{n-1})$$

$$= k_1^2 \sigma^2 + \dots + k_n^2 \sigma^2 + 0$$

$$= \sum_{i=1}^{n} k_i^2 \sigma^2$$

$$= \sigma^2 / \sum_{i=1}^{n} x_i^2$$

Here, we will use assumptions E2 and E3. According to E2:

$$E(e_i) = \sigma^2 \text{ for every } i$$

and according to E3:

$$E(e_i e_j) = 0 \text{ for } i \neq j \qquad \text{Equation 4.8}$$

Thus, variance of $b^{\wedge}$ is given by the ratio of the variance of $e$ to the sum of the squared deviations of $X$ from its mean. Let us understand this result properly. If we take different samples, we would get different values of $b^{\wedge}$. The variance of $b^{\wedge}$ measures the spread of these values around $b$, the true population parameter that we are trying to estimate. Obviously, the more closely clustered are the values of $b^{\wedge}$ around $b$, the more accurate is our estimator. But being more closely clustered just means having a lower variance. Therefore, larger the variance of $b^\wedge$, less accurate is $b^\wedge$ as an estimator of $b$. It might be unbiased, that is, on an average, $b^\wedge$ might be equal to $b$. But this does not preclude individual values of $b^\wedge$ lying far off from $b$. The larger is this spread, the lesser is the accuracy of the estimator. The variance of the estimator is inversely related to its accuracy. Let us examine Equation 4.8 in the light of this comment.

Suppose we divide the numerator and the denominator of the expression for variance of $b^\wedge$ by $n$, keeping the fraction unchanged.

$$\text{Var}(b^\wedge) = (\sigma^2 / n) / (\sum_{i=1}^{n} x_i^2 / n)$$

The numerator is the variance of $e$ divided by the sample size, while the denominator is the variance of $X$. Remember that our model (the sample regression function) for $Y$ is:

$$Y_i = a + bX_i + e_i$$

Suppose the variance of $e$ is large relative to the variance of $X$. It then means that we will see $Y$ varying a lot, even if $X$ does not. Given a fixed sample, our ability to estimate the change in $Y$ per unit change in $X$ will be imprecise, because $Y$ will be increasing or decreasing a lot independently of the change in $X$. But in terms of our formula, this just implies that the numerator of the fraction above is much larger than the denominator, implying a larger variance of $b^\wedge$. On the other hand, if the variance of $X$ is much larger than the variance of $e$, we would be able to identify more precisely the impact of the change in $X$ on the change in $Y$. This also underlies the importance of the variability in $X$. If all the values of $X$ are identical, then $\sum_{i=1}^{n} (X_i - \overline{X})^2$ would be zero, leading to an infinitely large variance for $b^\wedge$. This just means that if the observed values of $X$ do not change at all, our ability to estimate how much $Y$ changes if $X$ changes by one unit is infinitely low. Therefore, it is important to ensure at least some variability in $X$.

Now, we are ready to answer our question: Is there any other linear unbiased estimator that can estimate $b$ more precisely compared to the OLS estimator? If we can find any such estimator, it would be more attractive to use it, rather than the OLS estimator. Therefore, it is important to see if we can find any other linear unbiased estimator that will have a lower variance than the OLS estimator $b\hat{}$. Theorem 4.4 answers this question in the negative.

### Theorem 4.4

Efficiency: The OLS estimator has the lowest variance within the class of linear unbiased estimators.

Let $\beta\hat{}$ be a different linear estimator of $b$. We then have:

$$\beta\hat{} = \sum_{i=1}^{n} w_i Y_i$$

$$E(\beta\hat{}) = \sum_{i=1}^{n} w_i E(Y_i)$$

$$= \sum_{i=1}^{n} w_i (a + bX_i)$$

$$= a \sum_{i=1}^{n} w_i + b \sum_{i=1}^{n} w_i X_i$$

Since $\beta\hat{}$ is an unbiased estimator of $b$, we must have $E(\beta\hat{}) = b$. But this implies that:

$$\sum_{i=1}^{n} w_i = 0 \text{ and } \sum_{i=1}^{n} w_i X_i = 1$$

Since all the $Y_i$'s are independent, we have:

$$\text{Var}(\beta\hat{}) = \sum_{i=1}^{n} w_i^2 \text{Var}(Y_i)$$

$$\text{Var}(Y_i) = E(Y_i - E(Y_i))^2$$

$$= E(a + bX_i + e_i - (a + bX_i))^2$$

$$= E(e_i)^2$$

$$= \sigma^2$$

Therefore:

$$\text{Var}(\beta^{\wedge}) = \sigma^2 \sum_{i=1}^{n} w_i^2$$

$$= \sigma^2 \sum_{i=1}^{n} (w_i - (x_i / \sum_{i=1}^{n} x_i^2) + (x_i / \sum_{i=1}^{n} x_i^2)^2$$

$$= \sigma^2 \sum_{i=1}^{n} (w_i - (x_i / \sum_{i=1}^{n} x_i^2))^2 + \sigma^2 \sum_{i=1}^{n} x_i^2 / (\sum_{i=1}^{n} x_i^2)^2$$

$$+ 2\sigma^2 \sum_{i=1}^{n} (w_i - x_i / \sum_{i=1}^{n} x_i^2)(x_i / \sum_{i=1}^{n} x_i^2)$$

The last term is zero. To see this, note that:

$$\sum_{i=1}^{n} (w_i - x_i / \sum_{i=1}^{n} x_i^2)(x_i / \sum_{i=1}^{n} x_i^2) = \sum_{i=1}^{n} w_i x_i / \sum_{i=1}^{n} x_i^2 - \sum_{i=1}^{n} x_i^2 / (\sum_{i=1}^{n} x_i^2)^2$$

$$= (\sum_{i=1}^{n} w_i x_i - 1) / \sum_{i=1}^{n} x_i^2$$

but:

$$\sum_{i=1}^{n} w_i x_i = \sum_{i=1}^{n} w_i (X_i - \overline{X}) = \sum_{i=1}^{n} w_i X_i - \overline{X} \sum_{i=1}^{n} w_i = 1$$

As a result:

$$= \sigma^2 \sum_{i=1}^{n} (w_i - x_i / \sum_{i=1}^{n} x_i^2)^2 + \sigma^2 (1 / \sum_{i=1}^{n} x_i^2)$$

What is the value of $w_i$ that would minimize var$(\beta^{\wedge})$? This requires the first term on the L.H.S. to be equal to zero. But that
means that:

$$w_i = x_i / \sum_{i=1}^{n} x_i^2$$

Thus:

$$\beta^{\wedge} = \sum_{i=1}^{n} (x_i / \sum_{i=1}^{n} x_i^2) Y_i$$

which is the same estimator as $b^\wedge$ (see Theorem 4.2).

We have shown that no other linear unbiased estimator has a lower variance than the OLS estimator.

Finally, we must examine whether the OLS estimator is consistent.

### Theorem 4.5

Consistency of the OLS estimator

We will use Theorem 4.1 to prove the consistency of the OLS estimator. According to that theorem, in order to test whether $b^\wedge$ is a consistent estimator of $b$, we need to show that:

$$(a)\ \lim_{n\to\infty} E(b^\wedge) = b$$

and:

$$(b)\ \lim_{n\to\infty} \mathrm{var}(b^\wedge) = 0$$

In the present case, we need not test $(a)$, since we have already shown that $E(b^\wedge) = b$.

We have:

$$\mathrm{Var}(b^\wedge) = (\sigma^2 / n) / (\sum_{i=1}^{n} x_i^2 / n)$$

Therefore, as $n$ becomes larger, the numerator of the fraction becomes smaller, while the denominator becomes the fixed number $\sigma_x^2$, the variance of $X$. In the limit, as $n \to \infty$, $\mathrm{var}(b^\wedge) \to 0$, thereby confirming consistency of $b^\wedge$. This implies that as you keep on increasing the sample size, the spread of the values of $b^\wedge$ around $b$ keeps on becoming smaller. As the sample size increases, the values of $b^\wedge$ keep getting closer to $b$.

An alternative proof goes like this. We have

$$\beta^\wedge = \sum_{i=1}^{n} x_i y_i / \sum_{i=1}^{n} x_i^2$$
$$= \beta + \sum_{i=1}^{n} x_i e_i / \sum_{i=1}^{n} x_i^2$$

$$= \beta + (\sum_{i=1}^{n} x_i e_i)/n / (\sum_{i=1}^{n} x_i^2)/n$$

(dividing and multiplying the second term by $n$).

Now, let us consider what happens to this expression as $n \to \infty$.

As $n \to \infty$, $(\sum_{i=1}^{n} x_i e_i)/n$ will approach $\text{Cov}(x\ e)$, because of the law of large numbers. Similarly, $\sum_{i=1}^{n} x_i^2 / n$ will approach $\sigma_x^2$. Hence, we have:

$$\text{plim}\,\beta^\wedge = \beta + \text{Cov}(xe)/\sigma_x^2$$

If we assume just that $x$ and $e$ are uncorrelated, we can show that:

$$\text{plim}\,\beta^\wedge = \beta$$

What this proof says is that even when the strong assumption that $x$ and $e$ are independent does not hold, the OLS estimators will be consistent as long as $x$ and $e$ are uncorrelated. Remember that unbiasedness requires that $x$ and e are independent. If $x$ and $e$ are just uncorrelated rather than independent, OLS estimators will be biased but consistent.

### Theorem 4.6 (Gauss–Markov theorem)[9]

If assumptions E1, E2, E3 and E5 are satisfied, the OLS estimators are BLUE.

**Proof**: We have seen that if assumptions E1, E2, E3 and E5 are satisfied, the OLS estimator is unbiased, linear and efficient. That makes it BLUE. This theorem also works in the reverse: whenever one or more of the assumptions E1, E2, E3 and E5 are not satisfied, the OLS estimator is no longer BLUE.

The efficiency of OLS estimators means that they are the most precise ones within the class of linear unbiased estimators. Can we quantify this precision? We could use the formula for $\text{Var}(b^\wedge)$ to measure the precision of $b^\wedge$. However, the formula

$$\text{Var}(b^\wedge) = \sigma^2 / \sum_{i=1}^{n} x_i^2$$

is not very useful since we have no knowledge of the precise value of $\sigma^2$. $\sigma^2$ refers to the variance of the $e_i$'s which are unobserved. We will need to figure out a way to estimate $\sigma^2$. Therefore, when we do a regression with a bivariate model, we must obtain not only $a\hat{}$ and $b\hat{}$, but also $\sigma^{\hat{}2}$. How does one obtain $\sigma^{\hat{}2}$? It turns out that $\sigma^{\hat{}2}$ can be estimated by estimating the unobservable $e_i$'s first and then calculating their variance. How does one estimate the $e_i$'s? From the definition, we have:

$$e_i = Y_i - a - bX_i$$

A natural way to estimate the $e_i$'s is to replace the unobservable $a$ and $b$ by their estimates $a\hat{}$ and $b\hat{}$. Thus, we have a way to estimate the $e_i$'s:

$$e_i^{\hat{}} = Y_i - a\hat{} - b\hat{}X_i$$

The $e_i$'s have some very interesting properties. We will briefly discuss them, before finding their variance.

### 4.4.2 The Properties of $e_i^{\hat{}}$

**PE1**

$$\sum_{i=1}^{n} e_i^{\hat{}} = 0$$

This follows from the equation:

$$\sum_{i=1}^{n}(Y_i - a - bX_i) = 0$$

which was the first of the two normal equations used to solve for $a\hat{}$ and $b\hat{}$. Since $a\hat{}$ and $b\hat{}$ will necessarily satisfy this equation, we have:

$$\sum_{i=1}^{n}(Y_i - a\hat{} - b\hat{} \ X_i) = 0$$

But this is the same thing as saying that:

$$\sum_{i=1}^{n} \hat{e}_i = 0$$

Note: This property requires that the linear approximation contains a non-zero intercept, $a^{\wedge}$. The linear regression should not be passing through the origin.

**PE2**

$$\sum_{i=1}^{n} X_i \hat{e}_i = 0$$

This follows because the second normal equation is:

$$X_i \sum_{i=1}^{n} (Y_i - a - bX_i) = 0$$

Replacing $a$ and $b$ by $a^{\wedge}$ and $b^{\wedge}$ results in 2. Note that $\sum_{i=1}^{n}(X_i - \bar{X})e_i^{\wedge}$ measures the covariance between $X$ and $e_i^{\wedge}$. But:

$$\sum_{i=1}^{n}(X_i - \bar{X})e_i^{\wedge} = \sum_{i=1}^{n} X_i e_i - \bar{X}\sum_{i=1}^{n} e_i^{\wedge} = \sum_{i=1}^{n} X_i e_i^{\wedge}$$

in view of PE1. As a result, PE2 states that the covariance between $X$ and $e_i^{\wedge}$ will be zero.

Having estimated the $e_i$'s, we can estimate their variance as follows (in view of PE1):

$$\hat{\sigma}_e^2 = \sum_{i=1}^{n} \hat{e}_i^2 / (n-2) \qquad \text{Equation 4.9}$$

This then yields an estimator for the variance of $b^{\wedge}$, $\hat{\sigma}_{b^{\wedge}}^2$:

$$\sigma_{b^{\wedge}}^{\wedge 2} = (\sum_{i=1}^{n} e_i^{\wedge 2} / (n-2)) / \sum_{i=1}^{n} x_i^2 \qquad \text{Equation 4.10}$$

Equation 4.10 yields an estimate of the precision of $b^{\wedge}$. We will now see an example of the method for calculating the variance of $b^{\wedge}$.

**Example 4.7** Let us turn to Example 4.1, where we obtained $a\text{\textasciicircum}=$ 0.3115857 and $b\text{\textasciicircum}=0.00001256873$. Let us now estimate the variance of $b\text{\textasciicircum}$. First, note that we can obtain estimated values of EDI,

$$EDI\text{\textasciicircum}_i = a\text{\textasciicircum} + b\text{\textasciicircum} NASP\text{\textasciicircum}_i$$

that is, by substituting the successive values of $X$ in the estimated equation. We can then obtain

$$e\text{\textasciicircum}_i = NSDP_i - NSDP\text{\textasciicircum}_i$$

(the actual values of EDI minus the estimated values of EDI). By doing this, we get the following results as seen in Table 4.4:

**Table 4.4**
**The calculation of the variance of $b\text{\textasciicircum}$**

| [col.1] EDI $(Y_i)$ | [col.2] NSDP $(X_i)$ | [col.3] EDI^ | [col.4] $e\text{\textasciicircum}_i$ | [col.5] $e\text{\textasciicircum}_i \times e\text{\textasciicircum}_i$ | [col.6] $(X_i - \bar{X})$ | [col.7] $(X_i - \bar{X}) \times (X_i - \bar{X})$ |
|---|---|---|---|---|---|---|
| 0.67 | 22,835 | 0.598593 | 0.071407 | 0.005099 | 1,319.882 | 1,742,089 |
| 0.477 | 15,623 | 0.507947 | −0.03095 | 0.000958 | −5,892.12 | 34,717,050 |
| 0.321 | 7,598 | 0.407083 | −0.08608 | 0.00741 | −1,3917.1 | 1.94E+08 |
| 0.612 | 35,779 | 0.761282 | −0.14928 | 0.022285 | 14,263.88 | 2.03E+08 |
| 0.707 | 28,415 | 0.668726 | 0.038274 | 0.001465 | 6,899.882 | 47,608,376 |
| 0.381 | 15,904 | 0.511479 | −0.13048 | 0.017025 | −5,611.12 | 31,484,641 |
| 0.772 | 27,824 | 0.661298 | 0.110702 | 0.012255 | 6,308.882 | 39,801,997 |
| 0.481 | 12,577 | 0.469663 | 0.011337 | 0.000129 | −8,938.12 | 79,889,947 |
| 0.598 | 19,625 | 0.558247 | 0.039753 | 0.00158 | −1,890.12 | 3,572,545 |
| 0.661 | 20,618 | 0.570728 | 0.090272 | 0.008149 | −897.118 | 804,820.1 |
| 0.487 | 15,096 | 0.501323 | −0.01432 | 0.000205 | −6,419.12 | 41,205,071 |
| 0.771 | 38,488 | 0.795331 | −0.02433 | 0.000592 | 16,972.88 | 2.88E+08 |
| 0.654 | 30,158 | 0.690633 | −0.03663 | 0.001342 | 8,642.882 | 74,699,415 |
| 0.582 | 15,420 | 0.505396 | 0.076604 | 0.005868 | −6,095.12 | 37,150,459 |
| 0.662 | 22,001 | 0.58811 | 0.07389 | 0.00546 | 485.8824 | 236,081.7 |
| 0.741 | 25,898 | 0.637091 | 0.103909 | 0.010797 | 4,382.882 | 19,209,658 |
| 0.526 | 11,898 | 0.461128 | 0.064872 | 0.004208 | −9,617.12 | 92,488,952 |

Using Equation 4.10, the variance of $b\text{\textasciicircum}$ can be obtained as the sum of numbers in [col. 5] divided by 15 ($n-2$), the whole divided by the sum of elements in col. 7. The sum of elements in col. 5, $\sum_{i=1}^{17} e_i^{\wedge 2}$ equals 0.104827. This divided by 15 equals 0.006988. This is the numerator of the formula in 4.8. The denominator in 4.8 is the sum of elements in col. 7, which is

$$\sum_{i=1}^{17} x_i^2 = 1,189,834,342$$

Therefore, Var($b^\wedge$) = 0.006988 / 1189834342 = 0.00000000000587 which as you can see, is a very small number indeed. Thus, the precision of our estimator seems to be pretty good, as the variance is really a small number.

### 4.4.3 The Distribution of $b^\wedge$

We have now been able to establish the mean of the distribution of $b^\wedge$, since we know that $E(b^\wedge) = b$. We also know the variance of $b^\wedge$ from Equation 4.10. What is the form of the distribution of $b^\wedge$? At this point, the linearity property of $b^\wedge$ becomes relevant. We know from Theorem 4.2 that

$$b^\wedge = a_1 \times Y_1 + \ldots\ldots\ldots + a_n \times Y_n$$

From this it follows that the distribution of $Y$ will have an important bearing on the distribution of $b^\wedge$. Remember that for each $Y$, we have:

$$Y_i = a + bX_i + e_i$$

For a moment, we will think of the $X$'s as fixed, and then the distribution of $Y_i$'s will be the same as the distribution of the $e_i$'s. Assumption E4 states that the distribution of the $e_i$'s is normal. This then leads us to the conclusion that the $Y_i$'s will also be normally distributed. An important theorem in statistics says that if you multiply each of a series of independent normally distributed random variables with a constant and then sum them all, the resultant will also be a normally distributed random variable. We can apply this result to Theorem 4.2. Each of the $Y_i$'s are normally distributed, which then implies that $b^\wedge$ will also be normally distributed.

### 4.4.4 Hypothesis Testing for $b^\wedge$

At this point, a question must have started to bother you. We know that $b^\wedge$ is a random variable, which means that its value can fluctuate from sample to sample. As you can see, the estimated value of $b^\wedge$ that we have got is quite small, namely, 0.00001256873. It is quite likely that even if the true value of $b$ is actually zero, pure sampling fluctuations might lead us to obtain a value of 0.00001256873 that we have obtained in our sample. But if the true value of $b$ is equal to zero, it would mean that the net domestic income of a state has no impact on its index of educational development! Whether the value of the educational development index of states depends upon their income levels is an important policy issue and hence the possibility just mentioned needs to be taken seriously. How do we resolve the issue? It is here that Theorem 3.3 of Chapter 3 will be useful. That theorem states that if $(X_1, X_2, \ldots\ldots X_n)$ is a random sample coming from a normally distributed population with mean $\mu = E(X)$, and if:

$$s^\wedge = \sqrt{\sum_{i=1}^{n}(X_i - \overline{X})^2 / (n-1)}$$

the estimated standard deviation of $X$, then:

$$t = (X_i - E(X)) / s^\wedge$$

follows the Student's $t$ distribution with $n - 1$ degrees of freedom. We already know the following about $b^\wedge$:

**B1**

$$E(b^\wedge) = b$$

(due to the property of unbiasedness):

**B2**

$$\mathrm{Var}(b^\wedge) = \sigma_e^2 / \sum_i^n x_i^2$$

(just shown earlier).

**B3**

$b^\wedge$ is normally distributed.

Combining B1, B2 and B3, we have:

$$b^\wedge \sim N(b, \sigma_e^2 / \sum_{i=1}^{n} x_i^2)$$

Consequently:

$$\left\{ (b^\wedge - b) / \sqrt{\sigma_e^2 / \sum_{i=1}^{n} x_i^2} \right\} \sim N(0,1)$$

(is a standard normal variable).

Let

$$s^\wedge = \sqrt{\text{Var}(b^\wedge)} = \sqrt{(\sum_{i=1}^{n} e_i^{\wedge 2} / (n-2)) / \sum_{i=1}^{n} x_i^2}$$

which is the estimated standard deviation of $b^\wedge$, and is referred to as the 'standard error' of $b^\wedge$.

Using this, and by Theorem 3.3 of Chapter 3, we can argue that $t_{b^\wedge} = (b^\wedge - E(b^\wedge)) / s^\wedge$ will follow the student's $t$ distribution with $n - 1$ degrees of freedom. This argument allows us to test various hypothesis about the unobservable $(b^\wedge)$. In our particular example, we are interested in testing whether $E(b^\wedge) = 0$. As explained in Chapter 3, we will set up the null hypothesis:

$$H_o : b = 0$$

as against the alternative hypothesis:

$$H_A : b \neq 0$$

To test this, we set up the statistic:

$$t_{b^\wedge} = (0.00001256875 - 0) / \sqrt{0.00000000000587}$$
$$= 0.00001256875 / 0.0000024228 = 5.18$$

The size of the critical region for this value with 16 degrees of freedom is 0.00009. This means that we can reject the null hypothesis at 0.009 per cent level of significance, which is a pretty strong rejection! We should feel highly confident that $E(b^\wedge) \neq 0$.

## 4.4.5 Confidence Interval for $b^\wedge$

For 16 degrees of freedom, we have:

Probability$(-2.11905 \leq t_{b^\wedge} \leq 2.11905) = 0.95$

Probability$(-2.11905 \leq \dfrac{b^\wedge - b}{s^\wedge} \leq 2.11905) = 0.95$

Probability$(b^\wedge - 2.11905 \times s^\wedge \leq b \leq b^\wedge + 2.11905 \times s^\wedge) = 0.95$

The interval $(b^\wedge - 2.11905 \times s^\wedge, b^\wedge + 2.11905 \times s^\wedge)$ is the 95 per cent confidence interval for $b$, for 16 degrees of freedom. In general, a $(1 - \alpha)$ per cent confidence interval for $b$, for $n$ degrees of freedom, is:

$$(b^\wedge - t_{\alpha/2,n} \times s^\wedge, b^\wedge + t_{\alpha/2,n} \times s^\wedge)$$

where $t_{\alpha/2,n}$ is the $t$-value at $\alpha/2$ level of significance. How does one interpret the 95 per cent confidence interval? Clearly, it is not the interval such that there is a 95 per cent probability that $b$ lies in this interval. After all, the value of $b$, the fixed unknown, is a constant. It will either lie within an interval with probability one or zero. Hence, we cannot have an interval such that there is a 95 per cent probability that $b$ will lie within it. How does one then interpret a confidence interval? Suppose you take hundred different sets of values of $Y$ (with the assumption that $X$ is fixed from sample to sample) and compute hundred different values of $b^\wedge$ and $s^\wedge$. Using these and the $t$ value at 97.5 per cent level of significance and appropriate degrees of freedom, we can construct 100 different confidence intervals. Then, approximately 95 per cent of these intervals will contain the true value of $b$. This is the correct interpretation of the term '95 per cent confidence interval'.

## 4.4.6 The Importance of Relative Variation

The following exercise is important in order to understand the importance of the variance of the independent variable relative to the variance of the error term.

**Step 1:** We generate the values of $X$ (the independent variable) as 100 normally distributed random numbers with mean zero and variance 1.

**Step 2:** Generate 100 values of a normally distributed random variable with mean equal to zero and variance 1 and call them $e$, the error term.

**Step 3:** We generate 100 values of $Y$ where:

$$Y_i = 3 + 0.6 \times X_i + e_i$$

**Step 4:** Calculate the standard error of $b^\wedge$ and test the null hypothesis = 0 which we know is not true.

**Step 5:** Increase the variance of $e$ to 5, leaving the variance of $X$ unchanged, repeat steps 3 and 4.

**Step 6:** Set the variance of $e$ back to 1 and change the variance of $X$ to 5, repeat steps 3 and 4.

The following program carries out this exercise:

```
set.seed(123)
# variance of X and e equals 1
X=rnorm(100,0,1)
e=rnorm(100,0,1)
Y=3+0.6*X+e
summary(lm(Y~X))
# variance of X equals 1 and variance of e equals 5
X=rnorm(100,0,1)
e=rnorm(100,0,5)
Y=3+0.6*X+e
summary(lm(Y~X))
##variance of X equals 5 and variance of e equals 1
X=rnorm(100,0,5)
e=rnorm(100,0,1)
Y=3+0.6*X+e
summary(lm(Y~X))
```

The output of the program is very instructive:

```
> set.seed(123)
> # variance of X and e equals 1
> X=rnorm(100,0,1)
> e=rnorm(100,0,1)
> Y=3+0.6*X+e
> summary(lm(Y~X))
Call:
lm(formula = Y ~ X)
Residuals:
Min         1Q        Median      3Q        Max
-1.9073    -0.6835    -0.0875     0.5806     3.2904
Coefficients:
Estimate    Std. Error    t value    Pr(>|t|)
(Intercept)  2.89720      0.09755    29.699 < 2e-16 ***
X            0.54753      0.10688    5.123 1.51e-06 ***
---
Signif. codes: 0 '***' 0.001 '**' 0.01 '*' 0.05 '.' 0.1 ' ' 1
Residual standard error: 0.9707 on 98 degrees of freedom
Multiple R-squared: 0.2112, Adjusted R-squared: 0.2032
F-statistic: 26.24 on 1 and 98 DF, p-value: 1.508e-06
```

The estimated coefficient of $X$, $b^\wedge = 0.54753$. The estimated standard error is $0.10688$. The calculated $t$ value is:

$$0.54753 / 0.10688 = 5.123$$

and the size of the critical region is $0.00000151$. We can reject the null hypothesis at a 1 per cent level of significance. In fact, the R output says that we can reject the null hypothesis at a level of significance that is very close to zero:

```
> # variance of X equals 1 and variance of e equals 5
> X=rnorm(100,0,1)
> e=rnorm(100,0,5)
> Y=3+0.6*X+e
> summary(lm(Y~X))
Call:
```

```
lm(formula = Y ~ X)
Residuals:
Min         1Q        Median      3Q        Max
-12.20581   -3.26836   0.03999    3.70598   12.63279
Coefficients:
            Estimate   Std. Error   t value   Pr(>|t|)
(Intercept) 2.8484     0.5257       5.418     4.31e-07 ***
X           0.3547     0.5518       0.643     0.522
—
Signif. codes: 0 '***' 0.001 '**' 0.01 '*' 0.05 '.' 0.1 ' ' 1
Residual standard error: 5.215 on 98 degrees of freedom
Multiple  R-squared:  0.004198,  Adjusted  R-squared:
-0.005963
F-statistic: 0.4132 on 1 and 98 DF, p-value: 0.5219
```

This output is different from the previous one in that the variance of $e$ has been set to be five times the variance of the independent variable. As you can see, the standard error of $b^{\wedge}$ has been scaled up by a factor of five. Consequently, the estimated value of $b$ (0.3547) lies relatively far from the actual value which equals 0.6. Now, we cannot reject the null hypothesis that $b = 0$, even when we know that by construction, the null hypothesis is false. This is an instance of type II error (failing to reject the null when the null is false). The moral of the story is that if the variance of the error term (which can include all sorts of excluded variables) is rather high relative to the variance of the independent variable, there is a substantial chance of making a type II error:

```
> #variance of X equals 5 and variance of e equals 1
> X=rnorm(100,0,5)
> e=rnorm(100,0,1)
> Y=3+0.6*X+e
> summary(lm(Y~X))
Call:
lm(formula = Y ~ X)
Residuals:
```

| Min | 1Q | Median | 3Q | Max |
|---|---|---|---|---|
| -2.72598 | -0.51086 | -0.03146 | 0.62991 | 2.89563 |

Coefficients:

| | Estimate | Std. Error | t value | Pr(>\|t\|) |
|---|---|---|---|---|
| (Intercept) | 2.93695 | 0.09285 | 31.63 | <2e-16 *** |
| X | 0.63921 | 0.01876 | 34.08 | <2e-16 *** |

---

Signif. codes: 0 '***' 0.001 '**' 0.01 '*' 0.05 '.' 0.1 ' ' 1
Residual standard error: 0.9231 on 98 degrees of freedom
Multiple R-squared: 0.9222, Adjusted R-squared: 0.9214
F-statistic: 1161 on 1 and 98 DF, p-value: < 2.2e-16

As can be seen, when we increase the variance of $X$ relative to the variance of the error term, the precision of the estimators improves substantially. As a result, the estimated value lies relatively close to the actual value. Also, we can reject the null hypothesis $b = 0$ since the size of the critical region is very small.

When we specify a regression model, it is important to take care to ensure that a significant part of the variation in $Y$ is due to variation in $X$ rather than $e$. In particular, if we have omitted some variables that may influence $Y$, then their effect will also be contained in $e$. In that case, you are more likely to land up with the situation that the variance of $e$ is substantially greater than the variance of $X$. As we have seen above, the chance of committing a type II error (failing to reject the null of $b = 0$ even when it is false) goes up substantially.

### 4.4.7 Hypothesis Testing for $\hat{a}$

It can be shown that:

$$\text{Var}(a\hat{}) = \sigma^2 n^{-1} \sum_{i=1}^{n} x_i^2 / \sum_{i=1}^{n} (x_i - \bar{x})^2$$

Therefore, this can be estimated as:

$$\sigma_{a\hat{}}^{\hat{}} = \sigma\hat{}^2 n^{-1} \sum_{i=1}^{n} x_i^2 / \sum_{i=1}^{n} (x_i - \bar{x})^2$$

## Exercise 4.4

Estimate the variance of $a\wedge$ and test the null hypothesis:

$$H_o : E(a) = 0$$

against the alternative:

$$H_a : E(a) \neq 0.$$

### 4.4.8 The Goodness of Fit: $R^2$

The idea of OLS is based upon approximating the scatter with a linear approximation. Using this idea, we derived formulae for $a\wedge$ and $b\wedge$. With the help of these estimators, we obtained specific values of $a\wedge$ and $b\wedge$ and obtained a linear approximation. How well does this line approximate our observed data? Suppose we have got two such approximations. How does one compare with the other? These questions can be answered if we can have a summary measure of the quality of the approximation, or the so called 'goodness of fit'. One such measure is the $R^2$. We explain it below:

Consider $\sum_{i=1}^{n}(Y_i - \overline{Y})^2$. This is the numerator of the variance of $Y$

(variance of $Y = \sum_{i=1}^{n}(Y_i - \overline{Y})^2 / n$) of the variance of $Y$, which we will

call the Total Sum of Squares (TSS) of $Y$. This can be written as:

$$\sum_{i=1}^{n}(Y_i - \overline{Y})^2 = \sum_{i=1}^{n}(Y_i - Y_i^{\wedge} + Y_i^{\wedge} - \overline{Y})^2$$

(adding and subtracting $Y_i^{\wedge}$ should leave the equation unchanged) where:

$$Y_i^{\wedge} = a\wedge + b\wedge\, X_i$$

(the 'fitted' values of $Y$ obtained by substituting the observed values of $X$ into the linear approximation).

$$\sum_{i=1}^{n}(Y_i - \bar{Y})^2 = \sum_{i=1}^{n}(Y_i - Y_i^\wedge)^2 + 2 \times \sum_{i=1}^{n}(Y_i^\wedge - \bar{Y})(Y_i - Y_i^\wedge) + \sum_{i=1}^{n}(Y_i^\wedge - \bar{Y})^2$$

Equation 4.11

Let us understand the term $(Y_i^\wedge - \bar{Y})$. We have:

$$Y_i = Y_i^\wedge + e_i \text{ (since } e_i^\wedge = Y_i - Y_i^\wedge)$$

Therefore:

$$\sum_{i=1}^{n} Y_i / n = \sum_{i=1}^{n} Y_i^\wedge / n + \sum_{i=1}^{n} e_i^\wedge / n \qquad \text{Equation 4.12}$$

Since our linear approximation is not through the origin but contains an $a \neq 0$, PE1 applies, and hence we have:

$$\sum_{i=1}^{n} Y_i / n = \sum_{i=1}^{n} Y_i^\wedge / n \text{ or } \bar{Y} = \bar{Y}^\wedge$$

implying that the average of the actual values of $Y$ is the same thing as the average of the fitted values of $Y$. Also, because $Y_i = Y_i^\wedge + e_i^\wedge$, we can rewrite Equation 4.11 as:

$$\sum_{i=1}^{n}(Y_i - \bar{Y})^2 = \sum_{i=1}^{n}(e_i^\wedge)^2 + 2 \times \sum_{i=1}^{n}(Y_i^\wedge - \bar{Y})(e_i^\wedge) + \sum_{i=1}^{n}(Y_i^\wedge - \bar{Y}^\wedge)^2$$

Equation 4.13

Let us examine the middle term of Equation 4.12 a bit more closely:

$$\sum_{i=1}^{n}(Y_i^\wedge - \bar{Y})e_i^\wedge = \sum_{i=1}^{n}(Y_i^\wedge - \bar{Y}^\wedge)e_i^\wedge = \sum_{i=1}^{n} b^\wedge(X_i - \bar{X})e_i^\wedge$$

$$= b^\wedge \sum_{i=1}^{n} X_i e_i^\wedge + \bar{X} \sum_{i=1}^{n} e_i^\wedge$$

$$= 0$$

where the definition of $Y_i^\wedge$ (Since $Y_i^\wedge = a^\wedge + b^\wedge X_i$ ; we have $\bar{Y}^\wedge = a^\wedge + b^\wedge \bar{X}$) has been used along with PE2 As a result of this, we have:

$$\sum_{i=1}^{n}(Y_i - \overline{Y})^2 = \sum_{i=1}^{n}(e_i^{\wedge})^2 + \sum_{i=1}^{n}(Y_i^{\wedge} - \overline{Y^{\wedge}})^2 \qquad \text{Equation 4.14}$$

The term on the L.H.S. is the numerator of the variance of $Y$. We will call it the TSS. The first term on the right hand side is the numerator of the estimated variance of the error term, or that part of the data that cannot be 'explained' by our linear approximation. We will call it the Residual Sum of Squares (RSS). The final term on the right hand side is the numerator of the variance of the 'fitted values', or that part of the scatter that our model can 'explain'. We will call it the Explained Sum of Squares (ESS). Hence, we have the following important equation:

$$\text{TSS} = \text{RSS} + \text{ESS}^{10} \qquad \text{Equation 4.15}$$

Therefore:

$$1 = (\text{RSS/TSS}) + (\text{ESS/TSS})$$

ESS/TSS is that fraction of the variance of the total variation in $Y$ that can be explained by our model. RSS/TSS is that fraction of the total variation in $Y$ that cannot be explained by our model. Equation 4.15 is saying that these two fractions sum to 1. We can rewrite Equation 4.13 as:

$$(\text{ESS/TSS}) = 1 - (\text{RSS/TSS})$$

and it is customary to refer to ESS/TSS as $R^2$. The $R^2$ is a measure of the 'goodness of fit', or how well our linear approximation fits the data. We can calculate it for our example. In our example, $EDI_i$ is our dependent variable. Hence:

$$\text{TSS} = \sum_{i=1}^{n} e_i^{\wedge 2} \sum_{i=1}^{n}(EDI_i - \overline{EDI})^2$$

$$\overline{EDI} - 0.594294.$$

Hence:

$$\sum_{i=1}^{n}(EDI_i - \overline{EDI})^2 = 0.27829 = \text{TSS}$$

$$\text{RSS} = \sum_{i=1}^{n} e_i^{\wedge 2} = 0.104827$$

Therefore:

$R^2 = 1 - (\text{RSS} / \text{TSS}) = 1 - (0.104827 / 0.27829) = 0.623995$

This is to be interpreted as follows: The linear approximation:

$$\text{EDI} = 0.3115857 + 0.00001256873 \times \text{NSDP}$$

'explains' approximately 62 per cent of the variation in EDI across states in our sample. That is, the remaining 38 per cent variation is not accounted for by our linear approximation.

### Example 4.8

Let us look at one more example to fix ideas more clearly. The Table 4.5 gives data for literacy and infant mortality rates (both are expressed per thousand) for 33 states and Union Territories (UTs) in India for the year 2001.

We would like to study how the infant mortality rate is affected (if at all) by the literacy rate. Presumably, one should expect a lower rate of infant mortality in states /UTs with a higher level of literacy.

As a first step towards fitting the linear approximation, let us plot the scatter for the two variables. This is done in Figure 4.8.

The scatter clearly indicates a negative association between literacy rate and infant mortality rate. The overall pattern indicates that States/UTs that have a higher literacy rate (on the X-axis) generally tend have a lower infant mortality rate (on the Y-axis). In addition, the relationship seems to be described by a straight line. We posit the following population regression function:

$$IMR_i = \alpha + bLit_i + e_i$$

And the associated sample regression function:

$$IMR_i = \alpha + \beta Lit_i + \varepsilon_i$$

Here, $IMR_i$ refers to the infant mortality in state $i$, $Lit_i$ refers to the literacy rate in State/UT $i$. The next step is to find the values of $a^{\wedge}$

## Table 4.5
### The Literacy and Infant Mortality Rates (expressed in per thousand) for 33 States and Union Territories for the year 2001

| State/UT | Literacy Rate | Infant Mortality Rate | State/UT | Literacy Rate | Infant Mortality Rate |
|---|---|---|---|---|---|
| Andhra Pradesh | 61.11 | 66 | Mizoram | 88.49 | 19 |
| Arunachal Pradesh | 54.74 | 39 | Orissa | 63.61 | 91 |
| Assam | 64.28 | 74 | Punjab | 69.95 | 52 |
| Bihar | 47.53 | 62 | Rajasthan | 61.03 | 80 |
| Delhi | 81.82 | 29 | Sikkim | 69.68 | 42 |
| Goa | 82.32 | 19 | Tamil Nadu | 73.47 | 49 |
| Gujarat | 69.97 | 60 | Uttar Pradesh | 57.36 | 83 |
| Haryana | 68.59 | 66 | Uttaranchal | 72.28 | 48 |
| Himachal Pradesh | 77.13 | 54 | West Bengal | 69.22 | 51 |
| Jammu & Kashmir | 54.46 | 48 | Andaman and Nicobar Islands | 81.18 | 18 |
| Jharkhand | 54.13 | 62 | Chandigarh | 81.76 | 24 |
| Karnataka | 67.04 | 58 | Chhattisgarh | 65.18 | 77 |
| Kerala | 90.92 | 11 | Dadra and Nagar Haveli | 60.03 | 58 |
| Madhya Pradesh | 64.11 | 86 | Daman and Diu | 81.09 | 40 |
| Maharashtra | 77.27 | 45 | Lakshadweep | 87.52 | 33 |
| Manipur | 68.87 | 20 | Pondicherry (now Puducherry) | 81.49 | 22 |
| Meghalaya | 63.31 | 56 | | | |

and $b^\wedge$, which will allow us to estimate the parameters of the linear approximation. We will use the OLS formulae to obtain estimates of $a^\wedge$ and $b^\wedge$. The actual calculations are presented in Table 4.6. *IMR* is the dependent variable ($Y$) while *Lit* is the independent variable ($X$).

## Figure 4.8
### Scatter diagram of infant mortality rate versus literacy rate

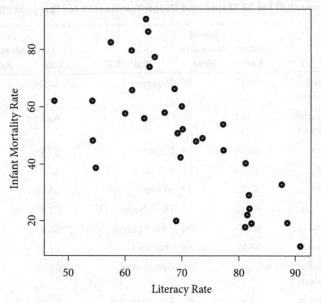

According to Equation 4.4:

$$b\wedge = \sum_{i=1}^{n} x_i y_i \bigg/ \sum_{i=1}^{n} x_i^2$$

The numerator is the sum of the elements in (col 5) which equals –5,390.73. The denominator is the sum of the elements in [col. 4] equals 3,855.925. The estimated value of $b\wedge$ turns out to be –1.39804. $a\wedge$ equals $\overline{y} - b\wedge \times \overline{X}$. This turns out to be 147.6601. This means that our linear approximation is:

$IMR\wedge = 147.6601 - 1.39804 \times Lit$

This means that for every one point increase in the literacy rate (the number of literates per thousand population), the IMR declines by approximately 1.4 points (infant deaths per thousand live births).

The next step is to examine the statistical significance of $a\wedge$ and $b\wedge$. The estimated variance of $b\wedge$, $\sigma_{b\wedge}^{\wedge 2}$, is given by:

**Table 4.6**
**The calculation required for the estimation of $a^\wedge$ and $b^\wedge$**

| States/UTs | $X$ Lit[1] | Y IMR [2] | $X_i =$ $(Xi - \overline{X})$ | | $X_i^2 =$ $(Xi - \overline{X})^2$ | $(Xi - \overline{X})$ $(Yi - \overline{Y})$ [5] |
|---|---|---|---|---|---|---|
| Andhra Pradesh | 61.11 | 66 | -8.91848 | 16.24242 | 79.53937 | -144.858 |
| Arunachal Pradesh | 54.74 | 39 | -15.2885 | -10.7576 | 233.7378 | 164.467 |
| Assam | 64.28 | 74 | -5.74848 | 24.24242 | 33.04508 | -139.357 |
| Bihar | 47.53 | 62 | -22.4985 | 12.24242 | 506.1818 | -275.436 |
| Delhi | 81.82 | 29 | 11.79152 | -20.7576 | 139.0398 | -244.763 |
| Goa | 82.32 | 19 | 12.29152 | -30.7576 | 151.0813 | -378.057 |
| Gujarat | 69.97 | 60 | -0.05848 | 10.24242 | 0.00342 | -0.59903 |
| Haryana | 68.59 | 66 | -1.43848 | 16.24242 | 2.069239 | -23.3645 |
| Himachal Pradesh | 77.13 | 54 | 7.101515 | 4.242424 | 50.43152 | 30.12764 |
| Jammu & Kashmir | 54.46 | 48 | -15.5685 | -1.75758 | 242.3777 | 27.36279 |
| Jharkhand | 54.13 | 62 | -15.8985 | 12.24242 | 252.7618 | -194.636 |
| Karnataka | 67.04 | 58 | -2.98848 | 8.242424 | 8.931042 | -24.6324 |
| Kerala | 90.92 | 11 | 20.89152 | -38.7576 | 436.4554 | -809.704 |
| Madhya Pradesh | 64.11 | 86 | -5.91848 | 36.24242 | 35.02846 | -214.5 |
| Maharashtra | 77.27 | 45 | 7.241515 | -4.75758 | 52.43954 | -34.4521 |
| Manipur | 68.87 | 20 | -1.15848 | -29.7576 | 1.342087 | 34.4737 |
| Meghalaya | 63.31 | 56 | -6.71848 | 6.242424 | 45.13804 | -41.9396 |
| Mizoram | 88.49 | 19 | 18.46152 | -30.7576 | 340.8275 | -567.831 |
| Orissa | 63.61 | 91 | -6.41848 | 41.24242 | 41.19695 | -264.714 |
| Punjab | 69.95 | 52 | -0.07848 | 2.242424 | 0.00616 | -0.176 |
| Rajasthan | 61.03 | 80 | -8.99848 | 30.24242 | 80.97273 | -272.136 |
| Sikkim | 69.68 | 42 | -0.34848 | -7.75758 | 0.121442 | 2.703398 |
| Tamil Nadu | 73.47 | 49 | 3.441515 | -0.75758 | 11.84403 | -2.60721 |

*(Table 4.6 Contd.)*

*(Table 4.6 Contd.)*

| | | | | | | |
|---|---|---|---|---|---|---|
| Uttar Pradesh | 57.36 | 83 | −12.6685 | 33.24242 | 160.4905 | −421.131 |
| Uttaranchal | 72.28 | 48 | 2.251515 | −1.75758 | 5.06932 | −3.95721 |
| West Bengal | 69.22 | 51 | −0.80848 | 1.242424 | 0.653648 | −1.00448 |
| Andaman & Nicobar Islands | 81.18 | 18 | 11.15152 | −31.7576 | 124.3563 | −354.145 |
| Chandigarh | 81.76 | 24 | 11.73152 | −25.7576 | 137.6284 | −302.175 |
| Chhattisgarh | 65.18 | 77 | −4.84848 | 27.24242 | 23.50781 | −132.084 |
| Dadra & Nagar Haveli | 60.03 | 58 | −9.99848 | 8.242424 | 99.9697 | −82.4118 |
| Daman & Diu | 81.09 | 40 | 11.06152 | −9.75758 | 122.3571 | −107.934 |
| Lakshadweep | 87.52 | 33 | 17.49152 | −16.7576 | 305.9531 | −293.115 |
| Pondicherry (now Puducherry) | 81.49 | 22 | 11.46152 | −27.7576 | 131.3663 | −318.144 |

$$(\sum_{i=1}^{n} e_i^{\wedge 2} / (n-2)) / \sum_{i=1}^{n} x_i^2 \text{ where } e_i^{\wedge} = IMR_i - IMR_i^{\wedge}$$

Using this formula, the estimated Variance ($b^{\wedge}$) can be calculated as 0.064364, while the estimated variance for $a^{\wedge}$ can be found to be 323.1581. We set up the null hypothesis:

$$H_o : E(b^{\wedge}) = 0$$

against the alternative:

$$H_A : E(b^{\wedge}) \neq 0$$

This hypothesis can be tested by calculating:

$$t_{b^{\wedge}} = b^{\wedge} / \sqrt{\sigma_{b^{\wedge}}^{2\wedge}}$$

which turns out to be −5.511. The size of the critical region turns out to be 0.00000497, which means that we can have a good deal of confidence while rejecting $H_o$ in favour of $H_A$. Similarly, we can test the hypothesis:

$$H_o : E(a^{\wedge}) = 0$$

against the alternative:

$$H_A : E(a^\wedge) \neq 0$$

The value of the associated $t$ statistic, $t_{a^\wedge} = 8.214$, with a critical region being of the size 0.00000000281. Again, we can confidently reject the null.

Having obtained our linear approximation, we must find out how good it is as a description of our data. That is, we should be calculating $R^2$. As an exercise, you are asked to show that the value of the $R^2$ in this case is 0.4948. How will you interpret this value?

A popular variation of the R-square is the adjusted R-square or the $\bar{R}^2$. The $\bar{R}^2$ is obtained from the R-square by replacing the RSS and TSS by unbiased estimates of the variance of the estimated residuals and the variance of Y. The unbiased estimator of the variance of the estimated residuals is:

$$\sigma_e^{\wedge 2} = \sum_{i=1}^{n} \varepsilon_i^{\wedge 2} / (n-2)$$

(since two parameters, $a^\wedge$ and $b^\wedge$ are estimated, the degrees of freedom are equal to $(n - 2)$), while the unbiased estimator of the variance of Y is:

$$\sigma_y^{\wedge 2} = \sum_{i=1}^{n} (Y_i - \bar{Y})^2 / (n-1)$$

Therefore, we have:

$$\bar{R}^2 = 1 - (\sigma_e^{\wedge 2} / \sigma_y^{\wedge 2}) = 1 - (\sum_{i=1}^{n} \varepsilon^{\wedge 2} / (n-2) / \sum_{i=1}^{n} (Y_i - \bar{Y})^2 / (n-1))$$

$$= 1 - ((n-1)/(n-2))(\sum_{i=1}^{n} \varepsilon^{\wedge 2} / \sum_{i=1}^{n} (Y_i - \bar{Y})^2 /)$$

Since $(n - 1) > (n - 2)$, R square $> \bar{R}^2$.

You would have clearly understood the basic idea of the regression model. In the remaining part of this chapter, we will explore some specialised topics in this approach.

Principles of Econometrics

A very important point to remember in the context of using the R-square and the adjusted R-square, is that the formulae are valid only for regression models that have an intercept. The derivation of R-square used the fact that $\sum_{i=1}^{n} \hat{\varepsilon}_i = 0$. This was obtained by differentiating $\sum_{i=1}^{n}(Y_i - \alpha - \beta X_i)^2$ with respect to $\alpha$, and replacing $\alpha$ by $\hat{\alpha}$ and $\beta$ with $\hat{\beta}$. If the regression model does not include an intercept, then the question of differentiating with respect to $\alpha$ does not arise and hence we cannot argue that $\sum_{i=1}^{n} \hat{\varepsilon}_i = 0$. In that case, the formulae for R-square and adjusted R-square (which is only a modification of R-square) cannot be interpreted to mean the ratio of the explained sum of squares to the total sum of squares. We will revisit this issue later in the section on regression through the origin.

## 4.5 TOPICS IN REGRESSION

### 4.5.1 Log–Log Regression

An important assumption that we have made so far is that $E(Y/X)$ is a linear function of $X$, that is $E(Y/X_i) = a + bX_i$. This requires that the value of slope of the function, $b$, be independent of $X$. However, that might not always be true. In particular, the slope of this function, the value of $b$, might depend upon the value of $X$. For example, if $Y$ is the output per hectare on identical plots of land and $X$ is the amount of fertilizers applied per hectare, at low levels of $X$, the output might show a large increase, which might then peter off as the amount of fertilizer input increases (*ceteris paribus*). In this case, the assumption of linearity of $E(Y/X)$ as a function of $X$ might not be valid. Another case might be that relating to the increase in market share of a firm as a result of repeated airing of the same advertisement. If the advertisement is a good one, it will have a large impact on the market share, which might peter off later as the advertisement is shown more are more often. How does one model such situations? Example 4.9 will explain this.

234

## Example 4.9

The 0–6 sex-ratio refers to the number of girls to the number of boys in the age group 0–6. Recently, this ratio has been falling, causing justified alarm all over the country. Suppose we wish to examine how the 0–6 sex-ratio across Indian states is related to the percentage of population below the poverty line across states. Do poorer states also have a worse sex-ratio at birth? We have data for the 0–6 sex-ratio from the Census of 2001. We also have got estimates for the percentage of population below the poverty line for the year 1999–2000. The data are given in Table 4.7.

**Table 4.7**
**The 0–6 sex ratio from the Census of 2001 and the estimates of the percentage population below the poverty line for the year 1999–2000**

| State | % below Poverty Line | 0-6 Sex Ratio | State | % below Poverty Line | 0-6 Sex Ratio |
|---|---|---|---|---|---|
| Jammu & Kashmir | 3.48 | 941 | Andaman and Nicobar Islands | 20.99 | 957 |
| Goa | 4.4 | 938 | Maharashtra | 25.02 | 913 |
| Chandigarh | 5.75 | 845 | West Bengal | 27.02 | 960 |
| Punjab | 6.16 | 798 | Manipur | 28.54 | 957 |
| Himachal Pradesh | 7.63 | 896 | Uttar Pradesh | 31.15 | 916 |
| Delhi | 8.23 | 868 | Nagaland | 32.67 | 964 |
| Haryana | 8.74 | 819 | Arunachal Pradesh | 33.47 | 964 |
| Kerala | 12.72 | 960 | Meghalaya | 33.87 | 973 |
| Gujarat | 14.07 | 883 | Tripura | 34.44 | 966 |
| Rajasthan | 15.28 | 909 | Assam | 36.09 | 965 |
| Lakshadweep | 15.6 | 959 | Sikkim | 36.55 | 963 |
| Andhra Pradesh | 15.77 | 961 | Madhya Pradesh | 37.43 | 932 |
| Dadra and Nagar Haveli | 17.14 | 979 | Bihar | 42.6 | 942 |
| Mizoram | 19.47 | 964 | Orissa | 47.15 | 953 |
| Karnataka | 20.04 | 946 | | | |

Let us set up a linear approximation as follows:

$$SR = a + b \times BPL$$

where $SR_i$ is the sex-ratio in state $i$, and $BPL_i$ is the percentage of population that is below the poverty level in state $i$.

Let us plot the scatter of sex ratio against the population below poverty line. This is done in Figure 4.9.

**Figure 4.9**
**Scatter plot of sex-ratio at birth versus percentage of population below the poverty line**

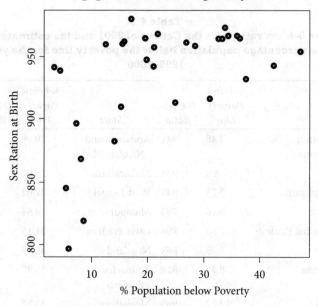

As we can see from the figure, the sex-ratio at birth is increasing with the population below the poverty line. This means that on an average, relatively poorer states do actually have a relatively better sex-ratio! There is another thing that we should note from the model: Sex-ratio at birth is not linearly related to the percentage of population below poverty line. As the percentage below poverty line starts to move up, the sex-ratio initially increases a lot, but at higher values of the population below poverty line, the increase in the sex-ratio is relatively smaller. That is, the rate of increase of the sex-ratio at birth per unit increase in the population below poverty line is dependent upon the level of the percentage of population below poverty line. If this level is small, the increase in sex-ratio is large, but if the level of population below poverty line is large, the increase in sex-ratio is small. Clearly, we cannot represent the scatter by a linear approximation. However, all is not lost. Let us posit a model of how the sex ratio changes with the level of population below poverty line. Suppose we posit the following model:

$$SR = A \times BPL^{\alpha}, 0 < \alpha < 1 \qquad \text{Equation 4.16}$$

Let us see how SR changes with *BPL*. We have:

$$dSR / dBPL = \alpha ABPL^{\alpha-1} = \alpha A / BPL^{1-\alpha} \qquad \text{Equation 4.17}$$

Equation 4.17 says that the rate of change of sex-ratio (SR) with respect to below the poverty line (BPL), given by $dSR / dBPL$ depends upon the value of BPL. Since BPL is in the denominator and its exponent $1 - \alpha$ is positive, as BPL increases, $dSR / dBPL$ must fall.[11] Thus, we can think of Equation 4.16 as a non-linear model for SR. How do we convert this non-linear model into a linear one? Ultimately, we want to fit a linear approximation. The non-linear model 4.15 can be converted into a linear one by taking natural logarithms of both the sides, which gives:

$$\ln(SR) = \ln(A) + \alpha \times \ln(BPL) + \varepsilon i \qquad \text{Equation 4.18}$$

where ln(SR) is the natural logarithm of SR, ln(BPL) is natural logarithm of BPL and ln(A) is the natural logarithm of A. This gives us the following sample regression function:

$$SR^*_i = a + b \times BPL^*_i + \varepsilon_i \qquad \text{Equation 4.19}$$

where $SR^*_i - \ln(SR_i)$, $BPL^*_i, = \ln(BPL_i)$ and $a = \ln(A)$. We now have a linear approximation but with the original variables expressed in terms of their natural logarithms. We plot the scatter diagram of log(SR) and log(BPL) in Figure 4.10.

**Figure 4.10**
**Scatter plot of log(*SR*) and log(*BPL*)**

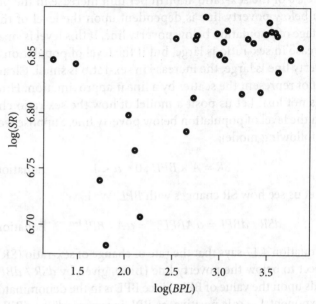

Figure 4.10 is much more amenable to fitting a linear approximation, compared to Figure 4.9. We can now proceed to carry out regression as usual, with the independent variable being the values of the natural logarithm of the percentage of population below the poverty line in each state, the dependent variable being the natural logarithm of the value of the sex-ratio in each state. You can then apply the usual formulae for estimating *a* and *b*, except that the data that you will use will be the natural logarithms of the original data. Let us use R to carry out the calculations through the following program:

```
d<-read.table("c:\\bplsr.txt",header=TRUE,sep="")
##command reads the data##
attach(d)
lbpl=log(BPL) ## takes natural logarithm of BPL##
lsr=log(SR) ## takes natural logarithm of SR##
summary(lm(lsr~lbpl)) ## fits a linear approximation with
lsr as dependent variable and lbpl as the
```

independent variable and prints out the summary re-
sults##

If you run this programme, you get the following output:
Call:
lm(formula = lsr ~ lbpl)
Residuals:

| Min | 1Q | Median | 3Q | Max |
|---|---|---|---|---|
| -0.108841 | -0.027009 | 0.008272 | 0.025741 | 0.080047 |

Coefficients:

| | Estimate | Std. Error | t value | Pr(>\|t\|) |
|---|---|---|---|---|
| (Intercept) | 6.71437 | 0.03312 | 202.737 | < 2e-16 *** |
| lbpl | 0.04212 | 0.01112 | 3.787 | 0.00071 *** |

Signif. codes: 0 '***' 0.001 '**' 0.01 '*' 0.05 '.' 0.1 ' ' 1
Residual standard error: 0.04292 on 29 degrees of freedom
Multiple R-squared: 0.3309, Adjusted R-squared: 0.3079
F-statistic: 14.34 on 1 and 29 DF, p-value: 0.0007103

The estimated value of $a$, $a^\wedge$ equals 6.71437 (given here as the 'intercept') while the estimated value of $b$, $b^\wedge$ equals 0.04212, given against *lbpl*. Since $b^\wedge$ is really the estimated value of the elasticity of the sex-ratio at birth with respect to the per cent population below the poverty line, the result says that the sex-ratio goes up by 4.21 percentage points for states as the per cent below poverty line increases by 1 per cent. The standard errors of $a^\wedge$ and $b^\wedge$ turn out to be 0.03312 and 0.0112. As we have seen above, these measure the precision of the estimates of $a^\wedge$ and $b^\wedge$, respectively. The $t$-values for $a^\wedge$ and $b^\wedge$ are 202.737 and 3.787 respectively. If we attempt to test the null $H_o$: $E(b^\wedge) = 0$ against the alternative $H_A$: $E(b^\wedge) \neq 0$, the null can be safely rejected since the size of the critical region is 0.00071, which is quite small. The value of the R-square is 0.3309, implying that 33 per cent of the variability in the sex-ratio is explained by the model. We will have the opportunity to meet the remaining statistics, that is, Adjusted R-squared, F-statistic in the fifth chapter where we study the multiple regression model. The output under the heading Residuals: gives the minimum value, the 1st quartile (the value of $X$ such that 25 per cent of the area of the distribution is to the left of $X$), the median, the 3rd quartile (value of $X$ such that 75 per cent of the area under the distribution is to the left of $X$) and the maximum value of the estimated $e_i^{\wedge}$. In the next graph in Figure 4.11, we show the scatter as well as the estimated linear approximation:

**Figure 4.11**
**Scatter plot of log($SR$) and log($BPL$) and the linear approximation**

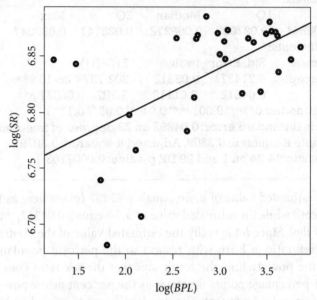

The line is the linear approximation. As you can see, it seems to describe the data reasonably well, though perhaps not as well as we would like.

### 4.5.2 Semi Log Regression

Sometimes, regression models are estimated where only the logarithm of the dependent variable is taken, but not of the independent variable. Such models are particularly useful for modelling variables that grow at a fixed per cent per unit of time. Let $Y_t$ be the value of $Y$ at time period $t$. Suppose $Y$ grows exponentially in time at the rate $\beta$ per unit of time. Then, we can posit the following model for $Y_t$:

$$Y_t = Y_0 e^{\beta t}$$

where $Y_0$ is the initial value of $Y$ and $e$ stands for the exponential function. This is a non-linear model. But we can linearise this by taking the natural logarithm of $Y$:

$$\ln(Y_t) = \ln(Y_0) + \beta t \text{ where } t = 1........T \qquad \text{Equation 4.20}$$

which is now a linear relationship with $\ln(Y_t)$ as the dependent variable and $t$ as the independent variable. Let us understand what $\beta$ signifies. Let us take the derivative of $\ln(Y_t)$ with respect to $t$.

$$\beta = \partial \ln(Y_t) / \partial t = (1 / Y_t)(\partial Y_t / \partial t) \qquad \text{Equation 4.21}$$

Let us look carefully at the term on the right hand side. This term is in the nature of $(\Delta Y_t / Y_t) / \Delta t$, the percentage change in $Y$ per unit of time. It is the proportionate change in $Y$ per unit change in time. $\beta$ multiplied by 100 gives percentage change in $Y$ per unit of time, the compound annual growth rate (CAGR). Equation 4.20 can be used to estimate the CAGR for any given time series.

### Example 4.10

Let us take an example. Table 4.8 gives the values of India's gross domestic product (GDP) at factor cost at constant prices with base 1999–2000 equal to100 (in Rs crore) from 1950–51 to 2007–08.

We will plot the data in the graph in Figure 4.12. As you can see from the graph, GDP at factor cost increases exponentially in

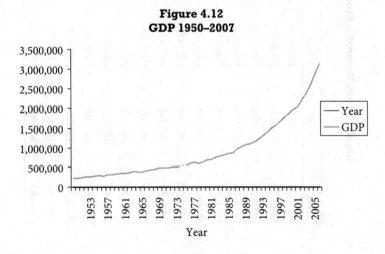

**Figure 4.12**
**GDP 1950–2007**

**Table 4.8**

**India's Gross Domestic Product (GDP in Rs Crores) at factor cost at constant prices from 1950–51 to 2007–08**

| Year | GDP | Year | GDP | Year | GDP | Year | GDP |
|------|-----|------|-----|------|-----|------|-----|
| 1950–51 | 224,786 | 1965–66 | 378,157 | 1980–81 | 641,921 | 1995–96 | 1,396,974 |
| 1951–52 | 230,034 | 1966–67 | 382,006 | 1981–82 | 678,033 | 1996–97 | 1,508,378 |
| 1952–53 | 236,562 | 1967–68 | 413,094 | 1982–83 | 697,861 | 1997–98 | 1,573,263 |
| 1953–54 | 250,960 | 1968–69 | 423,874 | 1983–84 | 752,669 | 1998–99 | 1,678,410 |
| 1954–55 | 261,615 | 1969–70 | 451,496 | 1984–85 | 782,484 | 1999–00 | 1,786,525 |
| 1955–56 | 268,316 | 1970–71 | 474,131 | 1985–86 | 815,049 | 2000–01 | 1,864,300 |
| 1956–57 | 283,589 | 1971–72 | 478,918 | 1986–87 | 850,217 | 2001–02 | 1,972,606 |
| 1957–58 | 280,160 | 1972–73 | 477,392 | 1987–88 | 880,267 | 2002–03 | 2,048,287 |
| 1958–59 | 301,422 | 1973–74 | 499,120 | 1988–89 | 969702 | 2003–04 | 2,222,758 |
| 1959–60 | 308,018 | 1974–75 | 504,914 | 1989–90 | 1,029,178 | 2004–05 | 2,388,384 |
| 1960–61 | 329,825 | 1975–76 | 550,379 | 1990–91 | 1,083,572 | 2005–06 | 2,612,847 |
| 1961–62 | 340,060 | 1976–77 | 557,258 | 1991–92 | 1,099,072 | 2006–07 | 2,864,310 |
| 1962–63 | 347,253 | 1977–78 | 598,885 | 1992–93 | 1,158,025 | 2007–08 | 3,122,862 |
| 1963–64 | 364,834 | 1978–79 | 631,839 | 1993–94 | 1,223,816 | – | – |
| 1964–65 | 392,503 | 1979–80 | 598,974 | 1994–95 | 1,302,076 | – | – |

time, and hence our model Equation 4.20 seems to be appropriate for describing GDP.

The R program given below will calculate the values of $\beta^\wedge$ and $\ln(Y_0)$:

```
d<-read.table("c:\\GDP.txt",header=TRUE,sep="")
attach(d)
t1=seq(1:58)
summary(lm(log(GDP)~t1))
```

The first line reads the data from the file GDP.txt that is saved in c:\. The second line separated out the variables in the file into separate columns. Since there are 58 observations, $t$ should go from 1 to 58. The third line generates a variable $t1$ taking values from 1 to 58. The last line does a linear regression of $\ln(GDP)$ on time and provides the summary. The summary is presented below:

```
Call:
lm(formula = log(GDP) ~ t1)
Residuals:
```

| Min | 1Q | Median | 3Q | Max |
|---|---|---|---|---|
| -0.16238 | -0.07473 | -0.01007 | 0.06805 | 0.26860 |

Coefficients:

| | Estimate | Std. Error | t value | Pr(>\|t\|) | |
|---|---|---|---|---|---|
| (Intercept) | 12.16 | 0.02.573 | 472.44 | <2e-16 | *** |
| t1 | 0.04358 | 0.0007587 | 57.44 | <2e-16 | *** |

```
---
Signif. codes: 0 '***' 0.001 '**' 0.01 '*' 0.05 '.' 0.1 ' ' 1
Residual standard error: 0.09673 on 56 degrees of freedom
Multiple R-squared: 0.9833, Adjusted R-squared: 0.983
F-statistic: 3300 on 1 and 56 DF, p-value: < 2.2e-16
```

As usual, the first line gives the minimum, the first quartile, the median, the third quartile and the maximum value of the estimated residuals. The value of the intercept $(\ln(Y_0))$ turns out to be 12.16, while the estimated value of $\beta$ can be seen to be 0.04358. This means that over the period 1950–51 to 2007–08, GDP at factor cost has been growing at an estimated compound annual rate (CAGR) of 4.358 per cent. The R-square of the regression is 0.9833, indicating a good fit.[12] We can see the fit and the actual data in Figure 4.13:

**Figure 4.13**
**Fitted and actual values of log(GDP) against time**

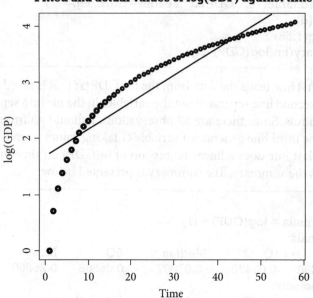

The dots are the actual values of log(GDP), while the solid line shows the estimated values of log(GDP). The estimated slope of this linear approximation, $\beta^{\wedge}$ gives the compound annual growth rate for GDP. In spite of the high R-square of the regression, you should be able to detect an obvious problem. Up to the first 20 years or so, the slope of the solid line is flatter than the slope of the dotted line. This means that during that period, the estimated CAGR is actually an underestimate of the real CAGR. Similarly, at observations roughly beyond the twentieth, the slope of the dotted line is flatter than the slope of the solid line. Thus, after that point, the estimated CAGR actually overestimates the actual CAGR. At the extremes of the dotted line, this under and over estimation is quite substantial.[13] Fortunately, we can deal with this by extending Equation 4.20 by rewriting it as follows:

$$\ln(Y_t) = \alpha + \beta t + \delta t^2 + e_t \qquad \text{Equation 4.22}$$

The difference between 4.19 and 4.21 is the existence of the term $\delta t^2$ in Equation 4.22. To understand Equation 4.22, let us examine the derivative of $\ln(Y_t)$ with respect to $t$:

$$\partial \ln(Y_t) / \partial t = (1 / Y_t) \times \partial Y_t / \partial t = \beta + 2\delta t$$

This equation implies that the direction as well as the magnitude of the per cent change $Y$ per unit change in time will depend not only on $\beta$ (as in 4.19) but also on $\delta$ as well as $t$. Suppose $\beta > 0$ and $\delta < 0$. For small values of $t$, $\partial \ln(Y_t) / \partial t$ will be positive while larger values of $t$, $\partial \ln(Y_t) / \partial t$ will be negative. Thus, the compound annual growth rate will be different at different points of time. On the other hand, the formulation in Equation 4.20 forces the compound annual growth rate to be fixed at all points in time. This will enable us to model the slow flattening out of the dotted line in Figure 4.13. Figure 4.14 demonstrates this.

**Figure 4.14**
**Fitted and actual values of log(GDP) using $t$ and $t^2$**

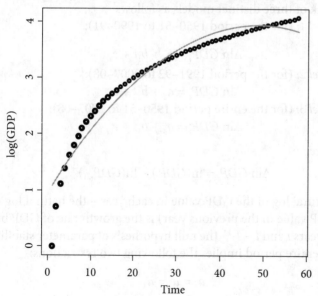

You will agree that the slope of the solid line in this figure is a better approximation to the slope of the dotted line, compared to the slope of the solid line in Figure 4.13. When we approximate the data by the formulation in Equation 4.20, we are fitting a 'linear trend' to $\ln(Y_t)$. On the other hand, when we do so using the formulation in Equation 4.22, we are fitting a 'quadratic trend' to $\ln(Y_t)$. When we come to Chapter 6 on multiple linear regressions, we will learn more about the mechanics of fitting models like those in 4.21, where $Y$ depends upon more than one explanatory variable.

### 4.5.3 Testing for Structural Change: The Chow Test

Sometimes, it might be relevant to ask if the parameters of the estimated model are stable throughout the sample period. For example, we know that 1990–91 was a significant year for the Indian economy, in that a programme of economic reforms was launched during this year. We might be interested in seeing the parameters of the equation describing economic growth as a function of time are stable for the entire period from 1950–51 to 2007–08 or undergo a change after 1990–91. In terms of the econometric model, we think of three distinct models as follows:

*Model 1:* (for the period 1950–51 to 1990–91):

$$\Delta\ln GDP_t = a_1 + b_1 t + e_{1t}$$

*Model 2:* (for the period 1991–92 to 2007–08):

$$\Delta\ln GDP_t = a_2 + b_2 t + e_{2t}$$

*Model 3:* (for the entire period 1950–51 to 2007–08):

$$\Delta\ln GDP_t = a_3 + b_3 t + e_{2t}$$

where:

$$\Delta\ln GDP_t = \ln(GDP_t) - \ln(GDP_{t-1})$$

(the natural log of the GDP value in each year – the natural log of the GDP value in the previous year) is the growth rate of GDP between years $t$ and $t-1$.[14] The null hypothesis of parameter stability for the entire period implies the following two restrictions:

$$a_1 = a_2 = a_3$$

and:

$$b_1 = b_2 = b_3$$

We can test these restrictions as follows:

**Step 1:** Estimate Model 1 for observations 1 to $n_1 = 1990$–91 and obtain the estimated residual sum of squares as below:

$$RSS_1 = \sum_{i=1}^{n_1} (Y_i - \hat{a}_1 - \hat{b}_1 X_i)^2 = \sum_{i=1}^{n_1} e_{1i}^{\wedge 2}$$

**Step 2:** Estimate Model 2 for observations $n_1 + 1$ to $T$ ($T = 2007$–08) and obtain the estimated residual sum of squares as follows:

$$RSS_2 = \sum_{i=n_1+1}^{T} (Y_i - \hat{a}_2 - \hat{b}_2 X_i)^2 = \sum_{i=n_1+1}^{T} e_{2i}^{\wedge 2}$$

**Step 3:** Estimate Model 3 for observations 1 to $T$ and obtain the estimated residual sum of squares as follows:

$$RSS_3 = \sum_{i=1}^{T} (Y_i - \hat{a}_3 - \hat{b}_3 X_i)^2 = \sum_{i=1}^{T} e_{3i}^{\wedge 2}$$

We will refer to $RSS_3$ as the restricted residual sum of squares ($RSS_R$), while we will refer to:

$$RSS_1 + RSS_2 = RSS_{UR}$$

as the unrestricted residual sum of squares. Under the null hypothesis, the sum of the squared errors in the two individual sub-periods should not be significantly different from the sum of squared errors for the entire period. On the other hand, the parameters are not stable across the two sub-periods the sum of squared errors in the two individual periods will differ substantially from the sum for the entire period with $RSS_{UR}$ being substantially smaller than $RSS_R$. If the parameters of the regression are different across the two sub-periods, we would get a lower residual sum of squares for the entire period by fitting separate regressions to each of the two periods, as compared to fitting one regression for the entire period. On the other hand, if there is no significant parameter change over the two sub-periods, then the sum of the *RSS* for the

247

two sub-periods—when we fit different regressions—will not differ significantly from the RSS obtained if we fit just one regression to the entire period. In effect, we are testing that the variance of the estimated errors is the same across the two sub periods, against the alternative that is not. Let $\sigma^2_{e1}$ be the population variance of the error term in the first sub-period and let $\sigma^2_{e2}$ be the population variance of the error term in the second sub-period. Let the hypothetical common variance be equal to $\sigma^2_e$. We can specify the null and the alternative hypothesis as:

$$H_o : \sigma^2_{e1} = \sigma^2_{e2} = \sigma^2_e$$
$$H_A : \sigma^2_{e1} \neq \sigma^2_{e2}$$

$RSS_1 / (n_1 - 2)$ is the unbiased estimator of the variance of the error term in the first sub-period and $RSS_2 / (T - n_1 - 2)$ is an unbiased estimator of the variance of the error term in the second sub-period and $RSS_3 / (T - 2)$ is the unbiased estimator of the variance of the error term in the entire period. Under the null hypothesis of the true variance of the error term being the same in both sub-periods:

$$(RSS_1 / \sigma^2_e) \times (n_1 - 2), (RSS_2 / \sigma^2_e) \times (T - n_1 - 2)$$

and:

$$(RSS_3 / \sigma^2_e) \times (T - 2)$$

are $\chi^2(n_1 - 2)$, $\chi^2(T - n_1 - 2)$ and $\chi^2(T - 2)$ and variables (Theorem 3.2 of Chapter 3).

We must now design a method to test the null against the above alternative. As a first step towards checking this, we form $(RSS_R - RSS_{UR})/\sigma^2_e$ which is a $\chi^2(2)$ variable. We would like to see if this difference is large relative to the value of $RSS_{UR}$. To this effect, we form the ratio:

$$\{(RSS_R - RSS_{UR}) / 2\} / \{RSS_{UR} / (T - 4)\} \tag{R1}$$

The numerator of this ratio has $\chi^2(2)$ variable divided by its degrees of freedom, while the numerator has a $\chi^2(T - 4)$ variable divided by its degrees of freedom. If we are assuming that the two relevant $\chi^2$ variables are independent, under the null hypothesis, the ratio R1 follows the *F* distribution with two and *T*– 4 degrees of freedom. Suppose we decide to use a critical region of size 5 per cent to evaluate the null. Then, we reject the null of parameter stability if the calculated value of R1 falls in the critical region. Otherwise, we fail to reject the null hypothesis. Remember that this is a one-tailed test, with the critical region being the 5 per cent region to the left of the distribution. We now proceed to test this hypothesis for our data.

The following R program will do the job:

```
ff<-read.table("c:\\gdp1.txt",header=TRUE,sep="")## 
reads the data
attach(ff)
gdp=ts(GDP) ## defines GDP as an object of time series 
class
dgdp=lag(log(gdp))-log(gdp)## generates the first differ-
ence of log(gdp)
##model 1
dgdp1=dgdp[1:40]## takes values of gdp from 1to 40¹⁵
t1=seq(1,40)
summary(lm(dgdp1~t1))
e1=residuals(lm(dgdp1~t1))
RSS1=sum(e1^2)
##model 2
dgdp2=dgdp[41:57]
t2=seq(1,17)
summary(lm(dgdp2~t2))
e2=residuals(lm(dgdp2~t2))
RSS2=sum(e2^2)
RSSUR=RSS1+RSS2
##model 3
t3=seq(1:57)
summary(lm(dgdp~t3))
e3=residuals(lm(dgdp~t3))
RSSR=sum(e3^2)
F=((RSSR-RSSUR)/2)/(RSSUR/(57-4))
F
qf(0.95,2,53)
```

This program yields the following output:

```
Call:
lm(formula = dgdp1 ~ t1)
Residuals:
  Min        1Q        Median     3Q        Max
  -0.09667   -0.01292   0.00019    0.02476   0.04935
Coefficients:
            Estimate    Std. Error   t value   Pr(>|t|)
(Intercept) 0.0298452   0.0102563    2.91 0.00601 **
t1          0.0004623   0.0004359    1.06 0.29566
—
Signif. codes: 0 '***' 0.001 '**' 0.01 '*' 0.05 '.' 0.1 ' ' 1
Residual standard error: 0.03183 on 38 degrees of freedom
Multiple R-squared: 0.02874, Adjusted R-squared: 0.00318
F-statistic: 1.124 on 1 and 38 DF, p-value: 0.2957
Call:
lm(formula = dgdp2 ~ t2)
Residuals:
  Min        1Q         Median     3Q        Max
  -0.032314  -0.010926   0.004997   0.011660  0.022161
Coefficients:
            Estimate    Std. Error   t value   Pr(>|t|)
(Intercept) 0.0391685   0.0084654    4.627 0.000329 ***
t2          0.0025662   0.0008261    3.106 0.007225 **
—
Signif. codes: 0 '***' 0.001 '**' 0.01 '*' 0.05 '.' 0.1 ' ' 1
Residual standard error: 0.01669 on 15 degrees of freedom
Multiple R-squared: 0.3914, Adjusted R-squared: 0.3509
F-statistic: 9.648 on 1 and 15 DF, p-value: 0.007225
Call:
lm(formula = dgdp ~ t3)
Residuals:
  Min        1Q         Median     3Q        Max
  -0.099581  -0.012769   0.001614   0.019730  0.044001
Coefficients:
            Estimate    Std. Error   t value   Pr(>|t|)
(Intercept) 0.0249024   0.0076338    3.262 0.00190 **
t3          0.0007332   0.0002290    3.202 0.00227 **
```

```
Signif. codes: 0 '***' 0.001 '**' 0.01 '*' 0.05 '.' 0.1 ' ' 1
Residual standard error: 0.02844 on 55 degrees of freedom
Multiple R-squared: 0.1571, Adjusted R-squared: 0.1418
F-statistic: 10.25 on 1 and 55 DF, p-value: 0.002268
> F
[1] 1.125329
> qf(0.95,2,53)
[1] 3.171626
>
```

As can be seen from the output, the calculated $f$ value which equals 1.125329 is less than the 5 per cent critical value, 3.171626. Therefore, we cannot reject the null hypothesis of no structural change. If we do choose to still reject it, what is the maximum probability of type I error? That can be obtained by calculating the area of the $F$ distribution to the left of 1.125329. This can be calculated as follows:

```
1-pf(1.125329,12,53)
```

which generates the value 0.36. Thus, the chance that we wrongly reject the null is quite high.

For this test to be valid, we require that the error terms in each sub-period be statistically independent within that sub-period. Unless that is true, $(RSS_{UR} / \sigma_e^2)(n_1 - 2)$, $(RSS_R / \sigma_e^2)(T - n_1 - 2)$ are not $\chi^2$ variables, since by definition, $\chi^2(n)$ is the sum of $n$ independent standard normal variables. This also applies to the next general application of the $F$ test that we discuss below.

The $F$ distribution is generally very important in the regression context. It can be used to evaluate tests on regression parameters. As an example, consider the following regression model:

$$Y_i = a + bX_i + e_i$$

Suppose we want to test the restriction $b = 0$ (of course you can also do this using the usual $t$ test). We can use the $F$ distribution to develop the test as follows:

**Step 1:** Estimate the model $Y_i = a + bX_i + e_{1i}$ and obtain the unrestricted residual sum of squares:

$$RSS_{UR} = \sum_{i=1}^{n} e_1^{\wedge 2} = \sum_{i=1}^{n} (Y_i - a^{\wedge} - b^{\wedge} X_i)^2$$

Note that $RSS_{UR}$ is a $\chi^2(n-2)$ variable.

**Step 2:** Estimate the model $Y_i = a + e_{2i}$ (imposing the restriction $b = 0$)and obtain the restricted sum of squares:

$$RSS_R = \sum_{i=1}^{n} (Y_i - a^{\wedge})^2$$

**Step 3:** If the restriction $b = 0$ is correct, the restricted sum of squares should not differ significantly from the unrestricted. However, if the restriction is not correct, then the unrestricted sum of squares must be significantly smaller than the restricted sum of squares. As usual, the null hypothesis is that the true population variance of the error term is the same for both the models against the alternative that it is larger for the restricted model compared to the unrestricted model. Let us refer to the hypothetical common variance as $\sigma_e^2$. We then proceed exactly in the same way as we did for the chow test. We form the ratio R2, which is:

$$(RSS_R - RSS_{UR}) / 1 / (RSS_{UR} / (n-2)) \qquad \text{R2}$$

The numerator in R2 is the difference between the restricted and unrestricted sum of squares, which, under the null hypothesis of identical variances, $\chi^2(1)$ is a variable,[16] divided by its degrees of freedom, 1, while the denominator is a $\chi^2(n-2)$ variable divided by its degrees of freedom. Therefore, under the null hypothesis that variance of the error term is the same in both the models, R2 follows the $F$ distribution with $(1, (n-2))$ degrees of freedom. As an example, consider the following regression output:

```
Call:
lm(formula = Y ~ X)
Residuals:
  Min       1Q        Median    3Q        Max
  -2.07943  -0.61830  -0.08883  0.58956   1.99548
Coefficients:
            Estimate   Std. Error   t value   Pr(>|t|)
(Intercept) 2.84471    0.08835      32.199    <2e-16 ***
X           -0.04150   0.09179      -0.452    0.652
—

Signif. codes: 0 '***' 0.001 '**' 0.01 '*' 0.05 '.' 0.1 ' ' 1
Residual standard error: 0.8824 on 98 degrees of freedom
Multiple  R-squared:  0.002081,  Adjusted  R-squared:
-0.008102
F-statistic: 0.2044 on 1 and 98 DF, p-value: 0.6522
```

We want to test the null hypothesis $\beta = 0$ against the alternative $\beta \neq 0$. The relevant test statistic is the $F$ statistic given in the bottom line of the output. The calculated $F$ statistic is distributed with 1 and 98 (in general, $n - 2$) degrees of freedom. The size of the critical region is 0.6522, and hence rejecting the null is not warranted. Therefore, we fail to reject the null $\beta = 0$.

### 4.5.4 Categorical Independent Variables or Dummy Variables

Sometimes, the independent variable is categorical[17] and not a variable which can take any values in a continuum. For example, you might be interested in asking whether average marks scored by girls are different from the average marks scored by boys for the 10th standard examination. Suppose you collect data on marks obtained by a randomly chosen set of 100 students and their genders. You would want to estimate the following regression:

$$M_i = \alpha + \beta d_i + e_i \qquad \text{Equation 4.23}$$

where $M_i$ refers to the marks obtained by the $i$th individual, $d_i$ stands for the gender of the individual and $e_i$ is the usual error term assumed to be normally distributed with mean equal to zero and a constant variance. The variable $d$ can only take two values, male or female. Suppose we let $d_i = 1$ if the $i$th individual is a male and $d_i = 0$ if the $i$th individual is a female. We will refer to $d$ as a 'dummy variable', because it acts as a quantifiable dummy for the variable gender that we cannot really quantify. This formulation gives us an empirical strategy to distinguish between the average marks for a male and average marks for a female. We have:

$$E(M) = \alpha + \beta E(d) \qquad \text{Equation 4.24}$$

For males, $d_i = 1$ and hence:
$E(M) = \alpha + \beta$ or the conditional mean of $M$, conditional on $d_i = 1$
$$\text{Equation 4.25}$$
While for females, $d_i = 0$ and hence:
$E(M) = \alpha$, or the conditional mean of $M$, conditional on $d_i = 0$
$$\text{Equation 4.26}$$

Hence, if $\beta > 0$, the mean marks for males are greater than for females. In general, this is a test whether the conditional mean for males is statistically significantly different from the conditional mean for females. If $\beta < 0$, then mean marks for females are greater than the mean marks for males. If $\beta = 0$, then there is no difference between the mean marks for males and females. Testing for $\beta = 0$ is equivalent to testing whether the means are different for boys as well as girls.

This enables us to set up a test of hypothesis: The null hypothesis that there is no significant difference between the mean marks for males and females is equivalent to testing the null hypothesis that $\beta^\wedge = 0$.

This introduces a matter of no small practical importance. An equivalent way to test for mean differences is to think of not one dummy variable, but two dummy variables $d_{1i}$ and $d_{2i}$ where $d_{1i} = 1$ if the $i$th person is a male and zero otherwise, while $d_{2i} = 1$ if the $i$th person is a female and zero otherwise.

The model then becomes:

$$M_i = \delta_1 d_{1i} + \delta_2 d_{2i} + e_i \qquad \text{Equation 4.27}$$

For males, we have:

$E(M) = \delta_1$, or the conditional mean of $M$, conditional on $d_1 = 1$

While for females, we have:

$E(M) = \delta_2$, or the conditional mean of $M$, conditional on $d_2 = 1$

Notice that Equation 4.27 does not have any intercept term unlike Equation 4.26. That is because, $\alpha$ in the case of Equation 4.26, measures the average marks scored by females, while $\alpha + \beta$ measures the average marks scored by males. On the other, in Equation 4.27, the average marks scored by females is $\delta_2$ while average marks scored by males are given by $\delta_1$. If we have an additional $\alpha$ in the model, it is not clear what it measures. We will have the following model:

$$M_i = \alpha + \delta_1 d_{1i} + \delta_2 d_{2i} + e_i \qquad \text{Equation 4.28}$$

The average education for males, according to Equation 4.28:

$$E(M) = \alpha + \delta_1$$

While that for females:

$$E(M) = \alpha + \delta_2$$

In any case, since $\alpha$ is there in both the cases, it does not help us distinguish between the two. Further, since we do not know what $\alpha$ measures, we cannot be sure what $E(M)$ is in both the cases. Thus, inclusion of an $\alpha$ in Equation 4.28 would create an 'identification' problem. Therefore, if we are going to include both $d_1$ and $d_2$ in Equation 4.28, we should not include an additional constant in the regression. However, if our regression equation has just one of the $d_1$ and $d_2$, we can measure the effect of the omitted category through the constant.

We can illustrate this better by taking a concrete (but entirely hypothetical) example. Suppose we want to examine whether boys perform better than girls on a musical test. So, we assemble a group of 10 boys and seven girls and administer the test. Here are the marks scored by each student (out of a maximum of 10) along with that student's gender (see Table 4.9).

## Table 4.9
## The scores of the students and their genders

| Student No. | Score | Gender (M for Male, F for Female) | Student No. | Score | Gender (M for Male and F for Female) |
|---|---|---|---|---|---|
| 1 | 6 | M | 10 | 3 | M |
| 2 | 4 | M | 11 | 2 | M |
| 3 | 7 | F | 12 | 7 | F |
| 4 | 8 | M | 13 | 6 | M |
| 5 | 7 | M | 14 | 8 | F |
| 6 | 6 | F | 15 | 4 | M |
| 7 | 2 | F | 16 | 5 | F |
| 8 | 4 | F | 17 | 5 | M |
| 9 | 7 | M | – | – | – |

Since gender is a categorical variable, we will introduce a dummy variable for gender, where the dummy variable $d_1 = 1$ if the student is a boy and $d_1 = 0$ if the student is a girl; similarly $d_2 = 0$ if the student is a boy and $d_2 = 1$ if the student is a girl. Table 4.9 can now be rewritten as (Table 4.10):

## Table 4.10
## The scores of the students and the associated value of the dummy variable gender

| Student No. | Score | $d_1$ | $d_2$ | Student No. | Score | $d_1$ | $d_2$ |
|---|---|---|---|---|---|---|---|
| 1 | 6 | 1 | 0 | 10 | 3 | 1 | 0 |
| 2 | 4 | 1 | 0 | 11 | 2 | 1 | 0 |
| 3 | 7 | 0 | 1 | 12 | 7 | 0 | 1 |
| 4 | 8 | 1 | 0 | 13 | 6 | 1 | 0 |
| 5 | 7 | 1 | 0 | 14 | 8 | 0 | 1 |
| 6 | 6 | 0 | 1 | 15 | 4 | 1 | 0 |
| 7 | 2 | 0 | 1 | 16 | 5 | 0 | 1 |
| 8 | 4 | 0 | 1 | 17 | 5 | 1 | 0 |
| 9 | 7 | 1 | 0 | – | – | – | – |

Since student number 1 is a male, we have given the value of $d_1$ for the first observation as 1, while the value of $d_2$ for this observation is zero. On the other hand, student number 3 is a female, we have $d_1 = 0$ and $d_2 = 1$ for this observation. Notice that $d_2 = 1 - d_1$. We will plot this in Figure 4.15.

**Figure 4.15**
**Score versus gender**

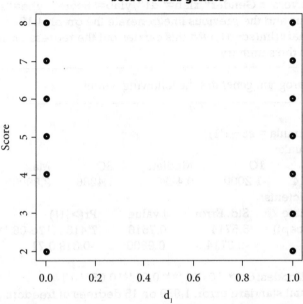

The scores for boys are plotted over $d_1 = 1$, while the scores for girls are plotted over $d_1 = 0$. We want to see whether the mean value of the numbers over $d_1 = 1$ is different from the mean of the numbers over $d_1 = 0$.

In order to test this, we first run the regression using Equation 4.23:

$$M_i = \alpha + \beta d_{1i} + e_i$$

We will set the null hypothesis that there is no significant difference between the average marks scored by girls and boys. As explained above, this translates into the restriction $\beta = 0$. We will now proceed to estimate this equation, using the following R commands:

```
sc<-c(6,4,7,8,7,6,2,4,7,3,2,7,6,8,4,5,5)  ## This command
reads the data on scores into a variable sc
d1<-c(1,1,0,1,1,0,0,0,1,1,1,0,1,0,1,0,1)  ## This generates
the dummy variable d1
d2=1-d1 ## This generates the dummy variable d2
par(bg="papayawhip",fg="purple1") ##
plot(d1,sc,type="p",col="red",lwd=6,main="Fig 4.13:
Score versus Gender",xlab="d1", ylab="Score",type="s")
## This and the previous line generate the graph 4.13
summary(lm(sc~d1)) ## this carries out the regression and
prints the summary
```

The program generates the following output:

```
Call:
lm(formula = sc ~ d1)
Residuals:
Min        1Q          Median      3Q        Max
-3.5714    -1.2000     0.4286      1.4286    2.8000
Coefficients:
Estimate     Std. Error    t value    Pr(>|t|)
(Intercept)  5.5714        0.7516      7.413 2.17e-06 ***
d1           -0.3714       0.9800      -0.379 0.71
—
Signif. codes: 0 '***' 0.001 '**' 0.01 '*' 0.05 '.' 0.1 ' ' 1
Residual standard error: 1.989 on 15 degrees of freedom
Multiple R-squared: 0.009486, Adjusted R-squared: -0.05655
F-statistic: 0.1437 on 1 and 15 DF, p-value: 0.71
```

The estimated regression has the value of $\beta^{\wedge}= -0.3714$. The estimated standard error is 0.9800, yielding a $t$ value equal to -0.379. The size of the critical region is rather large, being equal to 0.71. Hence, there is a large risk in rejecting the null since the probability of type I error is very large. Therefore, we cannot reject the null that there is no significant difference between the average marks scored by boys and girls. The estimated constant of the model is 5.5174. Thus, the conclusion we have is that the average marks scored by boys as well as girls are 5.5714.

## Exercise 4.5

Given below in Table 4.11 are series batting averages for the great Indian batsman, Sachin Tendulkar, for test match series played in India and abroad from 1988–89 to 2008–09. Examine if the average for the test series played abroad is different from the average for the test series played in India.

**Table 4.11**
**The batting averages of Sachin Tendulkar in test matches from 1989 to 2008–09 and the place of play**

| Series Average | Home/Away | Series Average | Home/Away |
|---|---|---|---|
| 35.83 | – | 181.00 | Home |
| 29.25 | – | 50.66 | Home |
| 61.25 | – | 66.83 | – |
| 11.00 | Home | 64.33 | – |
| 46 | – | 76.75 | Home |
| 0 | – | 84.66 | Home |
| 33.66 | – | 41.37 | – |
| 100.66 | Home | 66.83 | – |
| 62 | Home | 76.50 | Home |
| 101.5 | – | 25.00 | – |
| 54 | – | 17.75 | Home |
| 81.33 | Home | 76.60 | – |
| 67 | Home | 68.83 | – |
| 29 | Home | 17.50 | Home |
| 85.60 | Away | 27.50 | Home |
| 5 | Home | 284 | – |
| 27.66 | Home | 51 | Home |
| 40.16 | – | 37.80 | Home |
| 57.80 | – | 25 | – |
| 96.66 | – | 20.75 | – |
| 49.75 | Home | 33.16 | – |
| 111.50 | Home | 38 | Home |
| 20.50 | – | 127 | – |

*(Table 4.11 Contd.)*

*(Table 4.11 Contd.)*

| Series Average | Home/Away | Series Average | Home/Away |
|---|---|---|---|
| 75.66 | – | 69.50 | Home |
| 42.75 | Home | 70.42 | – |
| 108.75 | Home | 15.83 | – |
| 46.33 | – | 0 | Home |
| 36.50 | Home | 56.57 | Home |
| 18 | – | 52 | Home |

## 4.5.5 Regression Through the Origin

At times, the linear approximation that we envisage passes through the origin instead of having an intercept. That is, instead of having $Y = a + bX$, we think that a more suitable approximation might be given by $Y = bX$. Consider the scatter diagram in Figure 4.16.

From the scatter, it looks seems more appropriate to fit a linear approximation that passes through the origin, rather than one

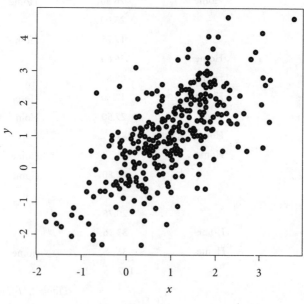

**Figure 4.16**
**Scatter of $Y$ against $X$**

that has a non-zero intercept. Now, the mechanics of the problem change. The sample regression function becomes:

$$Y_i = bX_i + e_i \qquad \text{Equation 4.29}$$

As a result:

$$\sum_{i=1}^{n} e_i^2 = \sum_{i=1}^{n} (Y_i - bX_i)^2 \qquad \text{Equation 4.30}$$

Differentiating this with respect to $b$, we have:

$$d\sum_{i=1}^{n} e_i^2 / db = -2X_i \sum_{i=1}^{n}(Y_i - bX_i) = 0 \qquad \text{Equation 4.31}$$

Therefore:

$$b^\wedge = \sum_{i=1}^{n} X_i Y_i / \sum_{i=1}^{n} X_i^2$$

The OLS estimator of $b$ when the linear approximation passes through the origin is different from the OLS estimator when the linear approximation has a non-zero intercept. However, one must be very careful while using the regression through origin. If the linear approximation has a non-zero intercept, and we attempt to fit an approximation without an intercept, the estimator of $b^\wedge$ will not be unbiased. If we indeed suspect that the linear approximation should pass through the origin, we should fit a linear approximation with a non-zero intercept and then test whether the estimated intercept, $a^\wedge$ is statistically significantly different from zero. Also, the conventional $R^2$ is not a valid measure of goodness of fit for regressions through the origin, as has been emphasised earlier. This is particularly important to remember since some computer packages that do regressions routinely report $R^2$ 'even for models that pass through the origin'. What we need is an alternate measure of goodness of fit for linear approximations passing through the origin. One such measure could be:

$$R_1^2 = \sum_{i=1}^{n} Y_i^{\wedge 2} / \sum_{i=1}^{n} Y_i^2$$

where $Y_t^\wedge = b^\wedge$, $X_i$ is the predicted value of $Y$. The closer the predicted values of $Y$ are to the actual values, higher will be the value of $R_i^2$. However, this value can exceed 1. An alternative measure that is sometimes used is:

$$R_2^2 = 1 - \sum_{i=1}^{n}(Y_i - Y_i^\wedge)^2 / \sum_{i=1}^{n} Y_i^2$$

The larger the gap between the actual and the predicted values of $Y$, the smaller $R_2^2$ will be.

It is worth reiterating that one must be careful to use the regression through the origin model only in cases where there is a compelling theoretical reason to do so.

### 4.5.6 Regression with Standardised Coefficients

There is one situation where the use of the regression through the origin model arises naturally. This is when the regression is done on standardised variables. Suppose $Y$ is variable with mean $\mu_y$ and variance $\sigma_y^2$. Then we can standardise $Y$ by subtracting $\mu_y$ from each value of $Y$ and dividing the resultant by $\sigma_y^2$. Let:

$$Y_y^* = (Y_i - \mu_y) / \sigma_y$$

We will call $Y_y^*$ the standardised value of $Y$. The advantage of standardizing $Y$ is that now, $Y$ is 'unit free' in that it is a deviation of $Y$ from its mean expressed in terms of the standard deviation of $Y$. Let us assume that instead of fitting the sample regression function:

$$Y_i^* = a + bX_i + e_i$$

We fit a function where instead of using $Y$ and $X$, we use their standardised values $Y^*$ and $X^*$. If we are using standardised variables, it is easy to see why the regression through the origin is the appropriate model. We carry out the following regression:

$$Y_i^* = bX_i^* + e_i$$

How do we interpret the coefficient $b$? $b$ measures the increase in standard deviation units that results from a one standard deviation increase in $X$. This coefficient is referred to as the 'beta coefficient'. The beta coefficients are particularly useful when we have more than one independent variable (we will look at such models in Chapter 7). In this case, the different independent variables will most surely be expressed in different units. The standardised regression model enables us to express all the coefficients in 'standard deviation units'. However, there is a caution that must be borne in mind: since this is a regression through the origin model, one must be careful in interpreting the $R^2$. This is particularly pertinent since some software routinely report the beta coefficients while also giving the usual $R^2$. Following is an example of regression on standardized variables:

```
X=c(2,4,5,4,5,7,5,6,8,6,7,4,5,8,7,5) ## This line reads in data on X
Y=c(5,3,6,8,3,6,8,5,4,5,7,2,4,8,7,5) ## This line reads in data on Y
X1=(X-mean(X))/sqrt(var(X))  ##This line creates standardised values of X
Y1=(Y-mean(Y))/sqrt(var(Y)) ## This line creates standardised values of Y
summary(lm(Y1~0+X1)) ## This line does a regression without an intercept
```

This program gives the following output:

```
Call:
lm(formula = Y1 ~ 0 + X1)
Residuals:
Min        1Q         Median      3Q         Max
-1.48576   -0.70986   -0.03302    0.56129    1.68386
Coefficients:
    Estimate    Std. Error    t valu      Pr(>|t|)
X1  0.3235      0.2443        1.324 0.205
Residual standard error: 0.9462 on 15 degrees of freedom
Multiple R-squared: 0.1047
```

## Exercise 4.6

Interpret the regression results above.

## 4.5.7 Prediction in the Two Variable Regression Model

After having estimated the regression coefficients, we have obtained an understanding of how the conditional mean of $Y$ given $X$ depends upon specific values of $X$. It is then natural to ask: What would be the value of the conditional mean of $Y$ given $X$, for a specific value of $X$, say $X_0$. This value may be one of those observed or might lie outside the set of values of $X$ that are observed. In the latter case, we may want to predict the value of $Y$, given the value of $X$. The prediction could be a point prediction or the prediction of an interval, within which the predicted value of $Y$ may lie with specified probability. For practical purposes, the prediction of just one point is not very useful, and we may want to also know how precise this prediction is, or the interval in which the actual values may end up lying, with some sense of the associated probability. To understand this better, suppose we have an estimated regression model:

$$Y_i = a^\wedge + b^\wedge X_i$$

From this, we have:

$$Y_0^\wedge = a^\wedge + b^\wedge X_0 = \overline{Y} - b^\wedge \overline{X} + b^\wedge X_0 = \overline{Y} - b^\wedge (X_0 - \overline{X})$$

The true value of $Y$ for $X = X_0$ is

$$Y_0 = a + bX_0 + e_0$$

averaging over $n$ sample observations, we have:

$$\overline{Y} = a + b\overline{X} + \overline{e}$$

So, we have:

$$Y_0 = \overline{Y} + b(X_0 - \overline{X}) + e_0 - \overline{e}$$

or:

$$Y_0 = \overline{Y} + b(X_0 - \overline{X}) + e_0 - \overline{e}$$

The estimated prediction error is:

$$e_o^\wedge = Y_o - Y_o^\wedge = -(b^\wedge - b)(X_o - \overline{X}) + e_o - \overline{e}$$

Let us examine some properties of the prediction error $e_o^\wedge$.

1. What is $E(e^\wedge)$?

$$E(e_o^\wedge) = -E((b^\wedge - b))(X_o - \overline{X}) + E(e_o) + E(\overline{e}) = 0$$

Since the expected value of the prediction error is zero, it is clear that $Y_o^\wedge$ is an unbiased estimator of $Y_o$.

2. What is the variance of the prediction error?

We have:

$$\text{Variance}(e_0^\wedge) = \sigma_e^2 \left( 1 + \frac{1}{n} + \frac{(X_o - \overline{X})^2}{\sum\limits_{i=1}^{n}(X_i - \overline{X})^2} \right)$$

**Exercise 4.7**
Prove the above statement.

3. What is the distribution of $e_o^\wedge$?

We know that $e_o^\wedge$ is a linear combination of three normally distributed random variables, $b$, $e_o$ and $\overline{e}$. As a result, $e_o^\wedge$ is itself normally distributed, with mean 0 and variance:

$$\sigma_e^2 \left( 1 + \frac{1}{n} + \frac{(X_o - \overline{X})^2}{\sum\limits_{i=1}^{n}(X_i - \overline{X})^2} \right)$$

This means that

$$\frac{e_o}{\sigma_e \sqrt{1+\dfrac{1}{n}+\dfrac{\sum\limits_{i=1}^{n}(X_o-\overline{X})^2}{\sum\limits_{i=1}^{n}(X_i-\overline{X})^2}}} \sim t$$

If we replace the unknown $\sigma_e^2$ by its sample estimate $S^2$, then:

$$\frac{e_o}{s \sqrt{1+\dfrac{1}{n}+\dfrac{\sum\limits_{i=1}^{n}(X_o-\overline{X})^2}{\sum\limits_{i=1}^{n}(X_i-\overline{X})^2}}} \sim t$$

distribution with $n - 2$ degrees of freedom.

Using all this, we can derive a 95 per cent confidence interval for $Y_0$:

$$(a^\wedge + b^\wedge X_0)(+/-)t_{0.025}s\sqrt{1+\frac{1}{n}+\frac{(X_o-\overline{X})^2}{\sum\limits_{i=1}^{n}(X_i-\overline{X})^2}} \qquad \text{Equation 4.32}$$

$$= (a^\wedge + b^\wedge X_0)(+/-)t_{0.025}\left(\sqrt{\frac{\sum\limits_{i=1}^{n}e_i^\wedge}{(n-2)}}\right)\sqrt{\frac{1+\frac{1}{n}+(X_o-\overline{X})^2}{\sum\limits_{i=1}^{n}(X_i-\overline{X})^2}}$$

Note that the width of the confidence interval increases the further $X_o$ is from $\overline{X}$.

To take an example, suppose we have the data on $Y$ and $X$ as shown in Table 4.12.

We carry out the following regression:

$$Y_i = \alpha + \beta X_i + e_i$$

The estimated coefficients are: $\alpha^\wedge = 3.94$ and $\beta^\wedge = 0.07$. The residual standard error, $\sigma_e^\wedge = 2.046$. The degrees of freedom are 8. Suppose we want to predict the value of $Y$ for $X = 3.5$. We have $\overline{X} = 3.3$, and hence $(X_o - \overline{X}) = (3.5 - 3.3) = 0.2$. We also see that $\sum_{i=1}^{n}(X_i - \overline{X})^2 = 18.1$.

Also, $\alpha^\wedge + \beta^\wedge (X = 3.5) = 3.94 + 0.07 \times (3.5) = 4.185$. The value of $t_{0.025}$ for 8 degrees of freedom is equal to $-2.30$. Substituting these values, we get a confidence interval:

**Table 4.12**
**The data on the values of X and Y**

| Y | X |
|---|---|
| 2 | 4 |
| 3 | 5 |
| 1 | 3 |
| 5 | 2 |
| 6 | 6 |
| 4 | 3 |
| 6 | 2 |
| 5 | 2 |
| 7 | 4 |
| 3 | 2 |

$$4.185(+/-)(-2.30) \times 2.046 \times \sqrt{1 + \frac{1}{10} + \frac{0.2}{18.1}}$$

$$= 4.185(+/-) \times (-4.26901) = (-0.77, 9.41)$$

The confidence interval for the predicted value of $y$ is quite wide. The precision of the forecast $Y^\wedge = 4.185$ is pretty low.

## CONCLUSION

In this chapter, we have learned the following:

1. Idea of an estimator and the following properties that any estimator considered to be desirable ought to have:
   a) Unbiasedness
   b) Efficiency
   c) Consistency
2. We learned the following about the OLS estimators:
   a) How to compute them
   b) The properties of OLS estimators
   c) Hypothesis tests for OLS estimators
   d) R square and adjusted $r$ square as measures of goodness of fit, along with their limitations.
   e) Logarithmic regression
   f) Semi-log regression
   g) Regression through the origin
   h) Standardised Regression coefficients
   i) Prediction from the OLS model.

You must make sure that you have understood these concepts well.

## NOTES

1. This way of approaching estimation of parameters is due to R. A. Fisher. Before him, Karl Pearson had assumed that the parameters computed from a large representative data set would be the same as the real thing. Pearson viewed statistical distributions as describing the actual collection of data that he would analyse. The actual parameters of this distribution could be estimated exactly, without any serious error from a large representative data set. On the other hand, for Fisher, parameter estimates based on a random sample would themselves be random variables and have a probability distribution. This chapter is firmly along Fisher's line of thinking.
2. The three criteria of efficiency, consistency and unbiasedness were initially proposed by Fisher.
3. Actually, you should not at all be surprised because of this result, $p^\wedge = \sum_{i=1}^{N} X_i / N$ is actually the sample mean, which we have already shown,

is an unbiased estimator of the population mean, $p$ in this case. In general, this is a great advantage when we are using sample means to estimate the population mean.

4. $E(\overline{X} - \mu)^2$ is the variance of $\overline{X}$, which as we know, equals $\sigma^2 / n$.

5. To be technically correct, consistency is a property not of the individual estimators themselves, but of the sequence of estimators, that converges in probability.

6. The proof of this theorem is not very hard; you can find an easy proof in Paul L. Meyer, *Introductory Probability and Statistical Applications* (New Delhi: Oxford and IBH, 1970), 285.

7. We have seen earlier (in Chapter 1) that distance between two points can also be measured by the absolute value of the difference of the two points. Just like the least squares estimator, we can also obtain an alternative estimator by minimizing the sum of absolute deviations rather than the sum of square of deviations. Such an estimator is called the Minimum Absolute Deviation (MAD) estimator. It can be shown that just as the OLS estimator models the conditional mean of $Y$ given $X$, the MAD estimator models the conditional median of $Y$ given $X$. Given a set of observations, let us define the $p$th quantile as the specific observation such that $p$ per cent of the observations are less than this specific observation. The median is the 50th quantile. In particular, the MAD estimators can be used to model any conditional quantile that one is interested in. For a reasonably accessible treatment, see R. Koenker and K. Hallock, 'Quantile Regression', *The Journal of Economic Perspectives* 15, no. 4 (Autumn 2001): 143–56.

8. The following expression for the variance of $b^\wedge$ is a powerful reason for using the OLS rather than the MAD estimator. For the OLS estimator, we can make a statement about the distribution of the variance of $b^\wedge$; we cannot do so for the MAD estimator since the above proof will not apply to the MAD case.

9. The name Gauss–Markov Theorem has an interesting history. We have already met the first author, C.F. Gauss. Andrei Markov (born 14 June 1856; died 20 July 1922) was a Russian mathematician who was born a year after Gauss's death. They could not have worked together to develop the theorem that has both their names in it (C.F. Gauss born 30 April 1777; died 23 February 1855). David (1998) refers to H. Scheffé's 1959 book *Analysis of Variance* for the first use of the phrase 'Gauss–Markoff theorem'. A search in JSTOR (a large electronic journal database) does yield a few earlier occurrences including one from 1951 by E.L. Lehmann, in *Annals of Mathematical Statistics* 22, no. 4 (1951): 587. For some years previously the term 'Markoff theorem' seems to have been in use. It was popularised by Jerzy Neyman who thought that this Russian contribution had been overlooked in the West. See Jerzy Newman, 'On the Two Different Aspects of the Representative Method', *Journal of the Royal Statistical Society* 97 (1934): 558–625. The theorem is in Chapter 7 of Markov's book "Probability Theory", translated into German as

*Wahrscheinlichkeitsrechnung* (Leipzig: Teubner, 1912). However R. L. Plackett (1949, *Biometrika*, 36: 149–157) pointed out that Markov had done no more than Gauss, nearly a century before, in his *Theoria combinationis observationum erroribus minimis obnoxiae* (Theory of the combination of observations least subject to error) (Gotiingen: Dietrich, 1821/23). Following Plackett, a few authors adopted the expression "Gauss theorem" but "Markov" was well-entrenched and the compromise "Gauss–Markov theorem" has become standard.

10. Please note that this requires our linear approximation to have a non-zero intercept as has been explained above; in case we choose to approximate our scatter by an approximation that passes through the origin, that is, with a zero intercept, this equation will not hold.

11. You should be able to see that $\alpha$ is the elasticity of sex-ratio at birth with respect to the population below poverty line. That is, it gives the per cent change in the sex-ratio per one per cent change in the per cent population below poverty line. To see this, assume $Y = f(X)$. Then, elasticity of $Y$ with respect to $X$ is given by $(dY / dX) \times (Y / X)$. In this case, this becomes

$$\alpha A \ / \ BPL^{1-\alpha} \times (BPL \ / \ SR) = \alpha A \ / \ BPL^{1-\alpha} \times (BPL \ / \ A \times BPL^{\alpha}) = \alpha$$

This is a very useful interpretation indeed.

12. It is usual to have very good fits for time series data. However, some of them might be spurious.

13. This should alert you to the dangers of relying solely on the R-square to decide on the goodness of model.

14. If $\{x_i\}_{t=1...T}$ refers to the values of a time series from $t = 1...T$, $\ln(x_t) - \ln(x_{t-1})$, (where $\ln(x_t)$ is the natural logarithm of $x_t$) closely approximates the percentage change in $x_t$.

15. One observation is lost when we take the first difference, so we have 57 and not 58 observations in all.

16. In general, if $k$ restrictions are imposed, the numerator will be a $\chi^2 (k)$ variable.

17. You can also have the dependent variable as a categorical variable; but then you cannot do an OLS. There are specialised methods like LOGIT or PROBIT and other models that can be used to model dependent variables that are categorical. A good reference is Damodar Gujarati, *Basic Econometrics*, 4th edition, Chapter 15 (New Delhi: Tata McGraw Hill, 2004).

# Chapter 5

# Multiple Linear Regression

## INTRODUCTION

In this chapter, we will study the multiple linear regression model. The regression model that we studied in Chapter 4 was a bivariate regression model, in that it took the form:

$$Y_i = a + bX_i + e_i \qquad \text{Equation 5.1}$$

In this regression, there is just one independent variable, $X$. However, we might be interested in the independent effects on $Y$ of more than one independent variable. For example, infant mortality might depend upon income and access to health facilities in addition to literacy. We might specify a more general linear regression model as:

$$Y_i = a + b_1 X_{i1} + b_2 X_{i2} + \ldots\ldots\ldots\ldots + b_n X_{in} + e_i \qquad \text{Equation 5.2}$$

where $Y_i$ is the $i$th observation on the dependent variable $Y$ and $X_{i1}, \ldots\ldots X_{in}$ are the $i$th observations on the independent variables $X_1, \ldots\ldots X_n$ respectively. $e_i$s are the stochastic disturbance terms that we have met in Chapter 4. We will assume that all the assumptions that we made regarding this term in Chapter 4 also continue to hold here. However, we will restate them in matrix form.

In the case of Equation 5.1, we interpreted $b$ to mean the change in $Y$ that results from a one unit change in $X$. In a similar manner, we can interpret $b_1$ as the change in $Y$ per unit change in $X_1$ keeping all the other independent variables constant. It is the marginal effect on $Y$ of a change in $X_1$ *ceteris paribus*. Since it allows us to estimate the marginal effects of each of the individual $X$ variables on $Y$ while controlling for the effects of the remaining variables, the multiple linear regression is extensively used in applied research. In this chapter, we will learn about estimating the parameters of a model like Equation 5.2. This is done in Section 5.1. In Section 5.2, we will learn how to calculate the standard errors for the estimated coefficients and carry out tests of significance. The Gauss–Markoff theorem for the multiple linear regression model is also proved in that section. In Section 5.3, we will also learn about measuring the goodness of such models. Models like Equation 5.2 also allow us to examine more complex hypotheses than permitted by Equation 5.1. For example, we might want to test whether $b_1 = b_2 = 0$ while allowing all the other $bs'$ to take unrestricted values. In this chapter, we will also learn about imposing such restrictions and testing for their statistical significance. This is done in Section 5.4.

In this chapter, we will study the following:

1. Estimating the parameters of a multiple linear regression model.
2. Obtain an expression for their standard errors and examine issues of unbiasedness and efficiency, proving that under the classical assumptions, the OLS estimators for the multiple linear regression are BLUE.
3. Testing restrictions in the context of the multiple linear regression model.
4. Examine the implications of multi-collinearity.
5. Develop tests for multicollinearity.
6. Discuss remedial measures for multi-collinearity.

## 5.1 INTRODUCTION TO MULTIPLE LINEAR REGRESSION

In this section, we will learn about estimating the parameters of equations like Equation 5.2. Suppose we have $T$ distinct observations on $Y$ and $X_1, \ldots \ldots X_n$, where $T > (n + 1)$, let us write out the model explicitly:

$$Y_1 = a + b_1 X_{11} + b_2 X_{12} + b_3 X_{13} + \ldots \ldots \ldots + b_n X_{1n} + e_1$$

$$Y_2 = a + b_1 X_{21} + b_2 X_{22} + b_3 X_{23} + \ldots \ldots \ldots + b_n X_{2n} + e_2$$

$$Y_3 = a + b_1 X_{31} + b_2 X_{32} + b_3 X_{33} + \ldots \ldots \ldots + b_n X_{3n} + e_3$$

$$\ldots \ldots \ldots \ldots \ldots \ldots \ldots \ldots \ldots \ldots \ldots \ldots \ldots \ldots \ldots \ldots$$

$$\ldots \ldots \ldots \ldots \ldots \ldots \ldots \ldots \ldots \ldots \ldots \ldots \ldots$$

$$\ldots \ldots \ldots \ldots \ldots \ldots \ldots \ldots \ldots \ldots \ldots$$

$$Y_T = a + b_1 X_{T1} + b_2 X_{T2} + b_3 X_{T3} + \ldots \ldots \ldots + b_n X_{Tn} + e_T$$

here $X_{23}$ for example, represents the 2nd observation on $X_3$. We can rewrite this in matrix notation as follows:

$$Y = XB + e \qquad \qquad \text{Equation 5.3}$$

where:

$$Y = \begin{pmatrix} Y_1 \\ Y_2 \\ .. \\ .. \\ .. \\ Y_T \end{pmatrix} \quad X = \begin{pmatrix} 1 & X_{11} & X_{12} & \cdots & X_{1n} \\ \vdots & X_{21} & X_{22} & \cdots & X_{2n} \\ \vdots & \vdots & \vdots & \cdots & \vdots \\ \vdots & \vdots & \cdots & \cdots & \vdots \\ 1 & X_{T1} & X_{T2} & \cdots & X_{Tn} \end{pmatrix}, \quad B = \begin{pmatrix} a \\ b_1 \\ b_2 \\ .. \\ .. \\ b_n \end{pmatrix} \text{ and } e = \begin{pmatrix} e_1 \\ e_2 \\ .. \\ .. \\ .. \\ e_T \end{pmatrix}$$

where $Y$ is a $(T \times 1)$ matrix, $X = (T \times n + 1)$ matrix, $B = (n + 1 \times 1)$ matrix and $e = (T \times 1)$ matrix. Writing Equation 5.2 in matrix notation allows us to write it more compactly. Note that the matrix $X$ has its first column as 1s. This is because there is a constant $a$ in model 5.2, so we have to estimate $n + 1$ parameters ($n$ $bs$ and one $a$).

## 5.1.1 Assumptions of the Multiple Regression Model

1. We will assume that $E(Y / X)$ is a 'linear function' of $X$, just as in Chapter 4.

Principles of Econometrics

2. $E(e_i) = 0$, $i = 1, 2....T$. That is, on an average, $e$ would equal zero.
3. Variance$(e_i) = \sigma_e^2$ $i = 1, 2....T$ is assumed to be constant, which is the assumption of 'homoskedasticity'.
4. We will also assume that all values of $e$ are uncorrelated with their previous or future values, which then implies that $Cov(e_i, e_j) = 0$, $i \neq j$. This is called the 'assumption of no auto-correlation'.
5. We will assume that each of the $e_i$ are normally distributed, so that the vector $e$ is normally distributed with mean 0 and variance $\sigma^2$, and with zero covariance.
6. We will assume that the random variables $(e_1, e_2,.....e_T)$ and the rows of $X$ are independent.
7. We will assume that the matrix $X$ is of rank $n + 1$. In other words, we will assume that none of the columns of $X$ can be obtained by a linear combination of other columns of $X$. This is required as we are going to estimate $n + 1$ coefficients which requires $n + 1$ independent equations, as we shall see ahead.

We proceed just like the model in Chapter 4, by minimizing the sum of squared errors from Equation 5.2. Note that:

$$\varepsilon' \times \varepsilon = \begin{pmatrix} \varepsilon_1 \\ \varepsilon_2 \\ .. \\ .. \\ .. \\ .. \\ \varepsilon_T \end{pmatrix}' \times \begin{pmatrix} \varepsilon_1 \\ \varepsilon_2 \\ .. \\ .. \\ .. \\ .. \\ \varepsilon_T \end{pmatrix} = \sum_{i=1}^{T} \varepsilon_i^2$$

which is the quantity that we wish to minimize.
Therefore, we must minimize:

$$\varepsilon'\varepsilon = (Y - X\beta)' (Y - X\beta)$$
$$= (Y' - \beta'X')' (Y - X\beta)$$
$$= (Y'Y - \beta'X'Y - Y'X\beta + \beta'X'X\beta) \quad \text{Equation 5.4}$$

Let us understand this expression better. $\varepsilon'\varepsilon$ is a single number being the product of a $(1 \times T)$ matrix with a $(T \times 1)$ matrix. Therefore, $(Y'Y - \beta'XY - Y'X\beta + \beta'X'X\beta)$ must also be a scalar. In fact, it is an expression involving the values of $Y$, the variable $X$ the values of which are fixed for repeated samples and the variables $\alpha$ and $\beta_1, \beta_2.........\beta_n$. Second, note that $\beta'X'Y$ and $Y'X\beta$ are both scalars and are equal to each other. Using this, we can express Equation 5.4 as:

$$Y'Y - 2\beta'X'Y + \beta'X'X\beta.$$

Let us rewrite the above expression fully:

$$Y'Y = [Y_1 . . . . . . . . . . . Y_T] \begin{pmatrix} Y_1 \\ .. \\ .. \\ .. \\ .. \\ Y_T \end{pmatrix} = Y_1^2 + Y_2^2 + ...... + Y_T^2 = \sum_{i=1}^{T} Y_i^2$$

$$2\beta'X'Y = 2 \begin{pmatrix} \alpha \\ \beta_1 \\ .. \\ \beta_n \end{pmatrix}' \begin{pmatrix} 1 & & 1 \\ X_{11} & \cdots & X_{T1} \\ \vdots & \ddots & \vdots \\ X_{1n} & \cdots & X_{Tn} \end{pmatrix} \begin{pmatrix} Y_1 \\ .. \\ .. \\ .. \\ Y_T \end{pmatrix}$$

$$= 2 \begin{pmatrix} \alpha \\ \beta_1 \\ .. \\ \vdots \\ \vdots \\ \beta_n \end{pmatrix}' \begin{pmatrix} Y_1 + Y_2 + ...................... + Y_T \\ X_{11}Y_1 + X_{21}Y_2 + ..... + X_{T1}Y_T \\ X_{12}Y_1 + X_{22}Y_2 + ..... + X_{T2}Y_T \\ .............................. \\ .............................. \\ .............................. \\ .............................. \\ X_{1n}Y_1 + X_{2n}Y_2 + ..... + X_{Tn}Y_T \end{pmatrix}$$

$$= 2 \times \begin{pmatrix} \alpha \\ \beta_1 \\ \beta_2 \\ \cdot\cdot \\ \cdot\cdot \\ \cdot\cdot \\ \beta_n \end{pmatrix}' \begin{pmatrix} \sum_{i=1}^{T} Y_i \\ \sum_{i=1}^{T} X_{i1} Y_i \\ \sum_{i=1}^{T} X_{i2} Y_i \\ \cdot\cdot \\ \cdots \\ \sum_{i=1}^{T} X_{in} Y_i \end{pmatrix}$$

$$= 2 \times (\alpha \sum_{i=1}^{T} Y_i + \beta_1 \sum_{i=1}^{T} X_{i1} Y_i + \beta_2 \sum_{i=1}^{T} X_{i2} Y_i + \ldots\ldots + \beta_n \sum_{i=1}^{T} X_{in} Y_i)$$

Similarly,

$$\beta' X' X \beta = \begin{pmatrix} \alpha \\ \beta_1 \\ \beta_2 \\ \cdots \\ \cdots \\ \beta_n \end{pmatrix}' \begin{pmatrix} 1 & & 1 \\ X_{11} & \cdots & X_{T1} \\ \vdots & \ddots & \vdots \\ X_{1n} & \cdots & X_{Tn} \end{pmatrix} \begin{pmatrix} 1 & & X_{1n} \\ 1 & \cdots & X_{2n} \\ \vdots & \ddots & \vdots \\ 1 & \cdots & X_{Tn} \end{pmatrix} \begin{pmatrix} \alpha \\ \beta_1 \\ \beta_2 \\ \cdot\cdot \\ \cdot\cdot \\ \beta_n \end{pmatrix}$$

Let us write these equations for the following simple model involving a constant and two independent variables, with $T$ observations on each :

$$Y_i = a + b_1 X_{i1} + b_2 X_{i2} + e_i$$

$$Y'Y = \sum_{i=1}^{T} Y_i^2$$

$$2\beta' X' Y = 2 \times (\alpha \sum_{i=1}^{T} Y_i + \beta_1 \sum_{i=1}^{T} X_{i1} Y_i + \beta_2 \sum_{i=1}^{T} X_{i2} Y_i) \qquad \text{Equation 5.4A}$$

$$\beta'X'X\beta = \begin{pmatrix} \alpha \\ \beta_1 \\ \beta_2 \end{pmatrix}' \begin{pmatrix} 1.. & 1... & ....1 \\ X_{11} & ....... & X_{T1} \\ X_{12} & ....... & X_{T2} \end{pmatrix} \begin{pmatrix} 1 & X_{11} & X_{12} \\ ... & & \\ ... & ... & ... \\ ... & & \\ 1 & X_{T1} & X_{T2} \end{pmatrix} \begin{pmatrix} \alpha \\ \beta_1 \\ \beta_2 \end{pmatrix}$$

$$= \begin{pmatrix} \alpha \\ \beta_1 \\ \beta_2 \end{pmatrix}' \begin{pmatrix} T & \sum_{i=1}^{T} X_{i1} & \sum_{i=1}^{T} X_{i2} \\ \sum_{i=1}^{T} X_{i1} & \sum_{i=1}^{T} X_{i1}^2 & \sum_{i=1}^{T} X_{i1}X_{i2} \\ \sum_{i=1}^{T} X_{i2} & \sum_{i=1}^{T} X_{i1}X_{i2} & \sum_{i=1}^{T} X_{i2}^2 \end{pmatrix} \begin{pmatrix} \alpha \\ \beta_1 \\ \beta_2 \end{pmatrix}$$

$$= \alpha^2 T + \alpha\beta_1 \sum_{i=1}^{T} X_{i1} + \alpha\beta_2 \sum_{i=1}^{T} X_{i2} + \alpha\beta_1 \sum_{i=1}^{T} X_{i1}$$

$$+ \beta_1^2 \sum_{i=1}^{T} X_{i1}^2 + \beta_1\beta_2 \sum_{i=1}^{T} X_{i1}X_{i2} + \alpha\beta_2 \sum_{i=1}^{T} X_{i2}$$

$$+ \beta_1\beta_2 \sum_{i=1}^{T} X_{i1}X_{i2} + \beta_2^2 \sum_{i=1}^{T} X_{i2}^2$$

Putting everything together, we have

$$(Y - X\beta)'(Y - X\beta)$$

$$= \sum_{i=1}^{T} Y_i^2 - 2\left(\alpha \sum_{i=1}^{T} Y_i + \beta_1 \sum_{i=1}^{T} X_{i1}Y_i + \beta_2 \sum_{i=1}^{T} X_{i2}Y_i\right)$$

$$+ \alpha^2 T + \alpha\beta_1 \sum_{i=1}^{T} X_{i1} + \alpha\beta_2 \sum_{i=1}^{T} X_{i2} + \alpha\beta_1 \sum_{i=1}^{T} X_{i1}$$

$$+ \beta_1^2 \sum_{i-1}^{T} X_{i1}^2 + \beta_1\beta_2 \sum_{i=1}^{T} X_{i1}X_{i2} + \alpha\beta_2 \sum_{i=1}^{T} X_{i2}$$

$$+ \beta_1\beta_2 \sum_{i=1}^{T} X_{i1}X_{i2} + \beta_2^2 \sum_{i=1}^{T} X_{i2}^2$$

This expression involves three variables. The expression can be minimized by taking derivatives of $(Y - X\beta)'(Y - X\beta)$ with respect to $\alpha, \beta_1, \beta_2$, which will yield three equations in three unknowns. Estimates of the unknown parameters can be obtained by solving these equations simultaneously.

For example:

$$\partial((Y - X\beta)'(Y - X\beta))/\partial\alpha = -2\sum_{i=1}^{T} Y_i + 2\alpha T$$

$$+ 2\beta_1 \sum_{i=1}^{T} X_{i1} + 2\beta_2 \sum_{i=1}^{T} X_{i2} = 0$$

Equation 5.5

or:

$$\alpha = \sum_{i=1}^{T} Y_i / T - \beta_1(\sum_{i=1}^{T} X_{i1} / T) - \beta_2(\sum_{i=1}^{T} X_{i2} / T)$$

Equation 5.6

$$\partial((Y - X\beta)'(Y - X\beta))/\partial\beta_1 = -2\sum_{i=1}^{T} X_{i1}Y_i + 2\alpha\sum_{i=1}^{T} X_{i1}$$

$$+ 2\beta_1 \sum_{i=1}^{T} X_{i1}^2 + 2\beta_2 \sum_{i=1}^{T} X_{i1}X_{i2} = 0$$

Equation 5.7

or:

$$\beta_1 = (\sum_{i=1}^{T} X_{i1}Y_i / \sum_{i=1}^{T} X_{i1}^2) - \alpha(\sum_{i=1}^{T} X_{i1} / \sum_{i=1}^{T} X_{i1}^2) - \beta_2(\sum_{i=1}^{T} X_{i1}X_{i2} / \sum_{i=1}^{T} X_{i1}^2)$$

Equation 5.7A

$$\partial(Y - X\beta)'(Y - X\beta)/\partial\beta_2 = -2\sum_{i=1}^{T} X_{i2}Y_i + 2\alpha\sum_{i=1}^{T} X_{i2}$$

$$+ 2\beta_1 \sum_{i=1}^{T} X_{i1}X_{i2} + 2\beta_2 \sum_{i=1}^{T} X_{i2}^2 = 0$$

or:

$$\beta_2 = (\sum_{i=1}^{T} X_{i2} Y_i / \sum_{i=1}^{T} X_{i2}^2) - \alpha(\sum_{i=1}^{T} X_{i2} / \sum_{i=1}^{T} X_{i2}^2) - \beta_1(\sum_{i=1}^{T} X_{i1} X_{i2} / \sum_{i=1}^{T} X_{i2}^2)$$

Equation 5.8

We now have three equations and three unknowns, allowing us to solve for the three unknowns simultaneously. After substituting for $\alpha$, $\beta_1$ and $\beta_2$ in the Equations 5.6, 5.7A and 5.8, we get the following expressions:

$$\bar{Y} = \alpha + \beta_1 \bar{X}_1 + \beta_2 \bar{X}_2$$

$$\sum_{i=1}^{T} X_{i1} Y_i = \alpha \sum_{i=1}^{T} X_{i1} + \beta_1 \sum_{i=1}^{T} X_{i1}^2 + \beta_2 \sum_{i=1}^{T} X_{i1} X_{i2}$$

$$\sum_{i=1}^{T} X_{i2} Y_i = \alpha \sum_{i=1}^{T} X_{i2} + \beta_1 \sum_{i=1}^{T} X_{i1} X_{i2} + \beta_2 \sum_{i=1}^{T} X_{i2}^2$$

Letting lower case letters stand for deviations from the mean, the above three equations can be re-expressed as:

$$\hat{\alpha} = \bar{Y} - \hat{\beta}_1 \bar{X}_1 - \hat{\beta}_2 \bar{X}_2$$

$$\hat{\beta}_1 = \frac{(\sum_{i=1}^{T} x_{i1} y_i)(\sum_{i=1}^{T} x_{i2}^2) - (\sum_{i=1}^{T} x_{i2} y_i)(\sum_{i=1}^{T} x_{i1} x_{i2})}{(\sum_{i=1}^{T} x_{i1}^2)(\sum_{i=1}^{T} x_{i2}^2) - (\sum_{i=1}^{T} x_{i1} x_{i2})^2}$$

$$\hat{\beta}_2 = \frac{(\sum_{i=1}^{T} x_{i2} y_i)(\sum_{i=1}^{T} x_{i1}^2) - (\sum_{i=1}^{T} x_{i1} y_i)(\sum_{i=1}^{T} x_{i1} x_{i2})}{(\sum_{i=1}^{T} x_{i1}^2)(\sum_{i=1}^{T} x_{i2}^2) - (\sum_{i=1}^{T} x_{i1} x_{i2})^2}$$

Equation 5.9

An interesting question is: How does $\hat{\beta}_1$ in Equation 5.9 relate to $\hat{\beta}$ of Chapter 4 (Equation 4.4)? In other words, suppose instead of carrying out the regression:

$$Y_i = a + b_1 X_1 + b_2 X_2 e_i$$

we did the regression $Y_i = a + b_1^* X_1 + e_{i1}$. What would be the relationship between $b_1$ and $b_1^*$? Examine the expression for $\hat{\beta}_1$ in Equation 5.9. From Equation 4.4, we have:

$$\hat{\beta}_1^* = \sum_{i=1}^{T} x_{i1} y_i \Big/ \sum_{i=1}^{T} x_{i1}^2$$

We see that the two expressions are identical only if:

$$\sum_{i=1}^{T} x_{i1} x_{i2} = 0$$

But this requires the correlation between $X_1$ and $X_2$ to be equal to zero.

**Result**: We have an important result: If $X_1$ and $X_2$ are uncorrelated, the regression coefficient of $X_1$ in a regression of $X_1$ and $X_2$ on $Y$ will be the same as the coefficient of $X_1$ in the regression of $X_1$ alone on $Y$. If $X_1$ is correlated with $X_2$, there is no reason to expect the two coefficients to have identical magnitudes or even signs. Therefore, as you keep on adding new variables to a regression, the coefficients of the existing variables will also generally change.

We have derived the formulae for estimating the regression parameters for a three variable model. We will now proceed to develop a method for the more general model. Let us examine equations like Equation 5.7 closely. In Equation 5.7, values of $X_2$ have been multiplied throughout with the values of $Y$, $X_1$ and $\alpha$, before being summed and subsequently multiplied by 2. It is the same for Equation 5.6, where all the values of $Y$, $\alpha$ and $X_2$ have been multiplied by values of $X_1$ before being summed and then being multiplied by 2. You will see that this holds for Equation 5.5 as well since the first column of the $X$ matrix is all ones. Let $X_i$ be the $i$th column of the $X$ matrix (where all values are 1 for the first column labeled $X_0$). Let:

$$S = (Y - X\beta)' (Y - X\beta)$$

Then, we can see that:

$$\partial S / \partial \alpha = -2X_0'Y + 2X_0'X\beta$$
$$\partial S / \partial \beta_1 = -2X_1'Y + 2X_1'X\beta$$
$$\partial S / \partial \beta_2 = -2X_2'Y + 2X_2'X\beta$$
$$\partial S / \partial \beta_3 = -2X_3'Y + 2X_3'X\beta$$

........

.......

......

$$\partial S / \partial \beta_n = -2X_n'Y + 2X_n'X\beta$$

Setting all these derivatives equal to zero, we have

$$X_0'Y = X_0'X\beta$$
$$X_1'Y = X_1'X\beta$$
$$X_2'Y = X_2'X\beta$$
$$X_3'Y = X_3'X\beta$$

.......

......

......

$$X_n'Y = X_n'X\beta$$

What is $X_1'X\beta$? If we expand, we get:

$$X_1'X_0\alpha + X_1'X_1\beta_1 + X_1'X_2\beta_2 + \ldots\ldots + X_1'X_n\beta_n = X_1'Y$$

The entire system can be written as:

$$X_0'X_0\alpha + X_0'X_1\beta_1 + X_0'X_2\beta_2 + \ldots\ldots + X_0'X_n\beta_n = X_0'Y$$
$$X_1'X_0\alpha + X_1'X_1\beta_1 + X_1'X_2\beta_2 + \ldots\ldots + X_1'X_n\beta_n = X_1'Y$$
$$X_2'X_0\alpha + X_2'X_1\beta_1 + X_2'X_2\beta_2 + \ldots\ldots + X_2'X_n\beta_n = X_2'Y$$

...................................

...................................

...................................

$$X_n'X_0\alpha + X_n'X_1\beta_1 + X_n'X_2\beta_2 + \ldots\ldots + X_n'X_n\beta_n = X_n'Y$$

or, writing this in matrix notation:

$$\begin{pmatrix} X_0'X_0 & \cdots & X_0'X_n \\ \vdots & \ddots & \vdots \\ X_n'X_0 & \cdots & X_n'X_n \end{pmatrix} \begin{pmatrix} \alpha \\ \beta_1 \\ .. \\ \beta_n \end{pmatrix} = \begin{pmatrix} X_0'Y \\ X_1'Y \\ .... \\ X_n'Y \end{pmatrix}$$

or more compactly:

$$X'X\beta = X'Y$$

As a result:

$$\hat{\beta} = (X'X)^{-1}X'Y \qquad \text{Equation 5.10}$$

The assumption that $X$ be a full rank matrix is relevant here. If $X$ is not a full rank matrix, we will not be able to solve for $n + 1$ parameters in terms of $n + 1$ equations.

Also remember that in order to estimate $B$, we will use a set of sample observations on $X$ and $Y$. That makes the estimated value of $B$ a random variable, and the value that we obtain as a specific realization of that random variable. Hence, in order to emphasize that we have an estimator of the true population $B$, we will denote an estimator $B$ by $\beta$ and the OLS estimator, in particular, by $\hat{\beta}$ in Equation 5.10.

### Example 5.1

Suppose we are given the following data on the dependent variable $Y$ and two independent variables $X_1$ and $X_2$. Our objective is to estimate, using the Equation 5.10, the parameters of the following model (also see Table 5.1):

$$Y_i = a + b_1X_1 + b_2X_2 + e_i \qquad \text{Equation 5.11}$$

**Step 1:** First, let us form the matrix $X$. Remember that since there is a constant in Equation 5.11, the first column of $X$ will have to consist of a column of 1s. The second column will consist of data on the variable $X_1$ while the third column will have data on $X_2$. In other words, the $X$ matrix will be:

**Table 5.1**
**The data on the dependent variable *Y* and two independent**
**variables $X_1$ and $X_2$**

| Y | $X_1$ | $X_2$ |
|---|---|---|
| 12 | 5 | 5 |
| 14 | 4 | 3 |
| 13 | 3 | 7 |
| 10 | 2 | 8 |
| 14 | 4 | 6 |
| 15 | 6 | 4 |
| 12 | 3 | 9 |
| 11 | 1 | 10 |
| 16 | 3 | 13 |
| 12 | 5 | 9 |
| 14 | 2 | 8 |
| 18 | 4 | 9 |
| 17 | 3 | 10 |
| 12 | 1 | 9 |
| 10 | 1 | 8 |

$$
\begin{aligned}
X = 1 \quad & 5 \quad && 5 \\
= 1 \quad & 4 \quad && 3 \\
= 1 \quad & 3 \quad && 7 \\
= 1 \quad & 2 \quad && 8 \\
= 1 \quad & 4 \quad && 6 \\
= 1 \quad & 6 \quad && 4 \\
= 1 \quad & 3 \quad && 9 \\
= 1 \quad & 1 \quad && 10 \\
= 1 \quad & 3 \quad && 13 \\
= 1 \quad & 5 \quad && 9 \\
= 1 \quad & 2 \quad && 8 \\
= 1 \quad & 4 \quad && 9 \\
= 1 \quad & 3 \quad && 10 \\
= 1 \quad & 1 \quad && 9 \\
= 1 \quad & 1 \quad && 8
\end{aligned}
$$

**Step 2**: The 15 × 1 column vector $Y$ is as follows:

$$
\begin{aligned}
Y &= 12 \\
&= 14 \\
&= 13 \\
&= 10 \\
&= 14 \\
&= 15 \\
&= 12 \\
&= 11 \\
&= 16 \\
&= 12 \\
&= 14 \\
&= 18 \\
&= 17 \\
&= 12 \\
&= 10
\end{aligned}
$$

**Step 3**: Form the matrix $X'X$:

$$
\begin{aligned}
X'X &= 15 & 47 & \quad 118 \\
&= 47 & 181 & \quad 342 \\
&= 118 & 342 & \quad 1020
\end{aligned}
$$

Since $X$ is a 15 × 3 matrix, $X'$ is a 3 × 15 matrix and $X'X$ is a 3 × 3 matrix.

**Step 4**: Obtain $(X'X)^{-1}$:

$$
(X'X)^{-1} = \begin{pmatrix}
1.9396789 & -0.21743119 & -0.15149083 \\
-0.2174312 & 0.03944954 & 0.01192661 \\
-0.15149083 & 0.01192661 & 0.01450688
\end{pmatrix}
$$

Notice that $(X'X)^{-1}$ is a symmetric matrix.

**Step 5**: Pre-multiply $(X'X)^{-1}$ with $X'Y$ to obtain $\hat{\beta}_1$:

$$
\hat{\beta} = (X'X)^{-1}X'Y = \begin{pmatrix} \hat{\alpha} \\ \hat{\beta}_1 \\ \hat{\beta}_2 \end{pmatrix} = \begin{pmatrix} 7.0129587 \\ 0.9963303 \\ 0.4065940 \end{pmatrix}
$$

The same calculations can be carried out using R as follows:

```
y=c(12,14,13,10,14,15,12,11,16,12,14,18,17,12,10) ##Reads
the data as a column
x1=c(5,4,3,2,4,6,3,1,3,5,2,4,3,1,1)
x2=c(5,3,7,8,6,4,9,10,13,9,8,9,10,9,8)
X=cbind(1,x1,x2) ## Generates the X matrix
betahat=solve(t(X)%*%X)%*%t(X)%*%y      ##Calculates
(X'X)⁻¹ X'Y
betahat ## Prints β^
```

The output is as follows:

```
y=c(12,14,13,10,14,15,12,11,16,12,14,18,17,12,10)
> x1=c(5,4,3,2,4,6,3,1,3,5,2,4,3,1,1)
> x2=c(5,3,7,8,6,4,9,10,13,9,8,9,10,9,8)
> X=cbind(1,x1,x2)
> betahat=solve(t(X)%*%X)%*%t(X)%*%y
> betahat
[,1]
7.0129587
x1 0.9963303
x2 0.4065940
```

As you can see, the values of $\hat{\alpha}, \hat{\beta}_1, \hat{\beta}_2$ are identical with those generated previously.

The estimated model is:

$$Y_i = 7.012958 + 0.9963303X_{i1} + 0.4065940X_{i2} + \varepsilon_i$$

$$\hat{Y}_i = 7.010129587 + 0.9963303X_{i1} + 0.4565940X_{i2} \quad \text{Equation 5.11}'$$

## 5.1.2 Obtaining the Fitted Values of $Y$ from the Estimated Regression

Suppose we substitute the individual values of $X_1$ and $X_2$ in Equation 5.11. For example, since $X_{11} = 5$ and $X_{12} = 5$, we can obtain

$$\hat{Y}_1 = 7.012958 + 0.9963303 \times 5 + 0.4065940 \times 5 = 14.02758$$

How do we interpret this figure?
Our regression model is:

$$Y_i = 7.012958 + 0.9963303X_{i1} + 0.4065940X_{i2} + \varepsilon_i$$

This implies that even when $X_{11} = 5$ and $X_{12} = 5$, $Y_1$ will take values different from 14.02758 depending upon the values of $\varepsilon_i$ which we have assumed is a random variable that is normally distributed with zero mean, a constant variance and independence across $i$'s. Therefore, when $X_1 = 5$ and $X_2 = 5$, we have:

$$Y_1 = 14.02758 + \varepsilon_1$$

Which also has a normal distribution and:

$$E(Y_1 / X_1 = 5, X_2 = 5) = 14.02758 + E(\varepsilon_1 / X_1)$$
$$= 14.02758$$

In other words, 14.02758, which we will call $\hat{Y}_1$, is the conditional expectation of $Y$ given $X_1 = 5$ and $X_2 = 5$.

The values of $\hat{Y}_1$ for any values of $X_1$ and $X_2$ can be obtained by substituting those values of $X_1$ and $X_2$ values in Equation 5.11'. The values of $\hat{Y}_1$ which we obtain by substituting the values of $X_1$ and $X_2$ that were observed in the sample and used to calculate $\hat{\beta}$, are known as the fitted values. These values give us an estimate of how the conditional mean of $Y$ changes with various values of $X$. The entire set of fitted values can be obtained by post-multiplying the $X$ matrix by the estimated coefficient vector:

$$\hat{Y} = X\hat{\beta}$$

### Exercise 5.1

The values of $\hat{Y}_1$ for any values of $X_1$ and $X_2$ can be obtained by substituting those values of $X_1$ and $X_2$ values in Equation 5.9. The values of $\hat{Y}_1$ which we obtain by substituting the values of $X_1$ and $X_2$, that were observed in the sample and used to calculate $\hat{\beta}$, are known as the fitted values.

Find the values of $\hat{\alpha}, \hat{\beta}_1, \hat{\beta}_2$ in the following regression:

$$Y_i = a + b_1 X_{i1} + b_2 X_{i2} + e_i$$

And obtain the fitted values of $Y$, $\hat{Y} = X\hat{\beta}$

We have seen how we can estimate the parameters of the multiple linear regression model. Since the estimated parameters are random variables, we should be able to make statements about their mean and standard deviation. As far as the mean is concerned, we will argue that as long as the elements of the vector $X$ and $e$ are uncorrelated, we will have $E(\hat{\beta}) = \beta$, that is, just like in the case of the regression model involving one explanatory variable, the OLS estimators will be unbiased estimators of the population parameters. Apart from this, we also are required to make some statements about the variance of the estimated OLS coefficients. This is done in the next section.

## 5.2 THE GAUSS–MARKOV THEOREM AGAIN

At the outset, we will demonstrate that the OLS coefficients in the matrix $\hat{\beta}$ are unbiased estimators of the population parameters:

$$\hat{\beta} = (X'X)^{-1} X'Y$$
$$Y = XB + e$$

Therefore,

$$\hat{\beta} = (X'X)^{-1} X'(XB + e)$$
$$= B + (X'X)^{-1} X'e$$

Therefore,

$$E(\hat{\beta}) = B + E((X'X)^{-1} X'e)$$

Since we are assuming that the elements of $X$ are constants, we can take them out of the expectations operator. We then have:

$$E(\hat{\beta}) = B + (X'X)^{-1} X'E(e)$$
$$= B$$

Since the last term is zero. We have proved that $\hat{\beta}$ is an unbiased estimator for $B$:

**The variance of** $\hat{\beta}$:

The variance of $\hat{\beta}$ =

$$E[(\hat{\beta} - E(\beta))'(\hat{\beta} - E(\hat{\beta}))]$$
$$= E[(\hat{\beta} - B)'(\hat{\beta} - B)]$$

because of the unbiasedness of $\hat{\beta}$. What does this expression mean? Let us examine this in the context of model 5.4A. The matrix:

$$B = \begin{pmatrix} a \\ b_1 \\ b_2 \end{pmatrix}, \text{ and } \hat{\beta} = \begin{pmatrix} \hat{a} \\ \hat{\beta}_1 \\ \hat{\beta}_2 \end{pmatrix}$$

$$E[(\hat{\beta} - B)(\hat{\beta} - B)']$$

$$= E\left[ \begin{pmatrix} \hat{\alpha} - a \\ \hat{\beta}_1 - b_1 \\ \hat{\beta}_2 - b_2 \end{pmatrix} \begin{pmatrix} \hat{\alpha} - a \\ \hat{\beta}_1 - b_1 \\ \hat{\beta}_2 - b_2 \end{pmatrix}' \right]$$

$$= E\left[ \begin{pmatrix} (\hat{\alpha} - a)^2 & (\hat{\alpha} - a)(\hat{\beta}_1 - b_1) & (\hat{\alpha} - a)(\hat{\beta}_2 - b_2) \\ (\hat{\beta}_1 - b_1)(\hat{\alpha} - a) & (\hat{\beta}_1 - b_1)^2 & (\hat{\beta}_1 - b_1)(\hat{\beta}_2 - b_2) \\ (\hat{\beta}_2 - b_2)(\hat{\alpha} - a) & (\hat{\beta}_2 - b_2)(\hat{\beta}_1 - b_1) & (\hat{\beta}_2 - b_2)^2 \end{pmatrix} \right]$$

Let us examine this matrix more closely. The element in the first row first column of this matrix (element $(1, 1)$) is $E(\hat{\alpha} - a)^2$. But since $E(\hat{\alpha}) = a$, this is just the variance of the estimator $\hat{\alpha}$. Similarly, the $(2, 2)$ element is the variance of $\hat{\beta}_1$ while the $(3, 3)$ element is the variance of $\hat{\beta}_2$. The $(1, 2)$ element, $E[(\hat{\alpha} - a)(\hat{\beta}_1 - b_1)]$, is the covariance between $\hat{\alpha}$ and $\hat{\beta}_1$. The other off diagonal elements have the same interpretation. We can rewrite this matrix as the 'variance–covariance matrix', $\Sigma_{\hat{\beta}}$

$$\Sigma_{\hat{\beta}} = \begin{pmatrix} \sigma_{\hat{\alpha}}^2 & \sigma_{\hat{\alpha}\hat{\beta}_1} & \sigma_{\hat{\alpha}\hat{\beta}_2} \\ \sigma_{\hat{\beta}_1\hat{\alpha}} & \sigma_{\hat{\beta}_1}^2 & \sigma_{\hat{\beta}_1\hat{\beta}_2} \\ \sigma_{\hat{\beta}_2\hat{\alpha}} & \sigma_{\hat{\beta}_1\hat{\beta}_2} & \sigma_{\hat{\beta}_2}^2 \end{pmatrix}$$

Note that this matrix is symmetric in that the elements $(i, j)$ and $(j, i)$ are identical. Also, the elements on the principal diagonal are all strictly non-negative. In order to estimate the three variances and three co-variances, we must estimate the matrix $\Sigma_{\hat{\beta}}$. How is that achieved?

Note that

$$\begin{aligned} \Sigma_{\hat{\beta}} &= E[(\hat{\beta} - B)(\hat{\beta} - B)'] \\ &= E((X'X)^{-1}X'e)((X'X)^{-1}X'e)') \\ &= E((X'X)^{-1}X'e)(e'X(X'X)^{-1}) \\ &= (X'X)^{-1}X'E(ee')X(X'X)^{-1} \end{aligned}$$

since $(X'X)^{-1}$ matrix is symmetric, we have

$$(X'X)^{-1'} = (X'X)^{-1}$$

Let us now examine the $ee'$ matrix. In case of our example, $e$ is a $(15 \times 1)$ matrix and hence $ee'$ is a $15 \times 15$ matrix. We will call it $\Sigma_e$:

$$\Sigma_e = E \begin{pmatrix} e_1^2 & \cdots & e_1e_{15} \\ \vdots & \ddots & \vdots \\ e_{15}e_1 & \cdots & e_{15}^2 \end{pmatrix}$$

$$= \begin{pmatrix} E(e_1^2) & \cdots & E(e_1e_{15}) \\ \vdots & \ddots & \vdots \\ E(e_{15}e_1) & \cdots & E(e_{15}^2) \end{pmatrix}$$

The $(1, 1)$ element of this matrix is the variance of $e_1$. In general, the $(i, i)$ diagonal element of this matrix is the variance of $e_i$. Similarly, the off diagonal element $(i, j)$ is the covariance between $e_i$

and $e_j$. Since we have assumed that $\text{Variance}(e_i)' = \sigma_e^2$ for all values of $i$ (assumption 3, the assumption of homoskedasticity) and that $\text{Covariance}(e_i, e_j) = 0$ for $i \neq j$ (assumption of no autocorrelation). This implies that

$$\Sigma_e = \begin{pmatrix} \sigma_e^2 & \cdots & 0 \\ \vdots & \ddots & \vdots \\ 0 & \cdots & \sigma_e^2 \end{pmatrix}$$

$$= \sigma_e^2 \begin{pmatrix} 1 & \cdots & 0 \\ \vdots & \ddots & \vdots \\ 0 & \cdots & 1 \end{pmatrix}$$

Therefore:

$$\Sigma_{\hat{\beta}} = E[(\hat{\beta} - B)(\hat{\beta} - B)']$$
$$= (X'X)^{-1}(X'X)\sigma_e^2 I(X'X)^{-1})$$
$$= \sigma_e^2(X'X)^{-1}$$

Equation 5.12

We have now succeeded in obtaining an expression for $\Sigma_{\hat{\beta}}$ in terms of the observed $X$ matrix and the unobserved quantity $\sigma_e^2$. Remember that this expression is valid only if the assumptions of no autocorrelation and homoskedasticity hold. In reality, they might not hold. In that case, 5.12 will not be the correct expression for $\Sigma_{\hat{\beta}}$. As of now, we will assume that both these important assumptions are fulfilled.

To be able to obtain an estimate of $\hat{\Sigma}_{\hat{\beta}}$, we need to obtain an estimate of $\sigma_e^2$. Though we cannot observe $e$, we can estimate $e$ as follows:

Since:

$$Y = XB + e$$

$$e = Y - XB$$

and estimated values of $e$ can be obtained by replacing the vector $B$, which we do not have, with its estimate, $\hat{\beta}$, so that:

$$\hat{e} = Y - X\hat{\beta} \qquad \text{Equation 5.13}$$

Let us note an important result:

$$\begin{aligned}
\hat{e} &= Y - X\hat{\beta} \\
&= Y - X[(X'X)^{-1}X'Y] \\
&= [I - X\{(X'X)^{-1}X'\}]Y \\
&= MY \qquad \text{Equation 5.13a}
\end{aligned}$$

By defining $M$ as $[I - \{X(X'X)^{-1}X'\}]$, we have obtained a matrix that, when pre multiplied with $Y$, produces the matrix of estimated residuals.

In the case of Example 5.1, we can obtain $\hat{e}$ as:

$$\hat{e} = \begin{pmatrix} 12 \\ 14 \\ 13 \\ 10 \\ 14 \\ 15 \\ 12 \\ 11 \\ 16 \\ 12 \\ 14 \\ 18 \\ 17 \\ 12 \\ 10 \end{pmatrix} - \begin{pmatrix} 1 & 5 & 5 \\ 1 & 4 & 3 \\ 1 & 3 & 7 \\ 1 & 2 & 8 \\ 1 & 4 & 6 \\ 1 & 6 & 4 \\ 1 & 3 & 9 \\ 1 & 1 & 10 \\ 1 & 3 & 13 \\ 1 & 5 & 9 \\ 1 & 2 & 8 \\ 1 & 4 & 9 \\ 1 & 3 & 10 \\ 1 & 1 & 9 \\ 1 & 1 & 8 \end{pmatrix} \begin{pmatrix} 7.0129587 \\ 0.9963303 \\ 0.4065940 \end{pmatrix}$$

$Y$ is a $15 \times 1$ matrix, $X$ is a $15 \times 3$ matrix while $\hat{\beta}$ is a $3 \times 1$ matrix. Therefore, $\hat{e}$ will be the following $15 \times 1$ matrix:

$$\hat{e} = \begin{pmatrix} -2.0275802 \\ 1.7819381 \\ 0.1518924 \\ -2.2583713 \\ 0.5621561 \\ 0.3826835 \\ -1.6612956 \\ -1.0752290 \\ 0.7123284 \\ -3.6539562 \\ 1.7416287 \\ 3.3423741 \\ 2.9321104 \\ 0.3313650 \\ -1.2620410 \end{pmatrix}$$

The estimated variance of these residuals can be used to replace the unknown $\sigma_e^2$ in 5.12. How do we find an estimator for $\sigma_e^2$? From Equation 5.13a, we have:

$$\hat{e} = MY$$

Therefore:

$$\hat{e} = M(XB + e) = MXB + Me = [I_T - X(X'X)X']XB + Me$$
$$= XB - X(X'X)^{-1}X'XB + Me$$
$$= Me$$

The matrix $M$ is a symmetric matrix of dimension $(T \times T)$. An interesting property of the $M$ matrix is $MM' = MM = M^2 = M$. Such matrices are called idempotent matrices. Using this property, we have, therefore:

$$E(\hat{e}'\hat{e}) = E(e'M'Me) = E(e'Me)$$

In order to evaluate this expression, we will use the concept of the trace of a matrix. The trace of a square matrix is defined as the sum of its diagonal elements, that is, $\text{trace}(A) = \sum_{i=1}^{T} X_{ii}$. We have:

$$E(\hat{e}'\hat{e}) = E[tr(e'M'Me)] = E[tr(e'Me)] = E[tr(Me'e)] = tr[(Me\,(e'e)]$$

$$= tr[M(\sigma_e^2 I_T)] = \sigma_e^2 tr(M) = \sigma_e^2 tr[I_T - X(X'X)^{-1}X']$$

Since $tr(A - B) = tr(A) - tr(B)$, we have:

$$\sigma_e^2 tr[I_T - X(X'X)^{-1}X'] = \sigma_e^2 tr(I_T) - \sigma_e^2 tr[X(X'X)^{-1}X']$$

Further, since:

$$tr(ABC) = tr(CAB)$$

we have:

$$\sigma_e^2 tr(I_T) - \sigma_e^2 tr[X(X'X)^{-1}X'] = \sigma_e^2 tr(I_T) - \sigma_e^2 tr[X'X(X'X)^{-1}]$$

$$= \sigma_e^2 tr(I_T) - \sigma_e^2 tr(I_{n+1}) = \sigma_e^2[T - (n+1)]$$

Therefore:

$$E\left(\frac{\hat{e}'\hat{e}}{T-(n+1)}\right) = \left(\frac{1}{T-(n+1)}\right)\sigma_e^2[T-(n+1)]$$

$$= \sigma_e^2$$

Therefore, if we let:

$$\hat{\sigma}_e^2 = \frac{(Y - X\hat{\beta})'(Y - X\hat{\beta})}{T-(n+1)}$$

we will obtain an unbiased estimator of $\sigma_e^2$.

Hence:

$$\hat{\sigma}_e^2 = \hat{e}'\hat{e}\,/\,[T-(n+1)]$$

Let us use this to compute $\hat{\sigma}_e^2$ in our example. It should be noted that though we have 15 observations ($T = 15$) in this example, we have already estimated three parameters, so $[n + 1] = 3$ and hence our degrees of freedom are only $T - (n + 1) = 15 - 3 = 12$. In the case of Example 5.1, we have:

$$\sigma_e^2 = \sum_{i=1}^{15} \hat{e}_i^2 / (12) = \hat{e}'\hat{e} / [T - (n+1)] = 4.595962$$

For the data in example 5.1, we have

$$\hat{\sum}_\beta = \hat{\sigma}_e^2 (X'X)^{-1} = [\hat{e}'\hat{e} / \{T - (n+1)\}](X'X)^{-1}$$

$$= 4.595962 \times \begin{pmatrix} 1.9396789 & -0.21743119 & -0.15149083 \\ -0.2174312 & 0.03944954 & 0.01192661 \\ -0.15149083 & 0.01192661 & 0.01450688 \end{pmatrix}$$

$$= \begin{pmatrix} 8.9146905 & -0.9930550 & -0.69624608 \\ -0.9930550 & 0.18130859 & 0.05481423 \\ -0.06962461 & 0.05481423 & 0.06667307 \end{pmatrix}$$

Equation 5.14

The (1, 1), (2, 2) and (3, 3) elements of this matrix are the variances of $\hat{a}, \hat{\beta}_1$ and $\hat{\beta}_2$ respectively. In Chapter 4, we have seen that these can be interpreted as the estimates of the precision of these estimates. The off diagonal elements are the estimates of the co-variances.

So far, we have established the following:

$$\hat{\beta} \sim [B, \sigma_e^2 (X'X)^{-1}]$$
$$Y \sim (XB, \sigma_e^2 I)$$

In addition, since:

$$\hat{\beta} = (X'X)^{-1} X'Y$$

$\hat{\beta}$ is a linear combination of the elements of $Y$, and hence is a linear estimator. If we assume that $e$ is normally distributed and $X$ is fixed from sample to sample, then $Y$ must also be normally distributed. This in turn implies that the OLS estimators themselves are normally distributed, being linear functions of a normally distributed variable. As a result, we also have:

$$\hat{\beta} \sim N(B, \sigma_e^2 I_T)$$

## 5.2.1 Efficiency of $\hat{\beta}$

We know that $\hat{\beta}$ is an unbiased estimator of B. But that just means that 'on an average', $\hat{\beta}$ equals B. But this does not rule out individual values of $\hat{\beta}$ that are substantially different from B. Even if $\hat{\beta}$ is an unbiased estimator, the individual realization can lay far from B with significant probabilities if the variance of $\hat{\beta}$ is large. For an estimator to be the 'best', we would want it to not only be unbiased, but also have a smaller variance than any other unbiased estimator. Does our OLS estimator $\hat{\beta}$ satisfy this property?

We will now compare $\hat{\beta}$ with other competing linear and unbiased estimators. Let us think of a different estimator of B that is also linear and unbiased, say:

$$\beta^* = AY \qquad\qquad \text{Equation 5.15}$$

such that $E(\beta^*) = B$ where A is an $[(n + 1) \times T]$ matrix whose elements do not depend upon elements of Y or any unknown parameters.[1] When we were trying to find the BLUE estimator for b in Chapter 4, we were looking for the estimator with the lowest variance among the class of linear unbiased estimators. This is fine when we are comparing unbiased estimators for a single parameter. In the multiple linear regression model, $\hat{\beta}$ is an $[(n + 1) \times 1]$ vector. It has a variance–co-variance matrix, as we have seen above. Therefore, we need to compare variance–co-variance matrices. For example, consider the variance–co-variance matrix for $\beta^*$, say $\Sigma_{\beta^*}$. If we are saying that $\hat{\beta}$ is a 'better' estimator than $\beta^*$, we must be able to say in what sense $\Sigma_{\hat{\beta}}$ is 'smaller' than $\Sigma_{\beta^*}$. We need some 'matrix way' of saying 'smaller than'. It turns out that the matrix analogue to saying that a real number is non-negative is to define a matrix as positive 'semi-definite'. We say that a symmetric matrix $A$ is positive semi-definite if $x'Ax \geq 0$ for all $x$. We can use this concept to resolve our difficulty.

Let $a' = (a_1, a_2, \ldots \ldots a_{n+1})$ be a $(1 \times (n+1))$ vector of constants. Then, we can think of a linear combination of the elements of $B$ as follows:

$$a'B = (a_1 a + a_2 b_1 + a_3 b_2 + \ldots \ldots \ldots + a_{n+1} b_n)$$

Similarly, a linear combination of elements of $\hat{\beta}$ is given by:

$$a'\hat{\beta} = a_1 \hat{\alpha} + a_2 \hat{\beta}_1 + \ldots \ldots \ldots + a_{n+1} \hat{\beta}_n$$

The elements of $a$ can be chosen according to our convenience. Suppose we are interested only in $b_1$, then we can specify $a'$ as $(0,1,0,\ldots\ldots.0)$, so that:

$$a'B = (0,1,0,0,0\ldots\ldots0)B = b_1$$

Similarly, if we set:

$$a = (0,0,1,1,0,0,\ldots\ldots.0)$$

then:

$$a'B = b_2 + b_3$$

We say that $\hat{\beta}$ is a 'better' estimator than $\beta^*$ (remember at both are unbiased and linear) if:

$$\text{Variance}(a'\hat{\beta}) \leq \text{Variance}(a'\beta^*) \text{for all } a \qquad \text{Equation 5.16}$$

If $\Sigma_{\hat{\beta}}$ is the variance–co-variance matrix of $\hat{\beta}$ and $\Sigma_{\beta*}$ the variance–co-variance matrix of $\beta^*$, Equation 5.16 can be rewritten as:

$$a'\Sigma_{\hat{\beta}}a \leq a'\Sigma_{\beta*}a$$

or:

$$a'(\Sigma_{\beta*} - \Sigma_{\hat{\beta}})a \geq 0 \text{ for any } a \qquad \text{Equation 5.17}$$

If Equation 5.17 holds, then $\Sigma_{\beta*} - \Sigma_{\hat{\beta}}$ must be a positive semi-definite matrix. In other words, we say that $\hat{\beta}$ is a better estimator than $b$ if $\Sigma_{\beta*} - \Sigma_{\hat{\beta}}$ is positive semi-definite. If we have to show that $\hat{\beta}$

has the lowest variance within the class of linear unbiased estimators, we have to show that $\Sigma_{\beta*} - \Sigma_{\hat{\beta}}$ is a positive semi-definite matrix where $\beta^*$ is any other linear unbiased estimator of . In order to demonstrate this, we start defining a $[(n + 1) \times T]$ matrix $C$ such that $C = A - (X'X)^{-1} X'$ so that $A = C + (X'X)^{-1} X'$. Given this, we can rewrite (5.14) as

$$\beta^* = (C + (X'X)^{-1} X')Y$$

$$= (C + (X'X)^{-1} X')(XB + e)$$

$$= B + CXB + (X'X)^{-1} X'e + Ce$$

$$E(\beta^*) = B + CXB + (X'X)^{-1} X'E(e) + C(e)$$

$$= B + CXB$$

Since we assumed $\beta^*$ to be an unbiased estimator, $CX = 0$, which is a restriction that must be placed on the $C$ matrix if $\beta^*$ is an unbiased estimator of $B$. We now have:

$$\beta^* - B = (X'X)^{-1} X'e + Ce$$

The variance–co-variance matrix of:

$$\beta^* = \Sigma_{\beta^*} = E[(\beta^* - B)(\beta^* - B)']$$

$$= E[\{(X'X)^{-1} X'e + Ce\}\{(X'X)^{-1} X'e + Ce\}']$$

$$= E[(X'X)^{-1} X'ee'X(X'X)^{-1} + (X'X)^{-1} X'ee'C'$$

$$+ Cee'X(X'X)^{-1} + Cee'C']$$

$$= (X'X)^{-1} X'E(ee')X(X'X)^{-1} + (X'X)^{-1} X'E(ee')C'$$

$$+ CE(ee')X(X'X)^{-1} + CE(ee')C'$$

$$= \sigma_e^2 (X'X)^{-1} + \sigma_e^2 (X'X)^{-1} X'C' + \sigma_e^2 CX(X'X)^{-1} + \sigma_e^2 CC'$$

Since $CX = X'C' = 0$, we have:

$$\Sigma_{\beta^*} = \sigma_e^2 (X'X)^{-1} + \sigma_e^2 CC'$$

$$= \Sigma_{\hat{\beta}} + \sigma_e^2 CC'$$

$$\therefore$$

$$\Sigma_{\beta^*} - \Sigma_{\hat{\beta}} = \sigma_e^2 CC'$$

An important result from matrix algebra says that any matrix multiplied by its transpose must always be positive semi-definite. $CC' > 0$ unless the matrix $C = 0$. However, if $C = 0$, then:

$$\beta^* = (X'X)^{-1}X'Y = \hat{\beta}$$

In other words, unless $\beta^*$ is identical to $\hat{\beta}$, any other unbiased and linear estimator will have a variance larger than that for the OLS estimator. This proves that the OLS estimators for the multiple regression model are BLUE.

## 5.2.2 Asymptotic Properties of the OLS Estimator

In many cases, the small sample properties of OLS estimators may deviate from the ones established above. For example, if the stochastic error term is not normally distributed, the OLS estimators will also deviate from normality. The failure of assumption 6 implies that the OLS estimator is not an unbiased estimator of $B$, the vector of true parameter values. In a very large number of situations where we give up some of these assumptions, the small sample distribution of the OLS estimators is not even known. How do we evaluate the quality of the estimators? That is where we use the asymptotic properties: properties of the estimators as the sample size (hypothetically) tends to infinity. Asymptotically, econometric estimators often have convenient properties like normality. We use these asymptotic properties to approximate the properties of estimators in small samples. Let us now examine some of the asymptotic properties of the OLS estimators.

## 5.2.3 Consistency of $\hat{\beta}$

We know that OLS estimator $\hat{\beta}$ has the following two properties:

$$a)\ E(\hat{\beta}) = B$$
$$b)\ \text{Variance}(\hat{\beta}) = \sigma_e^2(X'X)^{-1}$$

However, unless we are willing to assume that the error term is normally distributed, the distribution of $\hat{\beta}$ is unknown. But we can say something (at least approximately) about the distribution of $\hat{\beta}$. Let us assume that $\frac{1}{T}(X'X)$ converges to a finite non-singular matrix[2] $\Sigma_{XX}$, as $T$ becomes infinitely large. This, put in words, means that as $T$ increases, the elements of $(X'X)$ do not increase at a greater rate than $T$ and that the explanatory variables are not linearly dependent in the limit. We know that:

$$\hat{\beta} = B + \left(\frac{X'X}{T}\right)^{-1} \frac{X'e}{T}$$

$$\text{plim }\hat{\beta} = B + \text{plim} \left(\frac{X'X}{T}\right)^{-1} \frac{X'e}{T}$$

$$= B + \text{plim} \left(\frac{X'X}{T}\right)^{-1} \text{plim} \frac{X'e}{T}$$

$$= B + \left(\text{plim} \frac{X'X}{T}\right)^{-1} \text{plim} \frac{X'e}{T}$$

$$= B + \Sigma_{XX} 0$$

$$= B$$

where use has been made of a theorem called Slutsky's theorem that says $\text{plim } g(Z_T) = g(\text{plim} Z_T)$ in the third and the fourth lines, and also of the fact that it is possible to show that $\text{plim } \frac{X'e}{T} = 0$ if $E(e) = 0$ and $E(e'e) = \sigma_e^2 I_T$.

## 5.2.4 Asymptotic Normality of $\hat{\beta}$

By the asymptotic distribution of a consistent estimator $\hat{\beta}$, we mean the distribution of $\sqrt{T}(\hat{\beta} - B)$ as $T$ goes to infinity. The reason for the factor $\sqrt{T}$ is that $(\hat{\beta} - B)$ has a degenerate distribution as $T$ tends to infinity. Multiplying $(\hat{\beta} - B)$ by $\sqrt{T}$ will generally result in a non-degenerate distribution. In that case, $\sqrt{T}$ is referred to as the rate of convergence and the corresponding estimator is said to be $\sqrt{T}$ consistent. We will again assume that $\frac{1}{T}(X'X)$ converges to a finite non-singular matrix[3] $\Sigma_{XX}$, as $T$ becomes infinitely large. It can then be shown that $\sqrt{T}(\hat{\beta}-B) \to N(0, \sigma_e^2\Sigma_{XX}^{-1})$. Thus, the OLS estimator is asymptotically normally distributed with the variance–co-variance matrix $\sigma_e^2\Sigma_{XX}^{-1}$ under fairly general conditions. In practice, we have a finite sample. This result can then be restated as:

$$\hat{\beta} \sim^a N\left(B, \sigma_e^2\frac{\Sigma_{XX}^{-1}}{T}\right)$$

where $\sim^a$ means 'approximately distributed as'.

## 5.3 HYPOTHESIS TESTING FOR THE MULTIPLE LINEAR REGRESSION MODEL

### 5.3.1 The t-test in a Multiple Regression Framework

In the beginning, we will learn about testing the significance of individual parameters. Suppose we want to test whether $\hat{\beta}_i$ is statistically significantly different from zero. That is, could $\hat{\beta}_1$ have come from a population where $E(\hat{\beta}_1) = b_1 = 0$? Since $e$ is assumed to be normally distributed and the $X$ variables are fixed from sample to sample, it follows that the OLS estimators are also normally distributed since they are linear functions of the values of the dependent variable which itself is normally distributed. In Chapter 4, we learned that in order to test the null hypothesis $b = 0$, we set up the test statistic $\hat{\beta}/\hat{\sigma}_{\hat{\beta}}$, which follows the students' $t$ distribution with $(T-1)$ degrees of freedom under the null hypothesis where $T$ is the total number of observations. In the case of the multiple linear regression model, we must divide $\hat{\beta}_i$ by $\hat{\sigma}_{\hat{\beta}_i}$. $\hat{\sigma}_{\hat{\beta}_i}$ can be obtained as the square root of the $(i+1, i+1)$ diagonal element of the variance–co-variance matrix $\hat{\Sigma}_{\hat{\beta}}$. This follows the Student's $t$ distribution with $T-(n+1)$ degrees of freedom, since we are now estimating $n+1$ parameters. For example, in the context of Equation 5.11, suppose we want to test the following null and alternative pair:

$$H_o : b_1 = 0$$
$$H_A : b_1 \neq 0$$

Under the null hypothesis:

$$(\hat{\beta}_1 - b_1) / \hat{\sigma}_{\hat{\beta}_1} = \hat{\beta}_1 / \hat{\sigma}_{\hat{\beta}_1}$$

follows a student's $t$ distribution with:

$$n - 3 = 15 - 3 = 12 \text{ degrees of freedom}$$

From step 5 of Example 5.1, we know that:

$$\hat{\beta}_i = 0.9963303$$

$\hat{\sigma}_{\hat{\beta}_1}$ can be obtained from the square root of the $(2, 2)$ element of $\hat{\Sigma}_{\hat{\beta}}$ in Equation 5.14, which yields:

$$\hat{\sigma}_{\hat{\beta}_1} = \sqrt{0.18130859} = 0.4258035$$

Using this, we construct the $t$ statistic as follows:

$$\hat{\beta}_1 / \hat{\sigma}_{\hat{\beta}_1} = 0.9963303 / 0.4258035 = 2.339$$

In order to make the decision of rejecting or failing to reject the null using 5 per cent level of significance, we must obtain two values $t_1$ and $t_2$ using the $t$ distribution such that:

$$P(t \le t_1) + P(t \ge t_2) = 0.05$$

Since the $t$ distribution is a symmetric distribution, we will have:

$$P(t \le t_1) = P(t \ge t_2) = 0.025$$

or:

$$P(t \le t_2) = 0.975$$

The values $t_1$ and $t_2$ can be obtained in R by typing in the following commands:

```
qt(0.025,12)
```

which gives the value −2.17883

and

qt(0.975,12)

which gives the value 2.17883.

Since $t > 2.17883$, we reject the null hypothesis that $b_1 = 0$ in favour of the alternative that $b_1 \neq 0$ at 5 per cent level of significance.

We can also think of a one-sided test as follows:

$$H_o : b_1 = 0$$
$$H_A : b_1 > 0$$

To test the null hypothesis against the above alternative using a 5 per cent level of significance, we find a value $t_1$ such that:

$$P(t \geq t_1) = 0.05$$

This value can be obtained using R by typing the following command:

qt(0.95,12)

which generates the value 1.782288. Since our value of $t > 1.782288$, we reject the null in favour of the alternative at 5 per cent level of significance.

Suppose now that we want to test:

$$H_o : b_1 = 1$$

against the alternative:

$$H_A : b_1 \neq 1$$

First, we set up the test statistics:

$$(\hat{\beta}_1 - 1) / \hat{\sigma}_{\hat{\beta}_1} = (0.9963303 - 1) / 0.4258035 = -0.008618295$$

which follows the student's $t$ distribution with 12 degrees of freedom under the null hypothesis. Hence, we know that:

$$P(t \leq -2.17883) = P(t \geq 2.17883) = 0.025$$

Since $-2.17883 < -0.008618295 < 2.17883$, we fail to reject the null at the 5 per cent level of significance.

A Note of Caution: The power of the $t$ statistic with 12 degrees of freedom to correctly reject the null hypothesis $H_o: b_1 = 1$ in favour of the alternative $H_A: b_1 \neq 1$ might be too low when the true value of $b_1 \neq 1$ but is very close to $b_1 = 1$, say 0.99.

### 5.3.2 The *F* test in a Multiple Regression Framework

Suppose we have the following regression model:

$$Y_i = a + b_1 X_{i1} + b_2 X_{i2} + \ldots\ldots + b_k X_{ik} + e_i \quad i = 1\ldots..n \qquad \text{Equation 5.18}$$

Suppose we want to test the following null hypothesis:

$$H_o: b_1 = b_2 = \ldots\ldots = b_k = 0$$

Against the alternative that at least one of the $b_i \neq 0$, $i = 1….k$
This is a generalization of the $F$ test from Chapter 4. This can be tested as follows:

**Step 1**: Carry out the regression:

$$Y_i = a + b_1 X_{i1} + b_2 X_{i2} + \ldots\ldots + b_k X_{ik} + e_i$$

and calculate the unrestricted residual sum of squares:

$$RSS_{UR} = \sum_{i=1}^{n} (Y_i - \hat{\alpha} - \hat{\beta}_1 X_{i1} - \hat{\beta}_2 X_{i2} - \ldots.. - \hat{\beta}_k X_{ik})^2$$

**Step 2**: Carry out the regression:

$$Y_i = a + e_i$$

and calculate the restricted residual sum of squares:

$$RSS_R = \sum_{i=1}^{n} (Y_i - \hat{\alpha})^2$$

The test boils down to the comparison of $RSS_{UR}$ and $RSS_R$. In effect, we test whether the variance of the error term for both the models is the same. If the restriction that all the $b_i$s are zero is valid, then the variance of the error term in the restricted and the unrestricted models must be the same. On the other hand, if the restriction is not true, then the restricted model involves an incorrect restriction and hence the variance of the error term from the restricted model must be greater than the variance of the error term from the restricted model. Let the common unknown variance under the null hypothesis be equal to $\sigma_e^2$. Under the null hypothesis, $(RSS_{UR} / \sigma_e^2) \times (n - k - 1)$ is a $\chi^2 (n - k - 1)$ variable,[4] while $(RSS_R / \sigma_e^2) \times (n - 1)$ is a $\chi^2 (n - 1)$ variable. As a result, $(RSS_R - RSS_{UR})/ \sigma_e^2$ is a $\chi^2(k)$ $(n - 1 - n + k + 1)$[5]

**Step 3**: Form the ratio:

$$F = [(RSS_R - RSS_{UR}) / k] / [RSS_{UR} / (n - k - 1)] \qquad \text{Equation 5.18a}$$

The numerator and the denominator of this ratio are $\chi^2$ variables divided by their respective degrees of freedom. As a result, under the null hypothesis that the true population variance of the error term is constant across the two models, R3 follows an F distribution with $k$ and $n - k - 1$ degrees of freedom respectively. Hence, the way to test the restriction that all the $b_i$'s are zero involves calculating R3 and comparing it to the appropriate table value. If the calculated R3 is greater than the table $F$ values, we reject the null hypothesis. Otherwise, we fail to reject the null.

R does this test for us. Consider the following program:

```
x1=rnorm(100)
x2=rnorm(100)
x3=rnorm(100)
e=rnorm(100)
y=2=0.3*x1+0.6*x2-0.4*x3+e
summary(lm(y~x1+x2+x3))
```

The program generates the following output:

```
Call:
lm(formula = y ~ x1 + x2 + x3)
Residuals:
    Min      1Q   Median      3Q      Max
-2.53390 -0.55882  0.05247  0.54112  2.63056
```

```
Coefficients:
              Estimate   Std. Error   t value    Pr(>|t|)
(Intercept)   1.9243     0.1039       18.517     < 2e-16 ***
x1            0.0899     0.1077       0.835      0.406
x2            0.6386     0.1113       5.740      1.11e-07 ***
x3           -0.4498     0.1045      -4.304      4.04e-05 ***
Signif. codes: 0 '***' 0.001 '**' 0.01 '*' 0.05 '.' 0.1 ' ' 1
Residual standard error: 1.029 on 96 degrees of freedom
Multiple R-squared: 0.3383, Adjusted R-squared: 0.3176
F-statistic: 16.36 on 3 and 96 DF, p-value: 1.154e-08
```

The $F$ statistic in the last line of the program is the relevant statistic. The null hypothesis is:

$$b_1 = b_2 = b_3 = 0$$

against the alternative that at least one of the $b_i$s is not equal to zero. The calculated value of the $F$ statistic (R3) is 16.36 and under the null hypothesis, it is distributed with

$$k = 3$$

and:

$$n - 1 - k = 100 - 4 = 96 \text{ degrees of freedom}$$

The size of the critical region is rather small, 0.00000001154, and hence we reject the null hypothesis (which, as we know from the way $Y$ has been generated, is the correct thing to do).

We can have a more general application. For example, we might be interested in testing not that all the $b_i$s are equal to zero, but that only $b_1 = b_3 = 0$. How do we proceed in this case?

**Step 1:** As usual, generate the unrestricted sum of squares by doing the following regression:

$$Y_i = a + b_1 X_{i1} + b_2 X_{i2} + b_3 X_{i3} + e_i$$

and calculate:

$$RSS_{UR} = \sum_{i=1}^{n}(Y_i - \hat{\alpha} - \hat{\beta}_1 X_{i1} - \hat{\beta}_2 X_{i2} - \hat{\beta}_3 X_{i3})^2$$

**Step 2:** Generate the restricted sum of squares by doing the regression:

$$Y_i = a + b_2 X_{2i} + e_i$$

and calculate:

$$RSS_R = \sum_{i=1}^{n} (Y_i - \hat{\alpha} - \hat{\beta}_2 X_{i2})^2$$

**Step 3:** Form the ratio:

$$R4 = [(RSS_R - RSS_{UR}) / 2] / [RSS_{UR} / (n - 4)]$$

Under the null hypothesis, R4 follows the $F$ distribution with 2 and $(n - 4)$ degrees of freedom.

If R4 exceeds the critical value at the appropriate level of significance, we reject the null hypothesis; otherwise we fail to reject it.

### Example 5.2

Suppose we have the following data on $X_1, X_2, X_3, Y$:

$X_1 = (23, 21, 34, 43, 25, 54, 35, 32, 36, 44, 20, 28, 30, 32, 36, 38, 45)$

$X_2 = (34, 33, 32, 26, 27, 28, 34, 35, 33, 37, 38, 32, 29, 34, 36, 28, 29)$

$X_3 = (22, 20, 18, 19, 18, 21, 25, 24, 27, 45, 34, 36, 45, 43, 40, 39, 25)$

$Y = (34, 45, 34, 56, 58, 43, 39, 35, 36, 32, 43, 44, 45, 41, 35, 32, 33)$

Suppose we wish to carry out the following regression:

$$Y_i = a + b_1 X_{i1} + b_2 X_{i2} + b_3 X_{i3} + e_i$$

and test the restriction that:

$$b_1 = b_3 = 0$$

We can carry out this test as follows:

**Step 1:** Calculate the

$$RSS_{UR} = \sum_{i=1}^{n} (Y_i - \hat{\alpha} - \hat{\beta}_1 X_{i1} - \hat{\beta}_2 X_{i2} - \hat{\beta}_3 X_{i3})^2$$

For our data, the following R program can be used to calculate $RSS_{UR}$:

```
X1=c(23,21,34,43,25,54,35,32,36,44,20,28,30,32,36,38,45)
X2=c(34,33,32,26,27,28,34,35,33,37,38,32,29,34,36,28,29)
X3=c(22,20,18,19,18,21,25,24,27,45,34,36,45,43,40,39,25)
Y=c(34,45,34,56,58,43,39,35,36,32,43,44,45,41,35,32,33)
e=resid(lm(Y~X1+X2+X3))
RSSUR=sum(e^2)
RSSUR
```

It generates a value of:

$$RSS_{UR} = 554.6743$$

**Step 2:** Estimate $RSS_R$

The above program can be modified to calculate $RSS_R$. The following lines should be added to the program above:

```
e1=resid(lm(Y~X2))
RSSR=sum(e1^2)
RSSR
```

This generates the value of:

$$RSS_R = 732.45$$

As we expect, the restricted sum of squares is larger than the unrestricted sum of squares. But the moot question is: is the difference between restricted and unrestricted sum of squares sufficiently large relative to the unrestricted sum of squares? How large should this be to be statistically significant? We know that under the null hypothesis that the population variances of the errors from the two models are identical, we have:

$$R3 = [(RSS_R - RSS_{UR})/2]/[RSS_{UR}/(n-4)]$$

follows the $F$ distribution with $(2, n-4)$ degrees of freedom.

So, we calculate R3 and compare it with the $F$ distribution at a 5 per cent level of significance. Remember that we have a one-tailed test.

The value of R3 can be obtained by adding the following code to the above program:

```
R3=((RSSR-RSSUR)/2)/(RSSUR/(length(Y)-4))
R3
```

The value that gets generated is 2.08336. The 95 per cent critical value for the $F$ distribution with 2 and 13 (17 − 4) degrees of freedom can be obtained by adding the following line:

```
qf(0.95,2,13)
```

This generates the critical value 3.8055. Since our R3 value is less than 3.8055, we cannot reject the null hypothesis that $b_1 = b_3 = 0$.

### 5.3.3 Goodness of Fit and Multiple Regression

In Chapter 4, we developed the measures of R-square and adjusted R-square ($\bar{R}^2$) in the context of the bivariate regression model:

$$Y_i = a + bX_i + e_i$$

We will now generalize the two measures for the multiple linear regression:

$$Y_i = a + b_1X_{i1} + b_2X_{i2} + \ldots\ldots + b_kX_{ik} + e_i \quad \text{Equation 5.19}$$

In Chapter 4, we had defined the R-square for the two-variable model as:

$$R^2 = 1 - (ESS / TSS)$$

where $ESS$ was the error sum of squares $\sum_{i=1}^{n} \hat{e}_i^2$ and $TSS$ was the total sum of squares, and:

$$\sum_{i=1}^{n}(Y_i - Ybar)^2$$

where:

$$Ybar = \sum_{i=1}^{n} Y_i / n$$

and *ESS* is the error sum of squares. The same formula remains valid; except that:

$$ESS = \sum_{i=1}^{n} \hat{e}_i^2 = \sum_{i=1}^{n}(Y_i - \hat{\alpha} - \hat{\beta}_1 X_{i1} - \hat{\beta}_2 X_{i2} - \ldots - \hat{\beta}_k X_{ik})^2$$

(which is nothing but the $RSS_{UR}$ that we have encountered above).

The formula for the adjusted sum of squares, $\bar{R}^2$ that we previously encountered was:

$$\bar{R}^2 = 1 - (\hat{\sigma}_e^2 / \hat{\sigma}_y^2)$$

where $\hat{\sigma}_e^2$ and $\hat{\sigma}_y^2$ are unbiased estimators of the variance of the error term and the variance of $Y$ respectively. In the context of the model 5.19, we have:

$$\hat{\sigma}_e^2 = \sum_{i=1}^{n}(Y_i - \hat{\alpha} - \hat{\beta}_1 X_{i1} - \ldots - \hat{\beta}_k X_{ik})^2 / (n - k - 1)$$

and:

$$\hat{\sigma}_y^2 = \sum_{i=1}^{n}(Y_i - Ybar)^2 / (n - 1)$$

Therefore:

$$\bar{R}^2 = 1 - [\{(\sum_{i=1}^{n}(Y_i - \hat{\alpha} - \hat{\beta}_1 X_{i1} - \ldots - \hat{\beta}_k X_{ik})^2 / \sum_{i=1}^{n}(Y_i - Ybar)^2\}$$
$$\times \{(n-1)/(n-k-1)\}]$$

It is obvious that for $k \geq 1$, $R^2 > \bar{R}^2$.

The adjusted R square has an interesting property that R square does not. Consider the following model:

$$Y_i = a + b_1 X_{i1} + b_2 X_{i2} + e_i \qquad \text{Equation 5.20}$$

Let us estimate the model and examine the $R^2$ and $\bar{R}^2$.

Now, suppose we add a new variable $X_3$ (possibly an irrelevant variable) to Equation 5.19 and estimate the following regression:

$$Y_i = a^* + b_3 X_{i1} + b_4 X_{i2} + b_5 X_{i3} + v_i \qquad \text{Equation 5.21}$$

Let us compare the R-square and adjusted R-square from Equations 5.19 and 5.20. You should be able to see that the R-square of Equation 5.20 (here, the second model) cannot be lower than the R-square of Equation 5.19 (here, the first model), even when the freshly added variable $X_3$ is irrelevant for $Y$. That is because, if $X_3$ is irrelevant, we have $b_3 = 0$. Equation 5.19 can be thought of as the restricted version of Equation 5.20, with the restriction $b_3 = 0$. If the restriction is true, then the residual sum of squares from Equation 5.19 will not be different from the residual sum of squares from Equation 5.20. In that case, the formula for R-square is the same for both the models and hence, the R-square will not change.

This is not true of the adjusted R-square. The adjusted R-square for Equation 5.20 is:

$$\bar{R}^2 = 1 - [\{(\sum_{i=1}^{n}(Y_i - \hat{\alpha} - \hat{\beta}_1 X_{i1} - \hat{\beta}_2 X_{i2})^2 /$$

$$\sum_{i=1}^{n}(Y_i - Ybar)^2\} \times \{(n-1)/(n-3)\}]$$

whereas the adjusted R-square for Equation 5.21 is:

$$\bar{R}^2 = 1 - [\{(\sum_{i=1}^{n}(Y_i - \hat{\alpha} - \hat{\beta}_1 X_{i1} - \hat{\beta}_2 X_{i2} - \hat{\beta}_3 X_{i3})^2 /$$

$$\sum_{i=1}^{n}(Y_i - Ybar)^2\} \times \{(n-1)/(n-4)\}]$$

Now, when $X_3$ is irrelevant, the sum of squared errors from the two models is the same. However, in the first model, the divisor to $(n - 1)$ is $(n - 3)$ while in the second model the divisor to $(n - 1)$ is $(n - 4)$. In case of the second model, a greater fraction is being subtracted from 1 in comparison to the first model. Therefore, the adjusted R-square from Equation 5.21 is smaller than the adjusted R-square from Equation 5.20. In other words, Equation 5.21 has been penalized for including an irrelevant variable. When we put in an irrelevant variable, we did not gain anything in terms of improving the fit of the model by reducing its residual sum of squares, but lost out on degrees of freedom. This is reflected in a lower adjusted R-square. In general, the adjusted R-square involves a trade-off between improving the fit of the model by including a variable and the loss of corresponding degrees of freedom. If you add an additional variable, the benefit is the reduction in the residual sum of squares, which tends to increase the adjusted R-square, and a loss in the degrees of freedom that reduces the adjusted R-square by increasing $k$ in the divisor $(n - k - 1)$ in $[(n - 1) / (n - k - 1)]$. The decision whether to include or not to include an additional variable in a regression model can be made on the basis of the adjusted R-square. This is important because very often, comparisons between models are based on their R-squares. A model with a higher R-square is preferred to a model with a lower R-square if the dependent variables are the same. But one can indulge in the game of maximizing R-square: introducing an irrelevant variable will never reduce the R-square and might improve it if by pure chance, the values are such that the sum of a squared error declines somewhat. This tendency can be curbed somewhat by using the adjusted R-square instead of the R-square. The adjusted R-square will show an improvement only if the residual sum of squares improves sufficiently to compensate for the loss of the additional degrees of freedom.

However, one must not forget an important limitation that we have seen in Chapter 4: the adjusted R-square cannot be used if the regression model does not have a constant. The adjusted R-square is only a modification of the R-square, and the formula for R-square cannot be used if the regression model does not have a constant. For models involving regression through the origin, the discussion in Chapter 4 remains valid.

### 5.3.4 Other Model Selection Criteria

The idea of imposing a penalty for reducing the degrees of freedom and comparing the resultant loss to the gain in the fit of the regression via a reduction in the residual sum of squares has yielded other criteria for model selection. We will examine three such criteria:

1. Akaike Information Criterion (AIC). The AIC is given as:

$$\text{AIC} = e^{\frac{2k}{n}} \frac{\sum\limits_{i=1}^{n} RSS}{n}$$

where $k$ is the number of regressors (including the constant) and $n$ is the total number of observations. It is easier to interpret the AIC if we take the natural logarithm of AIC:

$$\ln(\text{AIC}) = \left(\frac{2k}{n}\right) + \ln\left(\frac{RSS}{n}\right)$$

This formula is insightful. Increasing the number of explanatory variables for a fixed $n$ implies a decline in the degrees of freedom, which is a 'cost' that should be accounted for. The formula for $\ln(\text{AIC})$ does this in an explicit manner. As the number of regressors increases, $k$ increases and hence $\ln(\text{AIC})$ also increases. However, if the additional regressor leads to an improved fit for the regression, the RSS of the regression should decline. As a result, $\ln(\text{AIC})$ will tend to go down. This is the 'benefit' from including the additional regressor. Whether the overall $\ln(\text{AIC})$ declines through the inclusion of an additional explanatory variable depends upon whether the decline in the second factor outweighs the increase in the first factor. If the decline in the RSS through inclusion of an explanatory variable outweighs the penalty for including that variable, the variable should be retained in the model. In general, when one is comparing across models, the model with the least $\ln(\text{AIC})$ or AIC is desirable.

2. Schwarz Information Criterion (SIC): The SIC is similar to the AIC, except that the amount of penalty imposed for adding an explanatory variable follows a different pattern. The SIC is given as:

$$\text{SIC} = n^{\frac{k}{n}} \frac{RSS}{n}$$

Similar to the AIC, $\ln(\text{SIC})$ is insightful:

$$\ln(\text{SIC}) = \frac{k}{n} \ln n + \ln\left(\frac{RSS}{n}\right)$$

The interpretation of the $\ln(\text{SIC})$ is similar to that of $\ln(\text{AIC})$. In a set of competing models, the model with the least $\ln(\text{SIC})$

is preferable. The ln(SIC) imposes a stricter penalty on additional regressors.

3.  Mallow's $C_p$ Criterion: Suppose we have carried out a regression with $k$ explanatory variables, including the constant. Let $\hat{\sigma}_e^2$ be the estimate of $\sigma_e^2$. Now, let us choose fewer regressors than $k$, say $j$, $j \leq k$. Let $RSS_j$ be the residual sum of squares from the model having $j$ regressors. The Mallows criterion:

$$C_j = \frac{RSS_j}{\hat{\sigma}_e^2} - (n - 2j)$$

If the model with $j$ explanatory variables is adequate, we have:

$$E\left(\frac{RSS_j}{n-j}\right) = \sigma_e^2$$

or:

$$E(RSS_j) = (n - j)\sigma_e^2$$

As a result, it must be approximately true that:

$$E(C_j) = \frac{(n-j)\sigma_e^2}{\sigma_e^2} - (n - 2j) \approx j$$

When we are choosing between competing models, we should choose a model that has a value of $C_j$ that is as small as possible, preferably equal to $j$.

## Example 5.3

Let us use R to estimate a full regression. Let us illustrate using a 'growth regression'. For the past quarter century or so, economists have attempted to explain the sources of economic growth across a sample of countries. The classical Solow model links the per capita GDP of a country to its population growth and accumulation of physical capital and growth rate of GDP to technical progress. Mankiw et al. (1992)[6] consider an 'augmented' model that also includes a proxy for accumulation of human capital. We will estimate the augmented Solow model estimated by Mankiw et al. (1992). A data set consisting of 98 countries is available in R, in package AER. You must first load the package AER. If you want to see the various datasets that are available in AER, type in:

```
data()
```

and you will get a list of various datasets that are available in the package. If you want to see what is inside the dataset GrowthDJ, you should simply type in:

```
GrowthDJ
```

And you will see the different variables and the associated data.

We will regress the growth in GDP per capita over 1960–1985 for the sample 98 countries on the *gdp60* (GDP per capita in 1960), *invest* (the average of annual ratios of real domestic investment to real GDP), *popgrowth* (average annual population growth) and *school* (school enrollment rate). All the variables will be expressed in logs. In order to carry out the regression, you can type in the following commands:

```
data("GrowthDJ")
model<lm(log(gdp85/gdp60)~log(gdp60)+log(invest)+
log(popgrowth+0.05)+log(school))
summary(model)
```

Note that 0.05 has been added to population growth to account for depreciation of physical capital, which is an important variable in the Solow model.

The resultant output is as follows:

```
Call:
lm(formula = log(gdp85/gdp60) ~ log(gdp60) + log(invest) +
log(popgrowth + 0.05) + log(school))
```

```
Residuals:
    Min         1Q        Median      3Q         Max
 -0.956194   -0.186650   -0.009247   0.192474   0.931381
Coefficients:
                    Estimate   Std. Error   t value   Pr(>|t|)
(Intercept)         1.10825    0.40372       2.745    0.007184**
log(gdp60)         -0.31156    0.05053      -6.166    1.53e-08***
log(invest)         0.55266    0.08682       6.365    6.12e-09***
log(popgrowth + 0.05)
                   -0.14151    0.06349      -2.229    0.028088*
log(school)         0.22042    0.05913       3.728    0.000322***
---
```

Signif. codes: 0 '***' 0.001 '**' 0.01 '*' 0.05 '.' 0.1 ' ' 1
Residual standard error: 0.3373 on 99 degrees of freedom
(17 observations deleted due to missingness)
Multiple R-squared: 0.5203, Adjusted R-squared: 0.5009
F-statistic: 26.85 on 4 and 99 DF, p-value: 4.315e-15

Let us now interpret this regression output. The coefficient of log($gdp60$) is negative and statistically significant, since the associated $p$ = value is only 0.007184. This means that countries that had a relatively higher level of GDP per capita in 1960 experienced relatively slower growth in per capita GDP over the period 1960–1985. This phenomenon is known as convergence. Similarly, countries that had a higher level of physical capital accumulation or human capital accumulation grew faster than other countries. Countries that experienced higher levels of population growth grew less slowly. The multiple R-square of this regression is 0.5205, but when adjusted for the degrees of freedom, it drops to 0.5011. Since there were 17 cases of missing observations, those countries were dropped from the analysis. The F statistic that is reported here tests the null hypothesis that the coefficients on log($gdp60$), log($invest$), log($popgrowth$) and log($school$) are each equal to zero. That null hypothesis is rejected, since the associated $p$-value is very small. The augmented Solow model fits the sample of 98 countries quite well. However, Mankiw et al. (1992). claimed that the data do not fit the sample of OECD countries. The relevant data for the OECD countries (with population over 1 million) is also available in R in the dataset OECDGrowth. After loading the AER package, the commands to be typed in are:

```
data("OECDGrowth")
model<-lm(log(gdp85/gdp60)~log(gdp60)+log(invest)+
log(popgrowth+0.05)
+log(school))
summary(model)
```

The output is as follows:

```
Call:
lm(formula = log(gdp85/gdp60) ~ log(gdp60) + log(invest) +
log(popgrowth + 0.05) + log(school))
Residuals:
    Min       1Q      Median      3Q        Max
-0.198407  -0.071679  0.007549  0.034667  0.272718
Coefficients:
                  Estimate  Std.Error  t value   Pr(>|t|)
(Intercept)       3.54610   1.02356    3.464     0.00296**
log(gdp60)        -0.38451  0.05873    -6.547    4.98e-06***
log(invest)       0.57954   0.19592    2.958     0.00881**
log(popgrowth + 0.05)
                  -0.65349  0.27939    -2.339    0.03181*
log(school)       0.21056   0.12157    1.732     0.10137
—
Signif. codes: 0 '***' 0.001 '**' 0.01 '*' 0.05 '.' 0.1 ' ' 1
Residual standard error: 0.1261 on 17 degrees of freedom
Multiple R-squared: 0.7844, Adjusted R-squared: 0.7337
F-statistic: 15.47 on 4 and 17 DF, p-value: 1.659e-05
```

### Exercise 5.2
Interpret the above output.

Suppose you did not want to see the regression output but only store the regression coefficients in an object called c1. You can type:

```
c1=coef(model)
```

If you want to see this output, type:

```
c1
```

and you will see:

```
c1
(Intercept) log(gdp60) log(invest) log(popgrowth + 0.05)
log(school)
 3.546101  -0.3845054  0.5795382  -0.6534874  0.2105575
```

If you want to only extract the coefficient of log(*invest*), type in:

```
c1[2]
```

and you will get:

```
c1[2]
log(gdp60)
-0.3845054
```

You can also extract the AIC value of the above regression by typing the following command:

```
AIC(model)
```

The output is:

```
AIC(model)
[1] 122.6989
```

In Chapter 4, we have learnt about confidence intervals. You can generate 5 per cent confidence intervals for the coefficients estimated earlier by typing in:

```
confint(model)
```

The output is:

```
confint(model)
                           2.5%           97.5%
(Intercept)             1.38658148      5.70562093
log(gdp60)             -0.50842354     -0.26058733
log(invest)             0.16619318      0.99288326
log(popgrowth + 0.05)  -1.24295303     -0.06402172
log(school)            -0.04592787      0.46704297
```

In general, you can use the following commands:

```
print( ) ## prints simple display
eg. print(model)
summary() ## prints standard regression output
coef() ## extracting the regression coefficients
residuals() ##extracting residuals
fitted() ## extracting regression
predict() ## prediction for new data
plot() ## diagnostic plots
confint() ## confidence intervals for the regression coef-
ficients
deviance() ## residual sum of squares
vcov() ## estimated variance-covariance matrix
```

## Example 5.4

Let us take another example from labour economics. Suppose we want to understand the determinants of wages. This is generally done using a semi-logarithmic specification where the dependent variable is in a natural log form while the independent variables are in their original values. We will use the data set CPS1988 available in the package AER. This is a data frame, comprising 28,155 observations, collected in the March 1988 Current Population Survey (CPS) by the US Census Bureau. These are cross-sectional data on males aged 18 to 70, with annual income greater than US $50 in 1992, who are not self-employed or working without pay. The wages are deflated by the personal consumption expenditure deflater for 1992. A summary of the data set can be obtained by typing in:

```
data("CPS1988")
summary(CPS1988)
```

This data frame contains data on (*a*) wage (wages in dollars per week, deflated as mentioned above); (*b*) education (measured in years); (*c*) experience (measured in years); (*d*) ethnicity (Caucasian or African–American); (*e*) a variable, *smsa*, that indicates residence in a standard metropolitan statistical area; (*f*) a variable, *region*, indicating the region of the United States; and (*g*) parttime, indicating whether the individual works part time. If you want to see just the variable 'wage', you can see it by typing:

```
data("CPS1988")
attach(CPS1988)
wage
```

Alternatively, if one does not want to use the command attach(), one can extract the first column of the data frame (since the data on wage is stored in the first column), by typing:

```
data("CPS1988")
wage=CPS1988[1]
wage
```

Suppose now we want to carry out the following regression:

$$\log(wage) = a + a_1\text{experience} + a_2\text{experience}^2 + a_3\text{education} + a_4\text{ethnicity} + e \qquad \text{Equation 5.22}$$

One way in which this regression can be run is as follows:

```
data=CPS1988)
cps<lm(log(wage)~experience+I(experience^2)+education+
ethnicity
summary(cps)
```

Here, we have introduced the function I(). You must have observed that symbols like + have variety of uses in R. The + symbol can be used for arithmetic addition, and also to add variables to a regression model. If we want to use the arithmetic operators in their original meaning in a formula, they should be protected from the formula by placing them inside a function. That is the purpose of the I() function in this case. The output is :

```
Call:
lm(formula = log(wage) ~ experience + I(experience^2) +
education + ethnicity, data = CPS1988)
Residuals:
    Min        1Q      Median      3Q       Max
 -2.94281   -0.31625   0.05799   0.37560   4.38295
Coefficients:
                  Estimate   Std. Error  t value   Pr(>|t|)
(Intercept)       4.321e+00  1.917e-02   225.38    <2e-16 ***
experience        7.747e-02  8.800e-04    88.03    <2e-16 ***
I(experience^2)  -1.316e-03  1.899e-05   -69.31    <2e-16 ***
education         8.567e-02  1.272e-03    67.34    <2e-16***
ethnicityafam    -2.434e-01  1.292e-02   -18.84    <2e-16 ***
—
Signif. codes: 0 '***' 0.001 '**' 0.01 '*' 0.05 '.' 0.1 ' ' 1
Residual standard error: 0.5839 on 28150 degrees of freedom
Multiple R-squared: 0.3347, Adjusted R-squared: 0.3346
F-statistic: 3541 on 4 and 28150 DF, p-value: < 2.2e-16
```

Let us consider the variable 'ethnicity' a bit carefully. In the output, ethnicity does not show up as 'Caucasian' or 'African-American'. Here, ethnicity is modeled as a dummy variable, with 'Caucasian' taking the value zero and 'African-American' taking the value.

Therefore, the regression output takes 'Caucasian' as the base line and the ethnicity variable gives the difference in intercepts between the 'Caucasian' and the 'African-American' groups.[7] That is why 'ethnicity' has a 'afam' postfix in the output above. Suppose we want to fit separate regressions for the two different ethnicities. We can estimate the two regressions 'embedded' within the factor 'ethnicity'. That can be done by typing the following commands:

```
cps2<-lm(log(wage)~ethnicity/+(education+experience
+I(experience^2)-1),data=CPS1988)
summary(cps2)
```

Note that since we are fitting two separate regressions, we do not need a constant to differentiate between the two factor levels. The addition of −1 to the command line fits a regression without an intercept. The output is as follows:

```
Call:
lm(formula = log(wage) ~ ethnicity/+(education + experi-
ence +
 I(experience^2) - 1), data = CPS1988)
Residuals:
```

| Min | 1Q | Median | 3Q | Max |
|---|---|---|---|---|
| -2.93535 | -0.31675 | 0.05713 | 0.37539 | 4.44184 |

Coefficients:

| | Estimate | Std. Error | t value | Pr(>|t|) |
|---|---|---|---|---|
| ethnicitycauc | 4.310e+00 | 1.977e-02 | 217.97 | <2e-16*** |
| ethnicityafam | 4.159e+00 | 7.330e-02 | 56.74 | <2e-16*** |
| ethnicitycauc: education | 8.575e-02 | 1.313e-03 | 65.29 | <2e-16*** |
| ethnicityafam: education | 8.654e-02 | 5.099e-03 | 16.97 | <2e-16*** |
| ethnicitycauc: experience | 7.923e-02 | 9.231e-04 | 85.84 | <2e-16*** |
| ethnicityafam: experience | 6.190e-02 | 2.940e-03 | 21.05 | <2e-16*** |

---

ethnicitycauc:
I(experience^2) -1.360e-03 2.001e-05 -67.97 <2e-16 ***
ethnicityafam:
I(experience^2) -9.415e-04 6.069e-05 -15.51 <2e-16 ***
—

Signif. codes: 0 '***' 0.001 '**' 0.01 '*' 0.05 '.' 0.1 ' ' 1
Residual standard error: 0.5835 on 28147 degrees of freedom
Multiple R-squared: 0.9912, Adjusted R-squared: 0.9912
F-statistic: 3.954e+05 on 8 and 28147 DF, p-value: < 2.2e-16

---

The coefficient *ethnicitycaus* corresponds to the intercept for the regression on the Caucasian sub-sample; correspondingly, the *ethnicityafam* coefficient corresponds to the intercept for the regression on the African-American sub-sample. The coefficients post-fixed by 'caus' correspond to the coefficients in the regression on the Caucasian sub-sample while the coefficients with a post-fix 'afam' correspond to the coefficients in the regression on the African-American sub-sample.[8]

Earlier in this chapter, we learned of the mechanics of conducting a test of hypothesis based on comparing the residual sum of squares from the restricted and the unrestricted equations. This can be done more economically in R using the anova command. Suppose we want to test the null hypothesis that experience has no impact on wages. That is, in the context of the equation 5.21, the null hypothesis that we are testing becomes:

$$H_o : a_1 = a_2 = 0$$
$$H_A : a_1 \text{ and } a_2 \neq 0$$

Equation 5.21 is the unrestricted model while the restricted model is:

$$\log(wage) = a + a_3 \text{education} + a_4 \text{ethnicity} + e \quad \text{Equation 5.23}$$

To test the hypothesis, we must first estimate the restricted and the unrestricted models and then use the anova command to compare the residual sums of squares from the two models as given below:

```
cps<lm(log(wage)~education+experience+I(experience^2)+
ethnicity,data=CPS1988)
cps1<-lm(log(wage)~education+ethnicity,data=CPS1988)
anova(cps,cps1)
```

cps1 is the restricted model while cps is the unrestricted one. The anova command compares the two residual sums of squares. The following output results:

```
Model 1: log(wage) ~ education + ethnicity
Model2:log(wage)~education+experience+I(experience^2)
+ ethnicity
     Res.Df    RSS     Df    Sum of Sq    F        Pr(>F)
1    28152   12933.5
2    28150   9598.6   2      3334.9    4890.1   <2.2e-16***
—
Signif. codes: 0 '***' 0.001 '**' 0.01 '*' 0.05 '.' 0.1 ' ' 1
```

In this output, model 1 is the unrestricted model while Model 2 is the restricted one. The degrees of freedom for the first model are 28,150. This is so because in all, there are 28,155 observations, and we have estimated five parameters for the first model. Correspondingly, the second model has 28,152 degrees of freedom. The residual sum of squares from the unrestricted model, $RSS_{UR}$ = 9,598.6, while the residual sum of squares form the restricted model, $RSS_R$ = 12,933.5. Sum of squares represents:

$$RSS_R - RSS_{UR} = 12933.5 - 9598.6 = 3334.9$$

The $F$ statistic is the usual:

$$[(RSS_R - RSS_{UR}) / k] / [RSS_{UR} / (n - k - 1)]$$

Here, $k = 2$ and the resultant F is highly significant since the $p$ value is very small, resulting in our rejecting the null hypothesis.

## 5.4 THE MULTIPLE LINEAR REGRESSION MODEL AND THE PROBLEM OF MULTICOLLINEARITY

Generally, the data available to an econometrician does not come from any controlled laboratory experiment. The data available to an econometrician are usually generated by some real world happenings, where it is not possible to control the experimental design. As a result, the data are far from perfect. One of the problems of such experiments is that the explanatory variables may be correlated among themselves. For example, suppose we are analyzing the impact of family income and mother's education on the nutritional status of school going children, measured as the weight for age of the child. It might happen that wealthier families also have better educated mothers, and hence the two explanatory variables will be correlated. There is evidently a problem here. To see this more clearly, let us write down the regression equation that we are attempting to estimate:

$$WAG_i = a + b_1 MothEdu_i + b_2 FamY_i + e_i \qquad \text{Equation 5.24}$$

where $WAG_i$ is the weight for age for the $i$th child, $MothEdu_i$ is the years of education of the child's mother and $FamY_i$ is the annual family income for the child's family. $b_1$ represents the impact on the nutritional status of the child of a one unit increase in the years of mother's education, keeping family income constant. Similarly, $b_2$ gives the impact of one unit increase in the family income on the child's nutritional status, keeping the years of mother's education constant. However, since the two variables are correlated in our sample, our ability to actually observe a situation where one of the variables changes keeping the other variable constant, is rather limited. As a result, we might not be able to estimate $b_1$ and $b_2$ very precisely. The estimated values $\hat{\beta}_1$ and $\hat{\beta}_2$ will have large variances and low $t$ statistics. As a result, they might not appear individually statistically significant, even when the overall fit of the regression is good. Let us carry out an experiment in R to see this point more fully. We will artificially generate two independent variables, $X_1$ and $X_2$. $X_1$ will consist of a series of 100 normally distributed random numbers with mean equal to 0 and variance equal to 1. $X_2$ will consist of 100 normally distributed random numbers $+ 4 \times X_1$, so that we induce correlation between $X_1$ and $X_2$.

Finally, we will generate:

$$Y = 0.4 + 0.3 \times X_1 + 0.2 \times X_2 + e$$

where $e$ is a series of normally distributed random numbers with mean as zero and variance as 20.5, the usual random error term in the regression. We know that $X_1$ as well as $X_2$ have an independent impact on $Y$. But since $X_1$ and $X_2$ are correlated to each other, we might not be able to precisely estimate the individual marginal effects of $X_1$ and $X_2$ separately. The following set of commands will do this:

```
set.seed(123) ## This command makes sure that the same
set of random numbers are
 ## are generated everytime the programme is run
X1=rnorm(100,0,1)
X2=rnorm(100,0,1) + 4*X1
Y=0.4+0.3*X1+0.2*X2+rnorm(100,0,0.5)
summary(lm(Y~X1+X2))
```

Let us examine the output:

```
Call:
lm(formula = Y ~ X1 + X2)
Residuals:
    Min       1Q     Median      3Q        Max
 -0.93651  -0.33037  -0.06222  0.31068   1.03991
Coefficients:
            Estimate   Std. Error  t value    Pr(>|t|)
(Intercept) 0.46753    0.04807     9.726      5.24e-16 ***
X1          0.18579    0.20229     0.918      0.361
X2          0.21191    0.04950     4.281      4.37e-05 ***
—
Signif. codes: 0 '***' 0.001 '**' 0.01 '*' 0.05 '.' 0.1 ' ' 1
Residual standard error: 0.4756 on 97 degrees of freedom
Multiple R-squared: 0.8046, Adjusted R-squared: 0.8006
F-statistic: 199.7 on 2 and 97 DF, p-value: < 2.2e-16
```

As you can see from the output, the coefficient of $X_1$ is not statistically significant. But we know from the way that $Y$ is generated that the coefficient of $X_1$ is statistically significantly different from zero. Even when the OLS estimators continue to be unbiased, the variance of the OLS estimators tends to be too large, leading to a downward bias in the associated $t$ value. This is a serious problem, in that it can mislead the analyst in believing (wrongly) that the variable $X_1$ does not matter. An associated problem with a model where the explanatory variables are highly correlated among themselves is that the addition or deletion of a small number of observations will alter the results dramatically. Note that the adjusted R-square of the regression is pretty high. This means that if the relationship between $X_1$ and $X_2$ remains unchanged in the future we can get good forecasts for $Y$.

In what follows, we will attempt to understand this problem in greater detail, point out some diagnostic tests that will enable us to detect multicollinearity and suggest remedial measures.

### 5.4.1 Multicollinearity in a Linear Regression Model with Two Explanatory Variables

Suppose we have a linear regression model with two explanatory variables:

$$Y_i = a + b_1 X_{i1} + b_2 X_{i2} + e_i$$

We have from Equation 5.9:

$$\hat{\beta}_1 = \frac{(\sum_{i=1}^{T} x_{i1} y_i)(\sum_{i=1}^{T} x_{i2}^2) - (\sum_{i=1}^{T} x_{i2} y_i)(\sum_{i=1}^{T} x_{i1} x_{i2})}{(\sum_{i=1}^{T} x_{i1}^2)(\sum_{i=1}^{T} x_{i2}^2) - (\sum_{i=1}^{T} x_{i1} x_{i2})^2}$$

and:

$$\hat{\beta}_2 = \frac{(\sum_{i=1}^{T} x_{i2} y_i)(\sum_{i=1}^{T} x_{i1}^2) - (\sum_{i=1}^{T} x_{i1} y_i)(\sum_{i=1}^{T} x_{i1} x_{i2})}{(\sum_{i=1}^{T} x_{i1}^2)(\sum_{i=1}^{T} x_{i2}^2) - (\sum_{i=1}^{T} x_{i1} x_{i2})^2}$$

We say that there is perfect multi-collinearity between $X_1$ and $X_2$ if one of the two explanatory variables is proportionate to the other, that is $X_{i2} = \lambda X_{i1}$ for some constant $\lambda$. So we have:

$$\hat{\beta}_1 = \frac{(\sum x_{i1} y_i)(\lambda^2 \sum x_{i1}^2) - (\lambda \sum x_{i1} y_i)(\lambda \sum x_{i1}^2)}{(\sum x_{i1}^2)(\lambda^2 (\sum x_{i1}^2) - \lambda^2 (\sum x_{i1}^2)^2}$$

$$= \frac{0}{0}$$

which is an indeterminate expression. How does one interpret this? $\hat{\beta}_1$ is supposed to be the impact on $Y$ of a unit increase in $X_1$, keeping $X_2$ constant. However, that is not possible in the case of perfect multi-collinearity, since $X_2$ is a multiple of $X_1$. The impossibility for obtaining any estimate of $b_1$ is captured by the indeterminate result. But we can still estimate a combination of the parameters $b_1$ and $b_2$. That is, by rewriting the two-variable model in deviation form, we have:

$$y_i = \hat{\beta}_1 x_{i1} + \hat{\beta}_2 \lambda x_{i1} + \hat{e}_i$$
$$= (\hat{\beta}_1 + \lambda \hat{\beta}_2) x_{i1} + \hat{e}_i$$
$$= \hat{\delta} x_{i1} + \hat{e}_i$$

where $\hat{\delta} = (\hat{\beta}_1 + \lambda \hat{\beta}_2)$.

We can now estimate:

$$\hat{\delta} = \frac{\sum x_{i1} y_i}{\sum x_{i1}^2}$$

even when we cannot estimate $b_1$ and $b_2$ separately.

Now let us look at another situation which is not as stark.

We will now assume that $X_1$ and $X_2$ are imperfectly, but highly correlated. We have:

$$X_{i2} = \lambda X_{i1} + v_i$$

where $\lambda \neq 0$ and $v_i$ is a stochastic error term uncorrelated with $X_{i1}$. In such a situation of imperfect multi-collinearity, it is possible to estimate the values of $b_1$ and $b_2$. For instance, we have:

$$\hat{\beta}_1 = \frac{\sum(x_{i1}y_i)(\lambda^2\sum x_{i1}^2 + \sum v_i^2) - (\lambda\sum x_{i1}y_i + \sum y_iv_i)(\lambda\sum x_{i1}^2)}{\sum x_{i1}^2(\lambda^2\sum x_{i1}^2 + \sum v_i^2) - (\lambda\sum x_{i1}^2)^2}$$

Since:

$$\sum x_{i1}v_i = 0$$

by the assumption of no correlation between $X_{i1}$ and $v_i$. You can also derive a similar expression for $\hat{\beta}_2$. It is important to note that both $\hat{\beta}_1$ and $\hat{\beta}_2$ are unbiased estimators of $b_1$ and $b_2$ respectively.

The impact of multi-collinearity becomes evident if we examine the expressions for the variances of $\hat{\beta}_1$ and $\hat{\beta}_2$. It can be shown that:

$$\text{Variance of } \hat{\beta}_1 = \frac{\sigma_e^2}{\sum x_{i1}^2(1-r_{12}^2)}$$

and:

$$\text{Variance of } \hat{\beta}_2 = \frac{\sigma_e^2}{\sum x_{i2}^2(1-r_{12}^2)}$$

Also:

$$\text{Cov}(\hat{\beta}_1, \hat{\beta}_2) = \frac{-r_{12}\sigma_e^2}{(1-r_{12}^2)\sqrt{\sum x_{i1}^2 \sum x_{i2}^2}}$$

where $r_{12}$ is the coefficient of correlation between $X_1$ and $X_2$. Greater the correlation between $X_1$ and $X_2$, higher is the estimated variances of $\hat{\beta}_1$ and $\hat{\beta}_2$. This in turn means that the $t$ values will be rather small and the estimated coefficients will turn out to be statistically insignificant. The factor $\frac{1}{(1-r_{12}^2)}$ is called the 'Variance Inflation Factor (VIF)'. The reciprocal of the VIF is called the 'Tolerance Factor (TOL)'.

We can extend this result to the general regression model where there are $n$ explanatory variables (with $T$ observations on each) in addition to a constant. It can be shown that:

$$\text{Var}(\hat{\beta}_i) = \frac{\sigma_e^2}{\sum_{j=1}^{T} x_{ij}} \left(\frac{1}{1-R_i^2}\right)$$

Equation 5.25

328

where:

$\hat{\beta}_i$ is the estimated coefficient of the $i$th explanatory variable.

$R_i^2$ is the $R^2$ in the regression where $X_i$ is regressed on the other explanatory variables in the regression (excluding the constant). Equation 5.25 indicates that the variance of the estimated coefficient of the $i$th explanatory variable depends upon the variance of the error term, the variance of the $i$th variable and the variation in the $i$th variable that is not explained by the other explanatory variables included in the model.

Is multi-collinearity a 'problem'? High multi-collinearity does not violate any of the assumptions of the OLS model and hence OLS estimators are still unbiased, efficient and consistent. The estimators just have a very large standard error. But so would estimators that are based on a small sample size, or where the variance of the error term is quite high relative to the variance of the explanatory variables. Multi-collinearity should be interpreted just as another feature of the sample.

### 5.4.2 How does One Detect Multi-collinearity?

#### 1. High $R^2$ in Spite of Individually Insignificant t values

If the extent of multi-collinearity is high, most of the regression coefficients will turn out to be individually insignificant but the overall fit of the regression may be quite good. Indeed, the F test of joint significance of the regression coefficients might also reject the null hypothesis that all the coefficients (other than the constant) are jointly equal to zero.

#### 2. Simple Correlations among Regressors

A commonly used rule of thumb is to examine pair-wise correlations among the explanatory variables. If these correlations are greater than 0.8 or 0.9, then multi-collinearity is a serious problem. A modification of this rule compares the pair-wise correlations to the overall $R^2$ of the regression. Multi-collinearity is a concern when the pair-wise correlations are higher than the overall $R^2$. The significant weakness of this approach is its arbitrary nature. In particular, if there are three or more variables involved, even relatively low pair-wise correlations can lead to multi-collinearity.

## 3. The Variance Inflation Factor

You already are familiar with the concept of the variance inflation factor. The closer is the $R_i^2$ to 1, larger is the variance of the estimated coefficient $\hat{\beta}_i$. This suggests that the variance inflation factor could be used as an indicator of multi-collinearity. Some authors regard a VIF in excess of 10 as an indication of severe multi-collinearity. Though this is useful, we must remember that the variance of $\hat{\beta}_i$ depends not only on the VIF, but on $\sum_{j=1}^{T} x_{ij}^2$ and $\sigma_e^2$ as well. If the latter two can counter-balance it appropriately, a high VIF need not necessarily mean a high variance for $\hat{\beta}_i$.

## 4. Auxiliary Regressions and Theil's Multi-collinearity Effect

Another procedure that is sometimes suggested is to regress each of the $K$ explanatory variables in the regression on the remaining $K - 1$ variables (which do not include the constant). A high $R^2$ indicates that multi-collinearity could be a problem. This process has another advantage: the estimated coefficients can reveal the structure of multi-collinearity. Theil (1971)[9] proposes a measure of multi-collinearity that is based on difference between $R^2$ and $R_i^2$ (i = 1,...K) where $R_i^2$ is the '$R^2$' of the regression of the dependent variable on all the explanatory variables excluding $X_i$. Specifically, the multi-collinearity effect is measured by:

$$R^2 - \sum_{i=1}^{K}(R^2 - R_i^2)$$

If there is no multi-collinearity at all, this quantity equals zero. Larger is this quantity more severe is the problem of multi-collinearity.

## 5. Test based on the Determinant of (X' X)

If all the explanatory variables are standardized (that is, all $T$ values of $X_i$ are expressed in terms of:

$$\left(\frac{X_{ij} - \mu_i}{\sigma_i}\right) j = 1,...T$$

where $\mu_i$ is the arithmetic mean of $X_i$ and $\sigma_i$ is its standard deviation), then the elements of $(X'X)$ are simple correlation coefficients between the different explanatory variables. If det $(X'X)$ = 0, then one or more exact linear relationships may hold between the explanatory variables. On the other hand, if det $(X'X)$ = 1, the explanatory variables are uncorrelated.[10]

## Example 5.5

To illustrate the issues involved, let us use data pertaining to the US economy, published by Klien and Goldberger (1955),[11] and reproduced in Judge et al., (1988).[12] The data relates to the relationship between aggregate US consumption $(C)$, as a function of wage income $(W)$, nonwage-nonfarm income $(P)$, and farm income $(A)$ for the period 1921–50 (with the war years 1942–44 excluded). The data are reproduced in Table 5.2:

**Table 5.2**

**The Klein–Goldberger data on the relationship between aggregate US consumption (C), as a function of wage income (W), nonwage-nonfarm income (P), and farm income (A) for the period 1921–50**

| Year | C | W | P | A |
|------|-------|-------|-------|------|
| 1928 | 58.2 | 39.21 | 17.73 | 4.39 |
| 1929 | 62.2 | 42.31 | 20.29 | 4.60 |
| 1930 | 58.6 | 40.37 | 18.83 | 3.25 |
| 1931 | 56.6 | 39.15 | 17.44 | 2.61 |
| 1932 | 51.6 | 34.00 | 14.76 | 1.67 |
| 1933 | 51.1 | 33.59 | 13.39 | 2.44 |
| 1934 | 54.0 | 36.88 | 13.93 | 2.39 |
| 1935 | 57.2 | 39.27 | 14.67 | 5.00 |
| 1936 | 62.8 | 45.51 | 17.20 | 3.93 |
| 1937 | 65.0 | 46.06 | 17.15 | 5.48 |
| 1938 | 63.9 | 44.16 | 15.92 | 4.37 |
| 1939 | 67.5 | 47.68 | 17.59 | 4.51 |
| 1940 | 71.3 | 50.79 | 18.49 | 4.90 |
| 1941 | 76.6 | 57.78 | 19.18 | 6.37 |
| 1945 | 86.3 | 78.97 | 19.12 | 8.42 |
| 1946 | 95.7 | 73.54 | 19.76 | 9.27 |
| 1947 | 98.3 | 71.92 | 17.55 | 8.87 |
| 1948 | 100.3 | 74.01 | 19.17 | 9.30 |
| 1949 | 103.2 | 75.51 | 20.20 | 6.95 |
| 1950 | 108.9 | 80.97 | 22.12 | 7.15 |

Let us carry out the following regression:

$$C_t = a + b_1 W_t + b_2 P_t + b_3 A_t + e_t$$

In order to carry out the regression in R, we will input the data into excel, and then read it in R before carrying out the regression:

```
kgdata<-read.table("c:\\kgdata.txt",header=TRUE,sep="")
attach(kgdata)
model<-lm(C~W+P+A)
summary(model)
```

The data have been saved in a .txt file (tab delimited) in C:\. Since the column names are included, *header=TRUE* is required. The *sep= ""* indicates that the columns are separated by spaces. The data gets assigned to an object called *kgdata*. The line *attach(kgdata)* will put the individual variables in the data, that is, *C, W, P, A* in the computer's search path. The rest of the command you are familiar with. The following is the output of this program:

```
Call:
lm(formula = C ~ W + P + A)
Residuals:
```

| Min | 1Q | Median | 3Q | Max |
|---|---|---|---|---|
| -15.1119 | -0.6438 | 0.2393 | 1.1091 | 5.1411 |

Coefficients:

| | Estimate | Std. Error | t value | Pr(>\|t\|) |
|---|---|---|---|---|
| (Intercept) | 8.1328 | 8.9211 | 0.912 | 0.375 |
| W | 1.0588 | 0.1736 | 6.100 | 1.54e-05*** |
| P | 0.4522 | 0.6558 | 0.690 | 0.500 |
| A | 0.1211 | 1.0870 | 0.111 | 0.913 |

```
Signif. codes: 0 '***' 0.001 '**' 0.01 '*' 0.05 '.' 0.1 ' ' 1
Residual standard error: 4.527 on 16 degrees of freedom
Multiple R-squared: 0.9527, Adjusted R-squared: 0.9438
F-statistic: 107.4 on 3 and 16 DF, p-value: 8.216e-11
```

A few things are immediately apparent. First, the overall F value is highly significant, and the R-square is also quite high. Thus, the overall fit of the regression is pretty good. But when the individual coefficients are examined, only the coefficient for *W* (wage income) is significant. The coefficients for *P* and *A* are not statistically significant, in spite of the theoretical expectation that these variables should be significant in explaining aggregate consumption. The coefficient of *W* seems to be too high: a one dollar increase in wages seems to be raising aggregate consumption by more than one dollar!

Considering the nature of the data, we should expect close relationships between wage income, nonwage–nonfarm income and farm income over time. As a result, we should expect a degree of multicollinearity in the data, and we should expect that the counter-intuitive results that we have obtained have something to do with this. Let us now apply the various tests that we have discussed so far to this data set.

## 1. High $R^2$ in Spite of Individually Insignificant t values

The regression has a high R square (0.95), but only W has a statistically significant coefficient. On this criterion alone, we should suspect multicollinearity.

## 2. Simple Correlations among Regressors

Let us examine the simple correlations among regressors.

The cor() command in R will compute the correlations:

```
X=cbind(C,W,P,A) ## puts C,W,P and A into a single matrix
cor(X)
```

The output is:

|   | C | W | P | A |
|---|---|---|---|---|
| C | 1.0000000 | 0.9753285 | 0.7265437 | 0.8935914 |
| W | 0.9753285 | 1.0000000 | 0.7184674 | 0.9151739 |
| P | 0.7265437 | 0.7184674 | 1.0000000 | 0.6306067 |
| A | 0.8935914 | 0.9151739 | 0.6306067 | 1.0000000 |

As you can see, some of the correlations are quite high. The correlation between *A* and *W* is 0.915. The correlation between *C* and *A* is 0.8935. The smallest pair-wise correlation is between *A* and *P*, which equals 0.63.

## 3. The Variance Inflation Factor

Since the pair-wise correlations are high, the Variance Inflation factors are also expected to be high. As we have seen above, if the $X$ matrix is standardized, then the variance inflation factors are the diagonal elements of $(X'X)^{-1}$. Let us standardize $X$ and find the required diagonal elements of $(X'X)^{-1}$.

This can be achieved in R:

```
kgdata<-read.table("c:\\kgdata.txt",header=TRUE,sep="")
attach(kgdata)
k=length(W) ## k returns the length of the series W
W1=((W-mean(W))/sqrt(k-1))/sqrt(var(W))
P1=((P-mean(P))/sqrt(k-1))/sqrt(var(P))
A1 =((A-mean(A))/sqrt(k-1))/sqrt(var(A))
X1=cbind(W1,P1,A1) ## puts the individual standardized
series into a matrix
t(X1)%*%X1 ## generates (X´ X)
X11=solve(t(X1)%*%X1)
X11
```

The output is as follows:

```
k=length(W)
W1=((W-mean(W))/sqrt(k-1))/sqrt(var(W))
P1=((P-mean(P))/sqrt(k-1))/sqrt(var(P))
A1 =((A-mean(A))/sqrt(k-1))/sqrt(var(A))
X1=cbind(W1,P1,A1)
t(X1)%*%X1
```

|     | W1        | P1        | A1         |
|-----|-----------|-----------|------------|
| W1  | 1.0000000 | 0.7184674 | 0.9151739  |
| P1  | 0.7184674 | 1.0000000 | 0.6306067  |
| A1  | 0.9151739 | 0.6306067 | 1.0000000  |

```
X11=solve(t(X1)%*%X1)
X11
```

|     | W1        | P1         | A1         |
|-----|-----------|------------|------------|
| W1  | 7.734853  | -1.8151714 | -5.9340763 |
| P1  | -1.815171 | 2.0861792  | 0.3456389  |
| A1  | -5.934076 | 0.3456389  | 6.2127495  |

As you can see, the matrix $(X'X)$ has correlations between the variables $W$, $P$ and $A$ as its elements while the matrix $(X'X)^{-1}$ has as its diagonal elements the variance inflation factors. For uncorrelated variables, the variance inflation factor is 1.0. Values in excess of 1.00 imply that the variable in question may not be orthogonal to the rest and hence, multi-collinearity is present to some extent. Values of variance inflation factor in excess of 5.00 are regarded as indications of severe multi-collinearity by some authors. There is clearly a problem of multi-collinearity with this data set.

## 4. Theil's Multi-collinearity Effect

This approach gauges the severity of multi-collinearity using the measure:

$$R^2 - \sum_{i=1}^{n}(R^2 - R_i^2)$$

where $R^2$ is the R-square of the original regression (in this case, the regression $C_t = a + b_1 W_t + b_2 P_t + b_3 A_t + e_t$, which equals 0.95) and $R_i^2$, which is the regression of the dependent variable on all the explanatory variables excluding the $i$th variable:

```
kgdata<-read.table("c:\\kgdata.txt",header=TRUE,sep="")
attach(kgdata)
summary(lm(C~P+A)) ## regression excludes W
summary(lm(C~W+A)) ## regression excludes P
summary(lm(C~P+W)) ## regression excludes A
```

The output is as follows:

```
Call:
lm(formula = C ~ P + A)
Residuals:
```

| Min | 1Q | Median | 3Q | Max |
|---|---|---|---|---|
| -12.0420 | -5.7113 | -0.3472 | 5.1028 | 15.7401 |

Coefficients:

| | Estimate | Std. Error | t value | Pr(>\|t\|) |
|---|---|---|---|---|
| (Intercept) | 1.7258 | 15.6728 | 0.110 | 0.9136 |
| P | 2.2597 | 1.0349 | 2.183 | 0.0433 * |
| A | 5.7971 | 0.9941 | 5.831 | 2.00e-05 *** |

---

Signif. codes: 0 '\*\*\*' 0.001 '\*\*' 0.01 '\*' 0.05 '.' 0.1 ' ' 1
Residual standard error: 8.009 on 17 degrees of freedom
Multiple R-squared: 0.8426, Adjusted R-squared: 0.8241
F-statistic: 45.52 on 2 and 17 DF, p-value: 1.492e-07
> summary(lm(C~W+A))

Call:
lm(formula = C ~ W + A)
Residuals:

| Min | 1Q | Median | 3Q | Max |
|---|---|---|---|---|
| -15.68310 | -0.52096 | -0.04591 | 0.94216 | 5.13974 |

Coefficients:

| | Estimate | Std. Error | t value | Pr(>\|t\|) | |
|---|---|---|---|---|---|
| (Intercept) | 13.68520 | 3.78320 | 3.617 | 0.00213 | \*\* |
| W | 1.11288 | 0.15244 | 7.300 | 1.24e-06 | \*\*\* |
| A | 0.04917 | 1.06520 | 0.046 | 0.96372 | |

---

Signif. codes: 0 '\*\*\*' 0.001 '\*\*' 0.01 '\*' 0.05 '.' 0.1 ' ' 1
Residual standard error: 4.457 on 17 degrees of freedom
Multiple R-squared: 0.9513, Adjusted R-squared: 0.9455
F-statistic: 165.9 on 2 and 17 DF, p-value: 7.017e-12
> summary(lm(C~P+W))

Call:
lm(formula = C ~ P + W)
Residuals:

| Min | 1Q | Median | 3Q | Max |
|---|---|---|---|---|
| -15.1603 | -0.5751 | 0.2413 | 1.0667 | 5.1199 |

Coefficients:

| | Estimate | Std. Error | t value | Pr(>\|t\|) | |
|---|---|---|---|---|---|
| (Intercept) | 8.02772 | 8.60958 | 0.932 | 0.364 | |
| P | 0.44523 | 0.63348 | 0.703 | 0.492 | |
| W | 1.07534 | 0.08708 | 12.348 | 6.49e-10 | \*\*\* |

---

Signif. codes: 0 '\*\*\*' 0.001 '\*\*' 0.01 '\*' 0.05 '.' 0.1 ' ' 1
Residual standard error: 4.394 on 17 degrees of freedom
Multiple R-squared: 0.9526, Adjusted R-squared: 0.9471
F-statistic: 171 on 2 and 17 DF, p-value: 5.506e-12

The R-square of the original regression

$$C_t = a + b_1 W_t + b_2 P_t + b_3 A_t + e_t$$

was 0.9527. Theil's multi-collinearity effect is given by:

$$0.9527 - (0.9527 - 0.8426) - (0.9527 - 0.9513)$$
$$- (0.9527 - 0.9526) = 0.8411$$

The number 0.8411 is to be interpreted as follows: the effects of multi-collinearity leave the sum of individual contributions of the explanatory variables 0.84 short of what their total contribution would have been if they were uncorrelated.

## 5. Test based on the Determinant of (X'X)

This test is based on the determinant of the matrix $(X'X)$ where all the explanatory variables have been standardized. The matrix $(X'X)$ then becomes the matrix of correlations among explanatory variables. We have already seen how variables can be standardized using simple R commands. The determinant of $(X'X)$ can also be computed using R:

```
kgdata<-read.table("c:\\kgdata.txt",header=TRUE,sep="")
attach(kgdata)
k=length(W) ## k returns the length of the series W
W1=((W-mean(W))/sqrt(k-1))/sqrt(var(W))
P1=((P-mean(P))/sqrt(k-1))/sqrt(var(P))
A1 =((A-mean(A))/sqrt(k-1))/sqrt(var(A))
X1=cbind(W1,P1,A1) ## puts the individual standardized
series into a matrix
X2=t(X1)%*%X1 ## generates
det(X2) ## Computes the determinant of (X'X)
```

The output is:

```
det(X2)
[1] 0.07787287
```

Closer the value of det $(X'X)$ to zero the more severe is the problem of multi-collinearity. On the other hand, the closer it is to 1, less is the extent of multi-collinearity. As we can see from the output above, this value is rather small, indicating severe multi-collinearity.

## Exercise 5.3

Time series data for 1947–62 are given below in Table 5.3.[13]

**Table 5.3**
**Time series data for 1947–62 for the dependent variable Y and the independent variables $X_1$, $X_2$, $X_3$, $X_4$ and $X_5$**

| Year | Y | $X_1$ | $X_2$ | $X_3$ | $X_4$ | $X_5$ |
|------|-------|-------|---------|-------|-------|---------|
| 1947 | 60,323 | 830 | 234,289 | 2,356 | 1,590 | 107,608 |
| 1948 | 61,122 | 885 | 259,426 | 2,325 | 1,456 | 108,632 |
| 1949 | 60,171 | 882 | 258,054 | 3,682 | 1,616 | 109,773 |
| 1950 | 61,187 | 895 | 284,599 | 3,351 | 1,650 | 110,929 |
| 1951 | 63,221 | 962 | 328,975 | 2,099 | 3,099 | 112,075 |
| 1952 | 63,639 | 981 | 346,999 | 1,932 | 3,594 | 113,270 |
| 1953 | 64,989 | 990 | 365,385 | 1,870 | 3,547 | 115,094 |
| 1954 | 63,761 | 1,000 | 363,112 | 3,578 | 3,350 | 116,219 |
| 1955 | 66,019 | 1,012 | 397,469 | 2,904 | 3,048 | 117,388 |
| 1956 | 67,857 | 1,046 | 419,180 | 2,822 | 2,857 | 118,734 |
| 1957 | 68,169 | 1,084 | 442,769 | 2,936 | 2,798 | 120,445 |
| 1958 | 66,513 | 1,108 | 444,546 | 4,681 | 2,637 | 121,950 |
| 1959 | 68,655 | 1,126 | 482,704 | 3,813 | 2,552 | 123,366 |
| 1960 | 69,564 | 1,142 | 502,601 | 3,931 | 2,514 | 125,368 |
| 1961 | 69,331 | 1,157 | 518,173 | 4,806 | 2,572 | 127,852 |
| 1962 | 70,551 | 1,169 | 554,894 | 4,007 | 2,827 | 130,081 |

1. Carry out the following regression:

$$Y_t = a + b_1 X_{t1} + b_2 X_{t2} + b_3 X_{t3} + b_4 X_{t4} + b_5 X_{t5} + b_6 t + e_t$$

where $t = 1$ for 1947, $t = 2$ for 1948 and so on.

2. Interpret the regression output.

3. Comment on the severity of multi-collinearity using all the methods of detection examined in this chapter.

## 5.4.3 Remedial Measures

We now know how to check whether our regression suffers from multi-collinearity. Having detected multi-collinearity, what does one do about it?

What one does with the problem of multi-collinearity depends to a large extent on what we want to do with the regression. If the sole object of the regression model is to make predictions of the dependent variable, one can make out a case for not doing anything at all. After all, even when we cannot estimate all the individual coefficients precisely, a linear combination of parameters can be estimated precisely as we have seen earlier. Provided that the R square of this regression is high, we can use the estimated regression as a whole for predictions, even though we cannot draw any conclusions about the individual parameters.

If we want to say something more precise about the individual parameters, we can do the following:

## 1. Use of a-priori Information

Suppose we consider the model:

$$Y_i = a + b_1 X_{i1} + b_2 X_{i2} + e_i$$

Suppose $X_1$ and $X_2$ are highly correlated. But suppose, we have information (either from previous studies or from relevant theory) that:

$$b_1 = 0.7 \times b_2$$

Using this information, we can rewrite our model as:

$$Y_i = a + 0.7 b_2 X_{i1} + b_2 X_{i2} + e_i = a + b_2 (0.7 X_{i1} + X_{i2}) + e_i$$

$b_2$ can be estimated from this model and $\hat{\beta}_1 = 0.7 \hat{\beta}_2$ can be recovered from the estimated value of $b_2$.

The problem in this is how and from where do you acquire this *a-priori* information? Sometimes you may have it from previous empirical work. At other times, economic theory may prompt such *a-priori* information. Suppose we want to estimate the Cobb–Douglas production function:

$$ln(Y_i) = ln(A) + a ln(K_i) + b ln(L_i) + e_i$$

where $ln(Y_i)$, $ln(K_i)$ and $ln(L_i)$, are natural logarithms of output, capital stock and labour employed by the $i$th firm. Very often, since larger firms will have larger capital stock as well as have a greater number of workers employed, $K$ and $L$ might be highly correlated. However, the assumption of constant returns to scale will imply $b = (1 - a)$, which can be used as *a-priori* information. But this may not work generally. For example, in the case of the Cobb–Douglas production function, constant returns to scale is an assumption that we may want to *test*, rather than *impose*. In such circumstances, little *a-priori* information might be available.

## 2. Dropping One of the Variables:

One alternative that is often suggested is to drop some of the highly correlated variables. For example, if in the regression, $X_1$ and $X_2$ are highly correlated, one might drop $X_2$ from the analysis. However, great caution must be exercised in doing this. Dropping a variable might lead to 'omitted variable bias'. To see this, assume that we drop $X_2$ from the model:

$$Y_i = a + b_1 X_{i1} + b_2 X_{i2} + e_i$$

and estimate:

$$Y_i = a + b_1^* X_{i1} + v_i \text{ where } v_i = b_2 X_{i2} + e_i, \text{ since } b_2 \neq 0$$

The stochastic term $v$ in the new regression includes $X_2$, and is therefore correlated with $X_1$ (because $X_1$ and $X_2$ are correlated). We have seen in Chapter 4 that for the estimated coefficient $\hat{\beta}_1$ to be an unbiased estimator of $b_1$, the stochastic error term $v$ and the included variable $X_1$ are required to be uncorrelated. Clearly, this important requirement is violated by dropping $X_2$.

## 3. Transforming Variables

Let us think of a situation where we have time series data and want to estimate the time series regression:

$$Y_t = a + b_1 X_{t1} + b_2 X_{t2} + e_t$$

where $X_1$ and $X_2$ are highly correlated. Suppose we subtract each value of $Y$ from its previous value so that we have:

$$Y_t - Y_{t-1} = b_1(X_{t1} - X_{t-1,1}) + b_2(X_{t2} - X_{t-1,2}) + v_t,$$

$$v_t = e_t - e_{t-1}$$

In this model, we are regressing changes in $Y$, on the changes in the two explanatory variables. It is possible that even when the explanatory variables are correlated, changes in them are not correlated or are only weakly correlated. If this is true, we might be able to estimate the coefficients. However, this comes with a cost. In Chapter 4 as well as this chapter, we have stated one of the assumptions of the linear regression model: $\mathrm{Cov}(e_i, e_j) = 0$. Let us assume that this holds for the error term $e_t$ in the original regression. Let us also assume that the other requirement on $e_t$, $E(e_t) = 0$ is also satisfied for all $t$. But the transformed stochastic error term $v_t$ violates this assumption. To see why, note that $E(v_t) = E(e_t) - E(e_{t-1})$ = 0. Because of this:

$$\mathrm{Cov}(v_t, v_{t-1}) = E(v_t v_{t-1}) - E(v_t)E(v_{t-1}) = E(v_t v_{t-1})$$
$$= E((e_t - e_{t-1}) \times (e_{t-1} - e_{t-2}))$$
$$= E((e_t e_{t-1}) - (e_t e_{t-2}) - (e_{t-1})^2 + (e_{t-1}e_{t-2}))$$
$$= E(e_t e_{t-1}) - E(e_t e_{t-2}) - E(e_{t-1})^2 + E(e_{t-1}e_{t-2})$$
$$= -\sigma_e^2$$

Since the first, second and the fourth terms are $\mathrm{Cov}(e_t, e_{t-1})$, $\mathrm{Cov}(e_t, e_{t-2})$ and $\mathrm{Cov}(e_{t-1}, e_{t-1})$, all of which are equal to zero because of the assumptions of OLS. The implication of this is that in general, the estimate of the variance covariance matrix of the vector of OLS estimators is not given by $\sigma_e^2(X'X)^{-1}$, since this latter expression is obtained only when we assume that the stochastic error terms are independent. Thus, the $t$ values based on this 'incorrect' variance–co-variance matrix will not be right. In general, this implies that the OLS estimators of the transformed model are not efficient. Another transformation that is generally advocated is:

$$\frac{Y_t}{X_{t2}} = \frac{\alpha}{X_{t2}} + \beta_1 \frac{X_{t1}}{X_{t2}} + \beta_2 + \frac{e_t}{X_{t2}}$$

Again, the OLS estimators in this case are not likely to be efficient. This is because the variance of the error term of the transformed model, $\dfrac{e_t}{X_{t2}}$ is not the constant $\sigma_e^2$. This is because:

$$\text{var}\left(\frac{e_t}{X_{t2}}\right) = E\left(\frac{e_t}{X_{t2}}\right)^2 = \frac{1}{X_{t2}^2}E(e_t)^2 = \frac{\sigma_e^2}{X_{t2}^2}$$

This expression is not a constant, but changes with $X_{t2}$, violating the assumption of homoskedasticity. Again, it is not clear that the OLS estimators for the transformed model are efficient.

## 4. Pooled Regression: Using Time Series and Cross Section Data

Sometimes, econometricians will combine time series and cross-section data, known as pooling the data. Suppose we want to study the demand for two-wheelers in India in year $t$, as a function of the average price of two wheelers in year $t$ and per capita income in year $t$. Suppose we are estimating the following time series regression:

$$\ln(S_t) = a + b_1 \ln(P_t) + b_2 \ln(Y_t) + e_t$$

where $P_t$ is the average price of two wheelers in year $t$, $S_t$ is the quantity sold of two-wheelers in year $t$ and $Y_t$ is the per capita income in year $t$. A potential problem with estimating this regression is that prices and per capita income are likely to be quite highly correlated over time. However, it might be possible to estimate $b_1$ from cross sectional data on prices and quantities sold across different markets in a 'given year', since the per capita income in the country will be the same across different markets in any given year. Suppose we obtain $\hat{\beta}_1$. Then, we can obtain $\hat{\beta}_2$ by running the following regression:

$$S_t^* = a + b_2 \ln Y_t + e_t$$

where:

$$S_t^* = S_t - \hat{\beta}_1 \ln(P_t)$$

We can now obtain the estimate of $\hat{\beta}_1$.

However, we are implicitly assuming that the cross-sectional price elasticity of demand is the same as the time series price elasticity of demand. To the extent that this assumption is not justified, resolving multi-collinearity by using pooled regressions might be problematic.

### 5. Adding New Data

The problem of multi-collinearity is a feature of the specific sample that we are using. The problem is that the parameters cannot be estimated as precisely as could have been done had there been no multi-collinearity. But as has been emphasized earlier in this chapter, this problem arises even when the sample size is small. We have seen that increasing the sample size will reduce the variance of the OLS estimators. The same logic would hold in the case of multicollinearity. Because of the problem of high variance, the need for adding data may be felt more strongly than in the case of a regression where the variables are approximately uncorrelated. But finding additional data need not always be easy or even cost-effective. For example, the data may have been generated by a market survey, which could be very costly to replicate just for a few more observations.

## CONCLUSION

We have learned the following things in this chapter:

1. How to set up a multiple linear regression model.
2. How to estimate a multiple linear regression model.
3. Establishing the sampling properties of the OLS estimators and proof the Gauss-Markoff theorem in the case of the multiple linear regression model. We learned about the small sample as well as asymptotic properties of the OLS estimators.
4. Measuring of goodness of fit and other model selection criteria for the multiple linear regression model.
5. Testing of hypotheses and restrictions in the case of the multiple linear regression model.
6. The influence of multicollinearity, measures to detect the severity of multicollinearity and remedial measures.
7. Implementation of all the above in R.

In the next chapter, we will turn to two other common problems associated with the linear regression model: the problems of multi-collinearity and autocorrelation, apart from other problems of specification.

## NOTES

1. For $A = (X'X)^{-1}X'$, $\beta^* = \hat{\beta}$.
2. Non-singularity of $\Sigma_{xx}$ implies there is no multi-collinearity asymptotically. A sufficient condition for this to happen is the $X$ variables are i.i.d. (independently and identically distributed) from a distribution with a finite variance.
3. Non-singularity of $\Sigma_{xx}$ implies there is no multi-collinearity asymptotically. A sufficient condition for this to happen is the $X$ variables are i.i.d. (independently and identically distributed) from a distribution with a finite variance.
4. Since $k + 1$ parameters ($k$ $b_i$'s and one $a$) are being estimated, there are $(n - k - 1)$ degrees of freedom.
5. For two independent $\chi^2(m)$ and $\chi^2(n)$ variables, $\chi^2(m) - \chi^2(n)$ follows a $\chi^2$ distribution with $(m - n)$ degrees of freedom.
6. Mankiw, N.G., D. Romer and D.N. Weil. 1992. 'A Contribution to the Empirics of Economic Growth', *Quarterly Journal of Economics*, 107: 407–37.
7. R produces a dummy variable for all levels of a factor and by default uses the dummy variables for all factors except the reference category in order to avoid the dummy variable trap.
8. However, the R-square is not the usual R-square.
9. Theil, H. 1971. *Principles of Econometrics*, p. 179, New York: Wiley.
10. Even when useful, one must remember a limitation: the determinant of a matrix equals the product of its characteristic roots. Hence, a small determinant may arise not because there is multi-collinearity, but because one or several characteristic roots are small.
11. Klien, L. R. and A. S. Goldberger. 1955. *An Econometric Model of the United States, 1929–1952*. Amsterdam: North–Holland.
12. Judge, George G., R. Carter Hill, William E. Griffiths, Helmut Lütkepohl and Tsoung-chao Lee. 1988. *Introduction to the Theory and Practice of Econometrics*, p. 861. New York: John Wiley and Sons.
13. The data are from Longley, J. 1967. 'An Appraisal of Least–Squares Programmes from the Point of the User', *Journal of American Statistical Association*, 2: 891–41.

# Chapter 6

# Heteroskedasticity, Autocorrelation and Issues of Specification

## INTRODUCTION

In Chapters 4 and 5, we studied the Ordinary Least Squares (OLS) model. We learnt how to calculate the OLS coefficients and also what their small sample and asymptotic properties are. In particular, we proved that if we are willing to make appropriate assumptions on the stochastic error term as well as the set of explanatory variables, the OLS estimators are unbiased, efficient and consistent, apart from being normally distributed. More formally, we argued that:

$$\hat{\beta} \sim N(\beta, \sigma_e^2 (X'X)^{-1})$$

We also showed that the variance of any other linear unbiased estimator will be at least as 'large' as the variance of the OLS estimator.

There is no reason why all the assumptions that we have made on the stochastic error term as well as on the set of explanatory

345

Principles of Econometrics

variables ought to hold in practice. Violations of several assumptions are common in real life. Violations of assumptions have consequences for the properties of the OLS estimators, some of which are serious. In this chapter, we will be examining the failure of the following assumptions:

$$a)\mathrm{Var}(e_i) = \sigma_e^2 \text{ for all } i \text{ and}$$
$$b)\mathrm{Cov}(e_i, e_j) = 0 \text{ for } i \neq j$$

The violation of the first assumption is the failure of the variance of the stochastic error terms to be constant and is referred to as the 'problem of heteroskedasticity'. The failure of the second assumption is referred to as the 'problem of autocorrelation'. We will examine the implications of the two types of violations on the various properties of OLS estimators. If we can demonstrate that OLS estimators lose some of their desirable properties when these failures occur, we will decide on appropriate remedial measures. We will also have to evolve appropriate ways of detecting whether a violation has actually taken place. In Section 6.1, we will examine the implications of the failure of the first assumption. In Section 6.2, we will develop some diagnostic tests for testing for the problem of heteroskedasticity. In Section 6.3, we will develop some remedial measures to deal with the problem of heteroskedasticity. In Section 6.4, we will study the implications of the problem of autocorrelation. In Section 6.5, we will develop some diagnostic methods to test for autocorrelation and in Section 6.6, we will develop some remedial measures for the problem of autocorrelation. In Section 6.7, we will consider issues of specification of the regression equation. We will examine problems arising from mis-specification and badly measured data in that section. We will also examine the implication of non-random sample selection methods as well as influential observations. We will examine the implications of various types of specification errors and discuss specification tests. We will also learn about the proxy variable and instrumental variables solution to omitted variables bias which is endemic in applied work. In short, this chapter will cover the following:

1. The problem of heteroskedasticity, its implications, tests for heteroskedasticity and remedial measures.
2. The problem of autocorrelation, its implications, tests for autocorrelation and remedial measures.
3. Implications of omitted variables.
4. Implications of including irrelevant variables.
5. Implications of errors in measurement of dependent as well as independent variables.
6. Functional form misspecification and tests for functional form misspecification.
7. Non-random sample selection and its implications for OLS estimators.
8. The method of proxy variables and instrumental variables as a solution to the problem of omitted variables.

## 6.1 HETEROSKEDASTICITY

In this section, we will examine the implications of the problem of heteroskedasticity for OLS estimators. Let us start with the simple two-variable model that we encountered in Chapter 4. That model is:

$$Y_i = a + bX_i + e_i \qquad \text{Equation 6.1}$$

We will continue to assume the following:

1. $E(e_i) = 0$ for all $i$.
2. The stochastic error terms are normally distributed.
3. The explanatory variable $X$ is fixed from sample to sample.
4. $\text{Cov}(e_i, e_j) = 0$ for $i \neq j$.

We will modify assumption E2 from Chapter 4.
Assumption E2 reads:

$$\text{Variance}(e_i) = \sigma^2, \, i = 1, 2 \ldots T \text{ is constant}$$

that is, we assume that all the $T$ error terms have the same variance. We will now modify this assumption and allow each of the $T$

stochastic error terms to have a different variance. Hence, we will rewrite E2 as:

$$E2': \text{Variance}(e_i) = \sigma_i^2, i = 1, 2....T$$

One possible modification of this is to assume that the variance of the error term depends upon the values of the explanatory variable in some manner, say:

$$\text{Variance}(e_i) = \sigma_i^2 = \sigma^2 \exp(\alpha_2 X)$$

Since the variance of the stochastic error term depends upon the explanatory variable in this specification, we cannot assume that the explanatory variable and the error term are independent. Instead, we will now require:

$$E(e_i \mid X_i) = 0 \text{ for all } i$$

Let us now examine the various properties of the OLS estimator of $b$ in particular, whether the OLS estimator continues to be BLUE even when we bring in this modification of assumption E2.

### 6.1.1 Is the OLS estimator $\hat{\beta}$ an Unbiased Estimator of $b$?

We know from Chapter 4 that:

$$\hat{\beta} = \frac{\sum\limits_{i}^{T} x_i y_i}{\sum\limits_{i=1}^{T} x_i^2}$$

where $x_i = (X_i - \bar{X})$ and $y_i = (Y_i - \bar{Y})$.

Therefore, we have:

$$\hat{\beta} = \frac{\sum\limits_{i=1}^{T} x_i y_i}{\sum\limits_{i=1}^{T} x_i^2} = \frac{\sum\limits_{i=1}^{T} x_i (Y_i - \bar{Y})}{\sum\limits_{i=1}^{T} x_i^2} = \frac{\sum\limits_{i=1}^{T} x_i y_i}{\sum\limits_{i=1}^{T} x_i^2} = \frac{\sum\limits_{i=1}^{T} x_i (a + bX_i + e_i)}{\sum\limits_{i=1}^{T} x_i^2}$$

$$= b + \frac{\sum\limits_{i=1}^{T} x_i e_i}{\sum\limits_{i=1}^{T} x_i^2}$$

$$E(\hat{\beta}) = b + \frac{E\left(\sum\limits_{i=1}^{T} x_i e_i\right)}{\sum\limits_{i=1}^{T} x_i^2}$$

Now, as long as assumptions 1 and 3 hold, we have:

$$E(\hat{\beta}) = b + \frac{\sum\limits_{i=1}^{T} x_i E(e_i)}{\sum\limits_{i=1}^{T} x_i^2} = b$$

The important point is that the assumptions E2 or E22 did not come into play anywhere while proving the unbiasedness of the OLS estimator.

Result: Even when there is heteroskedasticity, OLS estimators will continue to be unbiased.

You can also see that $\hat{\beta}$ 'continues to be a linear estimator of b even when the assumption E2 is replaced by E2'. Also, it can be shown that $\hat{\beta}$ continues to be consistent and asymptotically normally distributed'. We must ask whether it is an efficient estimator as well.

## 6.1.2  Is the OLS Estimator Efficient?

Since $\hat{\beta}$ is an unbiased estimator of $b$, we have

$$\text{Variance}(\hat{\beta}) = E(\hat{\beta} - b)^2 = E\left(\frac{\sum\limits_{i=1}^{T} x_i e_i}{\sum\limits_{i=1}^{T} x_i^2}\right)^2$$

$$= \frac{E(x_1^2 e_1^2 + x_2^2 e_2^2 + \ldots x_T^2 e_T^2 + 2x_1 x_2 e_1 e_2 + \ldots 2x_{T-1} x_T e_{T-1} e_T)}{\left(\displaystyle\sum_{i=1}^{T} x_i^2\right)^2}$$

$$= \frac{x_1^2 E(e_1^2) + \ldots x_T^2 E(e_T^2)}{\left(\displaystyle\sum_{i=1}^{T} x_i^2\right)^2}$$

Since we have assumed that:

$$\text{Cov}(e_i, e_j) = 0$$

Now, had assumption E2 continued to hold, each of the:

$$E(e_i^2) = \sigma_e^2$$

and then we would have had the result we obtained in Chapter 4:

$$\text{Variance}(\hat{\beta}) = \frac{\sigma_e^2 \displaystyle\sum_{i=1}^{T} x_i^2}{\left(\displaystyle\sum_{i=1}^{T} x_i^2\right)^2} = \frac{\sigma_e^2}{\displaystyle\sum_{i=1}^{T} x_i^2} \qquad \text{Equation 6.2'}$$

However, now assumption E2 has been replaced by assumption E2′ which means that:

$$E(e_i^2) = \sigma_i^2$$

As a consequence, we have:

$$\text{Variance}(\hat{\beta}) = \frac{x_1^2 \sigma_1^2 + x_2^2 \sigma_2^2 + \ldots x_T^2 \sigma_T^2}{\left(\displaystyle\sum_{i=1}^{T} x_i^2\right)^2} \qquad \text{Equation 6.2}$$

As you can see from the above, the variance of the OLS estimator is different when there is heteroskedasticity. The proof for the efficiency of the OLS estimators requires that the variance of $\hat{\beta}$ be equal to:

$$\frac{\sigma_e^2}{\displaystyle\sum_{i=1}^{T} x_i^2}$$

Since this condition is no longer satisfied in the presence of heteroskedasticity, OLS estimators are not efficient.

**Result:** When the disturbances are heteroskedastic, OLS estimators are unbiased, consistent but not efficient.

The problem of heteroskedasticity has further implications apart from the loss of a desirable small sample property. Tests of hypotheses can become a problem if we are not careful. For example, the true variance of $\hat{\beta}$ is:

$$\frac{x_1^2\sigma_1^2 + x_2^2\sigma_2^2 + \ldots \ldots x_n^2\sigma_T^2}{\left(\displaystyle\sum_{i=1}^{T} x_i^2\right)^2}$$

and is not:

$$\frac{\sigma_e^2}{\displaystyle\sum_{i=1}^{T} x_i^2}$$

we cannot use:

$$\frac{\hat{\sigma}_e^2}{\displaystyle\sum_{i=1}^{T} x_i^2} = \frac{\displaystyle\sum_{i=1}^{T} \hat{e}_i^2 / (T-2)}{\displaystyle\sum_{i=1}^{T} x_i^2}$$

as an estimate of the variance of $\hat{\beta}$. This latter estimator is a biased estimator of the true variance. However, if we continue to use this estimate for the sample variance of $\hat{\beta}$ (many software are programmed to do unless instructed otherwise), and proceed to test the null and alternative hypotheses:

$$H_o : b = 0$$
$$H_A : b \neq 0$$

by comparing the test statistic:

$$\frac{\hat{\beta}}{\sqrt{\dfrac{\displaystyle\sum_{i=1}^{T} \hat{e}_i^2 / (T-2)}{\displaystyle\sum_{i=1}^{T} x_i^2}}}$$

to the $t$ distribution with $(T - 2)$ degrees of freedom at $\alpha$ per cent level of significance, we will be off the mark, since the $t$ statistic does not have the correct expression for the sample standard deviation for $\hat{\beta}$. We cannot say whether the bias is positive or negative *a-priori*. Hence, hypothesis testing will be a problem in the presence of heteroskedasticity, if we continue to use the incorrect expression for the variance of the OLS estimator. If we persist in using the usual testing procedure (that which we would use when there is no heteroskedasticity), the inference we draw on the basis of tests of hypothesis can be very misleading.

## 6.2 DETECTION OF HETEROSKEDASTICITY

We have learnt in Section 6.1 that the existence of heteroskedasticity will create problems for hypothesis testing. It follows that we need to be sensitive to whether our data are characterized by heteroskedasticity. We will examine below some methods for the detection of heteroskedasticity.

### 6.2.1 Graphical Method

In this method, the practitioner examines the plot of the values $\hat{e}_i^2$ of either against one of the explanatory variables or the dependent variable, to see if there are any systematic patterns in the data. This method is useful if the sample size is sufficiently large.[1] The presence of heteroskedasticity will be detected by patterns in the plot.

### 6.2.2 Park Test

A criticism of the graphical method is that it is too subjective. One practitioner can see a 'pattern' where another practitioner may fail to see one altogether. Park[2] developed a more formal method to test whether $\sigma_i^2$ was some function of the explanatory variable $X_i$. In order to explicitly model this dependence, Parks suggested the following functional form:

$$\sigma_i^2 = \sigma^2 X_i^\beta e^{v_i} \qquad \text{Equation 6.3}$$

where $v_i$ is the stochastic disturbance term and $e$ is the exponential function. Let us take natural logarithms of both sides:

$$\ln(\sigma_i^2) = \ln\sigma^2 + \beta \ln X_i + v_i \qquad \text{Equation 6.4}$$

This can be seen as a linear regression model where:

$$\ln(\sigma_i^2) = \alpha + \beta \ln X_i + v_i$$

where:

$$\alpha = \ln(\sigma^2)$$

The null hypothesis of no heteroskedasticity boils down to the null and alternative hypotheses:

$$H_o : \beta = 0$$
$$H_A : \beta \neq 0$$

## Implementation of the Parks Test

In order to implement the Parks test, we need to have an estimate of the unknown $\sigma_i^2$. This can be done in the following two-step procedure:

**Step 1:** In the first step, run the regression:

$$Y_i = a + bX_i + e_i$$

disregarding the problem of heteroskedasticity and obtain the regression residuals, $\hat{e}_i$.

**Step 2:** In the second step, run the regression:

$$\ln(\hat{e}_i^2) = \alpha + \beta \ln X_i + v_i$$

and test the null hypothesis:

$$H_o : \beta = 0$$

against the alternative:

$$H_A : \beta \neq 0$$

The problem of heteroskedasticity shows up when we fail to reject the null.

Let us take an example. Suppose we have data on $X$ and $Y$ and estimate the regression:

$$Y_i = a + bX_i + e_i$$

where:

$$\text{Variance}(e_i) = X_i$$

Hence, there is a clear case of heteroskedasticity. (In a real-life situation, we would obviously not know that heteroskedasticity exists so easily, we need to test for it). The following R program generates the desired data and then conducts the Parks test:

```
X=abs(rnorm(100)) ## generates X as abs.vals. Of 100 normal
random numbers
e=rnorm(100,0,X) ## variance of e is X square
Y=2+0.3*X+e ## the model for Y
summary(lm(Y~X)) ## First step regression
r=resid(lm(Y~X)) ## storing the residuals
r2=r*r ## generating residual square
summary(lm(log(r2)~log(X))) ## the second step regression
```

In this model, we have generated the stochastic disturbance term to be heteroskedastic. Line two of the program sets the variance of $e$ to equal $X$. The third line generates the values of $Y$. As you can see in the output ahead, in the first step regression, the estimated coefficient of $X$ has a rather large standard error, resulting in the coefficient turning out to be statistically significant at 5 per cent level of significance. We know from the way in which we have generated the data that this is not true. Also, note that the estimated value of the coefficient of $X$ is quite far from the true value which equals 3. This is a good example of the problem that heteroskedasticity causes. The regression in the second step regresses the logarithm of the squared residuals from the first regression on the logarithm of values of $X$. As you can clearly see, the coefficient of $\log(X)$ is statistically significant, confirming heteroskedasticity:

```
Call:
lm(formula = Y ~ X)
Residuals:
     Min       1Q     Median      3Q       Max
  -4.2547   -0.3423   -0.0573    0.2572    4.7221

Coefficients:
              Estimate  Std. Error  t value  Pr(>|t|)
(Intercept)    2.0572    0.1944     10.585   <2e-16 ***
X              0.3574    0.1916      1.866   0.0651 .
—
Signif. codes: 0 '***' 0.001 '**' 0.01 '*' 0.05 '.' 0.1 ' ' 1

Residual standard error: 1.197 on 98 degrees of freedom
Multiple R-squared: 0.0343, Adjusted R-squared: 0.02444
F-statistic: 3.48 on 1 and 98 DF, p-value: 0.06509
> r=resid(lm(Y~X)) ## storing the residuals
> r2=r*r ## generating residual square
> summary(lm(log(r2)~log(X))) ## the second step regression
Call:
lm(formula = log(r2) ~ log(X))
Residuals:
     Min       1Q     Median      3Q       Max
  -7.4310   -1.3267    0.3953    1.6311    4.9443
Coefficients:
              Estimate  Std. Error  t value  Pr(>|t|)
(Intercept)   -1.3410    0.2446     -5.482   3.27e-07 ***
log(X)         1.5872    0.1812      8.757   6.00e-14 ***
—
Signif. codes: 0 '***' 0.001 '**' 0.01 '*' 0.05 '.' 0.1 ' ' 1

Residual standard error: 2.115 on 98 degrees of freedom
Multiple R-squared: 0.439, Adjusted R-squared: 0.4333
F-statistic: 76.69 on 1 and 98 DF, p-value: 5.996e-14
```

Though intuitively appealing, there are some problems with this test. In particular, the stochastic error term entering in the second stage regression equation may itself be heteroskedastic. In that case, testing whether the coefficient of $\log(X)$ is statistically significant might be difficult. Nevertheless, this test continues to be a useful and intuitively appealing method.

### 6.2.3 Glesjer Test[3]

Glesjer suggests a closely related procedure. The Glesjer test consists of regressing the absolute values of the estimated residuals from stage 1 regression on various linear and non-linear functions of the explanatory variable, and testing for the significance of the coefficients just like in the Parks test. Just to cite some examples, the regression might take the following functional forms:

$$\left|\hat{e}_i\right| = a + bX_i + v_i$$

$$\left|\hat{e}_i\right| = a + b\sqrt{X_i} + v_i$$

$$\left|\hat{e}_i\right| = a + b\frac{1}{\sqrt{X_i}} + v_i$$

$$\left|\hat{e}_i\right| = a + b\frac{1}{X_i} + v_i$$

Though this test is a good practical diagnostic measure, the stochastic error term could be serially correlated, have a non-zero expected value and also can be heteroskedastic.

### 6.2.4 Goldfeld–Quandt Test

Suppose we have the following regression:

$$Y_i = a + bX_i + e_i$$

Suppose we suspect that the variance of the stochastic error term is not constant, but is positively related to the value of the explanatory variable, so that if we arrange the values of the explanatory variable in an ascending order, the variance of the error term will increase with successive values of $X$. The Goldfeld–Quandt procedure tests whether this is indeed the case. The steps that are involved are as follows:

**Step 1:** Suppose we have $T$ observations on $X$. Arrange the values of $Y$ and $X$ in an increasing order according to the values of $X$, beginning with the lowest value of $X$ and the associated value of $Y$, then the next lowest value of $X$ and the associated value of $Y$ and so on.

**Step 2:** Omit $m$ (where $m$ is a predetermined number) central observations so that we have $(T - m)$ observations left. Divide the $(T - m)$ observations into two subsamples, the first $(T - m) / 2$ observations that are in the first half, and the remaining $(T - m) / 2$ observations that are in the second half.

**Step 3:** Fit two separate regressions for the two sub-samples. The Goldfeld–Quandt test relies on testing whether the sample variance of the estimated residuals in the second sub-sample is in fact statistically greater than the sample variance of the estimated residuals in the first sub-sample. That is, we form the ratio of the (residual sum of squares in the second equation / the degrees of freedom) to the (residual sum of squares in the first equation / the degrees of freedom). Formally, we have:

$$\lambda = \frac{\dfrac{RSS_2}{df_2}}{\dfrac{RSS_1}{df_1}}, \qquad \text{Equation 6.5}$$

$$df_1 = df_2 = \frac{(T - m)}{2} - k$$

where $k$ is the number of parameters in the regression that is being estimated. In the two-variable case that we are considering here, $k = 2$. The null hypothesis is of homoskedasticity. It can be shown that if the error term is normally distributed, under the null hypothesis, $\lambda$ follows the $F$ distribution with numerator and denominator degrees of freedom:

$$df_1 = df_2 = \frac{(T - m)}{2} - k$$

In the spirit of Chapter 3, we reject the null hypothesis if the value of $\lambda$ is large enough so that the critical region associated with the one sided hypothesis is rather small, smaller than the conventional levels of 1 per cent or 5 per cent.

Why do we delete the $m$ central observations? Notice that the test statistic being compared is the ratio of the estimated variance of the error term in the second sub-sample to the estimated variance of the error term in the first sub-sample. Since we suspect that the variance of the error term is increasing in $X$, the null hypothesis of homoskedasticity will be rejected if this ratio is too large to be plausible under the null hypothesis. We omit the $m$ central observations to sharpen the difference between the two sub-samples. Clearly, the choice of the number $m$ is important. Goldfeld and Quandt themselves suggest that if $T = 30$, then $m$ should be 8, and if $T$ is 60, $m$ should be 16. Evidence by Harvey and Phillips (1974)[4] suggests that no more than a third of the observations be dropped.

This test too suffers from a few limitations. One practical limitation is that if there are more than one explanatory variable (excluding the constant) in the regression model, we might not be sure about which one of them is related to the variance of the stochastic disturbance term. In this scenario, we will have to carry out this test on each individual variable, making it a cumbersome procedure. However, a more significant limitation is the assumption that the disturbance term is normally distributed. Unless it is normally distributed, the ratio of the two residual sums divided by their degrees of freedom does not follow the $F$ distribution, which we know from the definition of the $F$ distribution. Hence, in models where the error term does not follow the normal distribution (especially where $n$ is not very large), the $F$ test will only yield approximate results. Also, the power of the test is likely to be low since in general, we are not likely to know how the variance of the error term depends upon the explanatory variable.

## Example 6.1

Let us take a hypothetical example where $X$ is a set of 100 normally distributed random numbers with mean 100 and variance 1. Let:

$$Y_i = a + bX_i + e_i$$

where $e_i \sim N(0, X_i)$, so that the variance of the stochastic error term increases with $X$. We will hypothetically set $a = 2$ and $b = 3$. We will generate the data as usual in R. After generating the data, we need to rank the observations of $Y$ and $X$ on the basis of values of $X$, starting from the smallest and going on to the largest. We will then delete $m$ central observations, fit separate regressions to the two sub-samples, compute $F$ and calculate the size of the critical region under the null hypothesis. The following R program will carry this out:

```
X=rnorm(100,100,1)
e=rnorm(100,0,X)
Y=3+2*X+e
dat=cbind(Y,X)
## The line below stores the data as a data frame
dat<-as.data.frame(dat,row.names=c("Y","X"),optional=TRUE)
attach(dat)
## The line below sorts Y and X in ascending order of X.
dat1=dat[order(X),]
dat
dat1
RSS1=deviance(lm(Y[1:40]~X[1:40],data=dat1))
RSS2=deviance(lm(Y[61:100]~X[61:100],data=dat1))
df1=38
df2=38
lambda=(RSS2/38)/(RSS1/38)
critreg=1-pf(lambda,38,38)
critreg
```

This program gives the following output:

```
critreg
[1] 0.003685032
```

As you can see, the size of the critical region is very small, which means that there is strong evidence against the null of no heteroskedasticity.

## 6.2.5 Breusch–Pagan–Godfrey Test

Because of the various limitations of the Goldfeld–Quandt test, another popular test called the Breusch–Pagan–Godfrey test is often deployed.

Suppose we have a regression model involving $k$ explanatory variables in addition to the constant:

$$Y_i = \alpha + \beta_1 X_{i1} + \beta_2 X_{i2} + .... + \beta_k X_{ik} + e_i$$ 

Equation 6.6

Let us assume that the variance of the stochastic error term $\sigma_i^2$ is described as:

$$\sigma_i^2 = f(a + a_1 Z_{i1} + a_2 Z_{i2} + ....... + a_m Z_{im})$$ 

Equation 6.7

where $f(\ )$ is some deterministic function (which means that there is no error term involved in the functional specification of Equation 6.7, and the $Z$'s are deterministic variables, but can be the same $X$ variables that appear in Equation 6.6.

The null hypothesis of no heteroskedasticity can be tested by:

$$H_o : a_1 = a_2 = ...... = a_m = 0$$

### *Implementation of the Test*

**Step 1:** Estimate Equation 6.7 by using OLS and store the residuals $\hat{e}_i$.

**Step 2:** Calculate:

$$\overline{\sigma}^2 = \frac{\sum_{i=1}^{T} \hat{e}_i^2}{T}$$

and construct the variables:

$$\rho_i = \frac{\hat{e}_i^2}{\overline{\sigma}^2}$$

Note that $\overline{\sigma}^2$ is a biased estimator of the variance of the error term, the unbiased estimator being:

$$\overline{\sigma}_1^2 = \frac{\sum_{i=1}^{T} \hat{e}_i^2}{T-k}$$

**Step 3**: Regress

$$\rho_i = \eta + \eta_1 Z_{i1} + \ldots\ldots + Z_{im} + \nu_i$$

**Step 4**: Let ESS be the explained sum of squares from step 3. Then, it can be shown that under the null hypothesis of no heteroskedasticity,

$$\frac{1}{2} ESS \underset{asy}{\sim} \chi_m^2$$

(which means that as the sample size becomes large, the distribution of $\frac{1}{2} ESS$ is chi-square with $m - 1$ degrees of freedom). If the value of $\frac{1}{2} ESS$ exceeds that of the chi-square with $(m)$ degrees of freedom, we reject the null hypothesis.

## Example 6.2

Let us generate hypothetical data for a regression with heteroskedastic disturbances, and apply the Breusch–Pagan–Godfrey test to it. As usual, we will write an R program for this:

```
X=rnorm(100,100,1)
Z=rnorm(100,100,1)
e=rnorm(100,0,2+0.3*X+0.5*Z)
Y=2+3*X+0.5*Z+e
e=resid(lm(Y~X+Z))
sigsqr=sum(e^2)/length(X)
rho=e^2/sigsqr
pred=fitted(lm(rho~X+Z))
ESS=(sum((pred-mean(rho))^2))/2
ESS
1-pchisq(ESS,2)
```

In this program, we have generated 100 values of $X$ and $Z$, each normally distributed random numbers with mean 100 and variance 1. The stochastic error term is generated as a set of 100 normally distributed random numbers with mean 0 and variance:

$$\sigma_{ie}^2 = 2 + 0.3 \times X_i + 0.5 \times Z_i$$

which is a clearly heteroskedastic term. The values of the dependent variable, $Y$ are generated as $Y_i = 2 + 3 \times X_i + 0.5 \times Z_i + e_i$. The next line extracts the residuals of the regression of $Y$ on $X$ and $Z$. The next two lines calculate the quantities mentioned in step 2. The subsequent line stores the fitted values of the regression of rho on $X$ and $Z$, after which, $\dfrac{ESS}{2}$ is calculated. The last line computes the size of the critical region. We reject the null hypothesis of homoskedasticity if the size of the critical region is rather small. If we run this program, we get the following output, giving us the size of the critical region:

```
[1]0.04138284
```

As we can see from the size of the critical region (roughly 4 per cent), the observed evidence is rather implausible given the null hypothesis. Hence, we can be justified in rejecting the null hypothesis.

Though a highly useful test, this test has a significant limitation in that the stochastic error term in the original regression is required to be normally distributed.

### 6.2.6 White's General Heteroskedasticity Test

Suppose we have the following regression model:

$$Y_i = \alpha + \beta_1 X_{i1} + \beta_2 X_{i2} + e_i \qquad \text{Equation 6.8}$$

The mechanics of the White test are as follows:

**Step 1:** Estimate Equation 6.8 from the given data and store the residuals, $\hat{e}_i$

**Step 2**: Carry out the following regression:

$$\hat{e}_i^2 = \eta + \lambda_1 X_{i1} + \lambda_2 X_{i2} + \lambda_3 X_{i1}^2 + \lambda_4 X_{i2}^2 + \lambda_5 X_{i1} X_{i2} + \nu_i \qquad \text{Equation 6.9}$$

In this equation, we use the original variables $X$, their squares (and higher powers might be used too), and the interaction terms indicated by the products of the explanatory variables.

**Step 4**: Under the null hypothesis of no heteroskedasticity,

$$T \times R^2 \sim_{asy} \chi_{df}^2$$

where $T$ is the sample size, $R^2$ is the R-Square of the regression in step 2, (often referred to as the auxiliary regression) and $df$ is the number of explanatory variables in Equation 6.9 excluding the constant. The White's test is an extremely general test. In order to carry it out, we do not need to make any specific assumptions about the nature of heteroskedasticity. However, it has a potentially serious shortcoming. The test may indicate heteroskedasticity but it may also indicate some specification error like say the omission of the interaction term from the original regression. If the size of the critical region associated with $T \times R^2$ is small, we either have heteroskedasticity or specification errors, the latter of which are dealt with in the Section VII. At this stage, one must remember that the White test is a test of heteroskedasticity and/or of specification errors. Hence, except in the context of a specific problem, not much can be said about the power of the White's test. Also, it is what is called a 'non-constructive' test, in that, once the null is rejected, it does not indicate what to do next.

There are inbuilt functions in R to conduct most of the usual tests of heteroskedasticity.

To carry out the Breusch–Pagan–Godfrey test, we can use the *bptest()* command:[5]

```
X=rnorm(100,100,1)
Z=rnorm(100,100,1)
e=rnorm(100,0,2+0.3*X+0.5*Z)
Y=2+3*X+0.5*Z+e
bptest(lm(Y~X+Z))
```

The output is:

```
studentized Breusch-Pagan test
data: lm(Y ~ X + Z)
BP = 5.7323, df = 2, p-value = 0.05692
```

In order to conduct the Goldfeld–Quandt test,[6] we have:

```
Z=rnorm(100,100,1)
e=rnorm(100,0,0.3*X)
Y=2+3*X+e
gqtest(lm(Y~X),fraction=1/3)
```

The fraction 1/3 suggests that the central 1/3rd observations are to be dropped. In the case of our example, this would mean that the central 33 observations will be dropped. The output is:

```
Goldfeld–Quandt test
data: lm(Y ~ X)
GQ = 0.8823, df1 = 32, df2 = 31, p-value = 0.6371
```

The first 34 observations have been used to estimate the first regression. The next 33 observations have been dropped and the last regression has been fitted on the last 33 observations. The null cannot be rejected.

In this section, we have examined various tests for heteroskedasticity. Suppose we have identified our regression model as one with heteroskedastic disturbances. We know that the OLS estimator is not efficient because of heteroskedastic disturbances. How do we remedy the situation? It is to the remedial measures that we now turn.

## 6.3 REMEDIAL MEASURES FOR HETEROSKEDASTICITY

Suppose we have the following regression:

$$Y_i = a + bX_i + e_i,$$   Equation 6.10

and the stochastic disturbance term is normally distributed, mutually uncorrelated, and has an expected value of zero for all $i$, but $E(e_i^2) = \sigma_i^2$. First, let us make a simplifying assumption, that we know $\sigma_i^2$. Let us divide each value of $Y$ by $\sigma_i^2$ so that:

$$\frac{Y_i}{\sigma_i} = \frac{a}{\sigma_i} + b\frac{X_i}{\sigma_i} + \frac{e_i}{\sigma_i}$$

Equation 6.11

or

$$Y_i^* = a^* + b^* X_i^* + v_i$$

Let us examine the variance of $v_i$. The variance of:

$$v_i = E\left(\frac{e_i}{\sigma_i}\right)^2 = \frac{1}{\sigma_i^2}E(e_i^2) = 1$$

This last step is possible since we have assumed that $\sigma_i^2$ is a known constant, and can be brought out of the expectations operator. The result we have got shows that the stochastic error term in the rescaled model Equation 6.11 is no longer heteroskedastic, since the variance of the error term is now constant and equal to 1 for all $i$. As a result, in order to obtain the OLS estimator of Equation 6.11, we minimize:

$$k = \sum_{i=1}^{T}(\delta_i Y_i - \delta_i \alpha - \delta_i X_i)^2 = \sum_{i=1}^{T}\delta_i^2(Y_i - \alpha - \beta X_i)^2$$

where:

$$\delta_i = \frac{1}{\sigma_i^2}.$$

Equation 6.12

Let us examine Equation 6.12 carefully. In Equation 6.12, the sum of squares that is being minimized is a weighted sum of squares, since each of the $(Y_i - \alpha - \beta X_i)^2$ is weighted by the inverse of the variance of $e_i$. We want to achieve an estimator that has as low a variance as possible. A way of achieving this is to give a lower weight to those observations that have a higher variance when computing the estimators, instead of the usual OLS method of giving equal importance to all observations. The resulting estimator that we get, which is:

$$\hat{\beta}^* = \frac{\sum\limits_{i=1}^{T}(X_i^* - \overline{X^*})(Y_i^* - \overline{Y^*})}{\sum\limits_{i=1}^{T}(X_i^* - \overline{X^*})^2} \qquad \text{Equation 6.12}'$$

which can be shown to be BLUE, since the variance of the stochastic error terms in the rescaled model is now constant.

To recapitulate, in Equation 6.12, each product involving $X_i$ and $Y_i$ in the numerator as well as the denominator has been 'weighted' by the inverse of $\sigma_i^2$. In the case of the simple OLS, each product involving $X_i$ and $Y_i$ carries equal weight, whereas for the estimator in Equation 6.12', this is not so. The method of estimation, exemplified in Equation 6.12 and which is known as 'Weighted Least Squares (WLS)' explicitly takes into account the information contained in the unequal variability of the dependent variable, and produces estimators that are BLUE. WLS is one example of a more general approach called 'Generalized Least Squares', that is used to estimate parameters when the assumptions of homoskedasticity or no autocorrelation is violated.

The variance of:

$$\hat{\beta}^* = \frac{\sigma_e^2}{\sum\limits_{i=1}^{T}\left(\delta_i X_i - \frac{\sum\limits_{i=1}^{T}\delta_i X_i}{\sum\limits_{i=1}^{T}\delta_i}\right)^2}$$

and tests of hypothesis can be conducted using this expression for its variance. An estimate for $\sigma_e^2$ can be obtained by:

$$\hat{\sigma}_e^2 = \frac{1}{T-2}\sum\limits_{i=1}^{T}\delta_i^2(Y_i - \hat{\beta}^* X_i)^2$$

Since in the rescaled model, all variables, including the constant are rescaled, the new model does not have an intercept. Also, the rescaled model is only deployed in order to obtain the GLS estimator and does not have an economic interpretation in its own right. The coefficients have to be interpreted in the context of the original unscaled model.

However, it is hard to think of many economic applications where $\sigma_i^2$ is known. How do we then estimate the GLS model discussed above? If the $\delta_i$s are unknown, can we replace them by their unbiased or consistent estimates? This is not as straightforward as it seems, because now we will have to estimate $T\,\hat{\delta}_i s$ from $T$ observations. For each observation $i$, there is only one $e_i$ from which to estimate its variance and hence $\hat{\delta}_i$. Therefore, it is not possible to have consistent estimates of $\hat{\delta}_i$ without making additional assumptions. A possible assumption that we can make is:

$$\text{Variance of } e_i = \sigma_e^2 \exp(\alpha_1 X_i) \qquad \text{Equation 6.13}$$

where $X$ is the explanatory variable in our model. This is an example of a model with 'multiplicative heteroskedasticity'. This form of heteroskedasticity is common in applied work. From Equation 6.13, we have:

$$\ln(e_i^2) = \ln(\sigma_e^2) + \alpha_1 X_i \,.$$

The parameter $\alpha_1$ can be estimated by running the regression:

$$\ln(e_i^2) = \ln(\sigma_e^2) + \alpha_1 X_i + \eta_i \qquad \text{Equation 6.14}$$

where $\eta_i$ is a stochastic disturbance term that is homoskedastic and uncorrelated with the explanatory variable.[7] Now, we can calculate the 'Feasible Generalized Least Squares' (FGLS) estimate of $b$ in Equation 6.10. Let us enumerate the steps involved:

**Step 1**: Estimate Equation 6.10 using OLS and obtain $\hat{\beta}$.

**Step2**: Compute:

$$\log(\hat{e}_i^2) = \log(Y_i - \hat{\alpha} - \hat{\beta} X_i)^2$$

**Step 3**: Estimate Equation 6.14 using OLS after replacing $\log(e_i^2)$ by $\log(\hat{e}_i^2)$, and obtain the consistent OLS estimator of $\alpha_1$.

**Step 4:** Calculate:

$$\hat{\delta}_i = \frac{1}{\exp(\text{fitted values of the auxiliary regression})}$$

and rescale Equation 6.10 as

$$\hat{\delta}_i Y_i = \hat{\delta}_i \hat{\alpha} + \hat{\delta}_i \hat{\beta} X_i + \hat{\delta}_i e_i$$

**Step 5:** Estimate the rescaled model by OLS, by regressing $\log(\hat{\sigma}_i^2)$ on a constant and the explanatory variable $X$. This yields the FGLS estimator of $\beta$, $\hat{\beta}^*$ and that of $\alpha, \hat{\alpha}^*$. We will call this the 'auxiliary regression'.

**Step 6:** A consistent estimate of $\sigma_i^2$ is given by:

$$\hat{\sigma}_e^2 = \frac{1}{(T-2)} \sum_{i=1}^{T} \hat{\delta}_i^2 (Y_i - \hat{\alpha}^* - \hat{\beta}^* X_i)^2$$

**Step 7:** The variance of the FGLS estimator can be obtained as:

$$\text{Variance}(\hat{\beta}^*) = \frac{\hat{\sigma}_e^2}{\sum_{i=1}^{T} \hat{\delta}_i^2 (X_i - \overline{X})^2}$$

FGLS estimators can be computed in R. To illustrate, let us use dataset 'Journals' from the R package AER, which has data on subscriptions, prices and other parameters on various economics journals. Suppose we want to regress logarithm of library subscriptions (*subs*) on the logarithm of price per citations (*citepr*).

$$\log(subs) = a + b \log(price / citation) + e_i \qquad \text{Equation 6.15}$$

First, let us plot the scatter diagram:

```
data("Journals",package="AER")
attach(Journals)
citeprice=price/citations
plot(log(subs)~log(citeprice),data=Journals)
gqtest(log(subs)~log(citeprice),order.by=~citeprice,
data=Journals,fraction=1/3)
```

This results in the following graphical output:

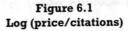

**Figure 6.1**
**Log (price/citations)**

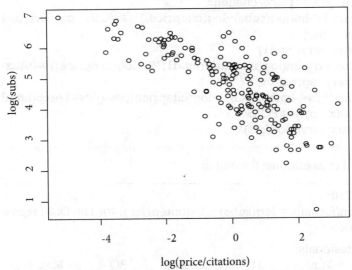

As you can see from Figure 6.1, the spread of the scatter increases as it moves from the left top corner to the bottom right corner. The Goldfeld–Quandt test confirms this suspicion through the following output:

```
. Goldfeld-Quandt test
data: log(subs) ~ log(citepri)
GQ = 2.136, df1 = 58, df2 = 58, p-value = 0.002226
```

Let us now obtain the FGLS estimate of $\beta$ in Equation 6.15. We will assume multiplicative heteroskedasticity, that is, variance of:

$$e_i = \sigma_e^2 \exp(\alpha_1 \, citeprice_i)$$

The following set of R commands will do the job:

```
data("Journals",package="AER")
attach(Journals)
citeprice=price/citations
mod1<-lm(log(subs)~log(citeprice))   ##OLS on original
equation
summary(mod1)
auxreg<-lm(log(residuals(mod1)^2)~log(citeprice)) ##Aux-
iliary regression
modfgls<-lm(log(subs)~log(citeprice),weights=1/exp(fitted
(auxreg)))##FGLS
summary(modfgls)
```

Let us examine the output:

```
Call:
lm(formula = log(subs) ~ log(citeprice)) ## The OLS regres-
sion

Residuals:
    Min        1Q      Median       3Q        Max
-2.72478   -0.53609    0.03721    0.46619    1.84808

Coefficients:
                Estimate   Std. Error   t value    Pr(>|t|)
(Intercept)     4.76621     0.05591      85.25     <2e-16 ***
log(citeprice)  -0.53305    0.03561     -14.97     <2e-16 ***
—
Signif. codes: 0 '***' 0.001 '**' 0.01 '*' 0.05 '.' 0.1 ' ' 1
Residual standard error: 0.7497 on 178 degrees of freedom
Multiple R-squared: 0.5573, Adjusted R-squared: 0.5548
F-statistic: 224 on 1 and 178 DF, p-value: < 2.2e-16

> auxreg<-lm(log(residuals(mod1)^2)~log(citeprice)) ##Aux-
iliary regression
>modfgls<-lm(log(subs)~log(citeprice),weights=1/exp(fitted
(auxreg)))##FGLS
> summary(modfgls)
```

```
Call:
lm(formula = log(subs) ~ log(citeprice), weights = 1/exp(fitted
(auxreg)))
Residuals:
    Min        1Q      Median       3Q        Max
  -5.4489    -1.3372    0.1184     1.3592     4.3704

Coefficients:
                 Estimate   Std. Error   t value    Pr(>|t|)
(Intercept)      4.77314     0.05450      87.59     <2e-16 ***
log(citeprice)  -0.50520     0.02982     -16.94     <2e-16 ***
—
Signif. codes: 0 '***' 0.001 '**' 0.01 '*' 0.05 '.' 0.1 ' ' 1

Residual standard error: 1.838 on 178 degrees of freedom
Multiple R-squared: 0.6172, Adjusted R-squared: 0.615
F-statistic: 287 on 1 and 178 DF, p-value: < 2.2e-16
```

The OLS estimator of $b = -0.53305$, while the FGLS estimator is $-0.5050$. The standard error of the FGLS estimator is in this case somewhat lower than that for the OLS estimator.[8] Unfortunately the FGLS estimator does not share the small sample properties of the GLS estimator, and is not BLUE. In fact, the FGLS estimator is not a linear estimator since the $e_i^2$ are non-linear functions of the $Y_i$'s unlike the OLS estimators that are linear functions of the dependent variable. We can draw some solace from the fact that as long as $E(e_i \mid X_i) = 0$, and that Variance$(e_i)$ is proportional to a constant $\sigma^2$ for all values of $i$, the FGLS estimator is consistent and asymptotically efficient.

One limitation of this method is that we are obliged to assume a specific functional form for heteroskedasticity as in Equation 6.13. So far, we have been attempting to rescale the original equation so as to obtain a fresh formulation that has homoskedastic disturbances. An alternative approach (explored by White [1980][9]) to dealing with heteroskedasticity would be to simply use an alternative expression for the variance of the OLS coefficients, rather than try to obtain a model with homoskedastic disturbances. This approach adjusts the OLS standard errors for heteroskedasticity.

## 6.3.1 White's Heteroskedasticity Consistent (HC) Standard Errors

Suppose we have the following regression model:

$$Y_i = a + bX_i + e_i \qquad \text{Equation 6.16}$$

where:

$$\text{Variance}(e_i) = \sigma^2_{e_i}$$

We know that:

$$\text{Variance}(\hat{\beta}) = \frac{\sum_{i=1}^{T} x_i^2 \sigma^2_{e_i}}{\left(\sum_{i=1}^{T} x_i^2\right)^2} \qquad \text{Equation 6.17}$$

Since the $\sigma^2_{e_i}$ are not directly observable, White suggests using the square of the estimated residual $\hat{e}_i^2$ in the place of $\sigma^2_{e_i}$, to obtain a consistent estimator of the variance of $\hat{\beta}$:

$$\text{Variance}(\hat{\beta}) = \frac{\sum_{i=1}^{T} x_i^2 \hat{e}_i^2}{\left(\sum_{i=1}^{T} x_i^2\right)^2} \qquad \text{Equation 6.18}$$

As the sample size increases, the probability that Equation 6.18 is at any given distance (however small) from Equation 6.17 tends to be zero.

This can be generalized to a regression model with $n$ independent variables in addition to the constant. Suppose we have the following regression model:

$$Y_i = \alpha + \beta_1 X_{i1} + \beta_2 X_{i2} + \ldots \ldots + \beta_n X_{in} + e_i \qquad \text{Equation 6.19}$$

Then, White's Heteroskedasticity Consistent Estimator of the variance of $\hat{\beta}_j$ is given by:

$$\text{Var}(\hat{\beta}_j) = \frac{\sum_{i=1}^{T} \hat{\phi}_{ji}^2 \, \hat{e}_i^2}{\left( \sum_{i=1}^{T} \hat{\phi}_{ji}^2 \right)^2}$$

Equation 6.20

where, as before, $\hat{e}_i^2$ is the squared $i$th residual from Equation 6.19, and $\hat{\phi}_{ji}^2$ is the $i$th residual in the auxiliary regression of explanatory variable $X_j$ on all other explanatory variables in Equation 6.19.

## Example 6.3

Nowadays, most econometric software will routinely produce White's heteroskedasticity consistent standard errors, along with the usual OLS standard errors. In R this is achieved by the function *vcovHC()* in the package 'sandwich', which needs to be loaded. The following commands calculate the White's heteroskedasticity consistent standard errors for the regression of journal subscriptions on price/citations that we have already encountered:

```
library(AER) ## loads package AER which has Journals data
library(sandwich) ## loads package sandwich
data("Journals")
attach(Journals)
citeprice=price/citations
vcovHC(lm(log(subs)~log(citeprice)),type="HC0")
                           ##prints White's
                           #heteroskedasticity consistent
                           #variance-covariance
                           #matrix
```

The output is the following 2 × 2 matrix:

```
(Intercept) log(citeprice)
(Intercept)    0.0030195502  0.0006803839
log(citeprice) 0.0006803839  0.0011404214
```

The $(1, 1)$ entry is the estimated heteroskedasticity consistent variance of $\hat{\alpha}$ while the $(2, 2)$ element is the estimated heteroskedasticity consistent variance of $\hat{\beta}$. These can then be used to calculate the t values for $\hat{\alpha}$ and $\hat{\beta}$.

## 6.4 AUTOCORRELATION

Suppose we have a linear regression model:

$$Y_i = a + bX_i + e_i \qquad \text{Equation 6.21}$$

Assume that the stochastic error term satisfies assumptions E1, E2, E4 and E5 from Chapter 4, but assumption E3 is violated so that instead of having $E(e_i, e_j) = 0$, we have $E(e_i, e_j) \neq 0$. This is referred to as the 'problem of autocorrelation'. The problem typically occurs in time series data, where the data are arranged in time. Typically, the error term might pick up the influence of factors that affects the dependent variable but have not been included in the regression equation. Suppose we are using monthly data to estimate the demand for ice-cream in Mumbai as a function of price of ice-cream and the average household income:

$$Q_t = a + b_1 P_t + b_2 Y_t + e_t \qquad \text{Equation 6.22}$$

where $Q_t$, $P_t$, $Y_t$ are the quantity sold, the price and household income respectively in month $t$. Weather is an important factor that influences the quantity of ice-cream that will be sold in any month $t$. Equation 6.22 does not incorporate the fact that during summer months, the sale of ice cream will be higher than that predicted on the basis of prices and income alone, while during the monsoons, it might be lower than that predicted by the factors that are included in Equation 6.22. Consequently, the values of $e_t$ would be mostly positive during the summer months and mostly negative during the monsoons. In other words, residuals from Equation 6.22 would tend to bunch together, meaning positive residuals would be followed by positive residuals, and negative residuals would be followed by negative residuals. This is an instance of 'positive autocorrelation'. On the other hand, if positive residuals are more likely to be followed by negative residuals and vice-versa, we have a case of 'negative autocorrelation'. The presence of autocorrelation is likely to indicate that the model is misspecified. Incorrect functional forms, inadequate dynamic specification can cause autocorrelation in addition to the omitted variable bias. That is why several of the tests of autocorrelation are also interpreted as tests of misspecification. We will study more about specification problems in Section VII.

### 6.4.1 First Order Autocorrelation

The most common form of autocorrelation that one encounters in applied work is 'first order autocorrelation'. Suppose we have the following regression specification:

$$Y_t = a + bX_t + e_t$$

$$e_t = \rho e_{t-1} + v_t \qquad \text{Equation 6.23}$$

where the stochastic error term $v_t \sim N(0, \sigma_v^2)$ and is not autocorrelated, and which satisfies assumptions E1 to E5 of Chapter 4, including the independence of $v_t$ and $e_{t-1}$. We will also assume that $\rho$ is a constant such that $|\rho| < 1$. This assumption is called the assumption of stationarity and implies that $E(e_t) = E(e_{t-1})$ and also that the variance of all the error terms is constant. Let us now examine the properties of $e_t$.

### 1. $E(e_t) = 0$

From Equation 6.23:

$$E(e_t) = \rho E(e_{t-1}) + E(v_t)$$

Because of the assumption of stationarity, we have:

$$E(e_t) = \rho E(e_{t-1}) + E(v_t) = \rho E(e_t) + E(v_t)$$

or:

$$E(e_t) = \frac{E(v_t)}{(1-\rho)} = 0 \text{ because } E(v_t) = 0$$

### 2. $E(e_t^2) = \dfrac{\sigma_v^2}{(1-\rho^2)}$

$$\text{Variance}(e_t) = \sigma_e^2$$
$$\text{Variance}(e_t) = \text{Variance}(\rho e_{t-1} + v_t)$$

Therefore, we have

$$\sigma_e^2 = \frac{\sigma_v^2}{1-\rho^2}$$

**3. $E(e_t e_{t-s}) = \dfrac{\rho^s \sigma_v^2}{(1-\rho^2)}$**

In order to demonstrate 3, let us first calculate $E(e_t e_{t-1})$. Multiplying both sides of $e_t = \rho e_{t-1} + v_t$ by $e_{t-1}$ and taking expectation of both sides, we have:

$$E(e_t e_{t-1}) = \rho E(e_{t-1}^2) + E(e_{t-1} v_t)$$
$$= \frac{\rho \sigma_v^2}{(1-\rho^2)}$$

Let us now calculate $E(e_t e_{t-2})$.

$$E(e_t e_{t-2}) = \rho E(e_{t-1} e_{t-2}) + E(e_{t-2} v_t)$$
$$= \frac{\rho^2 \sigma_v^2}{(1-\rho^2)}$$

Replacing 2 by $s$, we have:

$$E(e_t e_{t-s}) = \frac{\rho^s \sigma_v^2}{(1-\rho^2)}$$

The left hand side of 3 is nothing but the covariance between $e_t$ and $e_{t-s}$, that is error terms that are $s$ periods apart in time. Since we have assumed that $|\rho| < 1$, you can see that the covariance between $e_t$ and $e_{t-s}$ declines, the further apart are the terms.

## 6.4.2 Implications of Autocorrelation for OLS Estimators

As with heteroskedasticity, you should be able to see easily that the OLS estimators continue to remain unbiased, even when the stochastic error term is autocorrelated. This is because the assumption:

$$E(e_i, e_j) = 0$$

has no role to play in the proof for the unbiasedness of the OLS estimators. Just as in the case of heteroskedasticity, the failure of assumption:

$$E(e_i, e_j) = 0$$

comes into play for deriving the expression for the variance of the OLS estimators. As usual, we will concentrate on the derivation of the expression for Variance $(\hat{\beta})$.

$$\text{Variance } (\hat{\beta}) = E(\hat{\beta} - b)^2 = E\left(\frac{\sum_{i=1}^{T} x_i e_i}{\sum_{i=1}^{T} x_i^2}\right)^2 \cdot$$

$$= \frac{E(x_1^2 e_1^2 + x_2^2 e_2^2 + \ldots + x_T^2 e_T^2 + 2x_1 x_2 e_1 e_2 + \ldots + 2x_{T-1} x_T e_{T-1} e_T)}{\left(\sum_{i=1}^{T} x_i^2\right)^2}$$

$$= \frac{x_1^2 E(e_1^2) + \ldots + x_T^2 E(e_T^2) + 2x_1 x_2 E(e_1 e_2) + \ldots + 2x_{T-1} x_T E(e_T e_{T-1})}{\left(\sum_{i=1}^{T} x_i^2\right)^2}$$

$$= \frac{\sigma_e^2 \sum_{i=1}^{T} x_i^2 + 2x_1 x_2 E(e_1 e_2) + \ldots + 2x_{T-1} x_T E(e_T e_{T-1})}{\left(\sum_{i=1}^{T} x_i^2\right)^2}$$

Equation 6.24

Now, the terms involving $E(e_i e_j)$ do not disappear since they are non-zero. For example, in the case of first order autocorrelation, we would have (from the last line in Equation 6.24),

$$\text{variance}(\hat{\beta}) = \frac{\sigma_e^2 \sum_{i=1}^{T} x_i^2 + 2x_1 x_2 \dfrac{\rho\sigma_v^2}{(1-\rho^2)} + \ldots\ldots + 2x_{T-1} x_T \dfrac{\rho\sigma_v^2}{(1-\rho^2)}}{\left(\sum_{i=1}^{T} x_i^2\right)^2}$$

$$= \frac{\sigma_e^2 \sum_{i=1}^{T} x_i^2 + 2\dfrac{\rho\sigma_v^2}{(1-\rho^2)} \sum_{i=1}^{T-1} x_i x_{i+1}}{\left(\sum_{i=1}^{T} x_i^2\right)^2}$$

Equation 6.25

When there is no autocorrelation or heteroskedasticity, we have seen the usual expression is:

$$\text{Variance}(\hat{\beta}) = \frac{\sigma_e^2}{\sum_{i=1}^{T} x_i^2}$$

Equation 6.25 is the same as the usual expression only if $\rho = 0$. In general, Equation 6.24 will differ from the usual expression. It cannot be said that the variance obtained from Equation 6.24 will be greater or smaller than the variance based on the usual expression. Hence, there is no guarantee that the OLS estimators are efficient in the presence of autocorrelation. One thing is clear though: If, in the presence of autocorrelation, we continue to use the usual expression for the variance of OLS estimators, our inference and hypothesis testing procedures will be highly unreliable.

Just like first order autocorrelation, we can think of a higher order autocorrelation as in the expression below:

$$e_t = \rho_1 e_{t-1} + \rho_2 e_{t-2} + \ldots\ldots + \rho_q e_{t-q} + v_t$$

In this case, we say that we have autocorrelation of order $q$. The consequences of autocorrelation remain the same: OLS estimators are unbiased but not necessarily efficient, and tests of hypothesis and inference procedures can be unreliable if we continue to use the usual expression for the variance of the OLS estimators.

## 6.5 TESTS FOR DETECTING AUTOCORRELATION

Mirroring our discussion of heteroskedasticity, we must develop some tests for detecting autocorrelation.

### 6.5.1 Tests for First Order Autocorrelation

*Asymptotic Tests*

Suppose we have a linear regression model:

$$Y_i = a + bX_i + e_i \qquad \text{Equation 6.26}$$

And we want to test for first order autocorrelation. For the specification:

$$e_t = \rho e_{t-1} + v_t$$

the null hypothesis of no autocorrelation can be tested using the following null and alternative pairs:

$$H_o : \rho = 0$$

$$H_A : \rho \neq 0 \qquad \text{Equation 6.27}$$

One way of testing this is described below:

**Step 1:** Run the regression Equation 6.26, store the residuals $\hat{e}_i$.

**Step 2:** Run an auxiliary regression:

$$\hat{e}_t = \rho \hat{e}_{t-1} + v_t \qquad \text{Equation 6.28}$$

and obtain an estimate of $\rho$, $\hat{\rho}$.

**Step 3:** Obtain the $t$ statistic for $\hat{\rho}$, $t_{\hat{\rho}}$. The null hypothesis can be rejected at 5 per cent if $t_{\hat{\rho}} > 1.96$. Instead of Equation 6.27, suppose we have a one-sided alternative against the same null:

$$H_o : \rho = 0$$

$$H_A : \rho > 0$$

In this case, we will reject the null if the $\left| t_{\hat{\rho}} \right| > 1.64$.

## 6.5.2 An Alternative Asymptotic Test

An alternative way to test Equation 6.27 is to run the auxiliary regression in step 2, and calculate $(T - 1) \times R^2$ where $R^2$ is the r-square of the auxiliary regression. Under the null hypothesis, this statistic follows the $\chi^2$ distribution with 1 degree of freedom. We reject the null hypothesis is $(T - 1) \times R^2$ is greater than the $\chi^2$ value with 1 degree of freedom.

## 6.5.3 Durbin–Watson Statistic to Test for First Order Autocorrelation

The previous two tests are asymptotic tests. On the other hand, the Durbin–Watson test[10] is a test that has a known small sample distribution, albeit under fairly restrictive conditions. The restrictions are: (*a*) that we should be able to treat the *x* variable in Equation 6.26 as deterministic (fixed from sample to sample); and (*b*) The intercept in Equation 6.26 should not be omitted. The steps in the Durbin–Watson test are as follows:

**Step 1:** Carry out the regression in Equation 6.26 using OLS and store the residuals $\hat{e}_i$.

**Step 2:** From the residuals in step 1, construct the following statistic:

$$DW = \frac{\sum_{t=2}^{T}(\hat{e}_t - \hat{e}_{t-1})^2}{\sum_{t=1}^{T}\hat{e}_t^2} = \frac{\sum_{t=2}^{T}\hat{e}_t^2 + \sum_{t=2}^{T}\hat{e}_{t-1}^2 - 2\sum_{t=2}^{T}\hat{e}_t\hat{e}_{t-1}}{\sum_{t=1}^{T}\hat{e}_t^2}$$

$$\approx \frac{2\sum_{t=2}^{T}\hat{e}_t^2 - 2\sum_{t=2}^{T}\hat{e}_t\hat{e}_{t-1}}{\sum_{t=1}^{T}\hat{e}_t^2} = \frac{2\left(\sum_{t=2}^{T}\hat{e}_t^2 - \sum_{t=2}^{T}\hat{e}_t\hat{e}_{t-1}\right)}{\sum_{t=1}^{T}\hat{e}_t^2}$$

$$= 2\left(1 - \frac{\sum_{t=2}^{T}\hat{e}_t\hat{e}_{t-1}}{\sum_{t=1}^{T}\hat{e}_t^2}\right)$$

Note that:

$$\frac{\sum_{t=2}^{T} \hat{e}_t \hat{e}_{t-1}}{\sum_{t=2}^{T} \hat{e}_t^2}$$

is in effect the OLS estimator of $\rho$ in the auxiliary regression:

$$\hat{e}_t = \rho \hat{e}_{t-1} + v_t$$

As a result, we have:

$$\text{DW} = 2(1 - \hat{\rho})$$

The null hypothesis $\rho = 0$ implies DW = 2. The closer is $\rho$ to +1, closer is DW to 0, where the closer $\rho$ is to –1, closer is DW to 4. Thus, DW lies between 0 and 4, and the further it is from 2, the stronger is the evidence against the null of no autocorrelation. The complication is that under the null of no autocorrelation, the distribution of DW depends not only upon $T$ (the total number of observations) and the number of explanatory variables in the regression equation, but also on the actual values of the explanatory variables. However, it is possible to calculate upper and lower limits ($D_U$ and $D_L$) which depend only on the sample size and the number of explanatory variables. The true critical values are between these two limits. These values have been tabulated by Durbin and Watson (1950). The actual rules for rejecting or failing to reject the null (for a one-sided test of the null of no autocorrelation against the one sided alternative of positive autocorrelation) are as follows:

1. If DW is less than $D_L$, reject the null hypothesis.
2. If DW is larger than $D_U$, do not reject the null hypothesis.
3. If $D_L \leq \text{DW} \leq D_U$ you cannot be sure. This is called the zone of indecision. The larger the sample size, smaller is the zone of indecision.

If the null of no autocorrelation is being tested against the alternative of negative autocorrelation, the lower and the upper limits are given by $4 - D_L$ and $4 - D_U$.

The Durbin–Watson test statistic is routinely supplied by most software programs. In R, we can conduct the Durbin–Watson on artificially generated data test as follows:

```
library(lmtest) ##loads the package "lmtest"
e=rnorm(100)## generates 100 normally distributed ran-
dom numbers
x=rnorm(100) ## generates 100 normally distributed ran-
dom numbers
y=2+3*x+e ## generates the dependent variable y
dwtest(lm(y~x)) ##conducts the DW test
```

The output is:

```
Durbin-Watson test
data: lm(y ~ x)
DW = 2.0697, p-value = 0.6382
alternative hypothesis: true autocorrelation is greater than 0
```

The null hypothesis is of no autocorrelation whereas the alternative is that of positive autocorrelation. The calculated value of DW is 2.0697. The number of explanatory variables is 2, and $T = 100$. For this combination, $D_L = 1.503$ and $D_U = 1.583$. Since DW is greater than $D_U$, we do not reject the null.

Modern econometric packages are capable of calculating the exact DW test, and do not have to rely on the upper and lower limits. The R output has printed out a $p$-value which is 0.63 in this case. Clearly, we cannot reject the null.[11]

### 6.5.4 Durbin's $h$ test

A limitation of the DW test is that the explanatory variables in the regression should be non-stochastic. But sometimes, it is necessary to have the lagged value of the dependent variable as one of the explanatory variables. Suppose we have the specification:

$$Y_t = a + bY_{t-1} + \gamma X_t + e_t \qquad \text{Equation 6.29}$$

Suppose $Y_t$ is the markets share of a company in month $t$ and $X_t$ is the advertising expenditure in month $t$. The market share in month $t$ may depend upon the market share in the previous month as well as on the advertising expenditure in that month. We would then have to include the lagged value of the dependent variable as one of the explanatory variables. The problem with this specification is that the explanatory variables cannot be taken as non-stochastic. Durbin (1970)[12] suggested the following statistic:

$$h = \hat{\rho} \left( \frac{T}{1 - T \times \text{Variance}(\hat{\beta})} \right)^{\frac{1}{2}}$$

where:

$$\hat{\rho} = \frac{\sum_{t=2}^{T} \hat{e}_t \hat{e}_{t-1}}{\sum_{t=2}^{T} \hat{e}_t^2}$$

and Variance($\hat{\beta}$) is the estimated variance of the OLS estimator of $b$ in Equation 6.29. Under the null hypothesis of no autocorrelation, $h$ is asymptotically normal with mean zero and variance 1. A limitation of this is that $h$ cannot be calculated if:

$$T \times \text{Variance}(\hat{\beta}) \geq 1$$

In this case, Durbin suggests another asymptotically equivalent test. Regress the residuals $\hat{e}_i$ from Equation 6.29 on $\hat{e}_{t-1}$ and other explanatory variables, including the lagged dependent variable, and then test for the statistical significance of the estimated coefficient on $\hat{e}_{t-1}$ using usual $t$ statistics. If the coefficient of $\hat{e}_{t-1}$ is statistically significant, we reject the null of no autocorrelation.

## 6.6 REMEDIAL MEASURES FOR AUTOCORRELATION

Similar to the heteroskedastic case, we can obtain a GLS estimator that is BLUE by appropriately transforming the model with autocorrelated errors. To see this, suppose we have a regression model with first order autocorrelated errors:

$$Y_t = a + bX_t + e_t$$
$$e_t = \rho e_{t-1} + v_t$$

Equation 6.30

Which satisfies all assumptions E1 through E5 of Chapter 4. We can transform the regression equation in Equation 6.30 as follows:

1. Lag $Y_t$ by one period and multiply it by $\rho$, to obtain

$$\rho Y_{t-1} = \rho a + \rho b X_{t-1} + \rho e_{t-1}$$

Equation 6.31

2. Subtract Equation 6.31 from $Y_t$ to obtain

$$Y_t - \rho Y_{t-1} = (1 - \rho)a + b(X_t - \rho X_{t-1}) + v_t$$

or

$$Y_t^* = a^* + bX_t^* + v_t$$
$$Y_t^* = Y_t - \rho Y_{t-1}$$
$$X_t^* = (X_t - \rho X_{t-1})$$
$$a^* = (1 - \rho)a$$

Equation 6.32

Note that the transformed model Equation 6.32 has an error term which follows all the classical assumptions and hence the OLS estimator from this transformed model will be BLUE. $b$ can be estimated as:

$$\hat{\beta}^* = \frac{\sum_{t=1}^{T}(X_t^* - \bar{X}^*)(Y_t^* - \bar{Y}^*)}{\sum_{t=1}^{T}(X_t^* - \bar{X}^*)^2}$$

Equation 6.33

This will give us the 'Generalised Least Squares' or the GLS estimator in the case of first order autocorrelation in errors. However, one must account for the fact that we are losing one observation and whatever information that might have been contained in it. If we want to avoid that loss, we need to transform $Y_1$ as:

$$Y_1^* = \sqrt{1-\rho^2}\,Y_1,$$

$$X_1 \text{ as } X_1^* = \sqrt{1-\rho^2}\,X_1$$

and $e_1$ as:

$$e_1^* = \sqrt{1-\rho^2}\,e_1$$

This transformation is motivated by the fact that:

$$\text{Variance}(e_1^*) = (1-\rho^2)\frac{\sigma_v^2}{(1-\rho^2)} = \sigma_v^2$$

In earlier works, it was common to drop the first observation. Estimators where the first observation has been dropped are often referred to as 'Cochrane–Orcutt estimators'. On the other hand, estimators where the first observation has been transformed are sometimes referred to as 'Praise–Winsten estimators'.

The only hitch in this process is that we may not generally know the value of $\rho$. However, we can replace the unknown value of $\rho$ by its estimate and obtain Equation 6.32 as follows:

**Step 1**: Estimate:

$$Y_t = a + bX_t + e_t$$

by OLS and store the residuals $\hat{e}_i$.

**Step 2**: Estimate the regression:

$$\hat{e}_t = \rho\hat{e}_{t-1} + v_t$$

and obtain $\hat{\rho}$.

**Step 3**: Obtain:

$$X_t^* = (X_t - \hat{\rho}X_{t-1}), \ Y_t^* = (Y_t - \hat{\rho}Y_{t-1})$$

and using these, calculate Equation 6.33.

This gives you the 'Feasible Generalised Least Squares estimator' or FGLS estimator for the case of first order autocorrelation. Mirroring the case of the FGLS estimator under heteroskedasticity, the FGLS estimator under first order autocorrelation in errors is no longer BLUE in small samples, but asymptotically equivalent to the GLS estimator Equation 6.33.

### 6.6.1 Autocorrelation and Specification Problems

Often, autocorrelation can arise because of specification problems. For example, the true model describing the relationship between $Y$ and $X$ may be:

$$Y_t = a + b_1 X_t + b_2 X_t^2 + e_t \qquad \text{Equation 6.34}$$

where $b_1 > 0$, $b_2 < 0$.

The scatter diagram plotting $Y$ against $X$ will look somewhat like the one plotted in Figure 6.2.

**Figure 6.2**
**Scatter plot of $Y$ against $X$**

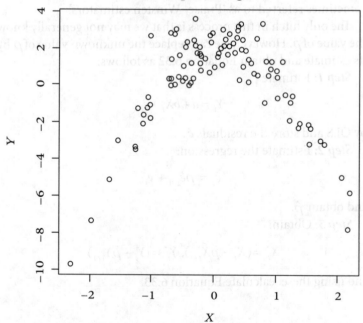

Suppose we wrongly estimate the following regression:

$$Y_i = a + bX_i + e_i$$

Figure 6.3 plots the estimated regression line against the scatter:

**Figure 6.3**
**XY scatter and estimated regression line**

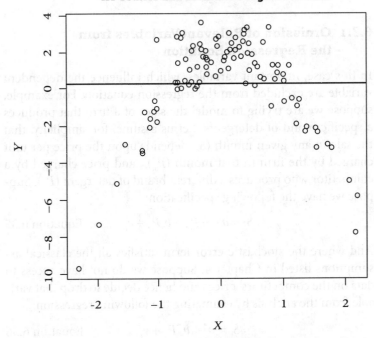

Since the estimated coefficient of $X$ is quite small, the estimated regression is only slightly upward sloping. But now you see how autocorrelation can arise because of an omitted variable, which is an instance of mis-specification. The positive and negative errors are all bunched together. This means that positive errors are more likely to be followed by positive errors while negative errors are more likely to be followed by negative errors, in other words, errors show positive autocorrelation. Thus, one of the causes of autocorrelation could be specification problems. In that case, one must look for a better specification rather than an alternate estimator. What are the various types of specification errors? How does one test them? We will examine these questions in the next section.

## 6.7 SPECIFICATION ERRORS

Generally, the following types of specification errors are common in applied work.

### 6.7.1 Omission of Relevant Variables from the Regression Equation

In this case, important variables, which influence the dependent variable are excluded from the regression equation. For example, suppose we are trying to model the sales of a firm that produces a specific brand of detergents. Let us assume, for simplicity, that the sale in any given month $(S_t)$ depends upon the price per unit charged by the firm in that month $(P_{ot})$ , and price charged by a competitor who produces a different brand of detergent $(P_{ct})$. Suppose we have the following specification:

$$S_t = a + b_1 P_{ot} + b_2 P_{ct} + e_t \qquad \text{Equation 6.35}$$

And where the stochastic error term satisfies all the classical assumptions listed in Chapter 4. Suppose we do not have access to data on the competitors' prices and hence decide to drop that variable from the analysis by estimating the following regression:

$$S_t = a^* + b_1^* P_{ot} + v_t \qquad \text{Equation 6.36}$$

Note that the stochastic error term in Equation 6.36 is:

$$v_t = b_2 P_{ct} + e_t$$

Let us find the OLS estimator of $b_1^*$:

$$\hat{\beta}_1^* = b_1 + \frac{\sum_{t=1}^{T} (P_{ot} - \bar{P}_{ot})(v_t - \bar{v}_t)}{\sum_{t=1}^{T} (P_{ot} - \bar{P})^2}$$

$$= b_1 + \frac{b_2 \sum_{t=1}^{T}(P_{ot} - \bar{P}_{ot})(P_{ct} - \bar{P}_{ct})}{\sum_{t=1}^{T}(P_{ot} - \bar{P}_{ot})^2} + \frac{\sum_{t=1}^{T}(P_{ot} - \bar{P}_{ot})e_t}{\sum_{t=1}^{T}(P_{ot} - \bar{P}_{ot})^2}$$

The second term in the line immediately above is the OLS estimator of $\gamma$ in the regression equation:

$$P_{ct} = \phi + \gamma P_{ot} + \eta_t \qquad \text{Equation 6.37}$$

As a result, we have:

$$\hat{\beta}_1^* = b_1 + b_2\hat{\gamma} + \frac{\sum_{t=1}^{T}(P_{ot} - \bar{P}_{ot})e_t}{\sum_{t=1}^{T}(P_{ot} - \bar{P}_{ot})^2}$$

$$E(\hat{\beta}_1^*) = b_1 + b_2\gamma \qquad \text{Equation 6.38}$$

Equation 6.38 implies that $\hat{\beta}_1^*$ is not an unbiased estimator of $b_1^*$ unless $b_2 = 0$ (in which case, the variable $P_{ct}$ does not play a role in determining detergent sales, or $\gamma = 0$ which requires that $P_{ct}$ be uncorrelated with $P_{ot}$. However, in this particular example, this is not likely to be the case. Both the firms are producing detergents and hence their price strategies are unlikely to be independent. In this scenario, the OLS estimator of $b_1^*$ will be biased.

We can write a program in R to see this graphically. Let us first describe the steps involved:

**Step 1:** Let us generate artificial data on two explanatory variables $X_1$ and $X_2$ which are correlated among themselves. We will then generate $Y$ as:

$$Y_t = 2 + 2X_{t1} + 3X_{t2} + e_t$$

**Step 2:** Carry out the regression:

$$Y_t = a + b_1 X_{t1} + b_2 X_{t2} + e_t$$

and obtain the estimated value of $b_1$.

We will repeat step 1 and 25,000 times, giving us 5,000 values of $\hat{\beta}_1$. We will plot the density function of these values and confirm that $\hat{\beta}_1$ is an unbiased estimator of $b_1$.

**Step 3:** Next, we will omit $X_2$ from the regression, estimate the regression:

$$Y_t = \phi + \delta_1 X_{t1} + e_t$$

and obtain an estimator of $\delta_1$. We will repeat steps 1 and 35,000 times, get 5,000 values of $\hat{\delta}_1$, and compare the density function of these values to the density function of $\hat{\beta}_1$.

The following R program will execute these steps:

```
dot=c(rep(0,5000)) # generates column of 5000 zeros
dot1=c(rep(0,5000)) #generates column of 5000 zeros
## a repeat loop starts from here
i=1
repeat {
x1=rnorm(100) #generates 100 values of x1 as normal ran-
dom numbers
#The next line generates x2 as a variable correlated with x1
x2=rnorm(100)+0.7*x1
e=rnorm(100) # generates 100 normal random terms
y=2+2*x1+3*x2+e # generates y
c1=coef(lm(y~x1+x2))
c2=coef(lm(y~x1))
beta1hat=c1[2]
beta1hat1=c2[2]
dot[i]=beta1hat
dot1[i]=beta1hat1
i=i+1
if(i>5000)
break
}
plot(density(dot,bw=1),main="")
plot(density(dot1,bw=1),main="")
```

The first plot statement plots the density function for $\hat{\beta}_1$ when $X_1$ as well as $X_2$ are included in the model. Figure 6.4 reproduces this graph:

**Figure 6.4**
**Density function of $\beta^*$ when both $X_1$ and $X_2$ are
included in the regression model**

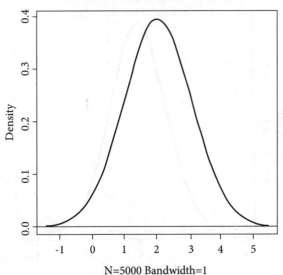

N=5000 Bandwidth=1

As you can see, $\hat{\beta}_1$ is an unbiased estimator of $b_1$, whose value is 2 by construction. This is what we would expect when there is omitted variable bias.

The last plot statement in the program plots the density of $\beta_1$ when $X_2$ is omitted from the regression. Figure 6.5 reproduces this graph.

As you can see from this graph, the density function of $\hat{\beta}_1$ has now shifted towards the right. $\hat{\beta}_1$ is no longer an unbiased estimator of $b_1$. What is the extent of the bias?

We know that in this specific case:

$$E(\hat{\beta}_1) = b_1 + b_2\gamma$$

where $\gamma$ is the slope co-efficient in the regression:

$$X_{t2} = \alpha + \gamma X_{t1} + e_t$$

By construction, we know that:

$$b_1 = 2,\ b_2 = 3,\ \gamma = 0.7$$

**Figure 6.5**
**Density function of $\beta^{*}$ when $X_2$ is omitted from the regression model**

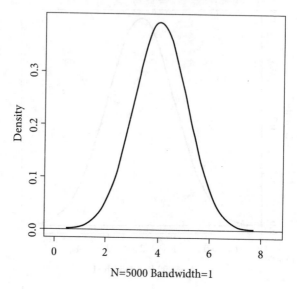

N=5000 Bandwidth=1

Therefore, we have:

$$E(\hat{\beta}_1) = 2 + 3 \times 0.7 = 4.1$$

when our regression suffers from the omitted variable bias. This is brought out by Figure 6.5 of the density function for $\hat{\beta}_1$. As you can see from Figure 6.5, this is likely to be disastrous, since the density function for $\hat{\beta}_1$ peaks over 4.1. This can be a disaster since the probability with which $\hat{\beta}_1$ takes its true value (which equals 2) is quite small! Further, it can be shown that when there is omitted variable bias, the OLS estimators are not even consistent. The result is worth reiterating: If we omit a relevant explanatory variable that is correlated with an included variable, the OLS estimators will be neither unbiased nor consistent. This is a very real problem in a great deal of applied work where the set of explanatory variables are not dictated by a well-specified theory but must be guessed. Suppose we do suffer from an omitted variable bias. Then, the OLS estimator cannot be saved. In that sense, the problem of omitted variable bias is qualitatively different from the problems of heteroskedasticity and autocorrelation. In the case of the latter two problems, the OLS estimators can be rescued by transforming the data and obtaining GLS or FGLS estimators. However, in the case of an omitted variable bias, the OLS estimator cannot be saved. An alternative estimator, the Instrumental Variables (IV) estimator, that is based on a new variable that is correlated with the explanatory variable but not correlated with the error term, is used. The discussion of this estimator is beyond the scope of this book, but a good discussion can be found in Wooldridge (2006).[13]

## 6.7.2 Inclusion of Irrelevant Variables in the Model

The reverse is a less serious problem. Suppose the true regression is:

$$Y_t = a + b_1 X_{t1} + e_t \qquad \text{Equation 6.39}$$

But we estimate the regression:

$$Y_t = a_1 + b_1^* X_{t1} + b_2^* X_{2t} + e_t$$

The true value of $b_2^* = 0$. We will be able to find unbiased estimators of all the parameters. If, however, there is some correlation between $X_{t1}$ and $X_{t2}$, then as we have seen in the section on multicollinearity in Chapter 5, the variance inflation factor will come into play and the variance of the OLS estimators will be larger than what would have been if we would not have included the irrelevant variable.

The question that then arises is: How do we select the regressors to be included in the regression equation? In Chapter 5, we have seen some model selection criteria like the Akaike Information Criterion (AIC) and Schwartz criterion (SC). However, a strong case can be made for selecting the set of explanatory variables on the basis of economic theory than on purely statistical criteria. Statistical criteria are probabilistic which means that there is always a small probability of rejecting the null wrongly. This can create problems. Suppose we have 20 variables that are mutually uncor-related as possible explanatory variables. We decide to add a vari-able in the regression model if the coefficient of that variable in the regression on the dependent variable is statistically significantly different from zero at a 5 per cent level of significance. This will automatically imply that one of the 20 variables is likely to be in-cluded, even if its true coefficient is zero, simply because we are al-lowing a 5 per cent type I error. Mechanical procedures for fitting regression models on a purely statistical basis is referred to as 'data mining'. Data mining is generally regarded as an avoidable mistake among econometricians.

One possible way of determining whether a variable $Z$ should enter a regression model that already has variables $X_1$ and $X_2$ is to use the $F$ statistic based on the residual sums of squares of the re-stricted and unrestricted models that we encountered in Chapter 5. Suppose we want to decide whether to include the variable $Z$ in the regression model.

Let us think of a regression model that has $Z$ in addition to $X_1$ and $X_2$ as the explanatory variables:

$$Y_i = a + b_1 X_{i1} + b_2 X_{i2} + \gamma Z_i + e_i$$

as the unrestricted model and:

$$Y_i = a + b_1 X_{i1} + b_2 X_{i2} + e_i$$

the model without $Z$ as the restricted model with the restriction $\gamma = 0$. This restriction can be easily tested using the $F$ test for comparison of restricted and unrestricted sums of squares that was explained in Chapter 5. This is an example of 'nested models', where one of the models can be derived as a special case of another. Sometimes, we need to compare non-nested models, where one of the models cannot be derived as a special case of another.

To understand the general idea of non-nested models, suppose we have two models explaining the same dependent variable:

Model 1: $Y_i = a_1 + b_1 X_i + e_i$
Model 2: $Y_i = a_2 + b_2 Z_i + v_i$

394

Both the models are attempting to explain the conditional expectation of $Y$ given $X$ and $Z$. However, neither can be derived as a special case of another. But note that since the dependent variable is the same in both the models, we can continue to use the R-square and the AIC and SC criteria that we have discussed in earlier chapters. An alternative method of choosing between models is the idea of 'encompassing', where Model 1 is said to encompass Model 2 if it can explain the results of Model 2, and vice-versa. We will discuss two tests for encompassing in non-nested models.

### Non-nested F test

Suppose we want to test the validity of Model 2. The following steps outline the test.

**Step 1:** Construct the so-called artificial nesting model for Model 2:

$$Y_i = a_3 + b_3 X_i + \delta Z_i + \eta_i$$

This model reduces to Model 2 if $b_3 = 0$. Please note that this artificial model has no particular economic relevance but is only used to test the relevance of Model 2.

**Step 2:** Estimate Model 2 as the restricted model and the artificial nesting model as the unrestricted model. Calculate the residual sums of squares from the two models as $RSS_R$ and $RSS_{UR}$ respectively.

**Step 3:** Calculate the F statistic as:

$$F = \frac{\dfrac{(RSS_R - RSS_{UR})}{1}}{\dfrac{RSS_{UR}}{(T-3)}}$$

which, under the null hypothesis $b_3 = 0$, follows the $F$ distribution with 1 and $(T-3)$ degrees of freedom where $T$ is the total number of observations. If the $F$ statistic calculated above exceeds the critical value at a given level of significance, the null hypothesis that Model 2 encompasses Model 1 can be rejected.

The validity of Model 1 can be tested in a similar manner, first by constructing an artificial encompassing model including $X$ as well as $Z$ and then testing for the restriction that the coefficient on $Z$ equals zero. It is of course possible that both the models are rejected or neither is rejected. Rejection of Model 1 does not constitute evidence in favour of Model 2 and vice-versa.

**The J Test**

Suppose we start with an artificial nesting model:

$$Y_i = \lambda(a_1 + b_1 X_i) + (1 - \lambda)(a_2 + b_2 Z_i) + e_i$$

If $\lambda = 1$, this reduces to Model 1, and if $\lambda = 0$, this reduces to Model 2. However, we cannot estimate it directly, since the parameters $\lambda$, $a_1$, $a_2$, $b_1$, $b_2$ cannot be separately identified. Davidson and MacKinnon (1981)[14] suggest the following methodology.

**Step 1:** Replace $a_1$ and $b_1$ in the artificial nesting model by their estimates from estimating Model 1 by OLS, so that the artificial nesting model becomes:

$$Y_i = \lambda \hat{Y}_{i1} + (1 - \lambda)(a_2 + b_2 Z_i) + e_i$$

where $\hat{Y}_{i1}$ are the estimated values of the dependent variable obtained by estimating Model 1.

**Step 2:** Test for $\hat{\lambda} = 0$ in the new equation. If the null hypothesis is not rejected, we have support for Model 2.

Another common form of mis-specification arises when the functional form of the regression equation is mis-specified. We now turn to this issue.

### 6.7.3 Incorrect Functional Form

Suppose the true functional form relating $Y$ and $X$ is non-linear as in the following case:

$$Y_i = a + b_1 X_{i1} + b_2 X_{i2}^2 + e_i \qquad \text{Equation 6.40}$$

But we estimate the regression:

$$Y_i = a^* + b_1^* X_{i1} + v_i \qquad \text{Equation 6.41}$$

We then have 'functional form misspecification'. In this case, we are omitting an explanatory variable that is obviously correlated with an included variable, leading to biased and inconsistent OLS estimators. In general, we say that a linear regression model suffers from functional form mis-specification, if it does not properly account for the relationship between the dependent and the observed explanatory variables. Omitting the higher power of the explanatory variable is not the only manner in which we may commit a functional form misspecification error. Suppose the true regression is:

$$Y_i = a + b\log(X_i) + e_i$$

but we estimate:

$$Y_i = a^* + b^* X_i + v_i$$

we will be guilty of functional form misspecification. However, since in this case, we are testing for:

$$Y_i = a + b\log(X_i) + e_i$$

against:

$$Y_i = a^* + b^* X_i + v_i$$

we are testing for non-nested models, which, as we have said above, is beyond the scope of this book. We will pay more attention to testing for omitting quadratic and higher powers of the explanatory variables, which is testing for nested models, and which we can examine here. One simple way to test whether quadratic and higher forms are to be included is simply to use the $F$ test of restrictions that we explained in Chapter 5.

To be specific, suppose we have the restricted model:

$$Y_i = a + b_1^* X_{i1} + e_i$$

against the alternative unrestricted model:

$$Y_i = a^* + b_1^* X_i + b_2 X_i^2 + \dots + b_q X_i^q + v_i$$

The null hypothesis:

$$H_0 : b_2 = b_3 = \dots = b_q = 0$$

can be tested by constructing the F statistic:

$$F = \frac{\dfrac{(RSS_R - RSS_{UR})}{(q-1)}}{\dfrac{RSS_{UR}}{(T-(q+1))}}$$

which, under the null hypothesis, follows the $f$ distribution with $q - 1$ and $(T - (q + 1))$ degrees of freedom, where $T$ is the total sample size. As explained in Chapter 5, if the critical region associated with this $F$ statistic is too small, we reject the null that no quadratic and higher power terms require to be included in the regression equation.

The problem with this test is that it can quickly use up degrees of freedom as the number of explanatory variables increases. Even in this example with just one explanatory variable, we are using up $q + 1$ degrees of freedom. Further, certain kinds of neglected non-linearities might not get picked up by adding quadratics of the explanatory variables.

### Ramsay Reset Specification Test

A closely related test is suggested by Ramsay (1969).[15] This is popularly known as the 'Regression Specification Error Test' (RESET) test.

The idea behind the Ramsay RESET test is that if the regression model:

$$Y_i = a + b_1 X_{i1} + b_2 X_{i2} + .... + b_k X_{ik} + e_i \qquad \text{Equation 6.42}$$

is the 'true' model, then no non-linear functions of the independent variables should be significant when added to Equation 6.42. The RESET test can be carried out through the following steps:

**Step 1**: Estimate Equation 6.42 and store the fitted values, $\hat{Y}_i$ and also store the residual sum of squares as $RSS_R$.

**Step 2**: Estimate the expanded model:

$$Y_i = a + b_1 X_{i1} + b_2 X_{i2} + .... + b_k X_{ik} + \delta_1 \hat{Y}_i^2 + .... + \delta_q \hat{Y}_i^q + v_i$$

Equation 6.43

and store the residual sum of squares $RSS_{UR}$. Though the expanded model looks rather odd, (since powers of the estimated values of the dependent variable are added as explanatory variables), note that we will not be interested in the estimated parameters from Equation 6.43, but use it only to test whether the formulation Equation 6.42 misses out important non-linearities. The higher powers of the estimated values of $Y$ are non-linear functions of the explanatory variables, which is the important thing.

*Step 3:* In order to test:

$$H_o : \delta_1 = \delta_2 = ..... = \delta_q = 0$$

we construct the $F$ statistic:

$$F = \frac{\dfrac{(RSS_R - RSS_{UR})}{q-1}}{\dfrac{RSS_R}{[T-k-(q+1)]}}$$

which, under the null hypothesis, follows the $F$ distribution with $q - 1$ and $[T - k - (q + 1)]$ degrees of freedom where $T$ is the total sample size. A value of $F$ that is significant implies evidence against the null.

We can conduct the RESET test using R. The test is a part of the package 'lmtest' and hence that package needs to be read in before conducting the test. Again, we will illustrate its use by using the journals data set from the AER package that we have been using in this chapter.

The following R code will take the RESET test:

```
library(lmtest)
data("Journals",package="AER")
attach(Journals)
citeprice=citations/price
resettest(lm(log(subs)~log(citeprice)))
```

The test yields the following output:

```
RESET test
data: lm(log(subs) ~ log(citeprice))
RESET = 1.4409, df1 = 2, df2 = 176, p-value = 0.2395
```

The resettest() command uses the quadratic and cubic powers of the fitted values of $y$ as a default. Here, since, the $p$-value is quite large, we cannot reject the null hypothesis.

### The Rainbow test [Utts (1982)[16]]

The Rainbow test takes a somewhat different approach to testing the functional form. Its basic idea is that even if a model is mis-specified, it might fit the data well in the center of the sample, but fail to fit well towards the extremes. The Rainbow test compares the fit in a sub-sample (most commonly in the middle 50 per cent range) and compares it with the fit for the full sample. The sample has to be ordered by an explanatory variable to be able to determine the 'middle'. The R function *raintest()* implements this procedure. We will carry this test out on our Journals data base:

```
library(lmtest)
data("Journals",package="AER")
attach(Journals)
citeprice=citations/price
raintest(lm(log(subs)~log(citeprice)),order.by=~citeprice)
```

We are ordering the data by *citeprice*. We are testing whether the model fits better in the middle of the explanatory variable, compared to the full sample.

The output is:

```
Rainbow test
data: lm(log(subs) ~ log(citeprice))
Rain = 1.0331, df1 = 90, df2 = 88, p-value = 0.4395
```

As we can see from the rather large $p$-value, it will be hard to reject the null of no significant difference in the fit of the model for the entire sample and the fit in the middle of the sample.

## 6.7.4 Errors of Measurement in the Data[17]

So far we have assumed that the dependent variable as well as the explanatory variables are measured with exactitude. This may not always be the case. If the data are measured with an error, the fact has important implications for the properties of the OLS estimators. We will now turn to the properties of the OLS estimators when the data are measured with error.

***Case I: The dependent variable is measured with error, but explanatory variables are accurately measured***

Suppose $Y_i^*$ is the 'true' data. Let us assume that we cannot observe $Y_i^*$ directly, but can only observe:

$$Y_i = Y_i^* + e_i$$

where $e_i$ is a random error term, uncorrelated with $Y_i^*$, and such that:

$$E(e_i) = 0, E(e_i, e_j) = 0 \text{ for } i \neq j \text{ and variance}(e_i) = \sigma_e^2$$

for all values of $i$ and $j$.

The regression model that we are trying to estimate is:

$$Y_i^* = a + bX_i + v_i \qquad \text{Equation 6.44}$$

Where the stochastic error term satisfies all the classical assumptions E1 to E5 from Chapter 4. But since we cannot observe $Y^*$ but only $Y_i$, we will actually estimate:

$$Y_i = \alpha + \beta X_i + v_i - e_i$$

$$= \alpha + \beta X_i + \eta_i \qquad \text{Equation 6.45}$$

where $\eta_i = v_i - e_i$.

Let us further assume that the stochastic disturbance terms $e$ and $v$ are uncorrelated.

Since the new composite error term in the regression Equation 6.45 also satisfies the assumptions E1 to E5, the OLS estimators will still be BLUE. However, the variance of the OLS estimator of $b$ from Equation 6.45 is:

$$\text{Variance}(\hat{\beta}) = \frac{\sigma_\eta^2}{\sum\limits_{i=1}^{T}(X_i - \bar{X})^2} = \frac{\sigma_v^2 + \sigma_e^2}{\sum\limits_{i=1}^{T}(X_i - \bar{X})^2} \geq \frac{\sigma_v^2}{\sum\limits_{i=1}^{T}(X_i - \bar{X})^2}$$

**401**

where the last term is what the variance of the OLS estimator of $b$ would have been, had there been no measurement error. Thus, if the dependent variable is measured with error, even when the error is not systematic, the OLS estimators will continue to be BLUE but the variance of the OLS estimator will be higher than what would have been if there had been no measurement error. This means that the associated $t$-values might be too small. This is the result of increased imprecision of our estimates since the data themselves are now more uncertain.

### Case II: The explanatory variable is measured with error, but dependent variable is accurately measured

Suppose the 'true' observations on the dependent variable are given by $X_i^*$ but we can only observe:

$$X_i = X_i^* + \omega_i$$

where $\omega_i$ is a stochastic disturbance that satisfies all the assumptions E1 to E5 of Chapter 4. Suppose our objective is to estimate the regression:

$$Y_i = a + bX_i^* + v_i \qquad \text{Equation 6.46}$$

where $v_i$ is a stochastic disturbance term satisfying all the classical assumptions E1 to E5 of Chapter 4 and is uncorrelated with the disturbance term $\omega_i$. Since we cannot observe $Y_i^*$ but only $Y_i$ we actually run the regression:

$$Y_i = a + b(X_i - \omega_i) + v_i = a + bX_i - b\omega_i + v_i$$

or:

$$Y_i = a + bX_i + \phi_i \qquad \text{Equation 6.47}$$

where $\phi_i = v_i - b\omega_i$.

Let us now examine the covariance between $X$ and $\phi$:

$$\text{Covariance}(X_i, \phi_i) = E((X - E(X))(\phi - E(\phi)))$$
$$= E(\omega_i(v_i - b\omega_i)) = E(\omega_i v_i) - bE(\omega_i^2)$$
$$= -b\sigma_\omega^2$$

Clearly, $X$ and $\phi$ in Equation 6.47 are correlated. That implies that the OLS estimator of $b$ in Equation 6.47 is neither unbiased nor consistent. We have an important conclusion: If the explanatory variables are measured with error, the OLS estimators are neither unbiased nor consistent. In this case, there is a serious problem with the OLS estimators.

### 6.7.5 Proxy Variables and Instrumental Variables

**Proxy Variables**

A possible solution to the problem of omitted variable bias is using a proxy variable. The proxy variable is a variable that is related to the missing variable which we would like to include in our analysis. Suppose we have the following regression model:

$$Y_i = a + b_1 X_i + b_2 Z_i + b_3 G_i + e_i$$

Let us assume that we are interested in obtaining unbiased and consistent estimates of $b_1$ and $b_2$.

Suppose we do not have data on $G$, which is correlated with $Z$. Hence, we cannot drop it from the regression, since that will induce an omitted variable bias. Let us assume that we have data on a proxy variable for $G$. Call this variable $G^*$. This variable should be related to $G$, though obviously it will be different from $G$. That is, the coefficient $\gamma$ in the following regression:

$$G_i = \eta + \gamma G_i^* + v_i$$

which captures the relationship between $G$ and $G^*$ and must be non-zero. Obviously, this regression cannot be carried out since we lack data on $G$ in the first place. We will now replace $G$ by $G^*$ and carry out the following regression:

$$Y_i = a + b_1 X_i + b_2 Z_i + b_3 G_i^* + e_i$$

Will we succeed in finding the effect of $X$ and $Z$ on $Y$, since $G$ and $G^*$ are not the same? In order for this to happen, the following assumptions need to be satisfied:

1. The error term $e$ must be uncorrelated with $X$, $Z$ and $G$.
2. The error term $v$ must be uncorrelated with $X$, $Z$ and $G^*$.

If these assumptions hold, then the proxy variable solution will work. By substitution, we have:

$$Y_i = a + b_1 X_i + b_2 Z_i + b_3(\eta + \gamma G_i^* + v_i) + e_i$$
$$= (a + b_3 \eta) + b_1 X_i + b_2 Z_i + b_3 \gamma G_i^* + b_3 v_i + e_i$$
$$= (a + b_3 \eta) + b_1 X_i + b_2 Z_i + b_3 \gamma G_i^* + \phi_i$$

where $\phi$ is the composite error term $b_3 v_i + e_i$

Since $v_1$ as well as $e_1$ satisfy the classical assumptions and are mutually uncorrelated, the coefficients $b_1$ and $b_2$ can be consistently estimated. However, the cost to pay is that the variance of the composite error term is:

$$b_3^2 \sigma_v^2 + \sigma_e^2 > \sigma_e^2, \text{ unless } b_3 = 0,$$

which means that the OLS estimators from the regression using the proxy variable as a solution will have a larger variance.

An alternative to the proxy variable method is to use 'Instrumental Variables'. Again, think of the regression where $Y$ depends upon two variables, $X$ and $Z$:

$$Y_i = a + b_1 X_i + b_2 Z_i + e_i \qquad \text{Equation 6.48}$$

Let us assume that we are interested in obtaining unbiased and consistent estimates of $b_1$. Suppose $X$ and $Z$ are correlated, but data on $z$ are not available. Clearly, we cannot omit $Z$, since we will have an omitted variable bias if we do that. For the proxy variable solution, we used a proxy for $X$. The 'Instrumental Variables' solution takes a different approach. We think of a variable $I$ such that $X$ and $I$ are correlated, but $I$ and $e$ are not. That is, we are looking for a variable $I$ that satisfies the following conditions:

1. $Cov(X, I) \neq 0$
2. $Cov(I, e) = 0$

We then call $I$ an Instrumental variable or an Instrument for $X$. Condition 1 is referred to as 'instrument relevance'; while condition 2 is called 'instrument exogeneity'. Instrument relevance can be tested by conducting the following regression:

$$X_i = \phi + \gamma I_i + v_i$$

Instrument relevance holds only if $\gamma \neq 0$.

In order to use the instrumental variable method, we use $I$ instead of $X$ in the regression Equation 6.48. The conditions of instrument exogeneity and instrument relevance allow us to identify $b_1$. We have:

$$\text{Cov}(I,Y) = b_1\text{Cov}(I,X) + \text{Cov}(I,e)$$

By the instrument exogeneity condition, we have:

$$\text{Cov}(I,e) = 0 \text{ and } \text{Cov}(X,Z) \neq 0$$

As a result, we have the Instrumental variable (IV) estimator of $b_1$:

$$\hat{\beta}_{1_{IV}} = \frac{\sum_{i=1}^{T}(I_i - \bar{I})(Y_i - \bar{Y})}{\sum_{i=1}^{T}(I_i - \bar{I})(X_i - \bar{X})}$$

It can be shown that the IV estimator is consistent for $b_1$, provided the instrument exogeneity and instrument relevance conditions are both satisfied. The IV estimator also has an approximate normal distribution in large samples. The asymptotic variance of:

$$\hat{\beta}_{1_{IV}} = \frac{\sigma_e^2}{T\sigma_x^2\rho_{xI}^2}$$

where $\sigma_e^2$ is the variance of the error term in Equation 6.48, $\sigma_x^2$ is the variance of $x$ and $\rho_{XI}^2$ is the square of the correlation coefficient between $X$ and $I$. How do we estimate this variance?

1. $\sigma_x^2$ can be simply estimated from the sample variance of $X$.

2. In order to obtain an estimate of $\rho_{XP}^2$, we run the following regression:

$$X_i = \omega + \varphi I_i + v_i$$

obtain the $R^2$, call it $R_{XI}^2$ and substitute that value for $\rho_{XI}^2$.

3. In order to obtain $\hat{\sigma}_e^2$, we obtain:

$$\hat{e}_i = Y_i - \hat{\alpha} - \hat{\beta}_{1_{IV}} X_i$$

and then find:

$$\hat{\sigma}_e^2 = \frac{\sum_{i=1}^{n} \hat{e}_i^2}{(n-2)}$$

The asymptotic standard error of the IV estimator is given by:

$$\frac{\hat{\sigma}_e}{\sum_{i=1}^{T} (X_i - \bar{X})^2 R_{XI}^2} \qquad \text{Equation 6.49}$$

This differs from the variance of the OLS estimator through the presence of the term $R_{XI}^2$. Since $R_{XI}^2 \leq 1$, we have:

$$\text{Variance}(\beta_{1_{OLS}}) \leq \text{Variance}(\beta_{1_{IV}})$$

If $R_{XI}^2$ is small, $I$ is a weak instrument for $X$ and the variance of the instrumental variable estimator can be quite large. Further, the IV estimator can have a large asymptotic bias, even if $I$ and $e$ are only weakly correlated. This aspect of the IV estimators needs to be kept in mind as far as practical work is concerned. Also, another thing to remember is that though the R-square of the IV regression will generally get reported, it has no natural interpretation unlike the R-square for the case of the OLS regression, since now $X$ and $e$ are correlated so we cannot get a decomposition of the total sum of squares into an 'explained' and an 'unexplained' part.

## 6.7.6 Missing Data and Non-random Samples

Often, data sets have gaps in them. For example, in the Indian context, data on some states for some years may not be available for a variety of reasons. Obviously, if the data for the dependent or an explanatory variable is missing, we cannot use that observation for calculating the regression coefficients. If the data are missing at random, the impact is to reduce the sample size, making the estimators less precise than they could have been.

The situation is more complex when missing data result in a non-random sample from the population. Suppose we are studying the relationship between household income (the explanatory variable) and household savings in financial assets (the dependent variable). We may decide to exclude households that have financial savings below a certain threshold. Or we may decide to exclude households whose income is below a certain threshold. The sample is no longer representative of the population. Fortunately, it turns out that non-random sampling of this form does not cause a bias or inconsistency in the OLS estimators, if the sample selection is based on the independent variable (the household income in our example). This is an example of 'exogenous sample selection'. The reason the OLS estimators are unbiased and consistent is that the conditional expectation of financial savings, conditional on household income is the same for any subset of the population described by income in this case, or any set of explanatory variables in the general case. The situation is quite different when the sample selection is based on the dependent variable. If we decide to exclude households that have financial savings below a certain threshold, we will get biased estimators. This is an example of 'endogenous sample selection'. A bias always occurs when the sample selection is based on the dependent variable. Other sampling schemes that are sometimes used deliberately also lead to non-random sampling. 'Stratified sampling' is an example in which the population is divided into non overlapping strata. The sample is divided into non-overlapping strata and some strata are samples more intensively than others. The data collection on the Consumption Expenditure Rounds of the National Sample Survey is an example of stratified sampling. If the stratification is exogenous (based on the explanatory variable), OLS estimators can still be used. However, when the stratification is endogenous (with respect to the dependent variable), special methods are required. For details, see Wooldridge (2002).[18]

Another problem that generally occurs in applied work, especially work involving small adaptable sets is the problem of 'outliers' or 'influential observations'. We will say that an observation is influential if dropping it from the analysis leads to a substantial change in the estimated coefficients. Since OLS estimators are derived by minimizing the sum of squares, large outliers would get a lot of weight. The problem of outliers is generally caused by two reasons:

1. Mistakes while entering the data
2. When one or more members of the population are very different from the rest of the population on some relevant aspects.

Outliers can provide important information by increasing the variation among the explanatory variables, but may also unduly skew the estimated coefficients.

There is a case for reporting the OLS results with and without including 'the influential observations'. But how does one identify such observations? The idea of 'Studentised residuals' is quite useful. Suppose we want to test if observation $t$ is an influential observation. We will explain the important steps below:

**Step 1**: Carry out a regression by including a dummy variable which equals 1 for the $t$th observation and zero for all other observations along with the other explanatory variables in the equation.

**Step 2**: The coefficient on the dummy variable has the following interpretation: It is the residual for observation $t$ from the regression line using only the other observations. The dummy coefficient can help us get an idea of how far the observation is from the regression line using all the other observations. The $t$ statistic associated with the dummy variable is equal to the Studentised residual for observation $t$. Examine the statistical significance of this $t$ statistic. A significant $t$ implies a large Studentised residual relative to its estimated standard deviation.

## CONCLUSION

We have learned the following things in this chapter:

1. We learnt the meaning of heteroskedasticity and that OLS estimators are unbiased but inefficient when the stochastic error term is heteroskedastic.
2. We learnt tests for detecting heteroskedasticity.
3. We learnt about GLS and FGLS estimators when disturbances are heteroskedastic, as also computation of White's heteroskedasticity consistent standard errors.
4. We learnt about the problem of autocorrelated disturbances and the implications of autocorrelated errors for OLS estimators. In particular, we learned that OLS estimators are unbiased but inefficient when the stochastic disturbance term is autocorrelated.
5. We examined tests for first order autocorrelation.
6. We learnt how to obtain GLS and FGLS estimators for disturbances that are first order autocorrelated.
7. We learnt how specification problems can lead to autocorrelated disturbances.
8. We learnt about various specification errors and their implications. We also studied some tests for functional form misspecification.
9. We learnt how to use R to carry out tests and obtain estimators in the case of heteroskedastic and autocorrelated errors.

## NOTES

1. $\hat{e}_i^2$ can be used as proxies for $e_i^2$. For the relationship between the two, see Malinvaud, E. 1970. *Statistical Methods of Econometrics*, pp. 88–89. Amsterdam: North Holland Publishing Company.
2. R.E. Park, 'Estimation with Heteroskedastic Error Terms', *Econometrica* 34, no. 4 (1966): 888. A generalization can be found in A.C. Harvey, 'Estimating Regression Models with Multiplicative Heteroskedasticity', *Econometrics* 44, no. 3 (1976): 461–65.
3. H. Glesjer, 'A New Test for Heteroskedasticity', *Journal of the American Statistical Association* 64 (1969): 316–23.

Principles of Econometrics

4. A. Harvey and G. Phillips, 'A Comparison of the Power of Some Tests for Heteroskedasticity in the General Linear Model', *Journal of Econometrics* 2 (1974): 307–16.
5. It is necessary to load the package 'lmtest' to be able to run this command; packages can be loaded from 'packages' in the console.
6. Again, it is necessary to load the 'lmtest' package.
7. However, it does not have a zero expected value, affecting the estimate of the constant in the regression, which fortunately, is irrelevant for the situation at hand.
8. Though asymptotically, the two estimators are equivalent, in small sample, the FGLS estimator does not share the small sample properties of the GLS, and we cannot say that it is BLUE. There is no guarantee that the FGLS out-performs the OLS in small samples (though it usually does).
9. H. White, 'A Heteroskedasticity—Consistent Covariance Matrix Estimator and a Direct Test for Heteroskedasticity', *Econometrica* 50 (1980): 1–25.
10. J. Durbin and G. Watson, 'Testing For Serial Correlation in Least Squares Regression-I', *Biometrica* 37 (1950): 409–28.
11. Notice that the data have been generated in a way that satisfies the null, since the stochastic error term is generated as 100 normally distributed random numbers.
12. J. Durbin, 'Testing for Serial Correlation I Least Squares Regression When Some of the Regressors are Lagged Dependent Variables', *Econometrica* 38 (1970): 410–21.
13. J.M. Woolridge, *Introductory Econometrics: A Modern Approach* (New Delhi: Thompson South–Western, 2006), 510–51.
14. R. Davidson and J.G. MacKinnon, 'Several Tests for Model Specification in the Presence of Alternative Hypotheses', *Econometrica* 49 (1982): 781–93.
15. J.B. Ramsay, 'Tests for Specification Errors in Classical Linear Least-Squares Analysis', *Journal of the Royal Statistical Association* 71, Series B (1969): 350–71.
16. J.M. Utts, 'The Rainbow Test for Lack of Fit in Regression', *Communication in Statistics-Theory and Methods* 11 (1982): 1801–1815.
17. J. Hausman, 'Mismeasured Variables in Econometric Analysis: Problems from the Right and Problems from the Left', *Journal of Economic Perspectives* 15, no. 4 (2001): 57–67. This reference can be consulted with immense profit.
18. J. Wolldridge, *Econometric Analysis of Cross Section and Panel Data*, Chapter 17 Cambridge, MA: MIT Press, 2002.

# Appendix

## AN INTRODUCTION TO R

R is a popular language for data analysis as well as graphics. It is best described as an integrated suite of software facilities for data manipulations, simulation, calculation and graphical display. It is an implementation of S, which was developed in the initial phases at Bell laboratories in the late 1970s. Robert Gentleman and Ross Ihaka initiated the R project (the R comes from the common R in the names of the two developers), at the University of Auckland, New Zealand in the early 1990s. Since the mid 1990s, R has been developed by an international team. R is an open-source software, which means that it permits users to use, change and improve the software and also redistribute it under certain conditions. The R project web page is: http://www.r-project.org. This is the main site for information on R. Here, you can get information on download-ing the software, the FAQ's, and also obtain relevant documenta-tion. For a direct download, you may visit http://cran.r-project. org/bin/windows/base/

In this short note, we will only present the basic rudiments of R that are required for the absolute beginner. The reader will learn much more about this versatile program as she works through the various applications of R in the main text. However, the reader can also consult a lot of freely downloadable documentation that exists on the internet. R comes with a number of manuals:

1. An Introduction to R
2. R Data Import/Export
3. R Language Definition

4. Writing R Extensions
5. R installation and Administration
6. R Internals

There are several collections of frequently asked questions at http://CRAN.R-project.org/faqs.html

The student will also benefit from the excellent book on applied econometrics with R by Klieber and Zeileis (2008).[1]

The simplest way to start R is in an interactive mode via the command editor. After R has been downloaded, double click on the R icon and the graphical user interface (GUI) window will appear. Statements in R can be typed directly at the > (greater than) prompt.

Once R has started you will see the following message:

R version 2.9.0 (2009-04-17)
Copyright (C) 2009 The R Foundation for Statistical Computing
ISBN 3-900051-07-0
R is free software and comes with ABSOLUTELY NO WARRANTY.
You are welcome to redistribute it under certain conditions.
Type 'license()' or 'licence()' for distribution details.
Natural language support but running in an English locale
R is a collaborative project with many contributors.
Type 'contributors()' for more information and
'citation()' on how to cite R or R packages in publications.
Type 'demo()' for some demos, 'help()' for on-line help, or
'help.start()' for an HTML browser interface to help.
Type 'q()' to quit R.

Now, we will see some basics of R.

## USING R AS A CALCULATOR

The standard arithmetic operators +, −, *, / and ^ are available in R. The only thing that you need to remember is that R is an object oriented language. It stores results as objects, and does not necessarily always show them unless specifically asked for.

For example:

```
> x<-1
> y<-2
> z<-x+y
```

will generate $z = 1 + 2$, but will not print out the value of $z$. You will have to explicitly ask for $z$ by typing in $z$:

```
>z
```

which will produce:

```
>[1] 3
```

On the other hand, by directly typing in:

```
3^2
```

you will get:

```
[1] 9
```

which is 3 raised to power of 2. The common mathematical functions in R are *log()*, *exp()*, *sin()*, *asin()*, *cos()*, *acos()*, *tan()*, *atan()*, *sign()*, *sqrt()*, *abs()*, *min()*, and *max()*. You can learn about any of the commands by using the help in R. For example, if you want to know about the command *abs()*, you can type:

```
>help(abs)
```

It is strongly recommended that you see the help documentation on functions like *log()* before using these commands.

## READING DATA INTO R VIA THE COMMAND EDITOR

Suppose we want to read the data (3, 4, 5, 3, 4, 5, 6, 9) into a variable called $x$ and then examine its mean and the variance. This can be achieved as follows.

345

The data can be read into a column vector $x$ in R as follows:

```
>x=c(3,4,5,3,4,5,6,9)
```

The mean and variance of $x$ can be easily computed:

```
> mean(x)
[1] 4.875
```

```
> var(x)
[1] 3.839286
```

You can also do arithmetic calculations on $x$:

```
> x^2+2*x
```

Each value of $x$ is squared and $2 \times x$ is added to it to produce the following output:

```
[1] 15 24 35 15 24 35 48 99
```

You can also work on a subset of $x$:

```
>x[1:4]
```

This will print the first four values of $x$:

```
[1] 3 4 5 3
```

You can also use logical relationships. For example, if you want to pick out the values of $x$ that are greater than 5 but less than 9, you can use the *which()* function:

```
>which(x>5 & x<9)
```

The output is:

```
[1] 7
```

Since the 7th value of *x*, which is 6, satisfies the condition of being greater than 5 and less than 9.

You can also assign names to the elements in *x*:

```
>names(x)<-c("a","b","c","d","e","f","g","h")
```

Now, if you type in *x* at the command prompt.

You will get the elements of *x* as well as the names assigned to them:

```
> x
a b c d e f g h
3 4 5 3 4 5 6 9
```

It is easy to plot graphs in R. *x* can be plotted as a simple graph by using:

```
>plot(x)
```

and the following plot will be produced:

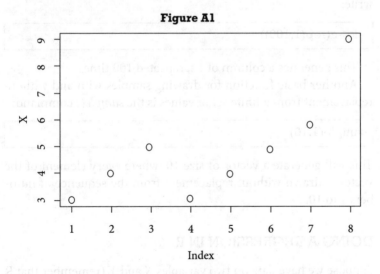

**Figure A1**

This plot can be embellished further, see the help on *plot()* by typing in:

```
>help(plot)
```

at the command prompt.

## GENERATING NUMBERS IN R

Suppose we want to generate a sequence of numbers from 1 to 100.
The command is:

```
>seq(1:100)
```

Suppose we want to generate 100 normally distributed random numbers with mean = 0 and variance 1, and store them in a variable called $e$:

```
>e=rnorm(100,0,1)
```

If want to generate a column of 100 1's, and name it $k$, we write:

```
>k<-c(rep(1,100))
```

This generates a column of 1's, repeated 100 times.
Another basic function for drawing samples with and without replacement from a finite set of values is the *sample()* command:

```
sample(1:10)
```

This will generate a vector of size 10, where every element of the vector is drawn without replacement from the sequence of numbers 1 to 10.

## DOING A REGRESSION IN R

Suppose we have data on two variables $X$ and $Y$ (remember that R is case sensitive):
$X = (20, 10, 25, 15, 20, 23, 13, 15, 20, 24, 34)$

$Y = (12, 32, 23, 22, 18, 17, 22, 18, 15, 12, 10)$

We want to run the following regression:

$$Y_i = \alpha + \beta X_i + e_i$$

and estimate the parameters $\alpha, \beta$:

This can be done by first reading the data into r and then by using the *lm()* (linear model) command:

```
>X=c(20,10,25,15,20,23,13,15,20,24,34)
> Y=c(12,32,23,22,18,17,22,18,15,12,10)
> lm(Y~X)
```

This gives the output:

```
Call:
lm(formula = Y ~ X)
Coefficients:
(Intercept) X
31.7746 -0.6782
```

where 31.7746 is an estimate of $\alpha$, while $-0.6782$ is an estimate of $\beta$. Not all the output produced by the *lm* command is printed here. To see more, you can type:

```
> summary(lm(Y~X))
```

which produces the standard regression output:

```
Call:
lm(formula = Y ~ X)
Residuals:
```

| Min | 1Q | Median | 3Q | Max |
|---|---|---|---|---|
| -6.2111 | -3.3547 | -0.2111 | 1.0534 | 8.1798 |

Coefficients:

| | Estimate | Std. Error | t value | Pr(>\|t\|) |
|---|---|---|---|---|
| (Intercept) | 31.7746 | 4.5951 | 6.915 | 6.95e-05 *** |
| X | -0.6782 | 0.2199 | -3.085 | 0.0130 * |

—

```
Signif. codes: 0 '***' 0.001 '**' 0.01 '*' 0.05 '.' 0.1 ' ' 1
Residual standard error: 4.637 on 9 degrees of freedom
Multiple R-squared: 0.5139, Adjusted R-squared: 0.4599
F-statistic: 9.515 on 1 and 9 DF, p-value: 0.01304
```

## FLOW CONTROL IN R

Like most programming languages, R too provides standard control structures like if/else statements, for loops, and while loops. The if /else statement has the following structure:

```
if(cond) {
expression1
} else {
Expression2
}
```

For example, suppose we have 100 normally distributed random numbers, with mean = 0 and variance = 1 and we would like to count the number of positive ones. We can use the following structure:

```
e=rnorm(100,0,1)
k=0
i=1
repeat {
if(e[i] >0) {
k=k+1
} else {
k=k
}
i=i+1
if(i>100)
break
}
k
```

Let us understand the structure of the program above. The first line generates 100 normally distributed random numbers with mean = 0 and variance = 1. The second line initializes a variable $k$ to zero. This variable is going to act as a counter. Basically, we are going to scan through all the 100 observations on $e$ and keep on adding 1 to $k$ whenever we encounter a positive number. $i = 1$ starts this loop. The *repeat* command repeats the commands that are enclosed between the first curly bracket and the one in the second last line, unless the *if(i>100)* statement is satisfied, at which point, the loop is broken. From the fifth to the ninth line of the program, the value of the $i$th observation is examined and if the value exceeds 0, 1 is added to $k$, otherwise, $k$ is left unchanged. The expression $i = i + 1$ increments the value of $i$ by 1, and the loop is repeated till $i$ does not exceed 100. When $i$ exceeds 100, the loop is broken, and the number $k$, which is the total number of observations that are positive, is printed. We have used the repeat loop repeatedly in the textbook:

```
ifelse(x>5,sqrt(x),x^2)
```

will square values of $x$ that are less than or equal to five and take square root of values that are greater than five.

## READING AND WRITING DATA IN R

Suppose we have data on two variables $X$ and $Y$ (with the variable names in the first row of the spreadsheet) in an Excel file called *mydata.xls* and we wish to read the data into R. The data may look like this (just the first six rows of the spreadsheet):

| X | Y |
|---|---|
| 1 | 4 |
| 2 | 5 |
| 6 | 7 |
| 2 | 5 |
| 2 | 3 |

A convenient (though not necessarily the only ) way is to follow the steps ahead:

**Step 1:** Save the spreadsheet as a Tab delimited (.txt) file, say by the name *mydata.txt*

**Step 2:** At the command prompt, type in:

```
data<-read.table("file name with path", header=TRUE,sep=" ")
```

The data in the spreadsheet will be read into the data frame 'data' (or any other name that you may choose). The *header=TRUE* line is necessary since the spreadsheet contains the variable names $X$ and $Y$ as 'headers' in the first row. The *sep=" "* line indicates that the columns are separated by spaces. The column names themselves should not have any spaces between them. For example, '*myname*' is allowed as a column name, but not '*my name*'.

**Step 3:** At this stage, R recognizes the object data, but not the individual variables $X$ and $Y$. Any effort to call them will result into R reporting that the variable does not exist. Hence, we now need to tell R to look at individual columns. This can be done by

*attach(data)*

which means that the data are added to the *search()* path and thus the variables contained in this data can be found when their name is used in a command. Data frames should be attached with care. In particular, attaching several data frames with variables having common names can create problems. An alternative is:

```
X=data$X
Y=data$Y
```

This will take the $X$ variable in the data frame data and assign it to a variable $X$ and similarly for $Y$.

Another alternative is:

```
X=dat[1]
Y=dat[2]
```

which will put the first column of the data frame *dat* into the variable $X$ and the second column of the data frame *dat* into the variable $Y$.

# WRITING DATA TO FILES

To export data frames in plain text format, the function *write.table()* is handy.

Suppose we want to write the data frame '*mydata*' to the file '*mydata.txt*'. We can use the following command:

```
write.table(mydata,file="mydata.txt",col.names=TRUE)
```

This will write the data frame *mydata* to a file *mydata.txt*, with column names in the first row.

# MANIPULATION OF MATRICES

Suppose $X$ is a matrix. Then, the transpose is generated by:

```
t(X)
```

Multiplication of two conformable matrices $X$ and $Y$ is done as:

```
X%*%Y.
```

The inverse of a square invertible matrix is calculated as:

```
solve(X)
```

The determinant of a matrix $X$ is obtained by:

```
det(X)
```

# FACTORS IN R

Factors are extensions of vectors designed to store categorical information in R. We might have qualitative variables like gender, union membership. etc., which are stored in R as factors. The following commands will help illustrate the idea:

```
f<-rep(0:1,c(2,4))
f<-factor(f,levels=0:1, labels=c("male","female"))
f
```

This will print the following output:

```
[1] male male female female female female
Levels: male female
```

## DATA SETS IN R

R has several interesting data sets that might be used for practice econometric techniques. In order to see all the available data sets, type:

```
data()
```

and you will get a list of all the datasets available in package 'data-sets'. If you want to see, say, the dataset 'longley', type:

```
library(datasets)
?longley
```

which will open a help document explaining the 'longley' data. To see the datasets available in all packages:

```
library(AER)
data()
```

This will list out a veritable treasure trove of data.

In this appendix, we have attempted to give the reader a flavour of R and also explain some of the functions that are used commonly in this text. However, the student should experiment with the R code given in the body of the text in all chapters. The best way to learn R is to start using it. The R help on various commands, along with the documentation as well as references cited here should help the student make more effective use of this highly versatile and flexible software.

## NOTES

1 Kleiber, Christian and Achim Zeileis, *Applied Econometrics with R* (New York: Springer, Science+Business Media, LLC, 2008).

# Sample Questions

## CHAPTER 1

Q1. Define the following:
  i) The expected value of a random variable
  ii) The variance of a random variable
  iii) Kurtosis of a random variable
  iv) Discrete and continuous random variables
  iv) The normal distribution
  v) The Poisson distribution
  vi) The Binomial distribution

Q2. If $(X_1, X_2, \ldots\ldots X_n)$ is a random sample of size $n$ from a normally distributed population having mean $= \mu$ and variance $= \sigma^2$,

show that $\left( \dfrac{\dfrac{\sum_{i=1}^{n} X_i}{n} - \mu}{\sigma} \right)$ will have mean $= 0$ and variance $= 1$. Will

this hold if the sample is not random? Discuss.

Q3. If $X_1, X_2, \ldots\ldots X_n$ are normally distributed random variables,

then $\sum_{i=1}^{n} \alpha_i \times X_i$ (where $\alpha_i$ are fixed constants) is also normally dis-

tributed. Show that the sample mean Xbar will be normally distributed.

Q4. Suppose, on any given day, at a busy supermarket, there are 0.5 shoplifting incidences. Shop lifting incidences occur randomly across days. The super market is open all days in the month. Estimate the probability that there will be between 12 to 20 shoplifting incidences in a month.

Q5. Which of the following functions are density functions?

  i) $f(x) = x(2 - x)$, $0 < x < 2$ and zero elsewhere

ii) $f(x) = x(2x-1)$, $0 < x < 2$, and zero elsewhere

Q6. Suppose a box contains 15 items out of which 5 are defective. If we pick a random sample of 6, what is the probability that :

   i)   Exactly five will be defective

   ii)  None will defective

   iii) Between 3 and 5 (both inclusive) will be defective

Q7. Suppose we toss a balanced coin $n$ times. Let $X$ be the total number of heads. Show that $E\left(\dfrac{X}{n}\right) = p$ and Variance $\left(\dfrac{X}{n}\right) = \dfrac{p(1-p)}{n}$

where $p$ is the probability of success.

Q8. If $X$ is a random variable following the Poisson distribution with parameter $\lambda$, show that $E(X) = \text{Variance}(X) = \lambda$.

# CHAPTER 2

Q1. We have a village with 20 households. The following ordered pairs describe the number of boys and girls respectively in each household (the first element is the number of boys, the second element is the number of girls:

   (0,2),(1,1),(2,1),(0,1),(1,0), (0,0),(2,1),(1,3), (0,4), (3,1), (3,2), (4,0), (3,1),(2,2),(0,0),(1,1),(2,0),(3,0),(0,3),(0,0)

   Let $X$ be the number of boys and $Y$ the number of girls. Find the joint distribution and the marginal distributions of $X$ and $Y$. Find $E(X/Y = 1)$.

Q2. Prove Theorem 2.6.

Q3. In what way is correlation a superior measure of association compared to covariance? What care should be exercised when interpreting correlation in time series data?

Q4. From Table 2.10, find $\sigma^2_{Y|X=0}$.

Q5. Suppose the experiment consists of throwing four balanced coins. Let $X$ be the number of heads on the first three tosses, while $Y$ is the number of heads on all four tosses. Find the correlation between $X$ and $Y$.

Q6. Suppose we have the following data on two random variables $X$ and $Y$:

**The values taken by the random variables $X$ and $Y$**

| X | Y | X | Y |
|---|---|---|---|
| 1 | 2 | -1 | -3 |
| 3 | 3 | -2 | -4 |
| 4 | 5 | 3 | 0 |
| 5 | 3 | 2 | 2 |
| 6 | 7 | 0 | 1 |

Find the correlation between $X$ and $Y$.

# CHAPTER 3

Q1. Define the following:
   i) The Standard Normal Distribution
   ii) The $\chi^2$ distribution with $n$ degrees of freedom
   iii) The $F$ distribution with $m$ and $n$ degrees of freedom
   iv) The Student's $t$ distribution

Q2. Suppose $X_1,........X_n$ is a random sample coming from a normally distributed population with variance $\sigma_x^2$. Prove that the statistic

$$\frac{(X_1 - Xbar)^2}{\sigma_x^2} + \frac{(X_2 - Xbar)^2}{\sigma_x^2} + ...... + \frac{(X_n - Xbar)^2}{\sigma_x^2} \text{ follows the } \chi^2 \text{ dis-}$$

tribution with $(n - 1)$ degrees of freedom.

Q3. Suppose we have two samples, each from a normally distributed population, $X = (23, 21, 24, 26, 29, 28, 24, 20, 27)$ and $Y = (22, 26, 29, 18, 17, 15, 26, 24, 27, 30)$. Say whether the two samples share a common population variance. Find the appropriate critical region using R.

Q4. Suppose the following sample comes from a normally distributed population with unknown mean $\mu$, and variance = 16: $(12, 18, 24, 7, 22, 12, 15, 23, 10, 8, 24, 28, 16)$. Calculate a 95 per cent confidence interval for $\mu$. Use R to find the appropriate critical values.

Q5. Suppose we are tossing 1,000 balanced coins. Using the Central Limit Theorem, construct the 95 per cent confidence interval for the total number of heads.

Q6. We have the following sample from a normally distributed population: (23, 22, 24, 12, 15, 22, 28, 26, 22, 19, 16, 28). Construct the 95 per cent confidence interval for the unknown population variance $\sigma_x^2$. (Hint: Use the $\chi^2$ distribution and R to obtain the relevant critical values).

Q7. In the text, we have said that we might fail to reject different null hypotheses that are mutually contradictory, and hence we cannot generally interpret the failure to reject a given null as evidence that the null is true. Using imaginary data, illustrate this point for the Z test.

Q8. We have the following sample from a normally distributed population:

(−10, 0, 12, −23, −15, 23, 24, 10, 6, −8, −12, 10, 14, 4, −7)

Construct the 95 per cent confidence interval for the unknown population mean $\mu$. (Hint: Use the $t$ distribution).

Q9. Given the following sample from a normally distributed population $X = (23, 22, 24, 16, 15, 12, 18, 19, 20, 22, 26, 10)$, test the null hypothesis that $\mu$, population mean = 15.

## CHAPTER 4

Q1. Assume we have an urn in which we have balls labelled 1 to N. Let the mean of all the balls in the urn be $\mu$. Suppose we take out a ball at random and call the number on that ball X. Show that X is an unbiased estimator of $\mu$. Suppose now, we take out $n$ balls at random and let Xbar be the arithmetic mean of all the numbers on the balls that we have drawn. Show that Xbar is also an unbiased estimator of $\mu$, but has a lower variance than X.

Q2. Suppose $X_1, X_2, \ldots\ldots X_n$ is a random sample of size $n$ from a population following Poisson distribution with parameter $\lambda$. Show

that $\dfrac{\sum\limits_{i=1}^{n} X_i}{n}$ is an unbiased and consistent estimator of $\lambda$.

Q3. Suppose we have a two variable regression model: $Y_i = a + bX_i + e_i$. Prove that $a^\wedge$ is an unbiased estimator of $a$ provided $b^\wedge$ is an unbiased estimator of $b$. What is the variance of $a^\wedge$?

Q4. What condition needs to be satisfied for $b^\wedge$ to be an unbiased and consistent estimator of $b$ in the linear regression model in Question 3?

Q5. What assumptions need to hold for the OLS estimators to be efficient ? What implications does the failure of these assumptions have for the computed $t$ ratios?

Q6. What do you mean by the term 'dummy variable' trap?

Q7. Explain why it is not appropriate to use the $R^2$ as a measure of goodness of fit for a linear regression model if the regression is through the origin.

Q8. What are the limitations of $R^2$ as a measure of goodness of fit? To what extent does the adjusted R-square overcome these? What are the limitations shared by both?

Q9. Suppose you are given the following data on $X$ and $Y$.

**The data on the values of $X$ and $Y$**

| Sr.no | Y | X | Sr.no | Y | X | Sr.no | Y | X |
|---|---|---|---|---|---|---|---|---|
| 1 | 20 | 25 | 11 | 24 | 23 | 21 | 23 | 25 |
| 2 | 24 | 27 | 12 | 26 | 22 | 22 | 22 | 22 |
| 3 | 32 | 27 | 13 | 22 | 20 | 23 | 26 | 27 |
| 4 | 33 | 28 | 14 | 18 | 19 | 24 | 29 | 21 |
| 5 | 35 | 20 | 15 | 15 | 17 | 25 | 25 | 19 |
| 6 | 20 | 26 | 16 | 26 | 12 | 26 | 20 | 20 |
| 7 | 21 | 29 | 17 | 22 | 16 | 27 | 18 | 18 |
| 8 | 18 | 26 | 18 | 20 | 18 | 28 | 26 | 16 |
| 9 | 15 | 15 | 19 | 18 | 20 | 29 | 24 | 15 |
| 10 | 20 | 14 | 20 | 16 | 21 | 30 | 22 | 15 |

i) Estimate the parameters $a$ and $b$ in the linear regression $Y_i = a + bX_i + e_i$

ii) Test the null hypothesis $b = 0$ against the alternative $b \neq 0$

iii) Calculate the R-square of the regression

iv) Carry out the regression using R

Q10. Suppose every odd numbered observation in the data in Question 9 is a measurement on $X$ and $Y$ for females while every even numbered observation on $X$ and $Y$ is a measurement for males. Test whether there is a statistically significant difference between the average value of $Y$ for males and females.

Q11. Suppose we have a linear regression model:

$$Y_i = a + bX_i + e_i$$

How will the OLS estimators of $a$ and $b$ be affected if every value of $X$ and $Y$ is multiplied by 10? How will they be affected if only the values of $X$ are divided by 10?

What are benefits of standardized regression coefficients?

Q12. When will you use log–log and semi-log regressions? In what way does the interpretation of coefficients differ from the usual regression case?

## CHAPTER 5

Q1. Stating the necessary assumptions, prove that the OLS estimators are BLUE.

Q2. What is the implication for OLS estimators of a non-normal stochastic disturbance term? Discuss the small sample as well as asymptotic implications.

Q3. Suppose you have a linear regression model:

$Y_i = \alpha + \beta_1 X_{i1} + \beta_2 X_{i2} + \beta_3 X_{i3} + e_i$. How would you test

$H_o : \beta_2 = \beta_3 = 0$

$H_A : \beta_2 \neq 0, \ \beta_3 \neq 0$

Q4. Explain how the AIC and SC can be used as model selection criteria.

Q5. What are the consequences of multicollinearity?

Q6. How will you detect multicollinearity?

Q7. Discuss remedial measures for multicollinearity.

Q8. Why do the coefficients of the variables included in a regression model change as we add or delete more explanatory variables?

# CHAPTER 6

Q1. Define heteroskedasticity. What are the implications of heteroskedastic disturbances for OLS estimators ?

Q2. Discuss any two tests of heteroskedasticity.

Q3. Explain in detail the method for calculating FGLS estimators in the case of heteroskedastic disturbances. What are their strengths and limitations?

Q4. What do you mean by White's heteroskedasticity consistent standard errors? Is it better to deal with heteroskedasticity by using White's standard errors rather than computer FGLS estimators, especially if the sample size is small?

Q5. What do you mean by autocorrelated disturbances? What are the implications of autocorrelated disturbances in the context of OLS estimators?

Q6. Discuss the Durbin–Watson test as a test for first order autocorrelation.

Q7. Discuss in detail the methodology for computing the Cochrane–Orcutt and the Praise–Winston FGLS estimators for autocorrelated disturbances.

Q8. What is omitted variable bias? What are its implications?

Q9. Discuss the Ramsay Reset Specification test in detail.

Q10. What are the implications of errors in measurement of the dependent variable? What happens if the independent variables are measured with error?

Q11. Discuss the proxy variable solution as well as Instrumental Variables as a possible solution to the problem of omitted variables, with special emphasis on the problem of weak instruments.

# Index

# About the Author

*Neeraj R. Hatekar* is Professor of Econometrics, Department of Economics, University of Mumbai. He is the Coordinator for the Centre for Computational Social Sciences, University of Mumbai. He has been the Smuts Visiting Fellow at the University of Cambridge and has taught courses on Indian economic development at the University. He is a prolific writer and has contributed to many peer-reviewed academic journals and the *Economic and Political Weekly*.